CIMA

Subject F3

Financial Strategy

Study Text

Published by: Kaplan Publishing UK

Unit 2 The Business Centre, Molly Millars Lane, Wokingham, Berkshire RG41 2QZ

Acknowledgements

We are grateful to the CIMA for permission to reproduce past examination questions. The answers to CIMA Exams have been prepared by Kaplan Publishing, except in the case of the CIMA November 2010 and subsequent CIMA Exam answers where the official CIMA answers have been reproduced.

British Library Cataloguing in Publication Data

A catalogue record for this book is available from the British Library.

ISBN: 978-1-78415-524-7

Printed and bound in Great Britain.

Contents

Introduction

How to use the materials

These official CIMA learning materials have been carefully designed to make your learning experience as easy as possible and to give you the best chances of success in your Objective Test Examination.

The product range contains a number of features to help you in the study process. They include:

- a detailed explanation of all syllabus areas;

- extensive 'practical' materials;

- generous question practice, together with full solutions.

This Study Text has been designed with the needs of home study and distance learning candidates in mind. Such students require very full coverage of the syllabus topics, and also the facility to undertake extensive question practice. However, the Study Text is also ideal for fully taught courses.

The main body of the text is divided into a number of chapters, each of which is organised on the following pattern:

- **Detailed learning outcomes.** These describe the knowledge expected after your studies of the chapter are complete. You should assimilate these before beginning detailed work on the chapter, so that you can appreciate where your studies are leading.

- **Step-by-step topic coverage.** This is the heart of each chapter, containing detailed explanatory text supported where appropriate by worked examples and exercises. You should work carefully through this section, ensuring that you understand the material being explained and can tackle the examples and exercises successfully. Remember that in many cases knowledge is cumulative: if you fail to digest earlier material thoroughly, you may struggle to understand later chapters.

- **Activities.** Some chapters are illustrated by more practical elements, such as comments and questions designed to stimulate discussion.

- **Question practice.** The text contains three styles of question:
  - Exam-style objective test questions (OTQs).
  - 'Integration' questions – these test your ability to understand topics within a wider context. This is particularly important with calculations where OTQs may focus on just one element but an integration question tackles the full calculation, just as you would be expected to do in the workplace.
  - 'Case' style questions – these test your ability to analyse and discuss issues in greater depth, particularly focusing on scenarios that are less clear cut than in the Objective Test Examination, and thus provide excellent practice for developing the skills needed for success in the Strategic Level Case Study Examination.

- **Solutions.** Avoid the temptation merely to 'audit' the solutions provided. It is an illusion to think that this provides the same benefits as you would gain from a serious attempt of your own. However, if you are struggling to get started on a question you should read the introductory guidance provided at the beginning of the solution, where provided, and then make your own attempt before referring back to the full solution.

If you work conscientiously through this Official CIMA Study Text according to the guidelines above you will be giving yourself an excellent chance of success in your Objective Test Examination. Good luck with your studies!

Quality and accuracy are of the utmost importance to us so if you spot an error in any of our products, please send an email to mykaplanreporting@kaplan.com with full details, or follow the link to the feedback form in MyKaplan.

Our Quality Co-ordinator will work with our technical team to verify the error and take action to ensure it is corrected in future editions.

Icon Explanations

Definition – These sections explain important areas of knowledge which must be understood and reproduced in an assessment environment.

Key point – Identifies topics which are key to success and are often examined.

Supplementary reading – These sections will help to provide a deeper understanding of core areas. The supplementary reading is **NOT** optional reading. It is vital to provide you with the breadth of knowledge you will need to address the wide range of topics within your syllabus that could feature in an assessment question. **Reference to this text is vital when self studying**.

Test your understanding – Following key points and definitions are exercises which give the opportunity to assess the understanding of these core areas.

Illustration – To help develop an understanding of particular topics. The illustrative examples are useful in preparing for the Test your understanding exercises.

 Exclamation mark – This symbol signifies a topic which can be more difficult to understand. When reviewing these areas, care should be taken.

 New – Identifies topics that are brand new in subjects that build on, and therefore also contain, learning covered in earlier subjects.

 Tutorial note – Included to explain some of the technical points in more detail.

Study technique

Passing exams is partly a matter of intellectual ability, but however accomplished you are in that respect you can improve your chances significantly by the use of appropriate study and revision techniques. In this section we briefly outline some tips for effective study during the earlier stages of your approach to the Objective Test Examination. We also mention some techniques that you will find useful at the revision stage.

Planning

To begin with, formal planning is essential to get the best return from the time you spend studying. Estimate how much time in total you are going to need for each subject you are studying. Remember that you need to allow time for revision as well as for initial study of the material.

With your study material before you, decide which chapters you are going to study in each week, and which weeks you will devote to revision and final question practice.

Prepare a written schedule summarising the above and stick to it!

It is essential to know your syllabus. As your studies progress you will become more familiar with how long it takes to cover topics in sufficient depth. Your timetable may need to be adapted to allocate enough time for the whole syllabus.

Students are advised to refer to the notice of examinable legislation published regularly in CIMA's magazine (Financial Management), the students e-newsletter (Velocity) and on the CIMA website, to ensure they are up-to-date.

The amount of space allocated to a topic in the Study Text is not a very good guide as to how long it will take you. The syllabus weighting is the better guide as to how long you should spend on a syllabus topic.

Tips for effective studying

(1) Aim to find a quiet and undisturbed location for your study, and plan as far as possible to use the same period of time each day. Getting into a routine helps to avoid wasting time. Make sure that you have all the materials you need before you begin so as to minimise interruptions.

(2) Store all your materials in one place, so that you do not waste time searching for items every time you want to begin studying. If you have to pack everything away after each study period, keep your study materials in a box, or even a suitcase, which will not be disturbed until the next time.

(3) Limit distractions. To make the most effective use of your study periods you should be able to apply total concentration, so turn off all entertainment equipment, set your phones to message mode, and put up your 'do not disturb' sign.

(4) Your timetable will tell you which topic to study. However, before diving in and becoming engrossed in the finer points, make sure you have an overall picture of all the areas that need to be covered by the end of that session. After an hour, allow yourself a short break and move away from your Study Text. With experience, you will learn to assess the pace you need to work at. Each study session should focus on component learning outcomes – the basis for all questions.

(5) Work carefully through a chapter, making notes as you go. When you have covered a suitable amount of material, vary the pattern by attempting a practice question. When you have finished your attempt, make notes of any mistakes you made, or any areas that you failed to cover or covered more briefly. Be aware that all component learning outcomes will be tested in each examination.

(6) Make notes as you study, and discover the techniques that work best for you. Your notes may be in the form of lists, bullet points, diagrams, summaries, 'mind maps', or the written word, but remember that you will need to refer back to them at a later date, so they must be intelligible. If you are on a taught course, make sure you highlight any issues you would like to follow up with your lecturer.

(7) Organise your notes. Make sure that all your notes, calculations etc. can be effectively filed and easily retrieved later.

Objective Test

Objective Test questions require you to choose or provide a response to a question whose correct answer is predetermined.

The most common types of Objective Test question you will see are:

- Multiple choice, where you have to choose the correct answer(s) from a list of possible answers. This could either be numbers or text.

- Multiple choice with more choices and answers, for example, choosing two correct answers from a list of eight possible answers. This could either be numbers or text.

- Single numeric entry, where you give your numeric answer, for example, profit is $10,000.

- Multiple entry, where you give several numeric answers.

- True/false questions, where you state whether a statement is true or false.

- Matching pairs of text, for example, matching a technical term with the correct definition.

- Other types could be matching text with graphs and labelling graphs/diagrams.

In every chapter of this Study Text we have introduced these types of questions, but obviously we have had to label answers A, B, C etc rather than using click boxes. For convenience we have retained quite a few questions where an initial scenario leads to a number of sub-questions. There will be questions of this type in the Objective Test Examination but they will rarely have more than three sub-questions.

Guidance re CIMA on-screen calculator

As part of the CIMA Objective Test software, candidates are now provided with a calculator. This calculator is on-screen and is available for the duration of the assessment. The calculator is available in each of the Objective Test Examinations and is accessed by clicking the calculator button in the top left hand corner of the screen at any time during the assessment.

All candidates must complete a 15-minute tutorial before the assessment begins and will have the opportunity to familiarise themselves with the calculator and practise using it.

Candidates may practise using the calculator by downloading and installing the practice exam at http://www.vue.com/athena/. The calculator can be accessed from the fourth sample question (of 12).

Please note that the practice exam and tutorial provided by Pearson VUE at http://www.vue.com/athena/ is not specific to CIMA and includes the full range of question types the Pearson VUE software supports, some of which CIMA does not currently use.

Fundamentals of Objective Tests

The Objective Tests are 90-minute assessments comprising 60 compulsory questions, with one or more parts. There will be no choice and all questions should be attempted.

Structure of subjects and learning outcomes

Each subject within the syllabus is divided into a number of broad syllabus topics. The topics contain one or more lead learning outcomes, related component learning outcomes and indicative knowledge content.

A learning outcome has two main purposes:

(a) To define the skill or ability that a well prepared candidate should be able to exhibit in the examination.

(b) To demonstrate the approach likely to be taken in examination questions.

The learning outcomes are part of a hierarchy of learning objectives. The verbs used at the beginning of each learning outcome relate to a specific learning objective, e.g.

Calculate the break-even point, profit target, margin of safety and profit/volume ratio for a single product or service.

The verb '**calculate**' indicates a level three learning objective. The following tables list the verbs that appear in the syllabus learning outcomes and examination questions.

CIMA VERB HIERARCHY

CIMA place great importance on the definition of verbs in structuring Objective Test Examinations. It is therefore crucial that you understand the verbs in order to appreciate the depth and breadth of a topic and the level of skill required. The Objective Tests will focus on levels one, two and three of the CIMA hierarchy of verbs. However they will also test levels four and five, especially at the management and strategic levels. You can therefore expect to be tested on knowledge, comprehension, application, analysis and evaluation in these examinations.

Level 1: KNOWLEDGE

What you are expected to know.

VERBS USED	DEFINITION
List	Make a list of.
State	Express, fully or clearly, the details of/facts of.
Define	Give the exact meaning of.

For example you could be asked to make a list of the advantages of a particular information system by selecting all options that apply from a given set of possibilities. Or you could be required to define relationship marketing by selecting the most appropriate option from a list.

Level 2: COMPREHENSION

What you are expected to understand.

VERBS USED	DEFINITION
Describe	Communicate the key features of.
Distinguish	Highlight the differences between.
Explain	Make clear or intelligible/state the meaning or purpose of.
Identify	Recognise, establish or select after consideration.
Illustrate	Use an example to describe or explain something.

For example you may be asked to distinguish between different aspects of the global business environment by dragging external factors and dropping into a PEST analysis.

Level 3: APPLICATION

How you are expected to apply your knowledge.

VERBS USED	DEFINITION
Apply	Put to practical use.
Calculate	Ascertain or reckon mathematically.
Demonstrate	Prove with certainty or exhibit by practical means.
Prepare	Make or get ready for use.
Reconcile	Make or prove consistent/compatible.
Solve	Find an answer to.
Tabulate	Arrange in a table.

For example you may need to calculate the projected revenue or costs for a given set of circumstances.

Level 4: ANALYSIS

How you are expected to analyse the detail of what you have learned.

VERBS USED	DEFINITION
Analyse	Examine in detail the structure of.
Categorise	Place into a defined class or division.
Compare/contrast	Show the similarities and/or differences between.
Construct	Build up or compile.
Discuss	Examine in detail by argument.
Interpret	Translate into intelligible or familiar terms.
Prioritise	Place in order of priority or sequence for action.
Produce	Create or bring into existence.

For example you may be required to interpret an inventory ratio by selecting the most appropriate statement for a given set of circumstances and data.

Level 5: EVALUATION

How you are expected to use your learning to evaluate, make decisions or recommendations.

VERBS USED	DEFINITION
Advise	Counsel, inform or notify.
Evaluate	Appraise or assess the value of.
Recommend	Propose a course of action.

For example you may be asked to recommend and select an appropriate course of action based on a short scenario.

Information concerning formulae and tables will be provided via the CIMA website, www.cimaglobal.com, and your EN-gage login.

F3
FINANCIAL STRATEGY

Syllabus overview

F3 focuses on the formulation and implementation of financial strategy to support the overall strategy of the organisation. Using insights gained from F1 and F2, it provides the competencies to evaluate the financing requirements of organisations and the relative merits of alternative sources of finance to meet these requirements. Finally, it develops the competencies required to value investment opportunities including the valuation of corporate entities for mergers, acquisitions and divestments.

Summary of syllabus

Weight	Syllabus topic
25%	**A.** Formulation of financial strategy
35%	**B.** Financing and dividend decisions
40%	**C.** Corporate finance

F3 – A. FORMULATION OF FINANCIAL STRATEGY (25%)

Learning outcomes
On completion of their studies, students should be able to:

Lead	Component	Indicative syllabus content
1 evaluate strategic financial and non-financial objectives of different types of entities.	(a) advise on the overall strategic financial and non-financial objectives of different types of entities	• Overall strategic financial objectives (e.g. value for money, maximising shareholder wealth, providing a surplus) of different types of entities (e.g. incorporated, unincorporated, quoted, unquoted, private sector, public sector, for-profit and not-for-profit). • Non-financial objectives (e.g. human, intellectual, natural, and social and relationship). • Financial strategy in the context of international operations.
	(b) evaluate financial objectives of for-profit entities	• Financial objectives (e.g. earnings growth, dividend growth, gearing) and assessment of attainment. • Sensitivity of the attainment of financial objectives to changes in underlying economic (e.g. interest rates, exchange rates, inflation) and business variables (e.g. margins, volumes).
	(c) advise on the use of sustainability and integrated reporting to inform stakeholders of relevant information concerning the interaction of a business with society and the natural environment.	• Limitations of financial statements for incorporated entities, prepared in accordance with International Accounting Standards (IAS), to reflect the value and stewardship of the non-financial capital base. • Principles and scope of reporting social and environmental issues (e.g. Global Reporting Initiative's Sustainability Reporting Framework and International Integrated Reporting Council guidance).
2 evaluate strategic financial management policy decisions.	(a) evaluate the interrelationship between investment, financing and dividend decisions for an incorporated entity	• Investment, financing and dividend decisions and the interrelationship between them in meeting the cash needs of the entity. • Sensitivity of forecast financial statements and future cash position to investment, financing and dividend decisions.

Learning outcomes

On completion of their studies, students should be able to:

Lead	Component	Indicative syllabus content
		• Consideration of the interests of shareholders and other stakeholders in investment, financing and dividend decisions (e.g. impact on investor and lender ratios, compliance with debt covenants and attainment of financial objectives). • Determine financing requirements and cash available for payment of dividends based on the overall consideration of the forecast future cash flows arising from investment decisions, business strategy and forecast business and economic variables.
	(b) advise on the development of financial strategy for an entity taking into account taxation and other external influences	• Lenders' assessment of creditworthiness (e.g. business plans, liquidity ratios, cash forecasts, credit rating, quality of management). • Financial strategy in the context of regulatory requirements (e.g. price and service controls exercised by industry regulators). • Consideration of taxation regulations (domestic and international) in setting financial strategy.
	(c) evaluate the impact of the adoption of hedge accounting and disclosure of financial risk on financial statements and stakeholder assessment.	• The accounting treatment of hedge accounting (cash flow, fair value and net investment), IFRS 9 (or IAS 39, before effective date for IFRS 9). • Impact of adoption of hedge accounting on financial statements and on stakeholder assessment. • Disclosure of financial risk, including policies for managing such risk (IFRS 7 *Financial Instruments: Disclosures*).

F3 – B. FINANCING AND DIVIDEND DECISIONS (35%)

Learning outcomes
On completion of their studies, students should be able to:

Lead	Component	Indicative syllabus content
1 evaluate the financing requirements of an entity and recommend a strategy for meeting those requirements.	(a) evaluate the impact of changes in capital structure for an incorporated entity on shareholders and other stakeholders	• Capital structure theories (traditional theory, Modigliani and Miller's (MM) theories with and without tax and practical considerations and calculations using MM formulae). • Calculation of cost of equity or weighted average cost of capital (WACC) to reflect a change in capital structure. • Modelling impact of choice of capital structure on financial statements and key performance measures (e.g. ratios of interest to investors and lenders and compliance with debt covenants). • Structuring the debt/equity profile of group companies, including tax implications and thin capitalisation rules
	(b) evaluate and compare alternative methods of raising long-term debt finance	• Criteria for selecting appropriate debt instruments (e.g. bank borrowings, bonds, convertible bonds, commercial paper). • Target debt profile (e.g. interest, currency and maturity profile) to manage interest, currency and refinancing risk. • Use of cross-currency swaps and interest rate swaps to change the currency or interest rate profile of debt. • Tax considerations in the selection of debt instruments. • Procedures for issuing debt securities (private placement and capital market issues, role of advisers and underwriters). • Debt covenants (e.g. interest cover, net debt/EBITDA, debt/debt and equity). • The lease or buy decision (for both operating and finance leases).

Learning outcomes

On completion of their studies, students should be able to:

Lead	Component	Indicative syllabus content
	(c) evaluate and compare alternative methods of raising equity finance.	• Methods of flotation and implications for the management of the entity and for its stakeholders. • Use of rights issues, including choice of discount rate, impact on shareholder wealth and calculation of the theoretical ex-rights price (TERP) and yield-adjusted TERP.
2 evaluate dividend policies for an incorporated entity that meet the needs and expectations of shareholders.	(a) evaluate alternatives to cash dividends and their impact on shareholder wealth and entity performance measures	• Impact of scrip dividends on shareholder value and entity value/financial statements/performance measures. • Impact of share repurchase programmes on shareholder value and entity value/financial statements/performance measures
	(b) recommend appropriate dividend policies, including consideration of shareholder expectations and the cash needs of the entity.	• Implications for shareholder value of alternative dividend policies including MM theory of dividend irrelevancy. • Development of appropriate dividend policy, taking into account the interests of shareholders and the cash needs of the entity.

F3 – C. CORPORATE FINANCE (40%)

Learning outcomes
On completion of their studies, students should be able to:

Lead	Component	Indicative syllabus content
1 evaluate opportunities for acquisition, merger and divestment.	(a) evaluate the financial and strategic implications of proposals for an acquisition, merger or divestment, including taxation implications.	• Recognition of the interests of different stakeholder groups. • Reasons for and against acquisitions, mergers and divestments (e.g. strategic position, synergistic benefits, Big Data opportunities, risks and tax implications). • Taxation implications (group loss relief, differences in taxation rates, withholding tax, double tax treaties). • Process and implications of a management buy-out, including potential conflicts of interest. • Role/function/implications of acquisition by private equity or venture capitalist. • Role and scope of competition authorities in relation to mergers and acquisitions.
2 evaluate the value of entities.	(a) calculate the value of a whole entity (quoted or unquoted), a subsidiary entity or division using a range of methods including taxation	• Asset valuation (e.g. historic cost, replacement cost and realisable value). • Forms of intangible asset (including intellectual property rights, brands etc) and methods of valuation. • Share prices (quoted on stock market or private sale for non-quoted entities). • Earnings valuation (e.g. price/earnings multiples and earnings yield). • Dividend valuation (e.g. dividend growth model, including estimating growth from past or forecast figures and including non-constant growth assumptions). • Discounted free cash flow valuation (including taxation, risk-adjusted discount rate, foreign currency cash flows and sensitivity analysis). • Ideas of diversifiable risk (unsystematic risk) and systematic risk.

Learning outcomes
On completion of their studies, students should be able to:

Lead	Component	Indicative syllabus content
		• Capital asset pricing model (CAPM), including the meaning and derivation of the component, and the ability to gear and un-gear betas. • Calculation of an appropriate cost of capital for use in discounted cash flow analysis (e.g. cost of equity or WACC) by reference to the nature of the transaction (e.g. division or an entire entity), including use of CAPM, dividend valuation model and MM WACC formula. • Efficient market hypothesis and its relevance for the valuation of quoted entities. • Impact of government incentives on entity value (e.g. capital or revenue grants).
	(b) evaluate the validity of the valuation methods used and the results obtained in the context of a given scenario.	• Strengths and weaknesses of each valuation method. • Validity of the results for use in decision making according to the nature of the target entity (e.g. a division, a whole entity, quoted or unquoted).
3 evaluate pricing issues and post-transaction issues.	(a) evaluate alternative pricing structures and bid process including taxation implications	• Forms of consideration and terms for acquisitions (e.g. cash, shares, convertibles and earn-out arrangements), and their impact on shareholders, including taxation impact. • Treatment of target entity debt (settlement, refinancing). • Methods/implications of financing a cash offer and refinancing target entity debt. • Bid negotiation (e.g. managing a hostile bid) including agency issues.
	(b) evaluate post-transaction issues.	• Potential post-transaction value for both acquirer and seller (e.g. taking into account synergistic benefits, forecast performance and market response). • Integration of management/systems and effective realisation of synergistic benefits. • Types of exit strategies and their implications.

Objectives

Chapter learning objectives

Lead	Component
A1: Evaluate strategic financial and non-financial objectives of different types of entities.	(a) advise on the overall strategic financial and non-financial objectives of different types of entities. (b) evaluate financial objectives of for-profit entities.

Indicative syllabus content

- Overall strategic financial objectives (e.g. value for money, maximising shareholder wealth, providing a surplus) of different types of entities (e.g. incorporated, unincorporated, quoted, unquoted, private sector, public sector, for-profit and not-for-profit).

- Non-financial objectives (e.g. human, intellectual, natural, and social and relationship).

- Financial strategy in the context of international operations.

- Financial objectives (e.g. earnings growth, dividend growth, gearing) and assessment of attainment.

- Sensitivity of the attainment of financial objectives to changes in underlying economic (e.g. interest rates, exchange rates, inflation) and business variables (e.g. margins, volumes).

1 Overview of chapter

Definitions of key terms

Mission: Fundamental objective(s) of an entity, expressed in general terms. (CIMA Official Terminology, 2005)

Mission statement: Published statement, apparently of the entity's fundamental objective(s). This may or may not summarise the true mission of the entity. (CIMA Official Terminology, 2005)

Objectives, hierarchy of: Arrangement of the objectives of an entity into a number of different levels, with the higher levels being more general and the lower levels more specific. These levels may be mission, goals, targets or, alternatively: strategic objectives, tactical objectives or operational objectives.

2 The mission and objectives of an entity

The mission and objectives of an entity will differ depending on:

* the type of entity (for example for-profit or not-for-profit)
* the needs of the entity's different stakeholders.

This chapter defines the different types of entity and considers who the entity's key stakeholders are. It then looks at different objectives, both financial objectives and non-financial.

Definitions of different types of entity

For-profit and not-for-profit entities

Most companies operate on a for-profit, or profit seeking basis. This means that their primary objective is to make a profit and therefore to satisfy their shareholders.

Most public sector entities operate on a not-for-profit basis, in that they usually have other primary objectives, often non-financial in nature.

Unincorporated and incorporated entities

An incorporated entity (sometimes called a company or corporation) is legally a separate entity from its owner(s).

Conversely, an owner and an unincorporated entity are legally the same, so the owner personally bears all the risks of the business.

Unincorporated entities are usually sole traders or partnerships.

Quoted and unquoted entities

Once an entity has been incorporated, it can apply to a stock exchange to have its shares quoted (or listed) on the exchange. It can be expensive to secure a stock exchange listing, so only large companies tend to become quoted.

A listing on an exchange makes it much easier for shareholders to buy and sell the entity's shares.

Private sector and public sector entities

A private sector entity is owned by private investors, whereas a public sector entity is owned by the government of a country.

Other types of entity

A **charitable entity (charity)** is a type of not-for-profit entity. It differs from other types of not-for-profit entities in that it centres on not-for-profit and philanthropic goals as well as social well-being (e.g. activities serving the public interest or common good).

An **association** or **union** is a group of individuals who enter into an agreement to form an entity to accomplish a purpose. Common examples include trade associations, trade unions and professional associations (like CIMA).

3 Objectives of different types of entity

It is generally accepted that the primary strategic objective of a for-profit entity (i.e. a commercial company) is the long-term goal of the **maximisation of the wealth of the shareholders**.

Entities such as public sector bodies (e.g. schools, hospitals), charities, trade unions and associations (such as accountancy bodies) are not run to make profits but to benefit prescribed groups of people. For example, the primary objective of a charity is to pursue whatever charitable objectives it was set up for.

Since the services provided are limited primarily by the funds available, secondary objectives are to raise the maximum possible funds each year (net of fund-raising expenses), and to use the funds efficiently to maximise the benefit generated.

Objectives of specific types of entity

There are some interesting extra points to note regarding objectives when we consider the issues facing the following specific types of entity:

Incorporated v unincorporated

An incorporated entity is likely to have several owners, and therefore there is the potential for greater conflict of stakeholder objectives than with an unincorporated entity.

Quoted v unquoted

A quoted company faces far more scrutiny from its many investors and from the financial market in general.

Also, because of this increased scrutiny, it is arguably more important that a quoted company sets appropriate non-financial objectives relating to its relationship with the environment and its staff.

Charities

Charites are usually established to raise money for a specific cause, and to spend the money raised in the most effective way.

However, increasingly charities are setting up retail outlets and trying to generate profits through trading. In some cases, the charities are making investments and therefore taking risks in order to try to increase returns. This sort of strategy used to be associated only with profit seeking organisations and would have once seemed inappropriate behaviour for charities. However, it has become the norm for most charities now.

4 Objectives and stakeholders

Definition of stakeholders

Stakeholders: Those persons and entities that have an interest in the strategy of an entity. Stakeholders normally include shareholders, customers, staff and the local community. (CIMA Official Terminology, 2005)

The decisions made by an entity's managers depend on the ultimate objectives of the entity.

Academic studies have shown that entities often have many, **sometimes conflicting,** objectives.

This is a consequence of having many stakeholders with both long- and short-term goals, such as:

- Equity investors (ordinary shareholders)
- The community at large
- Company employees
- Company managers/directors
- Customers
- Suppliers
- Finance providers
- The government

Stakeholder conflicts

Faced with a broad range of stakeholders, managers are likely to find they cannot simultaneously meet all the stakeholders' objectives.

For example the managers of a for-profit entity will find it difficult to maximise the wealth of their shareholders and keep all the other stakeholders content.

In this case, the main strategic objective may be interpreted as achieving the maximum profit possible, consistent with balancing the needs of the various stakeholders in the entity.

Such a policy may imply achieving a satisfactory return for shareholders, whilst (for example) establishing competitive terms and conditions of service for the employees, and avoiding polluting the environment.

Example of conflicts of objectives – agency theory

Agency theory: Hypothesis that attempts to explain elements of organisational behaviour through an understanding of the relationships between principals (such as shareholders) and agents (such as company managers and accountants). A conflict may exist between the actions undertaken by agents in furtherance of their own self-interest, and those required to promote the interests of the principals. (CIMA Official Terminology, 2005)

Agency theory

A possible conflict can arise when ownership is separated from the day-to-day management of an entity. In larger entities, the ordinary shares are likely to be diversely held, and so the actions of shareholders are likely to be restricted in practical terms. The responsibility of running the entity will be with the board of directors, who may only own a small percentage of the shares in issue.

The managers of an entity are essentially agents for the shareholders, being tasked with running the entity in the shareholders' best interests. The shareholders, however, have little opportunity to assess whether the managers are acting in the shareholders' best interests.

5 For-profit entities

Introduction to objectives of for-profit entities

As stated above, the primary objective of a for-profit entity is the maximisation of shareholder wealth.

However, this objective always has to be balanced with other objectives, driven by the needs of the other key stakeholder groups.

For-profit entities will therefore have a mix of financial and non-financial objectives.

Financial objectives of for-profit entities

The financial objectives of a for-profit entity will be created after considering the following factors:

Equity investors (ordinary shareholders)

Within any economic system, the equity investors provide the risk finance. There is a very strong argument for maximising the wealth of equity investors. In order to attract funds, the company has to compete with other risk-free investment opportunities, e.g. government securities. The shareholders require returns from the company in terms of dividends and increases in share prices.

Finance providers

Providers of loan finance (banks, loan creditors) will primarily be interested in the ability of the firm to repay the finance including interest. As a result it will be the firm's ability to generate cash both long and short term that will be the basis of the goals of these providers.

Risk exposure

Risk can be measured according to finance theory.

Some risks – for example exchange-rate risk and interest-rate risk – can be managed by the use of hedging mechanisms. Shareholders and entities can therefore choose how much risk they wish to be exposed to for a given level of return. However, risk can take many forms, and the theory does not deal with risk exposure to matters such as recruitment of senior personnel or competitor activity.

Directors should set risk policies according to an agreed risk appetite which reflects the risk appetite of the shareholders.

Examples of specific financial objectives of for-profit entities

In order to achieve the overall objective of maximising shareholder wealth, but also to address the other issues identified above, entities should set specific financial targets in order to both communicate direction and measure performance.

For example:

Profitability

e.g. annual 10% improvement in earnings, or earnings per share.

Dividends

e.g. annual 5% increase in dividends.

Cash generation

e.g. annual 10% improvement in operating cash flow.

Gearing

e.g. a maximum [debt to (debt + equity)] ratio of 40%.

In order to assess whether the entity has achieved its financial objectives, ratio analysis can be used (covered in more detail towards the end of this chapter).

More on financial objectives of for-profit entities

Financial performance indicators

Return to investors

The return from ownership of shares in a profit-making entity can be measured by the formula:

$$\text{Annual return to investors} = \frac{(P_1 - P_0) + \text{Dividend}}{P_0}$$

This is the capital appreciation on the shares (the difference between P_1 and P_0 – the share price at the end and the start of the year respectively), plus dividends received during the year. The measure reflects the fact that both share price growth and dividends are important to investors. In fact, investors can still make gains (through the capital appreciation of their shares) even if the entity never pays out a dividend.

Cash generation

Poor liquidity is a greater threat to the survival of an entity than is poor profitability. Unless the entity is prepared to fund growth with high levels of borrowings, cash generation is vital to ensure investment in future profitable ventures. In the private sector the alternative to cash via retained earnings is borrowing.

Value added

This is primarily a measure of performance. It is usually defined as revenues less the cost of purchased materials and services. It represents the value added to an entity's products by its own efforts. A problem here is comparability with other industries – or even with other entities in the same industry.

Profitability

Profitability may be defined as the rate at which profits are generated. It is often expressed as profit per unit of input (e.g. investment). However, profitability limits an entity's focus to one output measure – profit. It overlooks quality, and this limitation must be kept in mind when using profitability as a measure of success. Profitability as a measure of decision-making has been criticised because:

- it fails to provide a systematic explanation as to why one business sector has more favourable prospects than another;

- it does not provide enough insight into the dynamics and balance of an entity's individual business units, and the balance between them;

- it is remote from the actions that create value, and cannot therefore be managed directly in any but the smallest entities;

- the input to the measure may vary substantially between entities.

Nevertheless, it is a well-known and accepted measure which, once the input has been defined, is readily understood. Provided the input is consistent across entities and time periods, it also provides a useful comparative measure.

Return on assets (RoA)

This is an accounting measure, calculated by dividing annual profits by the average net book value of assets. It is therefore subject to the distortions inevitable when profit, rather than cash flows, is used to determine performance. Distorting factors for interpretation and comparison purposes include depreciation policy, inventory revaluations, write-off of intangibles such as goodwill, etc. A further defect is that RoA ignores the time value of money, although this may be of minor concern when inflation is very low.

RoA may not adequately reflect how efficiently assets were utilised: in a commercial context, taking account of profits but not the assets used in their making, for whatever reason, would overstate an entity's performance.

Market share.

Market share is often seen as an objective for an entity in its own right. However, it must be judged in the context of other measures such as profitability and shareholder value. Market share, unlike many other measures, can take quality into account – it must be assumed that if customers do not get the quality they want or expect, then the entity will lose market share.

Gaining market share must be seen as a long-term goal of entities to ensure outlets for their products and services, and to minimise competition. However, market share can be acquired only within limits if a monopoly situation is to be avoided.

Competitive position

The performance of an entity must be compared with that of its competitors to establish a strategic perspective. A number of models and frameworks have been suggested by organisational theorists as to how competitive position may be determined and improved. A manager needing to make decisions must know by whom, by how much, and why he is gaining ground or being beaten by competitors.

Conventional measures, such as accounting data, are useful but no one measure is sufficient. Instead, an array of measures is needed to establish competitive position. The most difficult problem to overcome in using competitive position as a success factor is in collecting and acquiring data from competitors.

Non-financial objectives of for-profit entities

The non-financial objectives of a for-profit entity will be created after considering the following stakeholder issues:

Company employees

Returns = wages or salaries. However, maximising the returns to employees does assume that finance can be raised purely on the basis of satisficing the returns to finance providers. The employees' other interests also include job security and good conditions of employment.

Company managers/directors

Such senior employees are in an ideal position to follow their own aims at the expense of other stakeholders. Their goals will be both long-term (defending against takeovers, sales maximisation) and short-term (profit margins leading to increased bonuses).

Suppliers

Suppliers to the organisation will have short-term goals such as prompt payment terms alongside long-term requirements including contracts and regular business. The importance of the needs of suppliers will depend upon both their relative size and the number of suppliers.

The government

The government will have political and financial interests in the firm. Politically it will wish to increase exports and decrease imports whilst monitoring companies via the competition authorities. Financially it requires long-term profits to maximise taxation income.

The community at large

The goals of the community will be broad but will include such aspects as legal and social responsibilities, pollution control and employee welfare.

Environmental concerns

In pursuit of shareholder wealth maximisation, historically decisions have often been made that led to pollution or other environmental problems. Increasingly, entities are becoming aware of their environmental responsibilities. Many entities now produce environmental reports alongside their financial statements to emphasise their commitment to environmental issues. This is covered in more detail in the later chapter: 'Integrated Reporting'.

Customer pressure

Entities are increasingly coming under pressure from knowledgeable customers. Customers are more and more keen to ensure that entities they trade with behave ethically and responsibly. Therefore, decision makers have to take account of customers' wishes, even if there appears to be a short-term conflict with the shareholder wealth maximisation objective.

Customer satisfaction.

If customers are not satisfied they will take their business elsewhere and the entity will lose market share and go into liquidation. Measuring customer satisfaction is difficult to do formally, as the inputs and outputs are not readily defined or measurable. Surveys and questionnaires may be used but these methods have known flaws, mainly as a result of respondent bias.

Examples of specific non-financial objectives of for-profit entities

Non-financial objectives can be used to direct managers' attention towards key stakeholder requirements, to ensure that the entity balances the needs of its different stakeholders and minimises the conflict between the different stakeholder groups.

Also, achievement of non-financial objectives can improve the image of the entity from the perspective of its stakeholders. This can have a knock-on effect on sales and profitability and hence can help to create additional wealth for shareholders in the longer term.

Non-financial objectives can be categorised under the following headings:

Human

This considers the relationship of the entity with its staff, so objectives could cover increasing the amount of training provided, or reducing the level of staff turnover

Intellectual

This considers the intangible assets of the entity, such as its brand and reputation. Objectives could focus on improving the brand recognition.

Natural

This considers the entity's responsibility towards the environment, so objectives might include reducing the level of pollution and increasing the amount of recycling.

Social

This considers the entity's responsibility towards its local community. A social objective could be to make sure at least 50% of the employees live within a 5 mile radius of the entity's premises.

Relationship

This considers the entity's responsibility towards key stakeholders such as suppliers and customers. A relationship objective could be to pledge to offer all suppliers longer term contracts and to pay them on time, in order to improve the relationships.

6 Not-for-profit entities

Objectives of not-for-profit entities

Not-for-profit entities such as public sector bodies (e.g. schools, hospitals), charities, trade unions and associations (such as accountancy bodies) are not run to make profits but to benefit prescribed groups of people. For example, the primary objective of a charity is to pursue whatever charitable objectives it was set up for.

Since the services provided are limited primarily by the funds available, secondary objectives are to raise the maximum possible funds each year (net of fund-raising expenses), and to use the funds efficiently to maximise the benefit generated.

This can be measured as the 'value for money' (VFM) generated.

Satisfying many different stakeholders

Before we look at VFM in detail, it is worth noting that not-for-profit entities will still have a mix of financial and non-financial objectives (just like for-profit entities discussed above) and will still have to try to satisfy many different stakeholder groups.

There will often be different views of what the objectives of a not-for-profit entity should be, and therefore, whether appropriate objectives have been achieved. What value does one put on curing an illness, or saving a life? Should the success of a hospital be measured by shorter waiting lists? These are societal matters, the discomfort being one of the reasons they are placed firmly in the public sector, rather than being left to the 'survival of the fittest' philosophy associated with the competitive markets.

A public sector college will set objectives relating to the number of students, the number of courses, the ratio of lecturers to students, and so on. It will also seek its customers' assessments of the standard of, for example its lecturing and catering, and compare them with preset targets. In the language of strategic financial management, these are answers to the question 'How well did we do what we chose to do?' that is, 'how **effective** were we in meeting the objectives?'

Public sector entities

Public sector entities are bodies such as nationalised industries and local government organisations. They represent a significant part of many countries' economies and sound financial management is essential if their affairs are to be conducted efficiently. The major problem here lies in obtaining a measurable objective.

Financial objectives in the public sector

For a stock market listed company we can take the maximisation of shareholder wealth as a working objective and know that the achievement of this objective can be monitored with reference to share price and dividend payments. For a public sector entity the situation is more complex.

The entity's mission statement will lay out its key objectives. However, generally such entities are run in the interests of society as a whole and therefore we should seek to attain the position where the gap between the benefits they provide to society and the costs of their operation is the widest (in positive terms).

The cost is relatively easily measured in accounting terms. However, many of the benefits are intangible. For example, the benefits of such bodies as the National Health Service or Local Education Authorities are almost impossible to quantify.

Such government organisations tend to use a low discount rate in investment appraisals (to take account of 'time preference') and have complex methods of quantifying non-financial benefits in a standard NPV analysis.

Economists have tried to evaluate many public sector investments through the use of cost benefit analysis, with varying degrees of success. Problems are usually encountered in evaluating all the benefits.

Regulation

It is worth remembering that organisations that have had a public sector history or are themselves natural monopolies are often regulated in order to ensure the public are not the victims of the monopoly power these companies enjoy. This regulation can take many forms but can include the capping of the selling prices, the taxing of super profits or simply a limit on the profits these entities are allowed to make.

Specific objectives of public sector entities

Traditionally, managers have focused on financial measures of performance and progress, but increasingly, entities in both the private and public sectors are using non-financial indicators to assess success across a range of criteria, which need to be chosen to help an entity meet its objectives.

A number of common objectives are discussed below, in the context of public sector entities.

Cash generation

Poor liquidity is a greater threat to the survival of an entity than is poor profitability. Unless the entity is prepared to fund growth with high levels of borrowings, cash generation is vital to ensure investment in future profitable ventures. In the private sector the alternative to cash via retained earnings is borrowing.

In the public sector this choice has not been available in the past, and all growth has been funded by government. However, in the face of government-imposed cash limits, local authorities and other public-sector entities are beginning to raise debt on the capital markets, and are therefore beginning to be faced with the same choices as profit-making entities.

Value added

Value added represents the value added to an entity's products by its own efforts.

A problem here is comparability with other industries – or even with other entities in the same industry.

Many public sector entities – for example those in the health service – are now publishing information on their own value added.

Profitability

Although the concept of profit in its true sense is absent from most of the public sector, profitability may be used to relate inputs to outputs if a different measure of output is used – for example: surplus after all costs, to capital investment.

Return on assets (RoA)

In the public sector, the concept of profit is absent, but it is still not unrealistic to expect entities to use donated assets with maximum efficiency. If depreciation on such assets were to be charged against income, this would depress the amount of surplus income over expenditure. Other points which may affect interpretation of RoA in the public sector are:

- difficulty in determining value;
- there may be no resale value;
- are for use by community at large;
- charge for depreciation may have the effect of 'double taxation' on the taxpayer.

Market share

Market share is a measure that is becoming increasingly relevant to the public sector – for example universities and health provision. Health providers must now 'sell' their services to trusts established to 'buy' from them. Those providers which are seen to fail their customers will lose market share as the trusts will buy from elsewhere (within certain limits).

Competitive position

The public sector is increasingly in competition with other providers of a similar service both in the private and public sectors.

For example hospitals now have to compete for the funds of health trusts. Their advantage is that it is easier to gain access to data from such competitors than it is in the private sector.

Risk exposure

Public sector entities tend to be risk averse because of the political repercussions of failure and the fact that taxpayers, unlike shareholders, do not have the option to invest their money in less (or more) risky ventures.

Assessing value for money in not-for-profit entities

Not-for-profit entities are often appraised according to the 'value for money' (VFM) that they generate.

Value for money may be defined as "performance of an activity in such a way as to simultaneously achieve economy, efficiency and effectiveness." (CIMA Official Terminology, 2005)

This means making the optimum use of available resources to achieve the intended outcome.

VFM has three constituent elements:

Economy: minimising the cost of resources used or required (inputs) – spending less

Efficiency: the relationship between the output from goods or services and the resources to produce them – spending well

Effectiveness: the relationship between the intended and actual results of public spending (outcomes) – spending wisely.

These elements can be referred to by the umbrella term **'cost effectiveness'**.

Besides these three 'Es, a fourth 'E' is applied in some places:

Equity: the extent to which services are available to and reach all people that they are intended to – spending fairly. Some people may receive differing levels of service for reasons other than differences in their levels of need.

Overview of VFM

Source: UK National Audit Office website

More detail on VFM

Measurement of VFM

In practice, value for money is difficult to measure, and it is a relative rather than an absolute measure.

Value for money audit or study

A value for money audit is defined as an "investigation into whether proper arrangements have been made for securing economy, efficiency and effectiveness in the use of resources." (CIMA Official Terminology, 2005)

A value for money study focuses on a specific area of expenditure, and seeks to reach a judgement on whether value for money has been achieved. Good value for money can be defined as the optimal use of resources to achieve the intended outcomes.

The purpose of a VFM study is not to question policy objectives, but to provide independent and rigorous analysis on the way in which money has been spent to achieve those policy objectives.

As well as reaching an overall conclusion on value for money, a VFM study will make recommendations on how to achieve better value for money and to improve the services under examination. In some circumstances, a follow-up study is conducted to measure progress against the recommendations made.

Typically, a study will use a mix of quantitative and qualitative methods. The methods commonly used include:

- Financial analysis

- Analysis of management information

- Interviews or focus groups with departmental and other staff

- General research

- Surveys of practitioners or service users

- Benchmarking with other organisations or other countries

Practical example: value for money (taken from the website of the UK National Audit Office)

A local authority sets up a new programme to reduce litter dropping. One of its early steps is to agree with stakeholders a set of outcomes for the programme. The effectiveness of the programme is to be judged on the extent to which it reaches its outcomes in a year.

In this case, the programme achieves 97% of its outcomes and councillors declare they have 'come within a whisker of winning the battle against litter'. The programme was effective.

However, the programme cost more than expected and overspent its budget by 25 per cent. This was because the programme managers allowed costs to over-run in their drive to meet the outcome. The programme was not economical.

The cost over-run prompts a review of the service. This concludes that, outcome for outcome, it was more expensive than similar programmes in neighbouring areas. The programme was not efficient.

If programme objectives had been exceeded sufficiently, the programme may have been cost-effective despite the overspend. However, programme managers could still be criticised for exceeding the budget.

The most disadvantaged parts of the area were also those with the biggest litter problems and these neighbourhoods improved more, from a lower base, than wealthier places. The programme was equitable.

7 International operations

Increasingly in the modern business environment, entities are expanding across national boundaries into many different countries.

Although there are risks associated with such strategies, the strategic and financial benefits to an entity can be enormous.

In many ways, the objectives of an entity trading internationally will be the same as those of an entity based in just one country. However, there are some additional considerations.

Strategic implications of international expansion

The main strategic implications of international expansion are:

Competition

Foreign markets may have weaker competition. A firm facing a competitive domestic market will benefit from finding a foreign market where it has a monopoly.

Country factors

Some countries have cheap sources of natural raw materials and cheap labour costs. Locating production facilities in these countries will bring significant cost savings. Also, some countries' governments offer grants and cheap loans to foreign investors to attract inward investment.

Benefits to the customer

Locating in a different country could move an entity closer to existing customers, so reducing delivery times and improving relationships. Also, it is likely to bring an entity closer to a pool of potential new customers.

Economies of scale

As the entity gets bigger, international expansion might be the best way of continuing to generate economies of scale.

Risk management

International expansion will leave an entity less exposed to a single economy. Factors such as interest rates, inflation, government policy and exchange rates from more than one economy will impact a business with international operations. This will reduce the economic and political risk to the entity.

Financial implications of international expansion

The primary corporate objective – to maximise shareholder wealth – has been referred to earlier in this chapter.

The main financial benefit of an international investment is the positive NPV and consequent gain to shareholders of undertaking an attractive project.

However, also consider the following other financial implications of international investment:

Impact on the financial statements

If the foreign project assets are denominated in foreign currency, they will have to be converted into the domestic currency for the purposes of consolidation. If exchange rates fluctuate from one year to the next, the value of these assets will also fluctuate, giving (unrealised) exchange gains or losses in the entity's accounts. This is known as translation risk, and it can be mitigated by raising finance in the foreign currency too (matching).

Impact on the cost of capital

International investments will often be more risky to an entity than its normal domestic investments. Therefore, it is likely that the entity's cost of capital will change to reflect this increased risk.

8 Financial performance evaluation

Introduction

Investors (both shareholders and lenders) will often appraise the financial performance of an organisation, to assess whether the organisation represents a good investment. If it is shown that the organisation's financial performance is declining, the shareholders may decide to sell their shares, and the lenders might change their assessment of the organisation's creditworthiness.

In an exam question, you might also be asked to use ratio analysis to assess whether an entity has met its financial objectives.

To appraise financial performance, it is necessary to first calculate ratios under the following headings:

- profitability ratios,
- lender ratios,
- investor ratios.

The calculation of these ratios is covered in the rest of this chapter.

However, as well as performing the calculations, it will also be important to be able to interpret the figures, so you will find detailed explanations of how to interpret the ratios throughout.

9 Profitability ratios

Several profit figures (gross profit, operating profit, net profit) can be identified in a typical statement of profit or loss.

Profitability is a key performance indicator for an entity. In order to assess performance accurately, it is important to compare figures consistently from one year to the next.

Definitions of different profit figures

Profit figures in the statement of profit or loss

Gross profit = Sales – Cost of Sales

$$\text{Gross profit margin} \quad = \quad \frac{\text{Gross profit}}{\text{Revenue}} \times 100$$

Generally, a high profit margin is perceived to be indicative of good performance.

Operating profit = profit from the trading activities of an entity i.e. sales – operating costs, but before finance costs (interest) and tax

Net profit = Profit after deduction of the finance costs (interest) and tax

EBITDA

EBITDA is an acronym for earnings before interest, tax, depreciation and amortization. In recent years many large entities have adopted EBITDA as a key measure of financial performance. Sceptics suggest that they do this in order to publicise a higher measure of earnings than profit from operations (this type of measurement is sometimes cynically referred to as EBB – earnings before the bad bits).

However, it does make some sense to measure EBITDA, provided that the user fully understands what is included and what is left out. Depreciation and amortization are accounting adjustments, not representing cash flows, that are determined by management. It can therefore be argued that excluding these items in assessing earnings eliminates a major area where management bias can operate. Unfortunately, EBITDA is consequently often misunderstood as being a measurement of cash flow, which of course it is not. Even though two categories of non-cash adjustment are eliminated, financial statements are prepared on an accruals basis. EBITDA makes no adjustments in respect of accruals or working capital movements, and so is emphatically not a cash flow measurement.

There are two measures critical to any analysis of profitability:

(1) **Return on Capital Employed (ROCE)**

(2) **Return on Equity (ROE)**

Return on capital employed (ROCE)

Return on capital employed (ROCE) is a measurement that is frequently used in the analysis of financial statements.

It shows the overall performance of the entity, expressed as a percentage return on the total investment. It measures management's efficiency in generating profits from the resources available.

ROCE is expressed as a percentage, and is calculated as follows:

$$\text{ROCE} = \frac{\text{Operating profit}}{\text{Capital employed}} \times 100$$

where Capital employed = The total funds invested in the business, i.e. shareholders' funds + long term debt, or total assets less current liabilities.

Return on equity (ROE)

ROE gives an indication as to how well the company has performed in relation to its shareholders, the most important stakeholder.

ROE is expressed as a percentage, and is calculated as follows:

$$\text{ROE} = \frac{\text{Net profit}}{\text{Equity}} \times 100$$

where Equity = The book value of shareholders' funds

It is useful to compare the ROE to the ROCE to measure the amount of the return underlying the business that pertains to the shareholder. Note, however, that they are not directly comparable, ROE being based on net profit and ROCE based on operating profit.

Asset turnover

$$\text{Asset turnover} = \frac{\text{Revenue}}{\text{Capital employed}}$$

This calculation is usually expressed as a simple ratio, rather than as a percentage. It shows how much revenue is produced per $ of investment in capital employed.

Return on capital employed – further analysis

When trying to analyse ROCE, it can be useful to break it down as follows into two component ratios:

ROCE = Operating profit margin × Asset turnover

The relationship becomes clear when we put the ratio calculations into the formula:

$$\frac{\text{Operating profit}}{\text{Capital employed}} \times 100 = \frac{\text{Operating profit}}{\text{Revenue}} \times 100 \times \frac{\text{Revenue}}{\text{Capital employed}}$$

Analysing the component ratios may throw some light on the cause of a change in ROCE.

For example, a fall in ROCE could be caused by:

- generating lower sales from the company's capital (lower asset turnover), and / or

- generating a lower profit margin on the sales which have been achieved (lower operating profit margin).

Test your understanding 1 (Integration question)

A company is considering two funding options for a new project. The new project may be funded by GBP10m of equity or debt. Below are the forecast financial statements reflecting both methods of funding.

Statement of financial position extract

	Equity GBPm	Debt GBPm
Long term liabilities (10% bonds)	0.0	10.0
Capital		
Share capital (50 pence)	11.0	3.5
Share premium	4.0	1.5
Reserves	5.0	5.0
	20.0	10.0

Statement of profit or loss extract

	GBPm
Revenue	100.0
Gross profit	20.0
Less expenses	(15.0)
(excluding finance charges)	
Operating profit	5.0

Corporation tax is charged at 30%.

Required:

(a) Calculate the operating profit margin and the asset turnover.

(b) Calculate Return on Capital Employed and Return on Equity, and compare the financial performance of the company under the two funding methods.

(c) What is the impact on the company's performance of financing by debt rather than equity?

Interpretation of profitability ratios

In general terms, high levels of profitability are desirable.

An entity with high profit margins and a high ROCE is usually perceived to be performing well. Similarly, if the ratios grow over time, this is usually perceived to be positive.

The ideal value for the profitability ratios will vary from industry to industry, so be sure to compare the figures to previous years and to other similar businesses if possible.

10 Lender ratios

Definition of gearing
CIMA's Official Terminology provides the following definition of gearing:
"... the relationship between an entity's borrowings, which includes both prior charge capital and long-term debt, and its shareholders' funds."

Gearing is the mix of debt to equity within a firm's permanent capital. There are two particularly useful measures:

(1) Capital gearing – a statement of financial position (balance sheet) measure.

(2) Interest cover – a statement of profit or loss measure.

Capital gearing – a measure of capital structure

There are two key measures of capital gearing:

$$\text{Capital gearing} = \frac{\text{Debt}}{\text{Equity}} \times 100$$

$$\frac{\text{Debt}}{\text{Debt} + \text{Equity}} \times 100$$

The calculation of capital gearing can be done in a number of different ways. In the exam, make sure that you show your workings, and use the same formula consistently.

The most commonly used formula in practice and in the exam is debt / (debt + equity) i.e. the second formula here.

Constituent elements of debt and equity

Debt includes redeemable preference shares, bank borrowings and bonds (overdrafts may be included if they are long-term finance sources).

Equity includes ordinary and irredeemable preference shares (plus reserves if the valuation is at book value).

Market values and book values

Wherever possible, market values should be used in preference to book values for the capital gearing ratio.

When using market values, care must be taken when calculating the market value of equity:

When equity is valued using book values it must include any reserves and retained profits that are attributable to the ordinary shareholders that is:

Book value of equity = ordinary share capital + reserves

When market values are used, reserves must be excluded since they are considered to be already incorporated into the market price of the shares, that is:

Market value of equity = Number of shares × Share price

Interest cover

The interest cover ratio indicates the number of times profits will cover the interest charge; the higher the ratio, the better.

$$\text{Interest cover} = \frac{\text{Profit before interest and tax}}{\text{Interest payable}}$$

The interest cover ratio is used by lenders to determine the vulnerability of interest payments to a drop in profit.

As an alternative to the formula shown here, investors often use EBITDA rather than profit before interest and tax in the formula, because EBITDA is a better approximation to the cash generated by the business (and available to pay interest with).

The debt ratio

Debt ratio

Another useful ratio is the ratio of long-term debt to total assets, which is calculated as follows:

$$\text{Debt ratio} = \frac{\text{Total long term debt}}{\text{Total assets}}$$

This can provide very useful information for creditors as it measures the availability of assets in the business in relation to the total debt.

Test your understanding 2 (Integration question)

Statement of financial position for X Co

	USDm
Non-current assets (total)	23.0
Current assets (total)	15.0
TOTAL ASSETS	**38.0**
Equity and Liabilities	
Ordinary share capital	10.0
Ordinary share premium	4.0
Preference share capital (irredeemable)	1.5
Reserves	1.5
Non-current liabilities	
10% bonds	8.0
Current liabilities	
Trade creditors	8.0
Bank overdraft	5.0
TOTAL EQUITY & LIABILITIES	**38.0**

X Co statement of profit or loss extract

	USDm
Operating profit (PBIT)	4.0
Finance Charges	(1.0)
Profit before tax (PBT)	3.0
Tax @ 30%	(0.9)
Net profit	2.1

Required:

(a) Calculate the interest cover for X Co, and the capital gearing ratio (on the assumption that the overdraft is to be used in the long term so should be included within debt).

(b) Comment on the results of your calculations in part (a).

11 Investor ratios

Investors will wish to assess the performance of the shares they have invested in (against competing entities in the same sector, against the market as a whole, and over time).

There are a number of ratios which will be of specific interest to investors (both debt investors and equity investors).

Market price per share

The market price per share used throughout the following ratio formulae is the ex-dividend market price.

Ex-dividend means that in buying a share today, the investor will not participate in the forthcoming dividend payment.

Sometimes in an examination, the market price may be quoted cum-dividend which means with dividend rights attached. Here the investor will participate in the forthcoming dividend if purchasing the share today. Arguably the investor will be willing to pay a higher price for the share, knowing that a dividend payment is forthcoming in the near future.

The relationship between the cum-dividend price and the ex-dividend price is then:

Ex-dividend market price = Cum-dividend market price − Forthcoming dividend per share

Earnings per share (EPS)

Before we can calculate any ratios we need to calculate a key measure of return, the Earnings per share (EPS).

$$EPS = \frac{\text{Earnings}}{\text{Number of ordinary shares in issue}}$$

where Earnings = Profit distributable to ordinary shareholders, i.e. after interest, tax and any preference dividend.

More details on EPS

An important point to remember is that EPS is a historical figure and can be manipulated by changes in accounting policies, mergers or acquisitions, etc.

Market analysts and company executives occasionally appear obsessed about EPS as a performance measure, an obsession which many think is quite disproportionate to its true value.

It is future earnings which should concern investors, a figure far more difficult to estimate.

P/E ratio

The P/E ratio is a measure of growth; it compares the market value (a measure of future earnings) to the current earnings.

$$P/E \text{ ratio} = \frac{\text{Current share price}}{\text{EPS}}$$

or, alternatively, Total market capitalisation / Total earnings.

The higher the P/E ratio, the greater the market expectation of future earnings growth. This may also be described as market potential.

Earnings yield

The P/E ratio is the reciprocal (in maths, a number or quantity divided into 1) of the earnings yield.

$$\text{Earnings yield} = \frac{\text{EPS}}{\text{Current share price}}$$

or, alternatively, Total earnings / Total market capitalisation.

The market price will incorporate expectations of all buyers and sellers of the entity's shares, and so this is an indication of the future earning power of the entity.

Dividend-payout rate

The cash effect of payment of dividends is measured by the dividend-payout rate.

$$\text{Payout rate} = \frac{\text{Dividend per share}}{\text{EPS}}$$

or, alternatively, Total dividend / Total earnings.

The relationship between the above investors' ratios is usually that an entity with a high P/E ratio has a low dividend payout ratio as the high growth entity needs to retain more resources in the entity. A more stable entity would have a relatively low P/E ratio and higher dividend-payout ratio.

When analysing financial statements from an investor's point of view it is important to identify the objectives of the investor. Does the investor require high capital growth and high risk, or a lower risk, fixed dividend payment and low capital growth?

Dividend yield

This is the relationship of the dividend paid to the current market value of a share.

$$\text{Dividend yield} = \frac{\text{Dividend per share}}{\text{Current share price}}$$

or, alternatively, Total dividend / Total market capitalisation.

However, the dividend represents only part of the overall return from a share.

The other part of the return is the capital gain from an increase in the value of the share. The capital gain from a share may well be far more significant than the dividend.

Dividend cover

Dividend cover measures the ability of the entity to maintain the existing level of dividend and is used in conjunction with the dividend yield.

$$\text{Dividend cover} = \frac{\text{Earnings per share}}{\text{Dividend per share}}$$

or, alternatively, Total earnings / Total dividend.

The higher the dividend cover the more likely it is that the dividend yield can be maintained.

Dividend cover also gives an indication of the level of profits being retained by the entity for reinvestment by considering how many times this year's dividend is covered by this year's earnings.

Test your understanding 3 (Integration question)

Lilydale Co has 5m ordinary shares in issue. Its results for the year are:

	USD000
Profit before tax	750
Tax	(150)
Profit after tax (PAT)	600
Ordinary dividend – proposed	(150)
Retained profit	450

The market price per share is currently 83 cents cum-dividend.

Required:

Calculate the following ratios:

(a) Price/earnings ratio

(b) Dividend payout rate

(c) Dividend yield, and

(d) Dividend cover.

Earnings growth and dividend growth

An analysis of growth rates of earnings and dividends can enable investors to make an assessment of the performance of an entity.

High growth rates in earnings and dividends are usually viewed positively.

Calculations

The growth rate for a single year is:

[(current figure / last year's figure) – 1] × 100%

Over a number of years (n), the implied compound annual growth rate is:

[$\sqrt[n]{}$ (current figure / earliest year's figure) – 1] × 100%

So for example, if earnings per share have grown from $0.28 to $0.33 over a 4 year period, the implied compound annual growth rate is:

[$\sqrt[4]{}$ (0.33 / 0.28) – 1] × 100% = 4.19% per year

Test your understanding 4 (Objective test question)

ALB Co has the following financial objectives:

- to achieve an average earnings growth of at least 6% per annum

- to keep its gearing, measured as [debt / (debt + equity)] by market value, below 35%

In the last three years, ALB Co's operating profit has grown from $4.0 million to $4.6 million, and its profit after tax has grown from $2.3 million to $2.9 million.

ALB Co has 1 million $1 shares in issue, trading at $1.88, and $1,000,000 of bonds, trading at $106 per cent.

Which of the objectives has ALB Co achieved?

A   Both objectives

B   Just the gearing objective

C   Just the earnings growth objective

D   Neither objective

12 Sensitivity of the attainment of financial objectives to changes in economic and business variables

Changes to economic and business variables

When economic variables (such as inflation rates and interest rates) and / or business variables (such as margins and volumes) change, it is important to be able to assess the likely impact on the entity and its chances of achieving its financial objectives.

For example a change in interest rates in the economy might cause an entity's financing costs to rise, and therefore might make it more difficult for the entity to achieve a profitability target.

More detail on interest rates and inflation

The effects of interest rate changes

Changes in interest rates affect the economy in many ways. The following consequences are the main effects of an increase in interest rates:

Spending falls – expenditure by consumers, both individual and business, will be reduced. This occurs because the higher interest rates raise the cost of credit and deter spending. If we take incomes as fairly stable in the short term, higher interest payments on credit cards/mortgages, etc., leave less income for spending on consumer goods and services. This fall in spending means less aggregate demand in the economy and thus unemployment results.

Asset values fall – the market value of financial assets will drop, because of the inverse relationship (between bonds and the rate of interest) explained earlier. This, in turn, will reduce many people's wealth. It is likely that they will react to maintain the value of their total wealth and so may save, thereby further reducing expenditure in the economy. This phenomenon seems to fit the UK recession of the early 1990s when the house-price slump deepened the economic gloom. For many consumers today a house, rather than bonds, is their main asset.

Foreign funds are attracted into the country – a rise in interest rates will encourage overseas financial speculators to deposit money in the country's banking institutions because the rate of return has increased relative to that in other countries. Such funds could be made available as loans to firms in that country by the banking sector.

The exchange rate rises – the inflow of foreign funds raises demand for the domestic currency and so pushes up the exchange rate. This has the benefit of lowering import prices and thereby bearing down on domestic inflation. However, it makes exports more expensive and possibly harder to sell. The longer-term effect on the balance of payments could be beneficial or harmful depending on the elasticity of demand and supply for traded goods.

Inflation falls – higher interest rates affect the rate of inflation in three ways. First, less demand in the economy may encourage producers to lower prices in order to sell. This could be achieved by squeezing profit margins and/or wage levels. Second, new borrowing is deferred by the high interest rates and so demand will fall. Third, the higher exchange rate will raise export prices and thereby threaten sales which in turn pressurises producers to cut costs, particularly wages. If workers are laid off then again total demand is reduced and inflation is likely to fall.

The effects of inflation

Inflation is defined simply as 'rising prices' and shows the cost of living in general terms.

If the rate of inflation is low, then the effects may be beneficial to an economy. Business people are encouraged by fairly stable prices and the prospect of higher profits. However, there is some argument about whether getting inflation below 3% to, say, zero, is worth the economic pain (of, say, higher unemployment). There is agreement, though, that inflation above 5% is harmful – worse still if it is accelerating. The main arguments are that such inflation:

Distorts consumer behaviour – people may bring forward purchases because they fear higher prices later. This can cause hoarding and so destabilise markets, creating unnecessary shortages.

Redistributes income – people on fixed incomes or those lacking bargaining power will become relatively worse off, as their purchasing power falls. This is unfair.

Affects wage bargainers – trades unionists on behalf of labour may submit higher claims at times of high inflation, particularly if previously they had underestimated the future rise in prices. If employers accept such claims this may precipitate a wage–price spiral which exacerbates the inflation problem.

Undermines business confidence – wide fluctuations in the inflation rate make it difficult for entrepreneurs to predict the economic future and accurately calculate prices and investment returns. This uncertainty handicaps planning and production.

Weakens the country's competitive position – if inflation in a country exceeds that in a competitor country, then it makes exports less attractive (assuming unchanged exchange rates) and imports more competitive. This could mean fewer sales of that country's goods at home and abroad and thus a bigger trade deficit. For example the decline of Britain's manufacturing industry can be partly attributed to the growth of cheap imports when they were experiencing high inflation in the period 1978–1983.

Redistributes wealth – if the rate of interest is below the rate of inflation, then borrowers are gaining at the expense of lenders. The real value of savings is being eroded. This wealth is being redistributed from savers to borrowers and from payables to receivables. As the government is the largest borrower, via the national debt, it gains most during inflationary times.

Parity theories

In economic theory, the impact of interest rates on the expected exchange rate is given by the parity theories: interest rate parity and expectations theory.

Interest rate parity

$$F_0 = S_0 \times \frac{(1 + r_{var})}{(1 + r_{base})}$$

where

S_0 = spot rate of exchange

F_0 = forward rate of exchange

r_{var} and r_{base} are the interest rates associated with the variable and base currencies respectively. For example, if an exchange rate is quoted as GBP/USD 1.65 (i.e. GBP 1 = USD 1.65) then the GBP is the base currency and the USD is the variable one.

The interest rate parity theory shows that the forward rate of exchange can be found by adjusting the spot rate of exchange to reflect the differential in interest rates between the two countries.

Test your understanding 5 (Objective test question)

BBL Co is based in country G, where the functional currency is the G$.

Some of BBL Co's suppliers are based in the UK, and they invoice BBL Co in British pounds (GBP). Therefore, the directors of BBL Co keep a close eye on the exchange rate between the G$ and the GBP, and they use the interest rate parity theory to estimate the likely future exchange rates.

The current spot rate is G$ / GBP 1.88 (that is G$ 1 = GBP 1.88), and the expected interest rates in the UK and country G respectively are 5% and 8% over the next year.

What is the forecast spot rate in one year's time using the interest rate parity theory and assuming that the current forward rate is the best forecast of the future spot rate?

A   G$ / GBP 1.18

B   G$ / GBP 1.83

C   G$ / GBP 1.93

D   G$ / GBP 3.01

Expectations theory

$$S_1 = S_0 \times \frac{(1 + r_{var})}{(1 + r_{base})}$$

where

S_0 = spot rate of exchange

S_1 = expected rate of exchange in one year

r_{var} and r_{base} are the interest rates associated with the variable and base currencies respectively. As with interest rate parity above, if an exchange rate is quoted as GBP/ USD 1.65 (i.e. GBP 1 = USD 1.65) then the GBP is the base currency and the USD is the variable one.

The expectations theory shows that the spot rate in the future can be forecast by adjusting the spot rate of exchange to reflect the differential in interest rates between the two countries.

Test your understanding 6 (Objective test question)

The financial director of JW Co is attempting to estimate the likely exchange rate in 1 year's time, so that he can assess the likely value of the entity's foreign currency income.

JW Co is based in country C (functional currency C$) and it makes some sales in the USA, denominated in US dollars (USD). Sales in 1 year's time are expected to be USD 400,000.

The spot rate of exchange is C$ / USD 23.35 (that is C$ 1 = USD 23.35). Interest rates in the USA and country C are expected to be 2% and 6% respectively over the next year.

What is the expected spot rate in 1 year's time, using the expectations theory, and what is the expected value of the USD sales when translated into C$?

A   Exchange rate: C$ / USD 24.27, value of sales: C$ 9.708 million

B   Exchange rate: C$ / USD 24.27, value of sales: C$ 16,481

C   Exchange rate: C$ / USD 22.47, value of sales: C$ 8.988 million

D   Exchange rate: C$ / USD 22.47, value of sales: C$ 17,802

The impact on financial ratios of changes in interest rates, exchange rates and inflation

A change in economic variables such as interest rates, exchange rates and inflation can have an impact on an entity's ability to meet its objectives.

For example, a change in exchange rates could impact selling prices and hence profitability ratios, and could prevent an entity from achieving an earnings objective.

If you are asked in the exam to assess the likelihood of an entity achieving a given objective, you should revise the financial statements to reflect the expected change and then recalculate the necessary ratios.

Test your understanding 7 (Objective test question)

Tillman Co is an unquoted manufacturing company based in country T, whose functional currency is the T$.

Extracts from its most recent financial statements are shown below:

Statement of profit or loss extract

	T$ m
Revenue	100.0
Gross profit	20.0
Less expenses	(15.0)
(excluding finance charges)	
Operating profit	5.0

Corporation tax is charged at 30%.

Tillman has T$ 8 million of long term borrowings, on which it paid interest of 10% last year, and it has 20 million T$ 1 shares in issue.

Tillman Co expects its interest rate to rise by two percentage points next year (to 12%). Also, a strengthening of the currency in Tillman Co's main export market will cause the T$ value of Tillman Co's gross profit to rise to T$ 25 million next year.

What is the likely impact on Tillman Co's earnings per share (EPS), assuming that all other factors remain the same next year?

A   Increase by 20%

B   Increase by 25%

C   Increase by 115%

D   Increase by 215%

The impact on financial ratios of changes in margins and volumes

A change in business variables such as margins and volumes of activity can also have an impact on an entity's ability to meet its objectives.

For example, a fall in sales volume can impact profitability ratios and could prevent an entity from achieving an earnings growth objective.

If you are asked in the exam to assess the likelihood of an entity achieving a given objective, you should revise the financial statements to reflect the expected change and then recalculate the necessary ratios.

Test your understanding 8 (Objective test question)

MATT Co is a manufacturing company based in country M, whose functional currency is the M$.

Extracts from its most recent financial statements are shown below:

Statement of financial position extract

	M$ m
Long term liabilities (10% bonds)	8.0
Capital	
Share capital (M$ 0.50 par)	10.0
Share premium	1.0
Reserves	3.0
	14.0

Statement of profit or loss extract

	M$ m
Revenue	100.0
Gross profit	20.0
Less expenses	(15.0)
(excluding finance charges)	
Operating profit	5.0

Corporation tax is charged at 30%.

MATT Co expects its volume of sales to increase by 5% next year, and its gross profit margin to reduce by 4 percentage points (so for example if the margin were currently 40%, it would reduce to 36% next year).

What is the likely impact on MATT Co's earnings per share (EPS), assuming that its capital structure, tax rate and other expenses stay constant?

A   Increase by 5%

B   Increase by 1%

C   Decrease by 20%

D   Decrease by 76%

13 The use of published accounts for ratio analysis

When external stakeholders, such as potential investors and lenders, try to assess the performance of an entity, the most readily available source of information is the published accounts of the entity.

In trying to interpret the ratios calculated from the published accounts figures, it is important to understand the limitations of the published figures.

Limitations of published accounts figures for ratio analysis

- Published accounts are historic records, not forward looking. However, the Operating and Financial Review (OFR), which companies are encouraged to present as part of their published accounts, will contain the directors' view of the company's prospects.

- The statement of profit or loss is prepared using the accruals concept, so it is difficult to relate the figures to the entity's cash position. However the inclusion of the cash flow statement in the published accounts helps to give an impression of the cash position.

- The published accounts have historically contained only financial information. In recent years entities have been encouraged to report on wider issues (such as environmental and social issues), so users of the accounts are able to see a fuller view of the entity's performance.

These points are covered more fully in the next chapter.

14 End of chapter objective test questions

Test your understanding 9 (Objective test question)

The share price of Woundale Co rose from $2.00 to $2.30 last year. During the year, the company paid out a dividend of $0.12 per share.

What was the annual return to investors last year?

A   15%

B   21%

C   30%

D   42%

Test your understanding 10 (Objective test question)

Q Co is an entity that was set up by the government of Country Q to produce electricity for the country's citizens.

Five years ago it was privatised as the government of Country Q opened up the energy market to competition. The shares of Q co are now owned by both private investors and institutions, and are traded on Country Q's stock market.

What kind of entity is Q Co?

A   Public sector, for-profit entity

B   Public sector, not-for-profit entity

C   Private sector, for-profit entity

D   Private sector, not-for-profit entity

Test your understanding 11 (Objective test question)

Value for money is an important objective for not-for-profit organisations.

Which action is LEAST consistent with increasing value for money?

A   Using a cheaper source of goods without decreasing the quality of not-for-profit organisation services

B   Searching for ways to diversify the finances of the not-for-profit organisation

C   Decreasing waste in the provision of a service by the not-for-profit organisation

D   Focusing on meeting the objectives of the not-for-profit organisation

Test your understanding 12 (Objective test question)

Blunderbuss Co is a listed company with 1 million $1 shares in issue and long term bank borrowings of $5 million. The bank interest rate in the most recent year was 8%, but this is expected to change to 10% for the whole of next year.

The company made an operating profit of $1.84 million last year.

What will be the change in the interest cover of Blunderbuss Co next year, on the assumption that operating profits will stay constant?

A   25% increase

B   20% decrease

C   25% decrease

D   20% increase

Test your understanding 13 (Objective test question)

Angela Co is a listed company.

It has 1 million $0.25 par value ordinary shares in issue, and $100,000 worth of $100 par value bonds.

The shares were originally issued at a premium of $0.05 per share, and the bonds were issued at a 10% discount to par value. The shares and the bonds are trading at $1.22 and $102 respectively.

What is the gearing ratio of Angela Co, calculated as [debt / (debt + equity)] and using market values?

A   7.7%

B   8.4%

C   23.1%

D   28.6%

Test your understanding 14 (Objective test question)

Your manager has asked you to compute the Return on Capital Employed for your company.

Which of the following profit figures would you use in the calculation?

A   Gross profit

B   Net profit

C   Operating profit

D   EBITDA

Test your understanding 15 (Objective test question)

Shepley High School had a problem with high levels of pupil absenteeism in the last academic year, so the senior management team decided to implement a new rewards programme in an attempt to reduce the number of pupils missing classes.

The plan was to reward all pupils with a sticker on a chart for every day that they attended all their classes. Then, at the end of each week, all pupils with five stickers on the chart (i.e. those with a perfect attendance record) were entered into a prize draw with a tablet computer as the prize for the winner.

The end of the academic year is now approaching, and the value for money (VFM) of the programme is being assessed.

Key observations:

- The cost of the programme has been lower than budgeted, because the school managed to get an unexpected bulk discount on purchases of the prize tablet computers.

- The level of absenteeism has remained almost constant compared with the previous year.

- A local newspaper has run a negative campaign about the programme, accusing the school of wasting money and 'bribing' pupils to attend classes. The head teacher has defended the programme, but has admitted that other schools in the area manage to achieve lower levels of absenteeism despite not running such expensive rewards programmes.

Which of the following is the best summary of the results of this Value for Money review?

A   Economy, effectiveness and efficiency have all been achieved

B   Economy and efficiency have been achieved, but not effectiveness

C   Economy and effectiveness have been achieved, but not efficiency

D   Only economy has been achieved

Test your understanding 16 (Objective test question)

The most recent statement of financial position of Johnson Co is as follows:

Assets	$000
Non-current assets	23,600
Current assets	8,400
	32,000
Equity and liabilities	
Capital and reserves	
$1 Ordinary shares	8,000
Retained earnings	11,200
	19,200
Non-current liabilities	
6% Unsecured bond	8,000
Current liabilities	4,800
	32,000

Johnson Co made an operating profit of $3.0 million and a net profit of $2.5 million in the year.

What is the return on equity of Johnson Co?

A   13.0%

B   15.6%

C   31.3%

D   37.5%

Test your understanding 17 (Objective test question)

The P/E ratios of AA Co and BB Co are 7.8 and 9.8 respectively.

Which TWO of the following statements are definitely correct based on this information?

A   AA Co's share price is lower than BB Co's

B   The market perception of BB Co is better than that of AA Co

C   AA Co is an unquoted company and BB Co is a quoted company

D   The risk associated with BB Co must be higher than the risk associated with AA Co

E   BB Co's earnings yield is lower than AA Co's

Test your understanding 18 (Objective test question)

Josh Co is an all equity financed company. It made sales in the most recent accounting period of $10.5 million, and achieved an operating profit margin of 12%.

The directors expect sales to increase by 10% next year, and the operating profit margin to fall to 10% in difficult trading conditions.

What is the likely change in operating profit, assuming all else remains the same?

A   No change

B $0.105 million decrease

C $0.100 million increase

D $1.050 million increase

Test your understanding 19 (Objective test question)

Ghoo Co is a company that has 50,000 shares in issue (nominal value $0.50 per share). The value of its capital employed in the most recent statement of financial position was $0.35 million.

Statement of profit or loss for the most recent accounting period

	$000
Revenue	285.1
Cost of sales	(120.9)
Gross profit	164.2
Operating expenses	(66.9)
Operating profit	97.3
Finance costs	(10.0)
Profit before tax	87.3
Taxation	(21.6)
Profit after tax	65.7

A trainee accountant has computed the return on capital employed (ROCE) and the earnings per share (EPS) of Ghoo Co.

Select the TWO numbers that are incorrect in the workings.

$$ROCE = \frac{\$87,300}{\$350,000} \times 100$$

$$EPS = \frac{\$65,700}{\$25,000}$$

Test your understanding 20 (Objective test question)

An investor in Hook Co has calculated that the company's dividend payout ratio is 25% and that the current dividend yield is 4%.

What is the P/E ratio of Hook Co?

A   100

B   16

C   6.25

D   29

Test your understanding 21 (Objective test question)

Cherry Co has the following accounting ratios, based on its most recent financial statements:

Gross profit margin = 18.6%

Operating profit margin = 10.4%

Asset turnover = 1.5

Interest cover = 4.3

What is the return on capital employed of Cherry Co?

A   It is impossible to tell from such limited information

B   15.6%

C   21.8%

D   27.9%

15 End of chapter case style questions

(a) You are a newly appointed Finance Manager of an Educational Institution that is mainly government-funded, having moved from a similar post in a service entity in the private sector. The objective, or mission statement, of this Institution is shown in its publicity material as:

'To achieve recognized standards of excellence in the provision of teaching and research.'

The only financial performance measure evaluated by the government is that the Institution has to remain within cash limits. The cash allocation each year is determined by a range of non-financial measures such as the number of research publications the Institution's staff have achieved and official ratings for teaching quality.

However, almost 20% of total cash generated by the Institution is now from the provision of courses and seminars to private sector entities, using either its own or its customers' facilities. These customers are largely unconcerned about research ratings and teaching quality as they relate more to academic awards such as degrees.

The Head of the Institution aims to increase the percentage of income coming from the private sector to 50% over the next 5 years. She has asked you to advise on how the management team can evaluate progress towards achieving this aim as well as meeting the objective set by the government for the activities it funds.

Required:

Discuss the main issues that an institution such as this has to consider when setting objectives. Advise on whether a financial objective, or objectives, could or should be determined; and whether such objective(s) should be made public.

(30 minutes)

(b) The following is a list of financial and non-financial performance measures that were in use in your previous profit-making entity:

Financial	**Non-financial**
Value added	Customer satisfaction
Profitability	Competitive position
Return on investment	Market share

Required:

Choose two of each type of measure, explain their purpose and advise on how they could be used by the Educational Institution over the next 5 years to assess how it is meeting the Head of the Institution's aims.

(30 minutes)

Note: A report format is not required in answering this question.

Test your understanding 23 (Case style question)

The directors of ABC, a conglomerate listed on a stock exchange, are appraising one of their wholly-owned subsidiaries, XYZ, with a view to disinvestment. The subsidiary is primarily involved in the manufacture and distribution of car care products.

Financial data for XYZ are shown in the table below.

Required:

(a) Calculate three ratios for each of the two years 20X1 and 20X2 which you consider to be appropriate for the evaluation of the subsidiary's gearing and profitability over the two-year period. Your selection of ratios should ensure measurement of the company's performance in both areas.

(30 minutes)

(b) Prepare a report for the management of ABC. This report should discuss the following:

(i) the performance of the subsidiary during the past two years, using the ratios calculated in part (a) to guide your comments;

(ii) the limitations of the type of historical analysis you have just provided;

(iii) suggestions for the parent company's future course of action in respect of the subsidiary, including comment on an appropriate procedure for valuing the company;

(iv) other, non-financial information which would be useful to the directors of ABC before they make any decision.

(30 minutes)

Summary accounts for XYZ

Statements of financial position at 31 December

	20X2	20X1
	$000	$000
Non-current assets (plant & equip)	2,650	2,255
Other long-term assets (Note 1)	750	675
Cash and marketable securities	195	162
Receivables	765	476
Inventory and work-in-progress	1,250	893
Other current assets	150	91
Total assets	5,760	4,552
Shareholders' funds	2,520	1,726
Long-term debt	2,250	1,976
Other long-term liabilities (Note 2)	275	206
Current liabilities	715	644
Total equity & liabilities	5,760	4,552

Extracts from the statement of profit or loss for the years ended 31 December

	20X2	20X1
	$000	$000
Turnover	6,575	5,918
Cost of goods sold	5,918	5,444
Other expenses	658	592
Other income	23	20
Earnings before finance charges and tax	22	(98)
Finance Charges	395	339
Tax on ordinary activities (Note 3)	(120)	(149)
Net loss	(253)	(288)

Notes:

(1) Other long-term assets are motor vehicles and office equipment.

(2) Other long-term liabilities are finance leases.

(3) The tax shown in the 20X1 profit and loss extract will be recovered in 20X2.

Other financial information

	$000
Depreciation 20X2	175
Net realisable value of inventory	1,091
Net realisable value of plant and equipment	3,907
Inventory and work-in-progress at 1 January 20X1	850
Receivables at 1 January 20X1	435

Test your understanding answers

Test your understanding 1 (Integration question)

(a) Asset turnover   = 100m/20m   = 5.0 times

Operating profit margin   = 5m/100m × 100   = 5%

	Equity finance	**Debt finance**
(b) Return on capital employed	= 5m/20m × 100	= 5m/20m × 100
	= 25%	= 25%

Working

	GBPm	GBPm
Operating profit	5.0	5.0
Interest	0.0	(1.0)
	5.0	4.0
Tax (@30%)	(1.5)	(1.2)
Net profit	3.5	2.8
Return on equity	= 3.5m/20m × 100	= 2.8m/10m × 100
	= 17.5%	= 28%

The financial performance of the two funding options is exactly the same for ROCE. This should not be a surprise given that ROCE is an indication of performance before financing, or underlying performance.

(c) When considering the ROE we see that the geared option achieves a higher return than the equity option. This is because the debt (10%) is costing less than the return on capital (25%). The excess return on that part funded by debt passes to the shareholder enhancing their return.

The only differences between ROCE and ROE will be due to taxation and gearing.

Test your understanding 2 (Integration question)

(a) **Capital gearing ratio**

Debt	= 5m + 8m		= USD13m
Equity	= 10m + 4m + 1.5m + 1.5m		= USD17m
Either	= 13m/17m × 100		= 76.5%
Or	= 13m/(13m + 17m) × 100		= 43.3%

Interest cover = 4m/1m = 4 times

(b) The capital gearing figure looks to be a high percentage, but without further analysis of trends and industry average figures, it is difficult to conclude whether the gearing is too high or whether it is at an acceptable level based on this value alone.

The interest cover measure attempts to equate the earning of profits with ability to pay interest as it falls due. There will be some correlation between the two; however, it is very risky to equate profits earned to cash flow.

However, a value of 4 indicates that the entity was easily able to meet its interest obligations in the most recent accounting period, and that the interest payments are not particularly vulnerable to a drop in profits.

Test your understanding 3 (Integration question)

$$EPS = \frac{\text{Profit distributable to ordinary shareholders}}{\text{Number of ordinary shares in issue}}$$

= 600,000 / 5m = USD 0.12

$$DPS \text{ (dividend per share)} = \frac{\text{Ordinary dividend}}{\text{Number of shares}}$$

= 150,000 / 5m = USD 0.03

Share price (ex-dividend) = 0.83 – 0.03 = USD 0.80

(a) Price/earnings ratio = 0.80 / 0.12 = 6.7

(b) Dividend payout rate = 0.03 / 0.12 = 25%

(c) Dividend yield = 0.03 / 0.80 = 3.75%

(d) Dividend cover = 0.12 / 0.03 = 4

Test your understanding 4 (Objective test question)

The answer is (C).

Earnings growth:

Focus on earnings, so profit after tax. From $2.3 million to $2.9 million amounts to approximately 26% growth in total (= [2.9/2.3] – 1).

Over three years, the annual growth is found by taking $[\sqrt[3]{1.26}] - 1 = 8\%$, so above the target of 6% – objective achieved

Gearing:

Debt value is $1 million × (106/100) = $1.06 million

Equity value is 1 million × $1.88 = $1.88 million

So [debt / (debt + equity)] = [1.06 / (1.06 + 1.88)] = 36%, so above the target of 35% – objective not achieved

Test your understanding 5 (Objective test question)

The answer is (B).

The G$ is the base currency and the GBP is the variable, so the forward rate is 1.88 × (1.05/1.08) = 1.83

Test your understanding 6 (Objective test question)

The answer is (D).

$$S_1 = 23.35 \times \frac{1.02}{1.06} = 22.47$$

so 400,000 USD equates to (400,000 / 22.47 =) C$17,802

Test your understanding 7 (Objective test question)

The answer is (C).

Earnings per share is (profit after tax (PAT) / no. of shares)

Current situation

Current profit before tax = T$ 5.0 m (operating profit) – T$ 0.8 m (interest) = T$ 4.2 m

Therefore PAT = 70% × T$ 4.2 m = T$ 2.94 m.

There are 20 million shares in issue, hence EPS = (T$ 2.94 m / 20 m) = T$ 0.147.

Next year's forecast

Gross profit will be T$ 25m and interest will be (12% × T$ 8 m =) T$ 0.96 m.

Profit before tax = T$ 25 m – T$ 15 m – T$ 0.96 m (interest) = T$ 9.04 m

Therefore PAT = 70% × T$ 9.04 m = T$ 6.33 m.

Hence EPS = (T$ 6.33 m / 20 m) = T$ 0.3165

This EPS of T$ 0.3165 is 215% of the previous year's T$ 0.147, so this is an increase of 115%.

Test your understanding 8 (Objective test question)

The answer is (D).

Earnings per share is (profit after tax (PAT) / no. of shares)

Current situation

Current profit before tax = M$ 5.0 m (operating profit) – M$ 0.8 m (interest) = M$ 4.2 m

Therefore PAT = 70% × M$ 4.2 m = M$ 2.94 m.

There are 20 million shares in issue, hence EPS = (M$ 2.94 m / 20 m) = M$ 0.147.

Next year's forecast

Revenue will be M$ 100 m × 1.05 = M$ 105 million.

Current gross profit margin is 20% (20 / 100) so next year's margin will be 16%.

Profit before tax = (16% × M$ 105 m) – M$ 15 m – M$ 0.8 m (interest) = M$ 1.0 m

Therefore PAT = 70% × M$ 1.0 m = M$ 0.70 m.

Hence EPS = (M$ 0.70 m / 20 m) = M$ 0.035

The EPS of M$ 0.035 is only 24% of the previous year's M$ 0.147, so this is a decrease of 76%.

Test your understanding 9 (Objective test question)

The answer is (B).

The annual return to investors is:

$$\text{Annual return to investors} = \frac{(P_1 - P_0) + \text{Dividend}}{P_0}$$

where P_0 is $2.00, P_1 is $2.30 and Dividend is $0.12.

Test your understanding 10 (Objective test question)

The answer is (C).

When the entity was privatised, it changed from being a public sector to a private sector entity. The fact that its shares are traded on the stock market and that it operates in a competitive market place suggests that it is a for-profit entity.

Test your understanding 11 (Objective test question)

The answer is (B).

VFM is about achieving economy, effectiveness and efficiency.

(A) achieves economy. (C) achieves efficiency and (D) achieves effectiveness.

Test your understanding 12 (Objective test question)

The answer is (B).

Interest cover is (operating profit / interest payable)

Last year = $1.84m / ($5m × 8%) = 4.60

Next year = $1.84m / ($5m × 10%) = 3.68

i.e. a decrease of 20%

Test your understanding 13 (Objective test question)

The answer is (A).

Market value of debt is $100,000 × (102/100) = $102,000

Market value of equity = 1 million × $1.22 = $1,220,000

Therefore, gearing is [102 / (102 + 1,220)] = 7.7%

Test your understanding 14 (Objective test question)

The answer is (C).

Test your understanding 15 (Objective test question)

The answer is (D).

Economy – achieved since the cost of the programme was below budget.

Effectiveness – not achieved since there has been no improvement in the level of absenteeism.

Efficiency – not achieved. Other schools manage to get better results at a lower cost, so this programme has not been an efficient use of resources.

Test your understanding 16 (Objective test question)

The answer is (A).

Return on equity uses the net profit figure. ($2.5 million) and the equity value is equal to the value of the ordinary share capital plus reserves ($19.2 million).

Test your understanding 17 (Objective test question)

The answer is (B) and (E).

A high P/E ratio shows that investors have confidence in the company.

Earnings yield is the reciprocal of P/E ratio, so a high P/E will correspond to a low earnings yield.

Test your understanding 18 (Objective test question)

The answer is (B).

Last year's operating profit was $10.5 million × 12% = $1.260 million

Next year's is expected to be ($10.5 million × 1.10) × 10% = $1.155 million

i.e. a decrease of $0.105 million

Test your understanding 19 (Objective test question)

The workings have been corrected below. The bold figures are the ones that were incorrect.

$$\text{ROCE} = \frac{\mathbf{\$97,300}}{\$350,000} \times 100$$

$$\text{EPS} = \frac{\$65,700}{\mathbf{50,000}}$$

Explanation:

ROCE uses operating profit, not profit after interest.

EPS uses the number of shares, not the value of them.

Test your understanding 20 (Objective test question)

The answer is (C).

Dividend payout ratio is (dividend per share / earnings per share), dividend yield is (dividend per share / share price) and P/E ratio is (share price / earnings per share).

Therefore, P/E ratio = (dividend payout ratio / dividend yield).

Alternatively, make up some numbers to help you manipulate the formulae.

For example, if dividend payout ratio is 25%, assume that dividend per share is $0.25 and EPS is $1. Then, if dividend yield is 4%, the share price must be $6.25 since we have already assumed that dividend per share is $0.25.

Hence P/E ratio = Share price / EPS = $6.25 / $1 = 6.25

Test your understanding 21 (Objective test question)

The answer is (B).

ROCE can be found by multiplying asset turnover and operating profit margin.

Test your understanding 22 (Case style question)

(a) The main issues to consider are:

- Who are the main stakeholders?

- Where is the financing coming from, and in what proportions?

- Are there other, higher level objectives that will supersede those set by the Institution, for example political aims/goals by the government?

- Does the objective need to be measurable?

- How can one objective meet all the competing aims of the stakeholders?

- Will information on the Educational Institution's performance be publicly available?

Setting a financial objective has the main advantage of being measurable. If it is made public, it can also be compared with other, similar, institutions if they also set and make public their objective and their subsequent performance. One objective will probably be insufficient, especially as the Institution has two main markets with very different requirements, costs and revenue structures.

The disadvantages of setting and making public an organisation's objectives are:

– The Educational Institution may not be allowed freedom to choose its own policies, for example on charging fees or selection of state-funded students.

– Political decisions may not affect all publicly funded institutions in the same way or to the same extent.

– Cost allocation between state-funded business and private-sector business may be difficult and politically sensitive.

(b) **Examiner's Note**

The question asks for comments on two performance indicators from each list, four criteria in all. In this answer comments are provided for all six criteria. Candidates may only receive marks for a maximum of two indicators from each list (i.e. no compensation between the lists.)

Introduction

Traditionally, financial measures have been the focus of management attention. Increasingly companies are using non-financial indicators to assess success across a range of criteria, which need to be chosen to help a company meet its objectives. However, an indicator, which is appropriate for one group of stakeholders in an organisation, may not be suitable for another group. Also, indicators that are suitable for short-term performance assessment may be unsuitable, or not optimum, for the long term.

The objective, or mission statement, of this institution is entirely qualitative (and subjective) and makes no concession to financial considerations or constraints.

Financial performance measures

Value added

This is primarily a measure of performance. It is usually defined as sales value less the cost of purchased materials and services. It represents the value added to a company's products by its own efforts. A problem here is comparability with other industries or even other companies in the same industry.

It is less common in the public sector, although the situation is changing and many public sector organisations are now publishing information on their own value added, for example, in the health service.

In respect of teaching, value added could be measured by the percentage of students who leave with a qualification. In post-graduate or executive education, it could be the increase in salary or improved jobs/job prospects obtained by graduates on obtaining their qualification. This may not precisely measure the qualitative aspects of the Institution's objectives, but could provide a close approximation.

In respect of research, the measure is much easier to apply and interpret. Research output can be measured by the number of staff publications in various categories of journal.

Profitability

Profitability may be defined as the rate at which profits are generated. It is often expressed as profit per unit of input (e.g. investment). However, profitability limits an organisation's focus to one output measure – profit. It overlooks quality and this limitation needs to be kept in mind when using it as a measure of success. Profitability as a measure of decision-making has been criticised because

- it fails to provide a systematic explanation as to why one business sector has more favourable prospects than another;

- it does not provide enough insight into the dynamics and balance of an enterprise's individual business units and the balance between them;

- it is remote from the actions that actually create value and cannot therefore be managed directly in all but the smallest of organisations;

- the input to the measure may vary substantially between organisations.

However, it is a well-known and accepted measure that, once the input has been defined, is readily understood. Provided the input is consistent across organisations and time periods it also provides a useful comparative measure. Although the concept of profit in its true sense is absent from most of the public sector, profitability may be used to relate inputs to outputs if a different measure of output is used, for example surplus after all costs to capital investment.

In the case of the educational institution, a problem may be determining the value of the initial investment, which may have been purchased by the government many years ago and appear to have cost nothing. A notional value could be attached to these assets for the purpose. Profits would be fees and other income less costs of salaries and other expenses. Notional rents or depreciation would also have to be estimated.

This measure would have little relevance to the Institution's only stated objective and its calculation is fraught with uncertainties and unknowns. This would be a measure that the organisation might wish to introduce some time in the future, but first it needs to estimate the value of its assets and the true nature of its costs.

Return on investment (ROI)

This is an accounting measure, which is calculated by dividing annual profits by the average net book value of assets. It is, therefore, subject to the distortions inevitable when profit rather than cash flows are used to determine performance. Distorting factors for interpretation and comparison purposes include depreciation policy, stock revaluations, write off of intangibles such as goodwill. A further defect is that ROI ignores the time value of money, although this may be of less concern when inflation rates, and therefore money discount rates, are very low.

Return on assets may not adequately reflect how efficiently assets were utilised; in a commercial context taking account of profits, but not the assets used in their making, for whatever reason, would overstate a company's performance. In the public sector, the concept of profit is absent, but it is still not unrealistic to expect organisations to use donated assets with maximum efficiency. If depreciation on such assets were to be charged against income, this would depress the amount of surplus income over expenditure. Other points which may affect interpretation of ROI in any public sector organisation, including educational institutions are: difficulty in determining value; assets may have no re-sale value; they are, or were originally intended, for use by the community at large and any charge for depreciation may have the effect of 'double taxation' on the taxpayer.

As with profitability, the relevance of this measure at the present time and to the stated objective is limited. First of all, it needs to estimate the value of its assets and the true nature of its costs.

Non-financial performance measures

Customer satisfaction

This measure can be linked to market share. If customers are not satisfied, they will take their business elsewhere and the company will lose market share or go into liquidation. Measuring customer satisfaction is difficult to do formally, as the inputs and outputs are not readily defined or measurable. Surveys and questionnaires may be used, but these methods have known flaws, mainly as a result of respondent bias. It can, of course, be measured indirectly by the level of sales and increase in market share.

In the United Kingdom, the Citizens' Charter was designed to help 'customers' of public services gain satisfaction and redress if they do not, for example refunds on late trains. There are many criteria for determining customer satisfaction in an educational institution, if we assume the 'customer' is the student. For example:

- Evaluations by students at the end of modules or entire programmes. There are problems of bias with this type of measure, but this is true of all surveys.

- Quality audits by government agencies and other regulatory bodies.

- Internal peer reviews.

However, the customer could also be the employer or sponsor of the graduating student. Surveys of satisfaction from this type of customer are less likely to be biased.

This type of measure will already be in place and possibly to a greater extent than in many private-sector institutions. If the Institution wishes to increase its proportion of private funding, then it needs to focus on developing its surveys of employers and likely providers of research funding.

Competitive position

The performance of a business needs to be compared with that of its competitors to establish a strategic perspective. A number of models and frameworks have been suggested by organisational theorists as to how a competitive position may be determined and improved. A manager needing to make decisions must know by whom, by how much and why he is gaining ground or being beaten by competitors.

Conventional measures such as accounting data are useful, but no one measure is sufficient. Instead, an array of measures is needed to establish competitive position. The most difficult problem to overcome in using competitive position as a success factor is in collecting and acquiring data from competitors.

The public sector is increasingly in competition with other providers of a similar service, both in the private and public sector. For example, universities must now compete for government funding on the basis of research output as well as meeting a range of targets for student recruitment. Their advantage is that it is easier to gain access to data from such competitors than is possible in the private sector, as all this information is ultimately in the public domain. Less publicly available is data on the amount of privately-funded teaching obtained by public-sector educational institutions.

This measure will also be already extensively used by the Institution, certainly in respect of its competitive position for students worldwide. Where it might need to develop its measures and improve its measurement data is in respect of privately-funded or sponsored students or courses.

Market share

Market share, a performance indicator that could conceivably be included under the financial heading as well as non-financial, is often seen as an objective for a company in its own right. However, it must be judged in the context of other measures such as profitability and shareholder value. Market share, unlike many other measures, can take quality into account as, it must be assumed, if customers do not get the quality they want or expect the company will lose market share.

Gaining market share must be seen as a long-term goal of companies to ensure outlets for their products and services and to minimise competition. However, market share can only be acquired within limits if a monopoly situation is to be avoided.

It is a measure that is becoming increasingly relevant to the public sector, for example universities and the health service. In educational institutions, the market share within the home country can be measured quite easily by reference to student numbers, in total and by programme/course. It is more difficult to compare market share worldwide. However, this measure of market share is on volume not value. Some institutions have high value programmes, such as MBAs, that distort this simple volume measure.

This institution needs to determine its mix of programmes and courses and set targets aimed at specific markets, for example to achieve x per cent of the market share of home-based MBA students by 2xxx. Such a target by itself will not be a guide to the quality of teaching and would need to be combined with other measures, such as customer satisfaction.

Test your understanding 23 (Case style question)

Key answer tips

Part (a): There are many other alternative ratios which could have been calculated (other than those below), as long as between them the five ratios cover the efficiency, profitability and liquidity of the company. It would also be possible to calculate different figures for each ratio, depending on whether the 'other financial information' was used, whether year-end or average statement of financial position figures were used, etc. What is important is that you show clearly how you have derived each of your chosen ratios, and that you do not overrun the time allowed for this part of the question.

(a) The following ratios can be calculated from the figures in the summary accounts:

Profitability ratios

		20X2	20X1
Return on Capital Employed =	Operating profit	22	(98)
	Capital employed	2,520+2,250	1,726+1,976
		= 0.0046	= (0.0265)
Operating profit margin	Operating profit	22	(98)
	Sales	6,575	5,918
		= 0.33%	= (1.66%)

Gearing ratios

At 31 Dec 20X2, gearing = $\dfrac{2{,}250}{2{,}250 + 2{,}520}$ = 47%

At 31 Dec 20X1, gearing = $\dfrac{1{,}976}{1{,}726 + 1{,}976}$ = 53%

(b)

Report

To: The Management of ABC

From: The Management Accountant

Date: X-X-20XX

Subject: Proposed disinvestment of XYZ

Introduction

This report has been prepared to appraise the financial performance of our wholly-owned subsidiary XYZ, with a view to recommending whether the company should be divested. The analysis has used XYZ's summary accounts for 20X1 and 20X2.

Analysis of recent performance

Gearing has fallen over the period as a result of the new equity injection exceeding the increase in net borrowings.

At 31 Dec 20X2, gearing = $\dfrac{2{,}250}{2{,}250 + 2{,}520}$ = 47%

At 31 Dec 20X1, gearing = $\dfrac{1{,}976}{1{,}726 + 1{,}976}$ = 53%

The company was struggling to pay its finance charge in 20X1 out of available profits; although the profitability situation has improved slightly in 20X2, finance charges payable still exceeds available profits so that a net loss is reported.

Limitations of historical analysis

The analysis above has been carried out on the summary accounts of XYZ for 20X1 and 20X2 which were presumably drawn up under the historical cost convention. In a period of changing prices such accounts can become misleading, for instance with the depreciation charge being calculated on the out-of-date historical cost of the fixed assets. Capital gearing ratios such as calculated above do not give the true picture; it would be more helpful if the summary accounts could be restated under a current cost basis.

There is the further conflict that a decision is to be made about the future based on an analysis of the past. The summary accounts give a historical record of what has happened over the last two years, but give no evidence of the company's likely future prospects. The decision as to whether XYZ should be divested should be taken on the basis of future opportunities and threats to which the company will be exposed.

A final weakness of analysis from accounts is that conventional accounting statements do not recognise a number of important assets that a company might have – a trained workforce, a new product about to be launched on to the market which has been fully researched, other sorts of inherent goodwill. It is impossible to look at the full picture of a company's situation while these assets have been ignored.

Future course of action

Given that ABC has subscribed an extra $1m of share capital of XYZ within the past 12 months, it seems premature to be considering divesting the company. It is perhaps more reasonable to allow the newly invested funds to settle down and reap the benefits for which, presumably, the investment was made. However, if ABC insists on divestment, there is a choice between closing the business (and selling the assets piecemeal) or selling the business as a going concern. If the assets are to be sold piecemeal, their relevant values are their net realisable values, e.g. inventory $1.091m and plant and equipment $3.907m. An aggregate total of the net assets valued at net realisable value would be the minimum acceptable offer.

In the more likely situation of selling the business as a going concern, the value of the business forgone if sold would be the aggregate of the forecast cash flows arising to ABC from XYZ, discounted at ABC's cost of capital. Such a computation requires many estimates to be made, including future growth of XYZ's business and of the car care products business sector as a whole. It may only be possible to identify a range of possible values, but even if it contains a degree of estimation the exercise will still be valuable.

Other valuable non-financial information

Several valuable items of non-financial information have already been identified above which would be useful to the directors of ABC before they make any decision:

(i)   the financial results of XYZ on a current cost basis, i.e. after the effects of price changes have been eliminated;

(ii) whether the company has significant intangible assets not currently recognised in the accounts;

(iii) the future prospects for the company and its place in its business sector if it is retained within the ABC group;

(iv) whether a prospective purchaser of the company has already been identified;

(v)   the effect on the morale of the remaining workforce if the company is closed or sold.

Please let me know if I can be of any further assistance.

Signed: The management accountant

Integrated reporting

Chapter learning objectives

Lead	Component
A1: Evaluate strategic financial and non-financial objectives of different types of entities.	(c) advise on the use of sustainability and integrated reporting to inform stakeholders of relevant information concerning the interaction of a business with society and the natural environment.

Indicative syllabus content

- Limitations of financial statements for incorporated entities, prepared in accordance with international accounting standards, to reflect the value and stewardship of the non-financial capital base.

- Principles and scope of reporting social and environmental issues (e.g. Global Reporting Initiative's Sustainability Reporting Framework and International Integrated Reporting Council guidance).

1 Overview of chapter

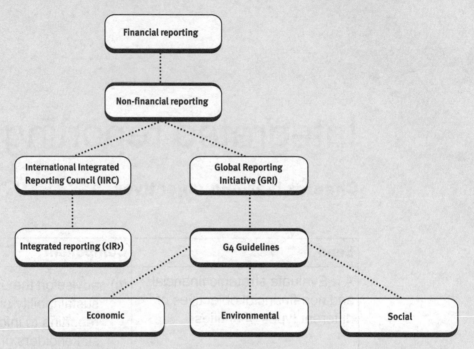

2 Financial and non-financial reporting

Financial reporting

According to the International Accounting Standards Board's (IASB's) conceptual framework, the objective of financial reporting is to 'provide information about the reporting entity that is useful to existing and potential investors, lenders and other creditors in making decisions about providing resources to the entity'.

Financial statements provide historic financial information, but they do not provide a full picture of how the entity is performing.

To help users make decisions, it may be helpful to provide information relating to other aspects of an entity's performance, such as:

- how the business is managed;
- its future prospects;
- the entity's policy on the environment;
- its attitude towards social responsibility etc.

There has been increasing pressure for entities to provide more information in their annual reports beyond just the financial statements since non-financial information can also be important to users' decisions.

Non-financial reporting

The important additional non-financial information can be reported in a number of ways.

For example, the Global Reporting Initiative (GRI) has produced guidelines that propose additional disclosures in addition to the standard disclosures required in the financial statements. In particular, the GRI guidelines suggest that entities should disclose economic, environmental and social performance indicators.

Alternatively, the International Integrated Reporting Council (IIRC) has produced a revolutionary framework known as the Integrated Reporting framework (<IR> framework). The <IR> approach proposes a fundamental change to the way that entities are managed and report to stakeholders.

This chapter first looks at the limitations of financial statements as a basis for performance appraisal. It then explains the GRI guidelines and the concept of Integrated Reporting (<IR>).

3 Limitations of financial statements in reflecting the value and stewardship of the non-financial capital base

Introduction

Capitalism relies on the efficient allocation of capital to deliver returns to investors over the short, medium and long term. It is the job of companies to manage the financial capital that investors provide and also to create and preserve the value generated from other forms of non-financial capital such as people, trademarks/copyrights and natural resources.

The western model of capitalism has been questioned following the onset of the banking crisis in 2007 because of its apparent dependence on short term financial factors over other forms of capital and longer time scales.

Financial statements have traditionally only reported the financial capital of companies in detail, and have not presented detailed information on the non-financial capital base.

Unfortunately, this type of corporate reporting no longer reflects the needs of users of accounting information in the 21st century.

Link to Integrated Reporting (<IR>)

Resilient capitalism needs financial stability and sustainability in order to succeed – and Integrated Reporting is intended to underpin both of these problems through communicating to providers of financial capital the information that they need.

At the heart of <IR> is the growing realisation that a wide range of factors determine the value of an organisation – some of these are financial or tangible in nature and are easy to account for in financial statements (e.g. property, cash), while many such as intellectual capital, competition and energy security are not.

<IR> reflects the broad and longer-term consequences of the decisions organisations make, based on a wide range of factors, in order to create and sustain value. <IR> enables an organisation to communicate in a clear, articulate way how it is drawing on all the resources and relationships it utilises to create and preserve value in the short, medium and long term, helping investors to manage risks and allocate resources most efficiently.

Link to the GRI guidelines

The GRI guidelines encourage organisations to disclose extra information when communicating with key stakeholders. Economic, environmental and social factors disclosed alongside the standard financial statements enable investors and other stakeholders to make a much better assessment of an organisation's overall performance.

The extra disclosures can be made in a separate environmental / sustainability or corporate social responsibility document, or as part of the management commentary presented with the financial statements. The disclosures are usually made by reference to the GRI guidelines, but this is not mandatory in all jurisdictions.

4 The Global Reporting Initiative (GRI)

Overall aim of the GRI

The GRI suggests that entities report performance indicators so that users can monitor their performance from economic, environmental and social perspectives.

GRI guidelines

- The most accepted framework for reporting sustainability is the Global Reporting Initiative's (GRI's) Sustainability Reporting Guidelines, the latest of which 'G4' – the fourth version of the guidelines – was issued in May 2013.

- The G4 Guidelines provide universal guidance for reporting on sustainability performance. They are applicable to all entities including SMEs and not-for-profit entities worldwide.

- The G4 Guidelines consist of principles and disclosure items. The principles help to define report content, quality of the report, and give guidance on how to set the report boundary. The disclosure items include disclosures on management of issues, as well as performance indicators themselves.

- Applying these guidelines is mandatory in some jurisdictions but voluntary in others.

Further information

The Global Reporting Initiative website is

www.globalreporting.org

The financial statements of companies that have applied the GRI guidelines are listed (in the 'Disclosure Database') with a link to their reports.

Background to and objectives of the G4 guidelines

Preface to the G4 guidelines

The following quote from the preface to the G4 guidelines explains the background to the G4 update of the GRI guidelines:

"The GRI Sustainability Reporting Guidelines are periodically reviewed to provide the best and most up-to-date guidance for effective sustainability reporting. The aim of G4, the fourth such update, is simple:

> to help reporters prepare sustainability reports that matter, contain valuable information about the organization's most critical sustainability-related issues, and make such sustainability reporting standard practice.

It is crucial for society and markets that sustainability reporting evolves in terms of content, and from an exceptional activity undertaken by a minority of leading companies to a standard practice.

Together with being more user-friendly than previous versions of the Guidelines, G4 has an increased emphasis on the need for organizations to focus the reporting process and final report on those topics that are material to their business and their key stakeholders. This 'materiality' focus will make reports more relevant, more credible and more user-friendly. This will, in turn, enable organizations to better inform markets and society on sustainability matters."

Materiality considerations

Materiality is placed at the centre of the new sustainability reporting guidelines issued by the Global Reporting Initiative (the so-called 'G4' guidelines).

G4 aims to improve the common language of corporate reporting, focusing heavily on the issues that are material to the organisation and important for stakeholders.

CEOs worldwide have identified the need to build public trust as a crucial part of improving operational effectiveness and engaging with customers following the financial crisis. Sustainability reporting, says the GRI, plays a key role in this, with non-financial reporting being singled out as a particularly effective means of communicating long-term commitment to sustainability.

G4 does not reward reporting of large quantities of indicators but requires companies to indicate and explain omissions of standard or material disclosures.

Overview of the GRI's G4 Guidelines document

The GRI's G4 Guidelines were published in May 2013, in a 94 page document in 7 sections. A brief, section-by-section overview of the contents of the G4 document is given immediately below, followed by a more detailed overview of the key elements.

Overview of the GRI's G4 Guidelines

Sections 1 and 2: The purpose of the Guidelines and how to use the Guidelines

These sections explain that there are two elements to the Guidelines, namely:

- Reporting Principles and Standard Disclosures (covered in Section 4 and the first part of Section 5), and
- Implementation Manual (covered in detail in Section 5).

They then give a step-by-step guide to using the Guidelines and preparing a sustainability report.

Section 3: Criteria to be applied by an organization to prepare Its sustainability report 'in accordance' with the Guidelines

This section explains that an entity can either prepare its sustainability report using Core disclosures or Comprehensive disclosures.

Both options can be applied by all entities, regardless of their size, sector or location.

The Core option provides the background against which an entity communicates the impacts of its economic, environmental and social and governance performance. The Comprehensive option builds on the Core option by requiring more extensive reporting of the entity's strategy and analysis, governance, and ethics and integrity.

A table in this section shows which of the detailed disclosures from the later Section 5 are needed for each of the Core and Comprehensive options.

Section 4: Reporting principles

In this section, the key reporting principles are outlined. These are essentially the required characteristics of the Report Content and the Report Quality.

The Principles for Defining Report Content are given as:

- Stakeholder Inclusiveness
- Sustainability Context
- Materiality
- Completeness

The Principles for Defining Report Quality are given as:

- Balance
- Comparability
- Accuracy
- Timeliness
- Clarity
- Reliability

Section 5: Standard Disclosures

This is the largest section of the G4 Guidelines document, covering 65 pages.

It covers in specific detail the Standard Disclosures required, after first explaining that there are two different types of Standard Disclosures (General Standard Disclosures and Specific Standard Disclosures), and outlining the subheadings that should be used within each type.

General Standard Disclosures

- Strategy and Analysis
- Organizational Profile
- Identified Material Aspects and Boundaries
- Stakeholder Engagement
- Report Profile
- Governance
- Ethics and Integrity

Specific Standard Disclosures

- Disclosures on Management Approach
- Indicators

Then, the Guidelines explain how to separate the Indicators into three Categories - Economic, Environmental and Social. The Social Category is further divided into four sub-Categories, which are Labor Practices and Decent Work, Human Rights, Society and Product Responsibility.

Sections 6 and 7: Quick links and definitions of key terms used

These final sections show how the G4 Guidelines link to other important sustainability reporting guidelines, such as the OECD Guidelines for Multinational Enterprises, and the UN's Guiding Principles on Business and Human Rights.

Then, the document finishes with a glossary of key terms.

Disclosures required by the GRI guidelines

The **Specific Standard Disclosures** are divided into two parts (Disclosures on Management Approach and Indicators). These disclosures cover the specific performance of the entity.

Disclosures on Management Approach (DMA)

The DMA is intended to give the entity an opportunity to explain how the economic, environmental and social impacts related to material Aspects are managed. The DMA also provides context for the performance reported by Indicators (see below).

Indicators

Indicators give information on the economic, environmental and social performance of an entity related to its material Aspects. Disclosures have to be made in each of these three categories (economic, environmental and social performance).

- **Economic**

  The **economic** dimension of sustainability concerns the entity's impacts on the economic conditions of its stakeholders, and on economic systems at local, national, and global levels.

  The **Economic Category** illustrates the flow of capital among different stakeholders, and the main economic impacts of the entity throughout society.

- **Environmental**

  The **environmental** dimension of sustainability concerns the entity's impact on living and non-living natural systems, including land, air, water and ecosystems.

  The **Environmental Category** covers impacts related to inputs (such as energy and water) and outputs (such as emissions, effluents and waste). In addition, it covers biodiversity, transport, and product and service-related impacts, as well as environmental compliance and expenditures.

- **Social**

  The **social** dimension of sustainability concerns the impacts the entity has on the social systems within which it operates.

  The **Social Category** includes the sub-Categories:

  (1) Labor Practices and Decent Work

  (2) Human Rights

  (3) Society

  (4) Product Responsibility

  Most of the content in the sub-Categories is based on internationally recognised universal standards or other relevant international references.

Examples of disclosures

The G4 guidelines encourage disclosure of various 'aspects' in the three key categories: Economic, Environmental and Social.

Based on the above guidance, the sort of disclosures entities might make to comply with the G4 guidelines are:

Economic

Aspect	Example of disclosures
Economic performance	Revenues / costs, levels of pension contributions, taxes paid and subsidies received
Market presence (i.e. the economic impact on the local area)	Comparison of wage rates to other firms locally, proportion of senior managers hired from the local community
Indirect economic impacts	Extent of investment in infrastructure projects
Procurement practices	Proportion of spending with local suppliers

Environmental

Key aspect	Example of disclosures
Materials	Materials used by weight or volume, and the proportion of materials used in production that are recycled
Energy	Total fuel consumption, reductions in the energy requirements of sold products and services
Biodiversity	The nature of significant impacts on biodiversity e.g. species affected and duration of impact
Emissions	Total emissions of greenhouse gases and ozone depleting substances, emissions reductions achieved as a direct result of initiatives to reduce emissions
Products and services (environmental aspects)	How the environmental impact of products services is mitigated, and what proportion of products and packaging materials is reclaimed
Supplier Environmental Assessment	The percentage of new suppliers that were screened using environmental criteria

Social – Labor practices and decent work

Key aspect	Example of disclosures
Employment (i.e. an overview of the entity's staff and policies)	Rate of staff turnover, number of new staff appointed, benefits provided to staff (e.g. life insurance, parental leave)
Training and education	Average hours of training provided per employee
Diversity and equal opportunity	Analysis of employees (and members of the entity's governance bodies) by age, gender, ethnic background, disability etc

Social – Human rights

Key aspect	Example of disclosures
Investment	The number / percentage of the entity's investments and contracts that underwent human rights screening
Freedom of association and collective bargaining	Measures taken to support rights to exercise freedom of association (e.g. joining a trade union) and collective bargaining
Assessment (of the entity's operations)	The number / percentage of the entity's operations that have been subject to human rights reviews (e.g. by groups such as Amnesty International)

Social – Society

Key aspect	Example of disclosures
Local communities	Operations with local community engagement and those with significant actual / potential negative impacts on local communities
Public policy	Financial donations to political parties analysed by country and by recipient
Anti-competitive behaviour	Number of legal actions faced by the entity relating to anti-competitive behaviour and violations of monopoly legislation

Social – Product responsibility

Key aspect	Example of disclosures
Customer health and safety	A summary of breaches of health and safety legislation reported by customers, and a summary of the results of any investigations
Marketing communications	A list of products sold by the entity that are banned or restricted in some markets, a summary of any investigations by the authorities into non-compliance with regulations on advertising / promotions
Customer privacy	The number of complaints received regarding customer privacy issues (for example leaks, thefts or losses of customer data)

Detailed list of aspects and categories of disclosures

Categories and aspects in the G4 guidelines

The examples in the tables above show some of the key disclosures under the G4 guidelines. For completeness, the lists below show all the aspects listed in the guidelines. For more examples, see the GRI's website (www.globalreporting.org).

Economic

- Economic Performance
- Market Presence
- Indirect Economic Impacts
- Procurement Practices

Environmental

- Materials
- Energy
- Water
- Biodiversity
- Emissions
- Effluents and Waste
- Products and Services
- Compliance

- Transport
- Overall
- Supplier Environmental Assessment
- Environmental Grievance Mechanisms

Social – the Social category is split into four sub-categories, each with several aspects associated with it as follows:

Labor Practices and Decent Work

- Employment
- Labor/Management Relations
- Occupational Health and Safety
- Training and Education
- Diversity and Equal Opportunity
- Equal Remuneration for Women and Men
- Supplier Assessment for Labor Practices
- Labor Practices Grievance Mechanisms

Human Rights

- Investment
- Non-discrimination
- Freedom of Association and Collective Bargaining
- Child Labor
- Forced or Compulsory Labor
- Security Practices
- Indigenous Rights
- Assessment
- Supplier Human Rights Assessment
- Human Rights Grievance Mechanisms

Society

- Local Communities
- Anti-corruption
- Public Policy
- Anti-competitive Behavior
- Compliance

- Supplier Assessment for Impacts on Society
- Grievance Mechanisms for Impacts on Society

Product Responsibility

- Customer Health and Safety
- Product and Service Labelling
- Marketing Communications
- Customer Privacy
- Compliance

General Standard Disclosures

As well as the Specific Standard Disclosures identified above, the GRI guidance proposes seven **General Standard Disclosures**. These disclosures cover general issues related to the entity, rather than information specific to its performance.

General Standard Disclosures

Strategy and Analysis

These disclosures provide a general strategic view of the entity's sustainability, in order to provide context for subsequent, more detailed reporting.

Organisational Profile

These disclosures provide an overview of organisational characteristics, in order to provide context for subsequent more detailed reporting.

Identified Material Aspects and Boundaries

These disclosures provide an overview of the process that the entity has followed to define the Report Content, the identified material Aspects and their Boundaries. (Note that the word Aspect is used throughout the Guidelines to refer to the list of subjects covered by the Guidelines.)

Stakeholder Engagement

These disclosures provide an overview of the entity's stakeholder engagement during the reporting period.

Engaging with stakeholders is the basis for good corporate governance but this is often something that entities either ignore or underestimate.

There are many ways to engage with stakeholders, especially as social media channels become more sophisticated. A direct dialogue with stakeholders is important for two reasons:

- as a PR and marketing exercise
- to take a direct pulse of the entity's performance and to assess how well its products are received.

Report Profile

These disclosures provide an overview of the basic information about the report, such as the reporting period, date of previous report and whether Core or Comprehensive disclosure has been used.

Governance

These disclosures provide an overview of the highest governance body of the entity (for example, the Board of Directors).

Ethics and Integrity

These disclosures provide an overview of the entity's values, principles, standards and norms, along with its internal and external mechanisms for seeking advice or reporting concerns on ethics and matters of integrity.

Principles for defining content of the GRI disclosures

Section 4 of the G4 Guidelines provides the following principles for defining report content:

Stakeholder inclusiveness

The reporting entity should identify its stakeholders and explain in the report how it has responded to their expectations and interests.

Sustainability context

The report should present the entity's performance in the wider context of sustainability.

Materiality

Organisations are faced with a wide range of topics on which they could report. Relevant topics are those that may reasonably be considered important for reflecting the organisation's economic, environmental and social impacts, or influencing the decisions of stakeholders, and, therefore, potentially merit inclusion in the report. Materiality is the threshold at which Aspects become sufficiently important that they should be reported.

Completeness

Coverage of **all** the material topics and indicators should be enough to reflect significant impacts and allow stakeholders to assess the reporting entity's performance.

Non-disclosure

In exceptional cases, if it is not possible to disclose certain required information, the report should clearly:

- Identify the information that has been omitted.
- Explain the reasons why the information has been omitted.

In addition, the applicable explanation of omission from the list below should be provided:

- A Standard Disclosure, part of a Standard Disclosure, or an Indicator is not applicable; the reason why it is considered to be not applicable should be disclosed

- The information is subject to specific confidentiality constraints; those constraints are to be disclosed by the organisation

- The existence of specific legal prohibitions; a reference to the specific legal prohibitions should be made

- The information is currently unavailable. In the case of the unavailability of data, the organization should disclose the steps being taken to obtain the data and the expected timeframe for doing so

The organisation should recognise, however, that a large number of omitted Standard Disclosures may invalidate its ability to claim that its sustainability report has been prepared 'in accordance' with the Guidelines.

Principles for defining report quality

As well as the principles for defining report content identified above, Section 4 of the G4 Guidelines provides the following principles for defining report quality:

Balance

The report should reflect both positive and negative aspects of an entity's performance to enable a reasoned overall assessment.

Comparability

Issues and information should be reported consistently. Reported information should be presented in a way which allows stakeholders to assess trends over time and compare the entity to other organisations.

Accuracy

The reported information should be sufficiently accurate and detailed for stakeholders to assess the entity's performance.

Timeliness

Reporting should occur regularly and in time for stakeholders to make informed decisions.

Clarity

Information should be understandable and accessible.

Reliability

The entity should gather, record, compile, analyse and disclose information and processes used in the preparation of a report in a way that they can be subject to examination and that establishes the quality and materiality of the information.

The process of putting together a report in accordance with the GRI guidelines

The GRI's 'G4' Guidelines document sets out the following four step approach to putting together a report.

Step 1: Identification

- Consider the GRI Aspects list and other topics of interest

- Apply the Principles of Sustainability Context and Stakeholder Inclusiveness: Identify the Aspects – and other relevant topics – based on the relevant economic, environmental and social impacts related to all of the organisation's activities, products, services, and relationships, or on the influence they have on the assessments and decisions of stakeholders

- Identify where the impacts occur: within or outside of the organisation

- List the Aspects and other topics considered relevant, and their Boundaries

Step 2: Prioritisation

- Apply the Principles of Materiality and Stakeholder Inclusiveness: Assess each Aspect and other topic considered relevant for:
  - the significance of the organisation's economic, environmental and social impacts
  - the influence on stakeholder assessments and decisions

- Identify the material Aspects by combining the assessments

- Define and document thresholds (criteria) that render an Aspect material

- For each material Aspect identified, decide the level of coverage, the amount of data and narrative explanation to be disclosed

- List the material Aspects to be included in the report, along with their Boundaries and the level of coverage

Step 3: Validation

- Apply the Principles of Completeness and Stakeholder Inclusiveness: Assess the list of material Aspects against Scope, Aspect Boundaries and Time to ensure that the report provides a reasonable and balanced representation of the organisation's significant economic, environmental and social impacts, and enables stakeholders to assess the organisation's performance

- Approve the list of identified material Aspects with the relevant internal senior decision-maker

- Prepare systems and processes to gather the information needed to be disclosed
- Translate the identified material Aspects into Standard Disclosures – DMA and Indicators – to report against.
- Determine which information is available and explain those for which it still needs to establish management approaches and measurements systems

Step 4: Review

- Apply the Principles of Sustainability Context and Stakeholder Engagement: Review the Aspects that were material in the previous reporting period
- Use the result of the review to inform Step 1 Identification for the next reporting cycle

5 International Integrated Reporting Council (IIRC)

Background

The International Integrated Reporting Council (IIRC) was formed in August 2010 and aims to create a globally accepted framework for a process that results in communications by an organisation about value creation over time. The IIRC brings together a cross section of representatives from corporate, investment, accounting, securities, regulatory, academic and standard-setting sectors as well as civil society.

The mission of the IIRC

The IIRC's mission is to create the globally accepted International <IR> Framework that elicits from organisations material information about their strategy, governance, performance and prospects in a clear, concise and comparable format.

The International <IR> Framework will underpin and accelerate the evolution of corporate reporting, reflecting developments in financial, governance, management commentary and sustainability reporting.

The IIRC will seek to secure the adoption of <IR> by report preparers and gain the recognition of standard setters and investors.

Objective

At the time of its formation, the IIRC's stated objective was to develop an internationally accepted integrated reporting framework by 2014 to create the foundations for a new reporting model to enable organisations to provide concise communications of how they create value over time.

After a consultation process, the IIRC published the first version of its 'International Integrated Reporting Framework' in December 2013.

The objective of integrated reporting is to try to create a more holistic and balanced view of the company being reported upon, bringing together material aspects such as strategy, governance, performance and prospects in a way that reflects the commercial, social and environmental context within which it operates.

The <IR> Framework is intended as a guidance for all businesses producing integrated reports. Its executive summary states:

"It is anticipated that, over time, <IR> will become the corporate reporting norm. No longer will an organisation produce numerous, disconnected and static communications. This will be delivered by the process of integrated thinking, and the application of principles such as connectivity of information."

Link between sustainability and <IR>

Sustainability reporting (in accordance with the GRI guidelines explained above) is an intrinsic element of integrated reporting.

Sustainability reporting is fundamental to an organisation's integrated thinking and reporting process, in providing input into the organisation's identification of its material issues, its strategic objectives, and the assessment of its ability to achieve those objectives and create value over time.

More on the link between sustainability and IR

From the **GRI 'G4' Guidelines**

"Sustainability reporting is a process that assists organizations in setting goals, measuring performance and managing change towards a sustainable global economy – one that combines long term profitability with social responsibility and environmental care. Sustainability reporting – mainly through but not limited to a sustainability report – is the key platform for communicating the organization's economic, environmental, social and governance performance, reflecting positive and negative impacts.

The Aspects that the organization deems to be material, in response to its stakeholders' expectations and interests, drive sustainability reporting. Stakeholders can include those who are invested in in the organization as well as those who have other relationships with the organization.

Integrated reporting is an emerging and evolving trend in corporate reporting, which in general aims primarily to offer an organization's providers of financial capital with an integrated representation of the key factors that are material to its present and future value creation.

Integrated reporters build on sustainability reporting foundations and disclosures in preparing their integrated report. Through the integrated report, an organization provides a concise communication about how its strategy, governance, performance and prospects lead to the creation of value over time. Therefore, the integrated report is not intended to be an extract of the traditional annual report nor a combination of the annual financial statements and the sustainability report. However, the integrated report interacts with other reports and communications by making reference to additional detailed information that is provided separately."

The concept of integrated reporting (<IR>)

Integrated Reporting (<IR>) is seen by the IIRC as the basis for a fundamental change in the way in which entities are managed and report to stakeholders.

A stated aim of <IR> is to support integrated thinking and decision-making. Integrated thinking is described in the <IR> Framework as "the active consideration by an organization of the relationships between its various operating and functional units and the capitals that the organization uses or affects".

Purpose and objectives of integrated reporting

The <IR> Framework sets out the purpose of an integrated report as follows:

"The primary purpose of an integrated report is to explain to providers of financial capital how an entity creates value over time. An integrated report benefits all stakeholders interested in an entity's ability to create value over time, including employees, customers, suppliers, business partners, local communities, legislators, regulators, and policy-makers."

The objectives for integrated reporting include:

- To improve the quality of information available to providers of financial capital to enable a more efficient and productive allocation of capital

- To provide a more cohesive and efficient approach to corporate reporting that draws on different reporting strands and communicates the full range of factors that materially affect the ability of an organisation to create value over time

- To enhance accountability and stewardship for the broad base of capitals (financial, manufactured, intellectual, human, social and relationship, and natural) and promote understanding of their interdependencies

- To support integrated thinking, decision-making and actions that focus on the creation of value over the short, medium and long term.

There are three fundamental concepts underpinning integrated reporting:

Value creation for the organisation and for others

An organisation's activities, its interactions and relationships, its outputs and the outcomes for the various capitals it uses and affects influence its ability to continue to draw on these capitals in a continuous cycle.

The capitals

The capitals are the resources and the relationships used and affected by the organisation, which are identified in the <IR> Framework as financial, manufactured, intellectual, human, social and relationship, and natural capital. However, these categories of capital are not required to be adopted in preparing an entity's integrated report , and an integrated report may not cover all capitals – the focus is on capitals that are relevant to the entity

The value creation process

At the core of the value creation process is an entity's business model, which draws on various capitals and inputs, and by using the entity's business activities, creates outputs (products, services, by-products, waste) and outcomes (internal and external consequences for the capitals).

More on value creation

Value creation

Value created by an organisation over time manifests itself in increases, decreases or transformations of the capitals caused by the organisation's business activities and outputs.

That value has two interrelated aspects – value created for:

*   The organisation itself, which enables financial returns to the providers of financial capital
*   Others (i.e., stakeholders and society at large).

Providers of financial capital are interested in the value an organisation creates for itself. They are also interested in the value an organisation creates for others when it affects the ability of the organisation to create value for itself, or relates to a stated objective of the organisation (e.g., an explicit social purpose) that affects their assessments.

The ability of an organisation to create value for itself is linked to the value it creates for others. This happens through a wide range of activities, interactions and relationships in addition to those, such as sales to customers, that are directly associated with changes in financial capital.

These include, for example, the effects of the organisation's business activities and outputs on customer satisfaction, suppliers' willingness to trade with the organisation and the terms and conditions upon which they do so, the initiatives that business partners agree to undertake with the organisation, the organisation's reputation, conditions imposed on the organisation's social licence to operate, and the imposition of supply chain conditions or legal requirements.

When these interactions, activities, and relationships are material to the organisation's ability to create value for itself, they are included in the integrated report. This includes taking account of the extent to which effects on the capitals have been externalised (i.e., the costs or other effects on capitals that are not owned by the organisation).

Because value is created over different time horizons and for different stakeholders through different capitals, it is unlikely to be created through the maximisation of one capital while disregarding the others. For example, the maximisation of financial capital (e.g., profit) at the expense of human capital (e.g., through inappropriate human resource policies and practices) is unlikely to maximise value for the organisation in the longer term.

The value creation process

The value creation process is depicted below, and is explained briefly in the following paragraphs:

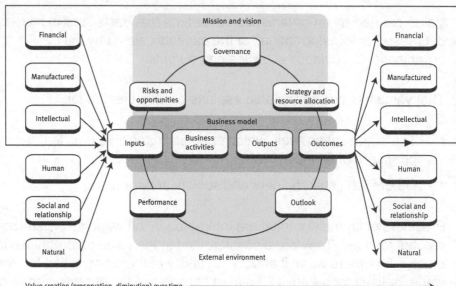

The **external environment**, including economic conditions, technological change, societal issues and environmental challenges, sets the context within which the organisation operates.

The **mission and vision** encompass the whole organisation, identifying its purpose and intention in clear, concise terms.

Those charged with **governance** are responsible for creating an appropriate oversight structure to support the ability of the organisation to create value.

At the core of the organisation is its **business model**, which draws on various capitals as **inputs** and, through its **business activities**, converts them to **outputs** (products, services, by-products and waste). The organisation's activities and its outputs lead to **outcomes** in terms of effects on the capitals. The capacity of the business model to adapt to changes (e.g., in the availability, quality and affordability of inputs) can affect the organisation's longer term viability.

Business activities include the planning, design and manufacture of products or the deployment of specialised skills and knowledge in the provision of services. Encouraging a culture of innovation is often a key business activity in terms of generating new products and services that anticipate customer demand, introducing efficiencies and better use of technology, substituting inputs to minimise adverse social or environmental effects, and finding alternative uses for outputs.

Outcomes are the internal and external consequences (positive and negative) for the capitals as a result of an organisation's business activities and outputs.

Continuous monitoring and analysis of the external environment in the context of the organisation's mission and vision identifies **risks and opportunities** relevant to the organisation, its strategy and its business model.

The organisation's **strategy** identifies how it intends to mitigate or manage risks and maximise opportunities. It sets out strategic objectives and strategies to achieve them, which are implemented through **resource allocation** plans.

The organisation needs information about its **performance**, which involves setting up measurement and monitoring systems to provide information for decision-making.

The value creation process is not static; regular review of each component and its interactions with other components, and a focus on the organisation's **outlook**, lead to revision and refinement to improve all the components.

More on the capitals

The stock and flow of capitals

All organisations depend on various forms of capital for their success. In the <IR> Framework, the capitals comprise financial, manufactured, intellectual, human, social and relationship, and natural, although as explained below, organisations preparing an integrated report are not required to adopt this categorisation.

The capitals are stocks of value that are increased, decreased or transformed through the activities and outputs of the organisation. For example, an organisation's financial capital is increased when it makes a profit, and the quality of its human capital is improved when employees become better trained.

The overall stock of capitals is not fixed over time. There is a constant flow between and within the capitals as they are increased, decreased or transformed. For example, when an organisation improves its human capital through employee training, the related training costs reduce its financial capital. The effect is that financial capital has been transformed into human capital. Although this example is simple and presented only from the organisation's perspective, it demonstrates the continuous interaction and transformation between the capitals, albeit with varying rates and outcomes.

Many activities cause increases, decreases or transformations that are far more complex than the above example and involve a broader mix of capitals or of components within a capital (e.g. the use of water to grow crops that are fed to farm animals, all of which are components of natural capital).

Categories and descriptions of the capitals

For the purpose of the <IR> Framework, the capitals are categorised and described as follows:

- **Financial capital** – The pool of funds that is:
  - available to an organization for use in the production of goods or the provision of services
  - obtained through financing, such as debt, equity or grants, or generated through operations or investments

- **Manufactured capital** – Manufactured physical objects (as distinct from natural physical objects) that are available to an organisation for use in the production of goods or the provision of services, including:
  - buildings
  - equipment
  - infrastructure (such as roads, ports, bridges, and waste and water treatment plants)

- Manufactured capital is often created by other organisations, but includes assets manufactured by the reporting organisation for sale or when they are retained for its own use.

- **Intellectual capital** – Organisational, knowledge-based intangibles, including:
  - intellectual property, such as patents, copyrights, software, rights and licences
  - 'organizational capital' such as tacit knowledge, systems, procedures and protocols

- **Human capital** – People's competencies, capabilities and experience, and their motivations to innovate, including their:
  - alignment with and support for an organization's governance framework, risk management approach, and ethical values
  - ability to understand, develop and implement an organization's strategy
  - loyalties and motivations for improving processes, goods and services, including their ability to lead, manage and collaborate

- **Social and relationship capital** – The institutions and the relationships within and between communities, groups of stakeholders and other networks, and the ability to share information to enhance individual and collective well-being. Social and relationship capital includes:
  - shared norms, and common values and behaviours
  - key stakeholder relationships, and the trust and willingness to engage that an organisation has developed and strives to build and protect with external stakeholders
  - intangibles associated with the brand and reputation that an organisation has developed
  - an organisation's social licence to operate
- **Natural capital** – All renewable and non-renewable environmental resources and processes that provide goods or services that support the past, current or future prosperity of an organisation. It includes:
  - air, water, land, minerals and forests
  - biodiversity and eco-system health.

Not all capitals are equally relevant or applicable to all organisations. While most organisations interact with all capitals to some extent, these interactions might be relatively minor or so indirect that they are not sufficiently important to include in the integrated report.

Role of the capitals in the <IR> Framework

The Framework does not require an integrated report to adopt the categories identified above or to be structured along the lines of the capitals. Rather, the primary reasons for including the capitals in the Framework are to serve:

- As part of the theoretical underpinning for the concept of value creation
- As a guideline for ensuring organisations consider all the forms of capital they use or affect.

Organisations may categorise the capitals differently. For example, relationships with external stakeholders and the intangibles associated with brand and reputation (both identified as part of social and relationship capital here), might be considered by some organisations to be separate capitals, part of other capitals or cutting across a number of individual capitals.

Similarly, some organisations define intellectual capital as comprising what they identify as human, 'structural' and 'relational' capitals.

Regardless of how an organisation categorises the capitals for its own purposes, the categories identified above are to be used as a guideline to ensure the organisation does not overlook a capital that it uses or affects.

How to prepare an integrated report

Introduction

An integrated report should be a designated, identifiable communication.

A communication claiming to be an integrated report and referencing the <IR> Framework should apply all the key requirements (identified using bold type below), unless the unavailability of reliable data, specific legal prohibitions or competitive harm results in an inability to disclose information that is material (in the case of unavailability of reliable data or specific legal prohibitions, other information is provided).

The integrated report should include a statement from those charged with governance that it meets particular requirements (e.g. acknowledgement of responsibility, opinion on whether the integrated report is presented in accordance with the <IR> Framework) – and if one is not included, disclosures about their role and steps taken to include a statement in future reports (a statement should be included no later than an entity's third integrated report referencing the <IR> Framework).

The <IR> Framework sets out several guiding principles and content elements that have to be considered when preparing an integrated report.

Guiding principles – these underpin the preparation of an integrated report, informing the content of the report and how information is presented

Content elements – the key categories of information required to be included in an integrated report under the Framework, presented as a series of questions rather than a prescriptive list of disclosures.

Illustration 1: Guiding principles illustration

Guiding principles

The following seven guiding principles should underpin the preparation and presentation of an integrated report:

Strategic focus and future orientation

An integrated report should provide insight into the organisation's strategy, and how it relates to the organisation's ability to create value in the short, medium and long term and to its use of and effects on the capitals. For example, highlighting significant risks, opportunities and dependencies flowing from the organisation's market position and business model, and giving the management's view of how the organisation balances short, medium and long term interests.

Connectivity of information

An integrated report should show a holistic picture of the combination, inter-relatedness and dependencies between the factors that affect the organisation's ability to create value over time. The more that integrated thinking is embedded into an organisation's activities, the more naturally will the connectivity of information flow into management reporting, analysis and decision-making, and subsequently into the integrated report.

Stakeholder relationships

An integrated report should provide insight into the nature and quality of the organisation's relationships with its key stakeholders. This reflects the importance of relationships with key stakeholders because value is not created by or within an organisation alone, but is created through relationships with others. However, it does not mean that an integrated report should attempt to satisfy the information needs of all stakeholders. An integrated report enhances transparency and accountability, which are essential in building trust and resilience, by disclosing how key stakeholders' legitimate needs and interests are understood, taken into account and responded to.

Materiality

An integrated report should disclose information about matters that substantively affect the organisation's ability to create value over the short, medium and long term. The materiality determination process for the purpose of preparing and presenting an integrated report involves:

- Identifying relevant matters based on their ability to affect value creation

- Evaluating the importance of relevant matters in terms of their known or potential effect on value creation

- Prioritising the matters based on their relative importance

- Determining the information to disclose about material matters

This process applies to both positive and negative matters, including risks and opportunities and favourable and unfavourable performance or prospects. It also applies to both financial and other information. Such matters may have direct implications for the organisation itself or may affect the capitals owned by or available to others.

Conciseness

An integrated report should be concise. It should give sufficient context to understand the organisation's strategy, governance and prospects without being burdened by less relevant information

Reliability and completeness

An integrated report should include all material matters, both positive and negative, in a balanced way and without material error.

Consistency and comparability

The information in an integrated report should be presented:

- On a basis that is consistent over time

- In a way that enables comparison with other organisations to the extent it is material to the organisation's own ability to create value over time.

Stakeholder considerations and the reporting boundary

Reporting boundary

Key to the materiality determination process is the concept of the reporting boundary. Determining the boundary for an integrated report has two aspects:

- The financial reporting entity (i.e., the boundary used for financial reporting purposes)

- Risks, opportunities and outcomes attributable to or associated with other entities/stakeholders beyond the financial reporting entity that have a significant effect on the ability of the financial reporting entity to create value.

The financial reporting entity is central to the reporting boundary because:

- It is the financial reporting entity in which providers of financial capital invest and therefore need information about

- Using the financial reporting entity enables the information in the financial statements to serve as an anchor or point of reference to which the other information in an integrated report can be related.

The diagram below depicts the entities/stakeholders that are considered in determining the reporting boundary:

Financial reporting entity

The financial reporting entity identifies which subsidiaries', joint ventures' and associates' transactions and related events are included in the organisation's financial report. The financial reporting entity is determined according to applicable financial reporting standards which revolve around the concepts of control or significant influence.

Risks, opportunities and outcomes

The second aspect of determining the reporting boundary is to identify those risks, opportunities and outcomes attributable to or associated with entities/stakeholders beyond the financial reporting entity that have a significant effect on the ability of the financial reporting entity to create value. These other entities/stakeholders might be 'related parties' for the purpose of financial reporting, but will ordinarily extend further.

The purpose of looking beyond the financial reporting boundary is to identify risks, opportunities and outcomes that materially affect the organisation's ability to create value. The entities/stakeholders within this portion of the reporting boundary are not related to the financial reporting entity by virtue of control or significant influence, but rather by the nature and proximity of the risks, opportunities and outcomes. For example, if aspects of the labour practices in the organisation's industry are material to the ability of the organisation to create value, then disclosure in the integrated report might include information about those aspects as they relate to suppliers' labour practices.

Illustration 2: Content elements illustration

Content elements

The following eight content elements are the key categories of information required to be included in an integrated report under the Framework.

They are fundamentally linked to each other and are not mutually exclusive. These content elements are not intended to serve as a standard structure for an integrated report with information about them appearing in a set sequence or as isolated, standalone sections. Rather, information in an integrated report is presented in a way that makes the connections between the content elements apparent.

The content elements are stated in the form of questions rather than as checklists of specific disclosures. Accordingly, judgement needs to be exercised in applying the guiding principles to determine what information is reported, as well as how it is reported.

Organisational overview and external environment

What does the organisation do and what are the circumstances under which it operates?

Governance

How does an organisation's governance structure support its ability to create value in the short, medium and long term?

Business model

What is the organisation's business model?

Risks and opportunities

What are the specific risk and opportunities that affect the organisation's ability to create value over the short, medium and long term, and how is the organisation dealing with them?

Strategy and resource allocation

Where does the organisation want to go and how does it intend to get there?

Performance

To what extent has the organisation achieved its strategic objectives for the period and what are its outcomes in terms of effects on the capitals?

Outlook

What challenges and uncertainties is the organisation likely to encounter in pursuing its strategy, and what are the potential implications for its business model and future performance?

Basis of preparation and presentation

How does the organisation determine what matters to include in the integrated report and how are such matters quantified or evaluated?

6 How should the extra information be presented?

Introduction

This chapter has so far explained the benefits of using either the GRI guidelines and / or the <IR> framework to enhance the quality of information presented to stakeholders. However, a question remains regarding what form the extra information should take, and whether it should be presented as a separate document or as part of the entity's published financial statements.

Within the introduction to the <IR> framework document, it says:

> "An integrated report should be a designated, identifiable communication, and should be more than just a summary of information in other communications. Critically, it must make explicit the connectivity of information to communicate how value is created over time.
>
> An integrated report may be either a standalone report or be included as a distinguishable, prominent and accessible part of another report or communication. For example, it may be included at the front of a report that also includes the entity's financial statements."

Therefore, the information is often presented as part of an entity's management commentary (MC) and included as part of the report containing the entity's financial statements.

Purpose of the Management Commentary (MC)

The International Financial Reporting Standards (IFRS) Practice Statement on Management Commentary provides a broad, non-binding framework for the presentation of management commentary that accompanies financial statements that have been prepared in accordance with International Financial Reporting Standards.

It sets out the principles, qualitative characteristics and elements that are necessary to provide users of financial statements with useful information. As the guidance is in the form of a practice statement (rather than an IFRS) compliance with it is voluntary, however where an entity chooses to apply the practice statement it should explain the extent to which it has been applied.

Management commentary is a narrative report that provides a context within which to interpret the financial position, financial performance and cash flows of an entity. Management are able to explain their objectives and strategies for achieving those objectives. Users routinely use the type of information provided in management commentary to help them evaluate an entity's prospects and its general risks, as well as the success of management's strategies for achieving the entity's stated objectives. For many entities, management commentary is already an important element of their communication with the capital markets, supplementing as well as complementing the financial statements.

The practice statement helps management to produce the management commentary that will be reported alongside the financial statements prepared in accordance with IFRS. The users are identified as existing and potential shareholders, together with lenders and creditors.

Framework for presentation of the MC

The following principles should be applied when considering the content of the management commentary:

(a) it should provide management's perspective of the entity's performance, position and progress;

(b) it should supplement and complement information presented in the financial statements;

(c) it should have an orientation to the future;

(d) it should possess the qualitative characteristics of relevance and faithful representation as described in the IASB's *Conceptual Framework for Financial Reporting*.

The management commentary should provide information to help users of the financial reports to assess the performance of the entity and the actions of its management relative to stated strategies and plans for progress. That type of commentary will help users of the financial reports to understand risk exposures and strategies of the entity, relevant non-financial factors and other issues not otherwise included within the financial statements.

Management commentary should provide management's perspective of the entity's performance, position and progress and therefore should derive from the information that is important to management in managing the business.

Test your understanding 1 (Integration question)

Many entities produce a 'Management Commentary' (known in the UK as the Operating and Financial Review).

Required:

(a) Explain why entities produce such a commentary together with a brief description of the typical information that it might contain.

(b) From the perspective of a user of financial statements, explain the advantages and disadvantages of such a report.

7 Future developments

Problems with the current approach to non-financial reporting

The sections above have highlighted the developments in non-financial reporting.

Due to the voluntary nature of these disclosures their impact and effectiveness will depend on various factors:

- **Relevance**: how much weight do/will investors, employees and consumers give to these factors, compared with that given to financial factors (so return on investment, employee benefits and price, respectively)?

- **Reliability**: how much can the performance measured in these areas be relied on? How sure can users of this information be that it is a faithful representation of what has occurred, as opposed to a selective view focusing on the successes? Are there external assurance processes that can validate the information, perhaps using the GRI guidelines?

- **Comparability**: is the information produced by different entities pulled together on a comparable basis, using similar measurement policies, so that the users can make informed choices between entities? If not, all that can be measured is an entity's performance compared with its own performance in previous periods.

The fact that there are two complementary sets of guidelines (GRI and <IR>) is certainly a problem, as is the fact that compliance with the guidelines is voluntary in many jurisdictions.

Future developments

The International Accounting Standards Board (IASB) and International Integrated Reporting Council (IIRC) have recently announced an agreement that will see the two organisations deepen their cooperation on the IIRC's work to develop an integrated corporate reporting framework. The agreement formalises the strong relationship that already exists at multiple levels between the two organisations

As part of the agreement, the two bodies will work together to communicate about work on their respective frameworks and to aim for complementarity and compatibility in the ongoing development of the two standards.

They have also agreed to work together to identify ways in which <IR> and financial reporting standards can be aligned to strengthen corporate reporting, and have committed to having regular, frequent and meaningful information exchanges on what they are each doing.

This will ensure that, where there are overlapping interests, they express a common opinion where possible.

It is likely that at some point in the future, regulation will be introduced to formalise this link between the two organisations.

Test your understanding 2 (Case style question)

Company B owns a chemical plant, producing paint.

The plant uses a great deal of energy and releases emissions into the environment. Its by-product is harmful and is treated before being safely disposed of. The company has been fined for damaging the environment following a spillage of the toxic waste product. Due to stricter monitoring routines set up by the company, the fines have reduced and in the current year they have not been in breach of any local environment laws.

The company is aware that emissions are high and has been steadily reducing them. They purchase electricity from renewable sources and in the current year have employed a temporary consultant to calculate their carbon footprint so they can take steps to reduce it.

Required:

(a) Explain why companies may wish to make social and environmental disclosures in their annual report. Discuss how this content should be determined.

(b) Discuss the information that could be included in Company B's environmental report.

(30 minutes)

8 End of chapter objective test questions

Test your understanding 3 (Objective test question)

HRJ Co is about to prepare a sustainability report for the first time, following the Global Reporting Initiative Guidelines.

The directors are currently preparing the section covering General Standard Disclosures.

Which TWO of the following headings should NOT appear in this section?

A   Society

B   Strategy and Analysis

C   Human Rights

D   Stakeholder Engagement

E   Governance

Test your understanding 4 (Objective test question)

Which THREE of the following are Content Elements as defined by the International Integrated Reporting Council's <IR> Framework?

A   Strategic focus and future orientation

B   Performance

C   Business model

D   Governance

E   Stakeholder relationships

Test your understanding 5 (Objective test question)

Eunice Co has followed the Global Reporting Initiative (GRI) G4 guidelines and is preparing to issue a sustainability report in accordance with the guidelines.

Which of the following statements relating to incomplete disclosure is correct?

A   Information may only be omitted if it is subject to either legal prohibitions or confidentiality constraints

B   Where legal restrictions prohibit disclosure, no further disclosure is required

C   Where information is omitted due to confidentiality constraints, these should be explained

D   Where information is unavailable, it is sufficient to state that this is the case

Test your understanding 6 (Objective test question)

Which THREE of the following are defined by the Global Reporting Initiative as being Principles for Defining Report Quality:

A   Timeliness

B   Materiality

C   Clarity

D   Reliability

E   Completeness

Test your understanding 7 (Objective test question)

Which THREE of the following are objectives of Integrated Reporting, as identified by the International Integrated Reporting Council (IIRC)?

A   To support integrated thinking and decision making

B   To communicate the impacts of economic, environmental and social and governance performance

C   To improve the quality of information available to providers of financial capital

D   To increase the quantity of information available to providers of financial capital

E   To provide a more cohesive and efficient approach to corporate reporting

Test your understanding 8 (Objective test question)

Which THREE of the following are Guiding Principles as defined by the International Integrated Reporting Council's <IR> Framework?

A   Conciseness

B   Materiality

C   Connectivity of information

D   Outlook

E   Basis of preparation and presentation

Test your understanding 9 (Objective test question)

Vinus Co is a UK based company. It is preparing a sustainability report in accordance with the Global Reporting Initiative's G4 guidelines.

The company recently made a political donation to the opposition party during the UK general election campaign.

Under which category would this information be disclosed in Vinus Co's sustainability report?

A   Economic

B   Social – Society

C   Social – Human rights

D   There is no requirement in the G4 guidelines to disclose political donations

Test your understanding 10 (Objective test question)

QQ Co has prepared a draft Integrated Report following the International Integrated Reporting Council's <IR> Framework.

Which THREE of the headings below have been placed in the wrong section of the report?

Guiding principles

A   Strategic focus and future orientation

B   Stakeholder relationships

C   Governance

D   Disclosures on Management Approach (DMA)

Content elements

E   Organisational overview and external environment

F   Strategy and resource allocation

G   Outlook

H   Consistency and comparability

Test your understanding 11 (Objective test question)

Which THREE of the following are defined by the Global Reporting Initiative as being Principles for Defining Report Content:

A   Sustainability context

B   Materiality

C   Stakeholder inclusiveness

D   Reliability

E   Balance

Test your understanding 12 (Objective test question)

Yootha Co is preparing an Integrated Report for the first time.

The directors feel that the eight 'Content Elements' headings listed in the <IR> Framework won't enable them to present the information about their company in the most user-friendly way. Hence, they are planning to use a different set of headings to structure their Integrated Report.

What does the <IR> Framework say about using different report headings?

A   Companies are not allowed to use different headings. The eight 'Content Elements' headings must be used to enable users to compare different companies' Integrated Reports easily.

B   Companies can use different report headings for the 'Content Elements'. The given headings are only provided as suggestions.

C   The eight 'Content Elements' headings must be used if a company is presenting Core Disclosures, but different headings can be used for Comprehensive Disclosures.

D   Different headings can be used in a company's first Integrated Reports, but by the time a company produces its third annual Integrated Report, the eight 'Content Elements' headings listed in the <IR> Framework have to be used.

9 End of chapter case style questions

Test your understanding 13 (Case style question)

It is becoming increasingly common for listed entities to provide non-financial disclosures intended to inform stakeholders about the business's environmental policies, impacts and practices. Supporters of such voluntary disclosures argue that stakeholders have a right to be informed about environmental issues in this way. However, there are also arguments against this type of disclosure.

Required:

Identify and explain the principal arguments against voluntary disclosures by businesses of their environmental policies, impacts and practices.

(15 minutes)

Test your understanding 14 (Case style question)

The directors of World Energy, a public limited company, feel that their financial statements do not address a broad enough range of users' needs. The company's main business is the generation and supply of electricity and gas.

They have reviewed the published financial statements and have realised that there is very little information about their corporate environmental governance.

The company discloses the following social and environmental information in the financial statements:

Corporate Environmental Governance

- the highest radiation dosage to a member of the public

- total acid gas emissions and global warming potential

- contribution to clean air through emission savings

The company wishes to enhance its disclosures but is unsure as to what the benefits would be for the company and what constitutes current practice. The problem that the directors envisage is how to measure and report the company's performance.

Required:

Explain the factors that provide encouragement to companies to disclose social and environmental information in their financial statements, briefly discussing whether the content of such disclosure should be at the company's discretion.

(30 minutes)

Describe how the current disclosure by World Energy of its 'Corporate Environmental Governance' could be extended and improved.

(30 minutes)

Test your understanding 15 (Case style question)

The directors of Glowball, a public limited company, have discussed a study by the Institute of Environmental Management which indicated that over 35% of the world's 250 largest corporations are voluntarily releasing green reports to the public to promote corporate environmental performance and to attract customers and investors. They have heard that their main competitors are applying the 'Global Reporting Initiative'(GRI) in an effort to develop a worldwide format for corporate environmental reporting.

However, the directors are unsure as to what this initiative actually means. Additionally they require advice as to the nature of any legislation or standards relating to environmental reporting as they are worried that any environmental report produced by the company may not be of sufficient quality and may detract and not enhance their image if the report does not comply with recognised standards.

Glowball has a reputation for ensuring the preservation of the environment in its business activities.

Required:

Prepare a report suitable for presentation to the directors of Glowball in which you discuss the current reporting requirements and guidelines relating to environmental reporting.

(30 minutes)

Test your understanding answers

Test your understanding 1 (Integration question)

(a) The need for management commentary

Financial statements, although useful, have limitations in that they are highly summarised and provide historic information. Management commentary (MC) aims to overcome these limitations by having a forward looking focus and enabling management to expand on the information presented in the financial statements.

The management commentary provides a narrative to the financial statements. It can therefore be used to explain the financial results within the context of the environment in which the entity operates. For example, whilst the financial results may not on their own be viewed as positive, the management commentary provides directors with the opportunity to explain that, within the context of the economic climate, the results should be considered positive.

The typical information contained within management commentary would be:

- description of the nature of the entity's activities

- the entity's objectives and strategies to achieve those objectives

- description of the entity's resources and the risks facing the business

- narrative review of the current year's results

- key performance indicators

- non-financial information such as employment and environmental policies

- outline plan for the future development of the business

(b) Advantages and disadvantages to users

Advantages

The MC will provide information regarding the future prospects of an entity. This should enhance the users' ability to make more appropriate investment decisions.

The narrative information should give users a better understanding of the performance and position of the entity.

Producing an MC voluntarily shows the entity as being transparent and willing to communicate. Users may wish to consider such factors, as well as financial information, when making investment decisions.

Users can gain information on non-financial factors addressed by the entity such as how the skills of the workforce contribute to the performance of the entity and whether the entity have a responsible attitude to the environment.

Disadvantages

Since the MC is voluntarily produced, it is unlikely to be prepared in a consistent manner between entities. Therefore users may not be able to perform any meaningful comparison between different entities.

Disclosing information regarding future prospects of an entity may raise the expectations of users. Users may be disadvantaged in the future if the performance does not meet these expectations.

The content of an MC is at the discretion of the directors. They may therefore choose to only disclose positive information. This reduces the reliability of the document for the users.

The content of the MC is not audited. Again, this reduces the level of reliance that users may be willing to place on the information.

Test your understanding 2 (Case style question)

(a) The way in which companies manage their social and environmental responsibilities is a high level strategic issue for management. Companies that actively manage these responsibilities can help create long-term sustainable performance in an increasingly competitive business environment.

Reports that disclose transparent information will benefit organisations and their stakeholders. These stakeholders will have an interest in knowing that the company is attempting to adopt best practice in the area. Institutional investors will see value in the 'responsible ownership' principle adopted by the company.

Although there is no universal 'best practice', there seems to be growing consensus that high performance is linked with high quality practice in such areas as recruitment, organisational culture, training and reduction of environmental risks and impact. Companies that actively reduce environmental risks and promote social disclosures could be considered to be potentially more sustainable, profitable, valuable and competitive. Many companies build their reputation on the basis of social and environmental responsibility and go to substantial lengths to prove that their activities do not exploit their workforce or any other section of society.

Governments are encouraging disclosure by passing legislation, for example in the area of anti-discrimination and by their own example in terms of the depth and breadth of reporting (also by requiring companies who provide services to the government to disclose such information). External awards and endorsements, such as environmental league tables and employer awards, encourage companies to adopt a more strategic approach to these issues. Finally, local cultural and social pressures are causing greater demands for transparency of reporting.

There is no IFRS that determines the content of an environmental and social report. While companies are allowed to include the information they wish to disclose, there is a lack of comparability and the potential that only the positive actions will be shown.

A common framework that provides guidelines on sustainability reporting would be useful for both companies and stakeholders.

The Global Reporting Initiative (GRI) provides guidelines on the content of a sustainability report, but these are not mandatory. However, a number of companies prepare their reports in accordance with the guidelines and the GRI is becoming the unofficial best practice guide in this area.

(b) Company B's environmental report should include the following information.

    (i) A statement of the environmental policy covering all aspects of business activity. This can include their aim of using renewable electricity and reducing their carbon footprint – the amount of carbon dioxide released into the environment as a result of their activities.

    (ii) The management systems that reduce and minimise environmental risks.

    (iii) Details of environmental training and expertise.

    (iv) A report on their environmental performance including verified emissions to air/land and water, and how they are seeking to reduce these and other environmental impacts. Company B's activities have a significant impact so it is important to show how this is dealt with. The emissions data could be graphed to show it is reducing. If they have the data, they could compare their carbon dioxide emissions or their electricity usage over previous periods. Presenting this information graphically helps stakeholders see how the business is performing in the areas it is targeting.

    (v) Details of any environmental offence that resulted in enforcement action, fine, etc. and any serious pollution incident. They can disclose how fines have been reducing and state that there have not been any pollution incidents in the current period.

    (vi) A report on historical trends for key indicators and a comparison with the corporate targets.

Test your understanding 3 (Objective test question)

The answer is (A) and (C).

These two sections should appear in the social category of the specific standard disclosures, not the general standard disclosures.

Test your understanding 4 (Objective test question)

The answer is (B), (C) and (D).

The other two headings are Guiding Principles, not Content Elements, as defined by the <IR> Framework.

Test your understanding 5 (Objective test question)

The answer is (C).

Where information is omitted due to confidentiality constraints, these should be explained.

Test your understanding 6 (Objective test question)

The answer is (A), (C) and (D).

The other two are Principles for Defining Report Content according to the GRI.

Test your understanding 7 (Objective test question)

The answer is (A), (C) and (E).

(B) is an objective of sustainability reporting.

(D) is irrelevant – investors are more interested in the quality, not the quantity, of information available.

Test your understanding 8 (Objective test question)

The answer is (A), (B) and (C).

The other two headings are Content Elements, not Guiding Principles, as defined by the <IR> Framework.

Test your understanding 9 (Objective test question)

The answer is (B).

Political donations have to be disclosed as part of the Public Policy aspect of the Social (Society) category.

Test your understanding 10 (Objective test question)

The answer is (C), (D) and (H).

(C) and (H) are simply the wrong way round i.e. Governance is really a content element and Consistency and comparability is a guiding principle.

(D) should not appear in an Integrated Report. However it would appear as a specific standard disclosure in a sustainability report prepared using the GRI Guidelines.

Test your understanding 11 (Objective test question)

The answer is (A), (B) and (C).

The other two are Principles for Defining Report Quality according to the GRI.

Test your understanding 12 (Objective test question)

The answer is (B).

Note that the Core and Comprehensive Disclosures mentioned in (C) relate to the GRI G4 guidelines, not the <IR> Framework.

Test your understanding 13 (Case style question)

Many of the arguments against disclosure stem from the fact that disclosure is still voluntary. Even in countries such as the UK, where many companies are now legally required to disclose relevant information, there may be few actual requirements as to what exactly should be disclosed.

Several problems result:

- The information disclosed may not be complete or reliable. Environmental disclosures normally appear in the Chairman's Statement, in the Operating and Financial Review or in a 'stand alone' environmental report. Therefore they do not normally have to be audited and can be framed in very general terms. Entities can present information selectively so as to present their activities in a positive light.

- A wide variety of information is disclosed and this may be both narrative and numerical (in the form of key performance indicators). This means that is difficult to compare the performance of different entities. Non-financial performance indicators may not be well understood by users and the basis of their calculation may not be adequately explained.

- The information may not be disclosed consistently from year to year. This means that users cannot assess any progress that is being made.

- Not all businesses disclose information. Those that do are often under particular pressure to prove their 'green' credentials (for example, large public utility companies whose operations directly affect the environment) or because they have deliberately built their reputation on environmental friendliness or social responsibility. This means that (understandably) the public may view environmental reporting as little more than a cynical public relations exercise and not pay much attention to any information presented.

Some believe that there are fundamental problems to do with disclosure itself, rather than with the relevance or reliability of the information:

- Separate environmental reports and/or disclosure in the Operating and Financial Review are no substitute for clear disclosure of environmental costs in the financial statements themselves. This would provide a far greater incentive for entities to act responsibly.

- Equally, disclosure does not solve the environmental problems that are disclosed. There is a school of thought that believes that encouraging and praising voluntary disclosure could create the impression that disclosure, in itself, is enough.

Management may also have arguments against disclosure:

- Producing environmental disclosures is time consuming and costly, particularly where these are intended to be genuinely useful. It may also harm a company's reputation, rather than enhancing it. A useful report must be even handed, and must publish bad news as well as good. Even if the company acts in good faith, there is a danger that disclosure will be seen as merely a public relations exercise.

- A company that presents itself as environmentally responsible in a 'standalone' report may find that this has an impact on the financial statements. Undertaking publicly to carry out particular courses of action (for example, to clean up environmental damage) will create a constructive obligation to do so, even where there is no legal obligation.

Test your understanding 14 (Case style question)

Answer to the first task

The way in which companies manage their social and environmental responsibilities is a high level strategic issue for management. Companies that actively manage these responsibilities can help create long term sustainable performance in an increasingly competitive business environment.

Greater transparency in this area will benefit organisations and their stakeholders. These stakeholders will have an interest in knowing that the company is attempting to adopt best practice in the area. Institutional investors will see value in the 'responsible ownership' principle adopted by the company. Although there is no universal 'best practice' there seems to be growing consensus that high performance is linked with high quality practice in such areas as recruitment, organisational culture, training and reduction of environmental risks and impact. Companies that actively reduce environmental risks and promote social disclosures could be considered to be potentially more sustainable, profitable, valuable and competitive.

Many companies build their reputation on the basis of social and environmental responsibility and go to substantial lengths to prove that their activities do not exploit their workforce or any other section of society. Governments are encouraging disclosure by passing legislation, for example in the area of anti-discrimination and by their own example in terms of the depth and breadth of reporting (also by requiring companies who provide services to the government to disclose such information).

External awards and endorsements, such as environmental league tables and employer awards, encourage companies to adopt a more strategic approach to these issues. Finally, local cultural and social pressures are causing greater demands for transparency of reporting.

There are arguments for giving organisations the freedom to determine the contents of such reports and for encouraging common practices and measures. Standardised reports may fail to capture important information in individual organisations and may lead to 'compliance' rather than 'relevance'. At the same time, best practice would encourage consistency, comparability and reliability, providing a common framework which companies and stakeholders might find useful.

Answer to the second task – Corporate environmental governance

The reporting of corporate environmental governance by World Energy could be improved by including the following information in the financial statements:

- a statement of the environmental policy covering all aspects of business activity

- the management systems which reduce and minimise environmental risks (reference should be made to internationally recognised environmental management systems)

- details of environmental training and expertise

- a report on their environmental performance including disclosing verified emissions to air/land and water, and how they are seeking to reduce these and other environmental impacts. Operating site reports could be prepared for local communities for businesses with high environmental impacts

- details of any environmental offence that resulted in enforcement action, fine, etc, and any serious pollution incident

- a report on historical trends for key indicators and a comparison with the corporate targets

- a simple environmental statement of comprehensive income and statement of financial position including income and value derived from the environment, expenditure on natural resources, licences etc, investment in anti-pollution equipment.

The environmental performance statements and report should be audited and verified to recognise environmental and auditing standards, and companies should perhaps have a health, safety and environment committee.'

Test your understanding 15 (Case style question)

Report to the Directors of Glowball – Environmental Reporting

Introduction

The following report details the current reporting requirements and guidelines relating to Environmental Reporting.

Current reporting requirements and guidelines

The initial goal of environmental reporting was simply to demonstrate a company's commitment to the environment. However, the debate has moved on and the central objective of any environmental report is now to communicate environmental performance.

Wider ranging objectives may also be attributed to the report, such as acknowledging shared responsibility for the environment, differentiating the company from its competitors, obtaining social approval for operating practices and demonstrating regulatory compliance.

Reports in practice vary from a simple public relations statement to a detailed examination of the company's environmental performance. Environmental accounting disclosure is an assortment of mandatory and voluntary requirements.

Not all companies report on environmental performance and those that do report often focus on only selected aspects of performance. It is typically only the leaders in environmental reporting that report in a comprehensive manner.

In the UK, environmental reporting is voluntary although disclosure of environmental matters such as the business's impact on the environment is encouraged in a company's 'Operating and Financial Review' by the ASB's Reporting Statement on best practice on the operating and financial review. Accounting standards on non-current assets, provisions, and research and development costs mention the need to disclose environmental effects.

This voluntary position contrasts with the situation in Denmark and the Netherlands, which have passed legislation making environmental disclosure mandatory for the larger companies. In the USA, the SEC/FASB environmental accounting standards are obligatory, although the standards may not be policed as closely as other accounting standards. The International Accounting Standards Board has not as yet issued a standard in this area. However, IAS 37 Provisions, Contingent Liabilities and Contingent Assets requires disclosure of potential environmental liabilities in certain circumstances.

There is a range of codes of practice and environmental reporting guidelines that have been published. The Global Reporting Initiative's Sustainability Reporting Guidelines, published by the Coalition of Environmentally Responsible Economies (CERES), has become the de facto standard worldwide. The GRI provides a set of principles to enable investors and others to assess environmental performance.

There is a whole range of governmental, academic, professional body and international agencies that have published reports and guidelines that can be accessed and downloaded from the Web. Under the Eco Management and Audit Scheme (EMAS), companies can sign up to agree to a specific code of practice, but the report must be validated by an accredited environmental verifier.

The Companies Act 2006 now requires the directors of UK quoted companies to report on environmental matters, the company's employees and social/community issues.

Conclusion

In summary, environmental reports can enhance a company's reputation and standing, and the use of environmental reporting will expand. Currently, except in a few specific countries, this form of activity reporting is voluntary and, therefore, the extent of disclosure varies significantly.

However, until regulation and standards are developed, the completeness and consistency of environmental reports will not be achieved. Similarly best practice in the attestation of the reports also needs establishing.

Environmental reporting is important to large companies as it is no passing phase. The main question is as to the form and content of the environmental report.

Development of financial strategy

Chapter learning objectives

Lead	Component
A2: Evaluate strategic financial management policy decisions.	(a) evaluate the interrelationship between investment, financing and dividend decisions for an incorporated entity
	(b) advise on the development of financial strategy for an entity taking into account taxation and other external influences.

Indicative syllabus content

- Investment, financing and dividend decisions and the interrelationship between them in meeting the cash needs of the entity.

- Sensitivity of forecast financial statements and future cash position to investment, financing and dividend decisions.

- Considerations of the interests of shareholders and other stakeholders in investment, financing and dividend decisions (e.g. impact on investor and lender ratios, compliance with debt covenants and attainment of financial objectives).

- Determine financing requirements and cash available for payment of dividends based on the overall consideration of the forecast future cash flows arising from investment decisions, business strategy and forecast business and economic variables.

- Lenders' assessment of creditworthiness (e.g. business plans, liquidity ratios, cash forecasts, credit rating, quality of management).

- Financial strategy in the context of regulatory requirements (e.g. price and service controls exercised by industry regulators).

- Consideration of taxation regulations (domestic and international) in setting financial strategy.

1 Overview of chapter

Definitions of key terms

Strategy: A course of action, including the specification of resources required, to achieve a specific objective. (CIMA Official Terminology, 2005)

Financial strategy is the aspect of strategy which falls within the scope of financial management, which will include decisions on investment, financing and dividends.

Strategic financial management: The identification of the possible strategies capable of maximising an entity's net present value, the allocation of scarce capital resources among the competing opportunities and the implementation and monitoring of the chosen strategy so as to achieve stated objectives. (CIMA Official Terminology, 2005)

The importance of financial strategy to an entity

An entity's financial managers must plan their courses of action to achieve the entity's financial objectives.

The key consideration is how should the entity generate cash, and what is the best use of this key finite resource?

For example, should new investments be undertaken, and how large a dividend should be paid?

This chapter identifies the three key decisions in financial strategy and looks at the links between them.

2 The key decisions of financial strategy

We saw in the earlier chapter, 'Objectives', that entities usually have financial objectives that encourage investment and growth.

However, before any investment decisions can be made, the entity's managers will have to assess whether they have enough cash to make the new investments, or whether additional finance will have to be raised.

Therefore, the three key decisions in financial strategy are:

- Investment – what projects should be undertaken by the organisation?
- Financing – how should the necessary funds be raised?
- Dividends – how much cash should be allocated each year to be paid as a return to shareholders, and how much should be retained to meet the cash needs of the business?

These three areas are very closely interlinked.

Investment decision

Financial managers have responsibility for the allocation of financial resources to achieve the organisation's objectives. An important part of their job is to understand the short, medium and long-term capital requirements for investment in fixed assets and working capital that fits with the overall strategy.

Whilst financial managers are unlikely to be solely responsible for the final choice of capital investment projects to be undertaken, they will be actively involved in the evaluation of possible investment opportunities.

More detail on the investment decision

When considering whether a project is worthwhile, a company must consider its implications. Any potential investment is likely to affect:

- **The liquidity of the company** – All projects involve cash flows in and out. The size and timing of such flows should be considered when appraising projects. If an aim of investment appraisal is to satisfy shareholders then it is important to remember that, if a company has no cash, it cannot pay a dividend.

- **The reported profit and earnings** – All projects will change the revenues, expenses and asset values shown in the financial accounts. If shareholders are concerned about such statistics as earnings per share, then the effect of investments on reported figures must be part of the investment appraisal.

- **The variability of cash flows and earnings** – Investors are concerned about the variability of returns from their investments. The greater the variability, the greater the risk, and therefore the greater the return they will require. Thus, when appraising potential projects, managers should consider not only the likely size and direction of cash flows and profits but also whether they are likely to add to or reduce the variability of such flows.

Financing decision

For both non-current asset and working capital investment, the financial manager must decide on the most appropriate type and source of funding.

This will include such considerations as:

- the extent to which requirements can be funded internally, from the organisation's operations. This will involve considerations of dividend policy and tax implications;

- if new, externally provided, finance is required, whether it should be in the form of equity or debt finance. This may affect the level of gearing (the ratio of debt to equity finance) which can have implications for returns required by the providers of capital;

- the extent to which working capital should be financed by long-term finance or short-term credit.

More detail on the financing decision

Financing decisions relate to acquiring the optimum finance to meet financial objectives and seeing that non-current assets and working capital are effectively managed.

Optimum level of cash to hold

The first decision that the financial manager will have to make is how much cash should be held by the business as a buffer against unexpected costs.

Key considerations are:

- **Trade off (too much cash v too little cash)**

  Holding too little cash will potentially leave the entity subject to liquidity problems and possible liquidation. However, holding too much cash has an opportunity cost (lost interest on deposits, or returns on attractive investments) and leaves an entity vulnerable to a takeover bid. The financial manager has to balance the trade-off between these issues and identify the optimum level of cash to hold.

- **Flexibility**

  Holding cash means that the entity can adjust its business plan (for example pursue a takeover opportunity or invest in a new project) rapidly without needing to raise finance first.

- **Expectations of shareholders**

  An entity needs to consider whether its shareholders could make better use of the cash themselves. The shareholders invest money in the expectation that the entity will invest it to create wealth. Theoretically, the entity should only hold cash if the managers expect to be able to use it to increase the wealth of the shareholders.

Sources of finance

The financial manager must possess a good knowledge of the sources of available funds and their respective costs, and should ensure that the entity has a sound capital structure, that is, a proper balance between equity capital and borrowings. Such managers also need to have a very clear understanding of the difference between profit and cash flow, bearing in mind that profit is of little avail unless the entity is adequately supported by cash to pay for assets and sustain the working capital cycle.

Financing decisions also call for a good knowledge of evaluation of risk: excessive borrowing carries high risk for an entity's equity because of the priority rights of the lenders.

A major area for risk-related decisions is in establishing foreign subsidiaries, where an entity is vulnerable to currency fluctuations. Foreign debt is often appropriate to create a hedge of the change in value of the net investment in the subsidiary as a result of currency movements.

> **Benefits of matching characteristics of investment and financing**
>
> The matching approach to financing is where the profile of the of the entity's financing matches the profile of the assets being funded.
>
> This principle can be applied to the matching of maturities.
>
> For example, using long-term finance to fund both non-current assets and permanent current assets, and financing fluctuating current assets by short-term borrowings.
>
> Another area where the matching principle can be applied is in relation to funding a foreign subsidiary.
>
> A matching foreign currency borrowing can be used to hedge the net investment in the subsidiary against currency movements.
>
> **Hedge:** Transaction to reduce or eliminate an exposure to risk. (CIMA Official Terminology, 2005)

Dividend decision

Dividends provide important returns to shareholders and can be seen as an indicator of success of the business. Shareholder returns comprise both increase in share price and cash in the form of dividends.

When deciding on the type of investment and level of finance needed, the financial manager must have regard for the potential effects on the risk and level of dividends payable to shareholders. If the shareholders are not happy with their return, they will be reluctant to invest further, which in turn will affect the funding available for future investment. However, the cash needs of the business must also be considered.

The business may wish to retain cash resources to finance investments rather than increase gearing by raising new funding. Cash resources may also be retained in order to provide rapid access to funds to respond to investment opportunities that might arise in the future or to provide flexibility in the face of poor trading conditions.

The dividend decision thus has two elements:

- the amount to be paid out, and
- the amount to be retained to support the growth of the entity (note that this is also a financing decision).

The level and regular growth of dividends represent a significant factor in determining a profit-making entity's market value, that is, the value placed on its shares by the stock market.

Links between the three key decisions

It is clear from the discussions above that the three areas are closely interrelated.

Investment decisions cannot be taken without consideration of where and how the funds are to be raised to finance them. The type of finance available will, in turn, depend to some extent on the nature of the project – its size, duration, risk, capital asset backing, etc.

Dividends represent the payment of returns on the investment back to the shareholders, the level and risk of which will depend upon the project itself, and how it was financed.

Debt finance, for example, can be cheap (particularly where interest is tax deductible) but requires an interest payment to be made out of project earnings, which can increase the risk of the shareholders' dividends.

3 The impact of investment, financing and dividend decisions on financial ratios

It is important to consider the inter-relationship between investment, financing and dividend decisions when assessing the impact of the decisions on the entity's ratios.

Examples of inter relationships

(1) An investment decision to undertake a profitable project, financed by raising new debt or equity finance, may impact several important investor and lender ratios such as earnings per share, earnings yield and interest cover.

Test your understanding 1 (Integration question)

Seed Co is considering an investment of $20m which is expected have an NPV of $8m, and is expected to increase profit before interest and tax by $4m per annum.

Extracts from the most recent financial statements of Seed Co:

Statement of financial position extracts	$m
Share capital ($1 shares)	16
Reserves	48
Long term borrowings	56
Statement of profit or loss extracts	**$m**
Profit before interest and tax	15.0
Interest	(4.0)
Profit before tax	11.0
Tax at 30%	(3.3)
Profit after tax (earnings)	7.7

The current share price of Seed Co is $2.70 per share.

The directors of Seed Co are considering two alternative ways of financing the new investment.

- borrow the $20m at an interest rate of 6% per annum,

- raise the funds using a 1 for 2 rights issue at $2.50 per share. Assume that this would cause the share price after the issue (BEFORE taking account of the project NPV) to fall to $2.63.

Required:

(a) Prepare profit forecasts for Seed Co for next year under both financing options, assuming that the new project goes ahead. Use the forecasts to calculate the impact of the project and each financing option on Seed Co's interest cover, earnings per share and earnings yield ratios.

(b) Based on the results of your calculations, discuss the likely reaction of the shareholders and the lenders to each of the possible financing options.

(2) Financing requirements and cash available for payment of dividends are determined based on the overall consideration of the forecast future cash flows arising from investment decisions, business strategy and forecast business and economic variables.

Test your understanding 2 (Objective test question)

The Finance Director of CP has calculated that the company needs to raise some additional long term funds to provide finance for the following three proposals.

- CP's trade payables are currently $3.15 million. Suppliers have expressed dissatisfaction that the company currently takes 45 days to pay. They would like to be paid 10 days quicker.

- The bank overdraft has been close to its limit for the last 6 months, and the bank is putting pressure on CP to reduce the overdraft from its current level of $2.2 million to $2 million.

- Over the past three years the annual revenue of CP has stagnated, so the directors are considering expanding operations. Capital expenditure of $1 million would be required to expand the existing distribution facilities.

How much finance needs to be raised in total to fund these three proposals?

A $1.90 million

B $3.65 million

C $4.35 million

D $6.35 million

(3) A change in dividend policy can have an immediate impact on some investor ratios such as dividend cover and dividend yield. However, there may also be other, less obvious, impacts. For example, reducing the level of dividend paid out one year could increase the amount of funds available for re-investment, so there might well be an increased level of growth in profit which could impact ratios such as earnings per share.

Illustration 1 (Integration question)

Elbow Co is an all equity financed company with a functional currency of British pounds (GBP). It has 10 million GBP 1 shares in issue. The directors of Elbow Co are considering a change in dividend policy at the end of this year.

Historically the company has paid out 30% of its profits as a dividend. However, the directors have identified a new project that they want to invest in. The necessary funds for investment could be found by cutting the dividend payout ratio to 10% of profits for this year only.

Forecast profits for the current year are GBP 10 million. Next year's profits will be 15% higher if the dividend is cut and the new project undertaken. Otherwise, profits will stay constant.

Required:

Calculate the dividend per share and the earnings per share for this year and next year, on the assumption that:

(a) the dividend is cut and the project is invested in.

(b) the dividend payout is left unchanged and the project is not undertaken.

Solution:

Current year:

The current year's profit is forecast to be GBP 10 million, so whether the dividend is cut and the project is undertaken or not, the earnings per share (EPS) will be

GBP 10m / 10m = GBP 1.

If the dividend is cut, to 10% of profits, the dividend per share (DPS) will therefore be 10% of this, i.e. GBP 0.10.

If the dividend is not cut, so remains at 30% of profits, the dividend per share (DPS) will be 30% of this, i.e. GBP 0.30.

Next year:

No project:

Next year's profit is forecast to stay at GBP 10 million if the project is not undertaken, so EPS will be

GBP 10m / 10m = GBP 1.

DPS is expected to stay at 30% of this, so will be GBP 0.30.

With project:

Next year's profit is forecast to grow by 15% (to GBP 11.5 million) if the project is undertaken, so EPS will be

GBP 11.5m / 10m = GBP 1.15

We are told that the dividend cut is expected to be for only one year, so DPS next year will revert to 30% of EPS, i.e. 30% × GBP 1.15 = GBP 0.345

4 Objectives and economic forces

When setting the company's financial strategy the financial manager is often influenced by external economic forces.

For example, significant expansion and an increase in dividends may become uneconomic if interest rates are set to rise (thus increasing the amount payable to banks and other debt finance providers).

External influences on financial strategy

Major influences include:

- The need to maintain good investor relations and provide a satisfactory return on investment

- Limited access to sources of finance, either due to weak creditworthiness or lack of liquidity in the banking sector and capital markets

- Gearing level. The main argument in favour of gearing is that introducing borrowings into the capital structure attracts tax relief on interest payments. The argument against borrowing is that it introduces financial risk into the entity. Financial managers have to formulate a policy that balances the effects of these opposing features.

- Debt covenants. These are clauses written into debt agreements which protect the lender's interests by requiring the borrower to satisfy certain criteria (e.g. a minimum level of interest cover)

- Government influence (see below)

- Regulatory bodies (see below)

- Major economic influences, such as interest rates, growth in GDP, inflation rates and exchange rates. The effects of interest rate and inflation changes on the economy are covered below.

- Accounting concepts.

Government influence

Governments often play a large part in influencing business activity. Some examples of the way in which governments can have an influence are as follows:

- Employment policy. Governments play a major role in attempting to stimulate employment. They can do this by funding vocational training programmes and funding employment programmes.

- Regional policy. Governments may make funds available to support regions of high unemployment and social deprivation.

- Taxation policy. The government raises taxes on the profits generated by profit-making entities and on shareholders' dividends.

- Legislation. Laws set out how people can and should behave towards one another, and particularly, how business should be conducted.

Regulatory requirements

Developing financial strategy in the context of regulatory requirements

The financial manager must have a proper understanding of those aspects of legislation which impact upon entities. Such legislation will include the Companies Acts, health and safety regulations, laws relating to consumer protection and consumer rights, laws relating to contract and agency, employment law and laws relating to protection of the environment and promoting competition.

Listed companies also have to comply with Stock Exchange regulations, and entities which operate in some high profile industries will also find regulatory bodies monitoring their performance. For example, in the UK, Oftel (telecommunications), Ofcom (media) and Ofwat (water) have been set up by the government to monitor and regulate their respective industries.

Regulatory bodies

A clear set of objectives is required for each regulatory body. In general terms, a regulatory body will have the power to impose price controls or service controls (i.e. to dictate prices or the quality of service delivered).

The objectives may be classified under three headings:

(1) The promotion of competition.

(2) The protection of customers from monopoly power.

(3) The promotion of social and macroeconomic objectives.

(1) Competition

Where a market is not competitive, or is in the early stages of becoming so, there is a need for regulators whose role is to try to balance the interests of the various stakeholders.

Important issues for regulation are the prevention of 'cross-subsidy', that is the transferring or offloading of portions of overhead costs from lower- to higher-margin products, the limitation of non-price barriers affecting the entry of new competitors, and assuring reasonable quality of product in relation to price. Non-price barriers could include trade restrictions, or restricted access to supplies or distribution channels.

(2) Monopoly power

Where market participants are judged to possess significant market power, and where there is no other protection for customers, controls on prices and on quality of service may be considered.

(3) Social objectives

Government objectives may include the availability and affordability of services in particular areas and to particular groups such as customers in remote rural areas. Regulators often use a 'public interest test' to assess whether an entity's strategy is acceptable – for example strategies compromising national security could be blocked.

5 The impact of taxation on financial strategy

The financial manager will have to consider the taxation implications of all his decisions when setting the entity's financial strategy. For companies with operations in several countries, there will be both domestic and international tax implications.

Specific tax rules differ from country to country, but some general points are explained below.

Domestic tax implications

Any profits generated by a new investment project will be taxable. However, tax allowable depreciation will normally be available on assets purchased, to reduce the overall tax liability.

Debt interest is tax deductible. Therefore if the entity decides to finance new investments through debt finance, there will be tax savings when the interest is paid. This is not the case with dividends to shareholders (if equity finance is used).

Dividends to shareholders will be taxed under income tax rules. However, if the entity chooses not to pay out a dividend, any increases in share price will be taxed under capital gains tax rules when the shares are sold. Therefore, most investors have a preference as to whether they'd like the entity to pay out a dividend or not.

Where the entity meets certain conditions its shares may be issued under special schemes that allow the investor tax relief on the investment, and/or when the shares are sold. An example is the Enterprise Investment Scheme in the UK, which is intended to encourage investors to subscribe for new shares in unquoted trading companies.

International tax implications

The main additional tax consideration for an entity with international operations is how to minimise the overall tax liability of the international entity.

For example, a decision will need to be made as to where the head office of the entity should be located. Multinational companies are often attracted to set up their operations in a low tax economy.

Also, the group's transfer pricing policy will be an important consideration. Tax authorities only allow transfer prices that are set at a fair, 'arm's length' level, so there is no opportunity to manipulate the entity's tax liability. The authorities will disallow any transfer prices that are considered to be set purely for the purposes of moving as much profit as possible into the lowest tax country.

The tax authorities also monitor royalties and management charges alongside transfer prices. Any royalties or management charges paid from one group company to another will not be allowed if the authorities feel that they are being used to increase profits in one group company (based in a low tax country) at the expense of another (based in a higher tax country).

6 The lender's assessment of creditworthiness

When an entity (a borrower) is seeking to raise debt finance, the lender (for example the bank) will carry out an assessment of the borrower to decide whether to lend.

Information presented by the borrower to the lender

In order to apply for the debt finance from a bank or other lender, an entity will have to put together a business plan. This will contain important information regarding the borrower's plans, such as:

- the purpose, amount and duration of the borrowing
- detailed cash flow forecasts, showing the likely cash flows of the borrower and aiming to show the lender that the prospects for the borrower are good
- an explanation of how the borrower is proposing to repay the borrowing.

Assessment of creditworthiness by the lender

The lender will carry out an assessment of the potential borrower by considering the following information:

- **Analysis of business plan**

  The lender will perform a detailed analysis of the business plan presented by the potential borrower. This will include detailed ratio analysis of the potential borrower's recent accounts and forecasts (see detail on ratio analysis below).

- **Business prospects of the potential borrower**

  An analysis of the business plan will give the lender an initial insight into the business prospects of the borrower. However, it will be important for the lender to carry out further analysis in an attempt to build up an independent assessment of the prospects of the borrower. For example, the lender will assess

  - the quality and track record of the borrower's management
  - the risk profile of the company

> – the prospects for the industry sector – e.g. competitor growth, market share trends etc

- **Security available**

  The lender will look at the statement of financial position of the potential borrower to assess whether there are assets that could be used to provide security for the borrowings. Lending the money secured on assets of the borrower would significantly reduce the risk to the lender.

- **Credit rating**

  The credit rating of the borrower is also an important factor. An entity with a poor credit rating will find it more difficult to borrow money. If the lender does decide to lend, a higher interest rate would be charged to compensate for the risk taken on by the lender.

- **Other borrowings and covenants**

  The risk to the lender will be higher if the potential borrower is already highly geared and has debt covenants attached to its existing borrowings.

  If the potential borrower has other borrowings and hence interest commitments, this could increase the risk to the new lender by reducing the amount of cash available to pay the interest on the new borrowing and possibly reducing the availability of assets to be used as security.

  The existence of covenants on existing borrowings could also cause problems for a new lender, especially if the covenants give priority to existing lenders over any new lenders.

Use of ratio analysis

The analysis undertaken by the lender will use many of the ratios that were covered in Chapter 1: 'Objectives'.

The key objective of the lender will be to assess the liquidity of the potential borrower i.e. whether the borrower's cash flows will be sufficient to pay the interest and repay the capital according to the proposed repayment schedule.

For example, the interest cover ratio will be particularly important, since it gives an idea of how likely it is that the firm will continue to be able to meet its interest payments even if profits fall.

Lenders might be even more interested in calculating interest cover with regard to EBITDA or cash (rather than profits) to give a more practical measure of cover.

Other ratios such as the stock market ratios (P/E ratio in particular) will also give the lender a feel for how the rest of the market views the firm. If the firm has a high P/E ratio, its growth prospects are good, so lending to such a firm would be perceived as low risk.

Rationale for analysing gearing

Analysis of capital structure

The gearing ratio is an important measure of risk. It is important to analyse, particularly for users such as shareholders and creditors, the ability to satisfy debts falling due after one year. There are two elements to consider: repayment of capital and payment of interest.

The assessment of an entity's gearing risk can be identified from two areas. The statement of financial position shows the current liquidity and capital structure of the entity, that is the short-term liquidity and the level of fixed prior charge capital. The statement of profit or loss shows the profitability of the entity generally, indicating its ability to generate cash, some of which may be available to repay debt.

The capital structure of the entity provides information about the relative risk that is accepted by shareholders and creditors. As long-term debt increases relative to share-holders' funds then more risk is assumed by long-term creditors and so they would require higher rewards, thereby decreasing resources available for the shareholders. As risk increases, creditors require higher interest in order to compensate for the higher risk.

However, the use of debt by management in their capital structure can assist in increasing profits available to shareholders. Cash received into the business from lenders will be used to generate revenue and profits. As interest costs are fixed, any profits generated in excess of the interest costs will accrue to the shareholders. There is, however, a negative side to the use of debt in the business. If the cash from the debt does not raise sufficient profits then the fixed interest cost must be paid first and so profits available to shareholders are decreased, and may be extinguished completely.

Interpretation of gearing ratios

Statement of financial position

A high proportion of debt finance in the entity's capital structure is seen as being risky by the entity's shareholders (which causes them to demand higher returns on their equity – see the later chapter: 'Financing – Capital structure' for more details).

However, it is difficult to give any practical guidance as to what a 'safe' level of gearing might be. Compare the gearing ratio to prior years and budgets, and to the gearing ratio of similar entities, to assess whether it looks too high.

Also, consider in particular the level of non-current assets on the statement of financial position which could be used for security. A high level of non-current assets (much higher than the current value of debt finance) indicates that potentially the entity should be able to raise more debt finance quite easily.

Statement of profit or loss

An interest cover ratio less than 1 indicates that the entity is having trouble servicing its debt finance. The higher the ratio is above 1, the easier it should be for the entity to continue paying its interest, so the less risky the entity appears to be.

However, note that a lack of cash, rather than a lack of profit, is usually the reason why a company fails to meet its interest obligations. This is why analysts often substitute EBITDA (or even cash flow) into the formula instead of profit, to give a more useful measure of cover.

Independent credit rating agencies

In order to help with the assessment of creditworthiness, credit ratings issued by an independent credit rating agency will often be considered.

Moody's and Standard and Poor's (S&P) are the two biggest credit rating agencies. Each of these agencies aims to provide a rating system to help investors determine the risk associated with investing in a specific company, investing instrument or market.

So for example, for a public issue of bonds, the company will obtain a specific rating for that issue from a rating agency before the issue takes place.

Setting credit ratings

These large credit rating agencies monitor the performance of all major businesses and rate them according to how likely it is that they will be able to afford to repay any debts.

The rating agency will focus on:

- Plans and forecasts of the company

- The strength and trends in the industry in which the company operates and the company's competitive position within that industry.

- Country risks – the political and regulatory risks

- The quality of the management team, including experience and track record

- Corporate attitude to risk taking

- Financial position – including capital structure and current debt profile

- Financial ratios

- Any parental support such as guarantees.

Updating of credit ratings

The ratings agencies are constantly assessing the performance of entities, and will update their ratings regularly.

For example, if an entity releases some worse-than-expected financial results, or if market analysts predict that an entity is likely to perform worse than previously thought, the ratings agencies may react by downgrading the entity's credit rating, or warning of a possibly future downgrade by issuing a Negative Outlook statement.

This could have a significant impact on the entity's plans to raise new finance e.g. the entity might have to delay a planned debt issue until such time that the rating rises again, or an issue currently in progress might not be fully subscribed.

The meaning of credit ratings

The different credit rating agencies use different terms to describe high risk and low risk companies or issues, as shown by the following table:

Moody's	S & P	Grade	Risk
Aaa	AAA	Investment	Lowest risk
Aa	AA	Investment	Low risk
A	A	Investment	Low risk
Baa	BBB	Investment	Medium risk
Ba, B	BB,B	Junk	High risk
Caa, Ca, C	CCC,CC,C	Junk	Highest risk
C	D	Junk	In default

A rating can refer to an entity's specific financial obligation or to its general creditworthiness.

Thus, for S&P, an 'AAA' rating signifies the highest investment grade and means that there is very low credit risk. 'AA' represents very high credit quality; 'A' means high credit quality, and 'BBB' is good credit quality. These ratings are considered to be investment grade, which means that the security or entity being rated carries a quality level that many institutions require when considering investments.

Ratings that fall under 'BBB' (for S&P) are considered to be speculative or junk grade. This is indicative of high risk.

The link between credit ratings and interest rates

An entity rated 'AAA' (the best rating) by Standard and Poor's is a very low risk investment.

Consequently, a lender would generally set a relatively low interest rate on a loan to an 'AAA' entity. By contrast, a lower rated entity would generally have to pay higher rates of interest (or might struggle to raise debt finance at all if its rating were especially low).

This is because risk and return are always linked: if an investor is likely to face high risks, he demands a high return to compensate him for this risk.

7 End of chapter objective test questions

Test your understanding 3 (Objective test question)

Which of the following financial ratios is likely to be of LEAST interest to a lender when assessing the creditworthiness of a borrower?

A   Interest cover

B   Gearing

C   Operating profit margin

D   EBITDA to finance charges ratio

Test your understanding 4 (Objective test question)

White Co has 1 million shares in issue. The shares have a nominal value of $1 and are currently trading at $2.00. White Co's P/E ratio is 7.05.

The directors are considering raising $400,000 in order to undertake a new project. It is expected that the new project will cause earnings to rise by $30,000 each year.

If White Co uses a 1 for 4 rights issue to raise the finance, what is the expected earnings per share (EPS) of White Co after the finance has been raised and the project undertaken?

A $1.60

B $1.41

C $0.28

D $0.25

Test your understanding 5 (Objective test question)

A company has 20 million $0.50 ordinary shares in issue and the current share price is $1.33.

A proposed new project is expected to have an IRR of 15% and an NPV of $8 million and requires an initial investment of $10 million.

If the market is efficient and the share price moves to reflect this information on the day that the project is announced, what is the theoretical movement in the share price on that day?

A   No change

B $0.40 increase

C $0.90 increase

D $0.20 increase

Test your understanding 6 (Objective test question)

Lazaretto Co is a listed company. It has 1 million $1 shares in issue, trading at $3.01, and 10,000, 5% coupon bonds with par value $100 and market value $95.

The company made an operating profit of $1.33 million last year.

The directors are considering issuing 5,000 new secured bonds at their par value of $100. The coupon rate will be 4%.

What will be the interest cover of Lazaretto Co in the year after the bonds are issued, on the assumption that operating profits will stay constant?

A   19.0

B   26.6

C   28.0

D   66.5

Test your understanding 7 (Objective test question)

Company X's bonds have a BBB credit rating according to Standard and Poor's credit rating agency, while Company Y's bonds have an A rating.

Which THREE of the following statements are true?

A   Both companies' bonds are investment grade

B   Both companies' bonds carry a low level of risk

C   The investors in Company X's bonds will require a higher rate of return than those in Company Y's bonds

D   The coupon rate on Company X's bonds will be higher than the coupon rate on Company Y's bonds

E   A movement to a BB rating would represent a downgrade for both companies

Test your understanding 8 (Objective test question)

The directors of McCombs Co, an unlisted company, have identified an attractive (positive NPV) project which is expected to generate positive cash flows for the company over a five year period. Finance is needed to fund the purchase of a new machine to use in the project.

Which of the following financing decisions would be most appropriate in these circumstances?

A   Extend the overdraft to fund the investment

B   Issue new shares to existing shareholders

C   Issue some new bonds on the market

D   Arrange a term loan with the bank

Test your understanding 9 (Objective test question)

Which TWO of the following actions are MOST likely to increase shareholder wealth?

A   The average cost of capital is decreased by a recent financing decision

B   The financial rewards of directors are linked to increasing earnings per share

C   The board of directors decides to invest in a project with a positive net present value

D   The annual report declares full compliance with the corporate governance code

Test your understanding 10 (Objective test question)

BB Co hopes to pay out an increased dividend to satisfy its shareholders, despite the fact that earnings have fallen by 3% this year.

Which of the following is NOT a likely consequence of this action?

A   The company will have less cash available for new investment projects

B   The shareholders' wealth will increase

C   The company is more likely to have to raise finance from new sources if it wants to make new investments

D   The gearing of the company will increase

Test your understanding 11 (Objective test question)

MFW is considering a $1 million expansion of its business.

The directors are considering either debt finance in the form of a 7% bond, or issuing 400,000 ordinary shares at a price of $2.50 to raise the necessary funds.

The expansion will generate $500,000 of extra operating profit each year.

MFW pays tax at 25%. Key investor ratios for MFW are currently as follows:

Gearing = (debt / equity) = $2.5m / $7.2m = 34.7%

Interest cover = (Earnings before interest and tax / Interest payable) = $2,522,000 / $223,000 = 11.3 times

Earnings per share (EPS) = (Profit after tax / No. of shares) = $1,724,000/3,000,000 = $0.575

Which of the following statements is correct?

A   Interest cover is reduced using either source of finance

B   EPS increases more by using debt

C   Equity reduces gearing and gives the best EPS

D   EPS and interest cover both worsen using debt

8 End of chapter case style question

Test your understanding 12 (Case style question)

CCC is a local government entity.

It is financed almost equally by a combination of central government funding and local taxation. The funding from central government is determined largely on a per capita (per head of population) basis, adjusted to reflect the scale of deprivation (or special needs) deemed to exist in CCC's region. A small percentage of its finance comes from the private sector, for example from renting out City Hall for private functions.

CCC's main objectives are:

- to make the region economically prosperous and an attractive place in which to live and work
- to provide service excellence in health and education for the local community.

DDD is a large listed entity with widespread commercial and geographical interests. For historic reasons, its headquarters are in CCC's region. This is something of an anomaly as most entities of DDD's size would have their HQ in a capital city, or at least a city much larger than where it is.

DDD has one financial objective: To increase shareholder wealth by an average 10% per annum. It also has a series of non-financial objectives that deal with how the entity treats other stakeholders, including the local communities where it operates.

DDD has total net assets of $1.5 billion and a gearing ratio of 45% (debt to debt plus equity), which is typical for its industry. It is currently considering raising a substantial amount of capital to finance an acquisition.

Required:

Discuss the criteria that the two very different entities described above have to consider when setting objectives, recognising the needs of each of their main stakeholder groups.

Make some reference in your answer to the consequences of each of them failing to meet its declared objectives.

(30 minutes)

MS is a private entity in a computer-related industry. It has been trading for six years and is managed by its main shareholders, the original founders of the entity.

Most of the employees are also shareholders, having been given shares as bonuses. None of the shareholders has attempted to sell shares in the entity so the problem of placing a value on them has not arisen. Dividends have been paid every year at the rate of 60 cents per share, irrespective of profits. So far, profits have always been sufficient to cover the dividend at least once but never more than twice.

MS is all-equity financed at present although $15 million new finance is likely to be required in the near future to finance expansion. Total net assets as at the last balance sheet date were $45 million.

Required:

Discuss and compare the relationship between dividend policy, investment policy and financing policy in the context of the small entity described above, MS, and DDD, the large listed entity described in the first part of this question.

(30 minutes)

Test your understanding answers

Test your understanding 1 (Integration question)

(a) **Pre-project ratios:**

Interest cover = $15m / $4m = 3.75 times

Earnings per share (EPS) = $7.7m / 16m = 48.1 cents per share

Earnings yield = EPS / Share price = $0.481 / $2.70 = 0.178, or 17.8%

Statement of profit / loss forecasts	$m – debt used	$m – rights issue
Profit before interest and tax ($15m + $4m)	19.0	19.0
Interest (W1)	(5.2)	(4.0)
Profit before tax	13.8	15.0
Tax at 30%	(4.1)	(4.5)
Profit after tax (earnings)	9.7	10.5

(W1) Interest on the new debt is 6% of $20m i.e. $1.2m. Assume that interest on the existing borrowings stays constant.

Share price workings:

Rights issue

If the rights issue goes ahead, the value of the shares after the rights issue will be the theoretical ex-rights price (TERP) of $2.63 (given). **N.B.** The calculation of this TERP will be covered in detail in the later chapter: 'Financing – Equity finance'.

Workings (for illustration only at the moment):

TERP = [(N × cum rights price) + issue price] / (N+1)

= [(2 × 2.70) + 2.50] / 3 = $2.63

However, since the rights issue will be used to fund the new project with an NPV of $8m, the value of the project will also be reflected in the new share price, increasing the share price to

$2.63 + [$8m / (16m shares + 8m new shares)] = $2.96

Debt finance

If debt finance is used to fund the new project, the share price should rise after the project has been taken on, to reflect the NPV of the new project.

Expected share price = $2.70 + ($8m / 16m shares) = $3.20

Post project ratios – using debt finance:

Interest cover = $19m / $5.2m = 3.65 times

Earnings per share (EPS) = $9.7m / 16m = 60.6 cents per share

Earnings yield = $0.606 / $3.20 = 0.189, or 18.9%

Post project ratios – using equity finance:

Interest cover = $19m / $4m = 4.75 times

Earnings per share (EPS) = $10.5m / (16m + 8m) = 43.8 cents per share

Earnings yield = $0.438 / $2.96 = 0.148, or 14.8%

(b) **Debt financing option**

If debt is used to fund the new project, the shareholders are likely to see the change in EPS and earnings yield as positive.

The EPS increases from 48.1 cents per share to 60.6 cents per share, and the earnings yield increases from 17.8% to 18.9%. This indicates that Seed Co will potentially be able to pay out a higher dividend to the shareholders in future.

On the other hand, the reduction in interest cover indicates that Seed Co will face a higher level of risk if the debt financing option is used i.e. the chance of Seed Co being unable to meet its interest obligations is higher. The higher risk to shareholders could lead to a fall in the share price if considered to be significant.

However, in practice it is unlikely that this issue will worry either the shareholders or the lenders greatly, given that the movement in interest cover is extremely small (3.75 to 3.65 times).

Overall, it is likely that both shareholders and lenders will be quite happy with the EPS, earnings yield and interest cover ratios if the debt finance option is used (assuming that the expected $4m increase in profit and $8m NPV are achieved).

Equity finance option

The lenders will be happy if the rights issue goes ahead, because there will be no additional interest payable and yet profits will increase, so the interest cover ratio will rise significantly. This means that the chances of Seed Co defaulting on its interest payments will be less if this option goes ahead.

At first glance, it appears that the shareholders will not be happy with this option, given that EPS reduces from 48.1 cents per share to 43.8 cents per share, and also given that earnings yield falls from 17.8% to 14.8%.

However, in this situation, where a 1 for 2 rights issue has been used, a shareholder who owned 2 shares before the rights issue will now own 3 shares (assuming he took up his rights). The rights issue itself makes no difference to the shareholder's return or wealth. However, the positive NPV of the project undertaken causes the shareholder return and wealth to increase.

The increase in earnings attributable to each shareholder's shareholding will be viewed positively by shareholders, who might expect to see increased overall dividends in the future.

Once again, overall it is likely that both shareholders and lenders will be quite happy with the EPS, earnings yield and interest cover ratios if this financing option is used (assuming that the expected $4m increase in profit and $8m NPV are achieved).

Test your understanding 2 (Objective test question)

The answer is (A).

Financing requirement is:

Reduction in payables = ($3,150,000 × 10/45) = $700,000

Reduction in overdraft = (2,200,000 – 2,000,000) = $200,000

New capital expenditure = $1,000,000

Therefore, total = $1,900,000

Test your understanding 3 (Objective test question)

The answer is (C).

Lenders are particularly interested in the level of gearing (B) and the ability of the borrower to meet its interest commitments ((A) and (D)).

Test your understanding 4 (Objective test question)

The answer is (D).

Currently P/E is 7.05 and share price is $2.00.

Therefore, EPS = (2.00 / 7.05 =) $0.284

With 1 million shares in issue, this amounts to total earnings of approximately $284,000

After the issue, the project will add $30,000 earnings to this, so earnings will become $314,000.

Total shares will be 1 million existing shares + 250,000 new ones (1 for 4 rights). Therefore 1,250,000 in total.

Hence EPS will be 314,000 / 1,250,000 = $0.25

Test your understanding 5 (Objective test question)

The answer is (B).

The NPV of the project is equal to the increase in wealth of the shareholders (i.e. the increase in share price).

Therefore, an NPV of $8 million, split between 20 million shares means an increase of 8/20 = $0.40 per share.

Test your understanding 6 (Objective test question)

The answer is (A).

Interest cover is (operating profit / interest payable)

= $1.33m / [(10,000 × $100 × 5%) + (5,000 × $100 × 4%)] = 19.0

Test your understanding 7 (Objective test question)

The answer is (A), (C) and (E).

Both companies' bonds are indeed investment grade bonds (A) - all ratings of BBB and above are investment grade. However, BBB is considered to be a medium level of risk, so both companies' bonds do not carry a low level of risk (B).

The investors in Company X's bonds will indeed require a higher rate of return (C) because of this higher level of risk, but that does not necessarily mean that the coupon rate on Company X's bonds will be higher than the coupon rate on Company Y's bonds (D) (for example the extra return could be paid in the form of a premium on redemption, rather than necessarily as an increased coupon rate).

BB is a lower grading than both A and BBB so a movement to a BB rating would represent a downgrade for both companies (E).

Test your understanding 8 (Objective test question)

The answer is (D).

An unlisted company cannot issue bonds (C). An overdraft (A) is too short term and equity (B) is too long term for the funding of a five year project.

Test your understanding 9 (Objective test question)

The answer is (A) and (C).

Test your understanding 10 (Objective test question)

The answer is (B).

Shareholder wealth is not affected by a dividend payment. Gearing will increase though, as there is less equity within the company. Also, the financing and investment policies will have to change since less cash is available within the company.

Test your understanding 11 (Objective test question)

The answer is (B).

Debt

Interest = $70,000 and value of debt increases by $1m, so the ratios become:

Gearing = (debt / equity) = $3.5m / $7.2m = 48.6%

Interest cover = (Earnings before interest and tax / Interest payable) = $3,022,000 / $293,000 = 10.3 times

Earnings per share (EPS) = (Profit after tax / No. of shares) = $2,047,000/3,000,000 = $0.682

Note that profit after tax = (EBIT – Interest) × (1-0.25)

Equity

400,000 extra shares and value of equity increases by $1m, so the ratios become:

Gearing = (debt / equity) = $2.5m / $8.2m = 30.5%

Interest cover = (Earnings before interest and tax / Interest payable) = $3,022,000 / $223,000 = 13.6 times

Earnings per share (EPS) = (Profit after tax / No. of shares) = $2,099,000/3,400,000 = $0.617

Test your understanding 12 (Case style question)

Answer to the first task:

The key criteria that need to be considered when objective setting are as follows:

Stakeholder expectations

All organisations need to identify key stakeholders, examine their expectations and try to set objectives to meet them. For CCC stakeholders include:

- Local residents want to see the provision of quality health

- Local businesses who will be interested in local infrastructure when deciding whether to invest in the area. In particular, CCC may be keen to ensure that DDD does not close its local offices, with resulting job losses, and move to the capital city.

- Central Government committees who make funding decisions based on local population and deprivation.

For DDD stakeholders include:

- Shareholders want to see their wealth increased through a mixture of growing dividends and an increasing share price. DDD has reflected this in the objective to increase shareholder wealth by 10% per annum.

- Customers will expect a certain level of quality and value for money, depending on the nature of products sold.

- The local communities affected by DDD will expect them to be good citizens and operate at high levels of corporate social responsibility.

Stakeholder power

All organisations will find conflicts between stakeholders, so they need to consider how to prioritise them. For a company like DDD the expectations of shareholders come first for the following reasons:

- This is usually reflected in companies' legislation where directors have a duty in law to put shareholder interests first. Many governance recommendations focus on protecting shareholder interests.

- Failure to deliver shareholder expectations will result in a falling share price and difficulties raising finance. Ultimately, shareholders have the power to remove directors should they feel dissatisfied.

However, this does not mean that other stakeholders' needs are ignored. Clearly, if customers are unhappy, then sales will be lost with a resulting fall in profitability and shareholder wealth.

For CCC the problem is more complex:

- It is much more difficult to prioritise stakeholder expectations. For example, given limited funds, should community health care needs come before educational ones?

- Even individual stakeholder groups have multiple conflicting objectives. For example, residents want to pay less tax and have better provision of services. Thus, even if some groups are satisfied, others may still vote for changes in CCC.

- With companies, customers pay directly for the products they receive, ensuring that customer needs are addressed. With CCC the bulk of its funding comes from central government, not the local community that benefits from CCC's actions. Thus the needs of the funding body may take priority over locals needs, otherwise funding may be cut. (**Note:** This is less likely here as funding is mainly driven by population size.)

Measurement issues

For an organisation like DDD, once shareholders have been prioritised, all decisions can be evaluated by reference to financial measures such as profitability. While non-financial targets will be incorporated as well, the 'bottom line' will be seen as key. Thus financial targets can be set for most objectives.

For CCC it is much more difficult to measure whether it is achieving its stated aims and hence to set targets.

For example, how do you assess whether somewhere is an 'attractive place to live and work' or whether health and education provision is 'excellent'?

Other issues

All organisations need to ensure that objectives set relate to controllable factors to ensure staff are motivated to meet them.

All organisations need to differentiate between cause and effect and have objectives for both. For example, DDD may have an objective of customer satisfaction, which will need to be translated into objectives for quality, cost, etc.

Answer to the second task:

As described above, companies make decisions with the primary objective of maximising shareholder wealth.

Investment decisions

Potential investments should thus be assessed using NPV or SVA, rather than ROCE to ensure that shareholder wealth is increased.

This should be the case for both MS and DDD, though the former will have more difficulty determining a suitable discount rate as it is unquoted.

Dividend decisions

Once shareholder value has been created, the firm needs to decide how to return those gains to shareholders – either as dividends or reinvested to enhance the share price further.

Modigliani and Miller argued that, given certain assumptions, dividend policy was irrelevant to shareholder wealth. If a dividend were cut, for example, shareholders could manufacture dividends by selling shares without any overall loss of wealth. Central to their theory was the idea that shareholders had perfect information and would understand why a dividend policy was changed.

In the case of MS, shareholders are also employees so will have full information regarding any change in dividend policy and will not thus perceive any information content in the dividends themselves. However, should the dividend be cut, shareholders who require income will not be able to sell shares to generate cash as the company is unquoted. MS should thus try to continue the stable dividend policy it has adopted to date, even though historical dividend cover is lower than the 'rule of thumb' of two.

In the case of DDD, major institutional shareholders will have good information from the company but may have tax preferences regarding income and capital gains so DDD should adopt a consistent dividend policy to meet their requirements. DDD will probably have attracted a certain clientele of shareholder based on previous policies.

Financing decisions

Both firms need to raise finance in order to undertake new investments to increase shareholder wealth. The issue here is whether the finance used ultimately affects shareholder wealth as well.

From a theoretical point of view, Modigliani and Miller argued that, in the absence of taxation and certain other assumptions, the choice between debt or equity finance was irrelevant. With corporation tax they concluded that debt finance was preferable, due to the benefits of the tax shield. With personal taxes the conclusions depend on the specific circumstances of the company and its shareholders. Incorporating real world factors, many analysts argue that there is an optimal gearing level for each company.

DDD is already at the typical gearing ratio for its industry so it would reasonable to assume that this is its optimal gearing level. Future financing should involve a mixture of debt and equity to maintain this ratio.

MS is all-equity financed at present so it should seek to raise at least some of the $15 million required using debt finance to take advantage of the tax relief and low costs involved.

Interrelationships

All three types of decisions are interrelated, thus the financing decision will affect the cost of capital and, as a consequence, the net benefits obtainable from a particular project, thereby influencing the investment decision, while the financing decision concerning gearing will affect both the other decisions.

The dividend decision, in determining the level of retentions, will affect the cash available for investment, and the extent to which external sources of funds need to be sought in financing to optimise operations.

4

Hedge accounting

Chapter learning objectives

Lead	Component
A2: Evaluate strategic financial management policy decisions	(c) Evaluate the impact of the adoption of hedge accounting disclosure of financial risk on financial statements and stakeholder assessment

Indicative syllabus content

- The accounting treatment of hedge accounting (cash flow, fair value and net investment), IFRS 9 (or IAS 39, before effective date for IFRS 9).

- Impact of adoption of hedge accounting on financial statements and on stakeholder assessment.

- Disclosure of financial risk, including policies for managing such risk (IFRS 7 Financial Instruments: Disclosures).

1 Overview of chapter

2 Introduction

The earlier chapters in this Text have looked at the financial strategy of an entity, and have considered the methods by which stakeholders can make an assessment of an entity's performance.

Integrated reporting and sustainability reporting can help to give an impression of the non-financial performance of an entity, while analysis of the financial statements is the best way of assessing the financial performance of an entity.

It is therefore critical that all an entity's financial instruments are disclosed appropriately in the financial statements, to allow stakeholders to build up an accurate picture of the entity's financial performance.

This chapter covers the main accounting standards associated with financial instruments, namely:

- IAS 39 **Financial Instruments: Recognition and Measurement**
- IFRS 7 **Financial Instruments: Disclosures**
- IFRS 9 **Financial Instruments**

IAS 39 deals with how financial instruments are measured and when they should be recognised in financial statements.

IFRS 7 deals with the disclosure of financial instruments in financial statements.

IFRS 9 will eventually supersede IAS 39. Its effective date for application is 1 January 2018, so for the moment we don't need to cover it in detail.

3 Hedge accounting introduction: Terminology

Definitions

Hedging

This is a method of managing risk by designating one or more hedging instruments so that their change in fair value is offset, in whole or in part, to the change in fair value or cash flows of a hedged item.

Hedged item

A hedged item as defined by IAS 39 can be any of the following:

* an asset, liability or firm commitment (see note below)
* a highly probable forecast transaction
* the net investment in a foreign operation

and must expose the entity to the risk of changes either:

* fair value, or
* future cash flows.

Note: The strict definition of a firm commitment per IAS 39 is 'a binding agreement for the exchange of a specified quantity of resources at a specified price on a specified future date or dates.' That is, a firm, binding order for goods or services where the price and quantity has been agreed.

Hedging instrument

A hedging instrument (according to IAS 39) is an instrument whose fair value or cash flows are expected to offset changes in the fair value or cash flows of a designated hedged item.

All derivative contracts with an external counterparty may be designated as hedging instruments except for some written options. A non-derivative financial asset or liability may not be designated as a hedging instrument except as a hedge of foreign currency risk.

Special hedge accounting rules apply to reflect the substance of the arrangement, i.e. to ensure that the gains and losses are offset.

4 Hedging instruments: Derivatives

Definition of derivatives according to IAS 39

A derivative is a financial instrument or certain other contract which has ALL THREE of the following characteristics:

(1) its value changes in response to the change in a specified rate or index (the 'underlying asset') such as an interest rate, financial instrument price, commodity price, foreign exchange rate, index of prices or rates, credit rating or credit index

(2) it requires little or no initial investment

(3) it is settled at a future date.

Some examples of derivatives are futures contracts, options, forward contracts, and interest rate and currency swaps.

Recognition and measurement of derivatives

All derivatives are categorised as fair value through the profit or loss (FVPL).

On initial recognition they are recorded at fair value which is usually zero as the derivative gains value as the underlying item's price moves.

At each reporting date, the derivative is restated to fair value and recorded as a financial asset or financial liability on the statement of financial position. Any gains/losses are taken to the statement of profit or loss.

There is an exception to this rule if the derivative is being used in some forms of hedging (see later notes).

Types of derivative

- **Forward** – the obligation to buy or sell a defined amount of a specific underlying asset, at a specified price at a specified future date.

- **Forward rate agreements** – a contract to fix the interest charge on a floating rate borrowing.

- **Futures contracts** – the obligation to buy or sell a standard quantity of a specific underlying item at a specified future date.

- **Swaps** – an agreement to exchange periodic payments at specified intervals over a specified time period.

- **Options** – the right, but not the obligation, to buy or sell a specific underlying asset on or before a specified future date.

Types of derivatives: Further detail

Forward contracts

The holder of a forward contract is obliged to buy or sell a defined amount of a specific underlying asset, at a specified price at a specified future date. For example, a forward contract for foreign currency might require GBP 100,000 to be exchanged for USD150,000 in three months' time. Both parties to the contract have both a financial asset and a financial liability. For example, one party has the right to receive USD150,000 and the obligation to pay GBP100,000.

Forward currency contracts may be used to minimise the risk on amounts receivable or payable in foreign currencies.

Example

On 1 January 20X9 a Country Z based company (currency Z$) buys goods from an overseas company whose currency is the euro (EUR). This results in a liability for EUR 8 million which must be settled on 31 March 20X9. The exchange rate on 1 January is Z$ / EUR 8 (that is Z$1 = EUR 8). The company takes out a forward exchange contract to buy EUR 8 million for Z$1 million on 31 March 20X9. This is at the exchange rate ruling at 1 January (i.e. Z$1 = EUR 8).

At 31 March the exchange rate is actually Z$ / EUR 8.5. If the company had not taken out the forward exchange contract it would have made an exchange gain of $58,824 (1,000,000 – 941,176). By taking out the forward exchange contract it has given up the chance to make this gain, but has also protected itself against the possibility of making a loss. In other words, it has used the forward exchange contract to eliminate exchange rate risk.

Forward rate agreements

Forward rate agreements can be used to fix the interest charge on a floating rate borrowing. For example, a company has a $1m dollar floating rate borrowing, and the current rate of interest is 7%. The rates are reset to the market rate every six months, and the company cannot afford to pay more than 9% interest. The company enters into a six month forward rate agreement (with, say, a bank) at 9% on $1m. If the market rates go up to 10%, then the bank will pay them $5,000 (1% of $1m for 6 months) which in effect reduces their finance cost to 9%. If the rates only go up to 8% then the company pays the bank $5,000.

Futures contracts

Futures contracts oblige the holder to buy or sell a standard quantity of a specific underlying item at a specified future date. Futures contracts are similar to forward contracts in that they aim to fix the price of a particular item. The difference is that futures contracts have standard terms and are traded on a financial exchange, whereas forward contracts are tailor made and are not traded on a financial exchange. Also, futures involve daily margin payments, settling any price movements in cash daily, making them much more complex to administer and account for. Questions on accounting entries in the exam are probably more likely to focus on forward contracts.

Swaps

Two parties agree to exchange periodic payments at specified intervals over a specified time period.

For example, in an **interest rate swap**, the parties may agree to exchange fixed and floating rate interest payments calculated by reference to a notional principal amount. This enables companies to keep a balance between their fixed and floating rate interest payments without having to change the underlying borrowings. In a **cross-currency swap** it is normal to exchange principal amounts as well as interest cash flows.

A 'pay-fixed, receive-floating' swap can be used to fix the interest rate on a floating rate borrowing and a 'pay-floating, receive-fixed' swap can be used to convert the interest profile of debt from fixed to floating. Swaps are covered in more detail in the later chapter: 'Financing - Debt finance'.

Options

These give the holder the right, but not the obligation, to buy or sell a specific underlying asset on or before a specified future date.

5 Hedge accounting rules

Conditions for hedge accounting

Hedge accounting may only be used if certain conditions are met:

- The arrangement must be designated as a hedge at the inception. There must be formal documentation which identifies:
  - hedged item;
  - hedge instrument;
  - nature of risk that is to be hedged;
  - how the entity will assess the hedging instrument's effectiveness.
- Hedge is expected to be highly effective (80% – 125%).
- Effectiveness is capable of reliable measurement.
- Assessment of effectiveness takes place on an ongoing basis.

Effectiveness of the hedge

The effectiveness of the hedge is calculated by comparing the movement in the value of the hedged item and the movement in value of the hedging instrument.

For example if the hedged item falls in value by $3.80 million and the hedging instrument increases in value by $4.70 million, the effectiveness would be measured in percentage terms as either:

$(3.80 / 4.70) \times 100\% = 80.85\%$, or

$(4.70 / 3.80) \times 100\% = 123.68\%$

so within the 80% – 125% range whichever way it is measured.

Types of hedge

There are three types of hedging arrangement:

- fair value hedge;
- cash flow hedge;
- net investment in a foreign operation.

More details on the three types of hedge

A **fair value hedge** is a hedge of the exposure to changes in fair value of a recognised asset or liability (or a previously unrecognised firm commitment or an identified portion of such an asset, liability or firm commitment) that is attributable to a particular risk and could affect profit or loss.

So for example it can be used to hedge against the risk of a change in the value of an asset such as inventory.

Also, a fair value hedge can be used when using a swap to switch the interest profile on a borrowing from fixed to floating rate.

A **cash flow hedge** is a hedge of the exposure to variability in cash flows that

(i)   is attributable to a particular risk associated with a recognised asset or liability or a highly probable forecast transaction and

(ii) could affect profit or loss.

So for example it can be used to hedge against the risk associated with the future interest payments on variable rate debt.

Also, a cash flow hedge can be used when using a swap to change the interest profile from floating to fixed rate (given that the cash flows being hedged are uncertain, being dependent on future interest rate movements).

A **hedge of a net investment in a foreign operation** (as defined in IAS 21 The Effects of Changes in Foreign Exchange Rates) is accounted for similarly to a cash flow hedge.

It is used to eliminate the risk associated with fluctuations in the value of a foreign investment due to movements in exchange rates.

Hedging the full risk or just a portion of the risk

A hedging instrument can be used to hedge a portion of the risk on a particular hedged item, or the whole risk.

Hedging a portion of the risk is particularly useful in helping to achieve hedge effectiveness when hedging forecast future cash flows that might not turn out to be as high as expected and in net investment hedges as the value of a subsidiary company is likely to change considerably from year to year (see examples later in this chapter).

Fair value hedge

According to IAS 39, a fair value hedge is 'a hedge of the exposure to changes in fair value of:

- a recognised asset or liability, or
- an unrecognised firm commitment, or
- an identified portion of such an asset, liability or firm commitment

AND:

- is attributable to a particular risk
- changes in fair value could affect profit or loss.'

The risk being hedged is often the change in the fair value of an asset or liability that is **already** recognised in the financial statements, in which case hedge accounting requires **both** the hedged item and the hedging instrument to be measured at fair value at each year end.

Alternatively, if the hedged item is a firm commitment which has not already been recognised in the accounts, the gain or loss on revaluation of this firm commitment must be recognised in the accounts. The net gain or loss is then accumulated over future periods and the fair value is recorded when the item is finally recognised in the accounts.

Fair value hedge rules

The changes in fair value of both the hedged item and the hedging instrument are recognised in profit or loss and will offset each other.

Illustration 1 (Integration question)

An entity owns inventories of 10,000 tons of steel which cost $100,000 on 1 December 20X5.

If the price of steel falls, the entity will suffer a loss when it sells the steel. To minimise this risk, it enters into a forward contract to sell 10,000 tons of steel for $120,000 on 1 February 20X6 i.e. at a price of $12 per ton.

At the year end of 31 December 20X5, the market value of the steel is $9 per ton and the forward price for 1 February 20X6 has moved to $11 per ton.

Required:

Show the impact of the fair value hedge on the financial statements of the entity at 31 December 20X5, assuming that the conditions for hedge accounting are satisfied.

Solution:

The hedged item is the steel. The hedging instrument is the forward contract (a derivative).

At the year end both the hedged item and hedging instrument will be measured at fair value and gains or losses recorded in the statement of profit or loss.

Hedged item (steel)		
10,000 tons × £9 per ton		$90,000
Cr	Inventory	$10,000
Dr	P&L (loss)	$10,000
Hedging instrument (forward contract)		
10,000 × (12–11)		$10,000
Dr	Derivative (financial asset)	$10,000
Cr	P&L (gain)	$10,000

The overall effect on profit is nil (gain of $10,000 on derivative less loss of $10,000 on inventory).

The above illustration shows that the value of the financial asset (the inventory in this case) is written down at the year end to fair value if the year end value is considered to be lower.

This treatment is in line with normal accounting rules – any reduction in value of an asset has to be recognised as soon as possible.

The interesting thing about hedge accounting is that the fair value adjustment at the year end is also made if the financial asset **increases** in value. This is contrary to normal accounting rules.

Recognition of the fair value increase using hedge accounting is shown in the illustration below.

e.g

Illustration 2 (Integration question)

An entity owns inventories of 10,000 tons of steel which cost $100,000 on 1 December 20X5.

If the price of steel falls, the entity will suffer a loss when it sells the steel. To minimise this risk, it enters into a forward contract to sell 10,000 tons of steel for $120,000 on 1 February 20X6 i.e. at a price of $12 per ton.

At the year end of 31 December 20X5, the market value of the steel is $12 per ton and the forward price for 1 February 20X6 has moved to $14 per ton.

Required:

Show the impact of the fair value hedge on the financial statements of the entity at 31 December 20X5, assuming that the conditions for hedge accounting are satisfied.

Solution:

The hedged item is the steel. The hedging instrument is the forward contract (a derivative).

At the year end **both** the hedged item and hedging instrument will be measured at fair value and gains or losses recorded in the statement of profit or loss.

Hedged item (steel)		
10,000 tons × £12 per ton		$120,000
Dr	Inventory	$20,000
Cr	P&L (gain)	$20,000
Hedging instrument (forward contract)		
10,000 × (12–14)		$20,000
Cr	Derivative (financial liability)	$20,000
Dr	P&L (loss)	$20,000

The overall effect on profit is nil (loss of $20,000 on derivative and gain of $20,000 on inventory).

Difference without hedge accounting

The above journal entries show the impact on the financial statements of using hedge accounting in this case.

If hedge accounting had not been used, the gain of $20,000 on the value of the inventory would not have been recorded in the financial statements (because under normal accounting rules inventory is stated at the lower of cost and realisable value).

Therefore, there would have been an unmatched loss on the derivative of $20,000 in the financial statements, creating greater volatility of reported results. Note that this is not a 'real' loss since it is matched by an equal and opposite profit on inventory that is not shown. Hedge accounting ensures that this confusion is avoided.

e.g

Illustration 3 (Integration question)

On 1 October 20X3, $5 million, 10-year, fixed rate bonds will be issued by FF at an annual rate of interest of 6%, payable semi-annually. On the same date, FF will enter into a receive-fixed, pay-variable $5 million interest rate swap arrangement with LL at current market rates.

This will require FF to pay an annual rate of LIBOR plus 3.75% and to receive a fixed rate of 6.5%, with semi-annual payments. The fair value of the swap on 1 October 20X3 is zero. The period of the swap will be ten years.

The annual LIBOR rate will be 2% on 1 October 20X3, but is expected to increase shortly thereafter. As a result of expected increases in LIBOR, the fair value of the 6% bonds will reduce to $4.8 million by 31 March 20X4.

The fair value of the swap at 31 March 20X4 will be $0.204 million, giving a loss to FF and a gain to LL.

Assume that

- there are minimal transaction costs on issuing the bonds and on the swap agreement.

- all necessary documentation to treat the swap as a hedge and establish its effectiveness can be set up on time.

- fair value hedge accounting is to be used by FF.

Required:

Set out and explain the journal entries for the year ending 31 March 20X4 for the 6% bonds and the swap arrangement, assuming that they take place as described.

Solution:

On the assumption that FF is to issue fixed rate debt, it would enter into a swap agreement to hedge the fair value of this debt which will change with market interest rates. This is therefore a fair value hedge.

In order for hedge accounting to apply, the hedge must meet the relevant criteria according to IAS 39. If, at any time, any of the criteria are not satisfied, then hedge accounting should be discontinued. The swap, as a derivative, would then be measured at 'fair value through profit or loss'.

There is a gain on the 6% bonds during the six month period to 31 March 20X4 as the fair value of a liability is reduced. This amounts to $5m – $4.8m = $0.2m.

The hedge effectiveness test is either:

$0.204m/$0.2m = 102% or $0.2m/$0.204m = 98.04%

These are within the 80%-125% permissible range and therefore the swap, although not fully effective, is deemed 'highly effective' and hedge accounting can be applied according to IAS 39.

The change in the fair value of the swap is recognised as a change in a derivative liability in the statement of financial position and is reported as a loss within profit or loss:

DR Profit or loss $0.204m

CR Swap derivative (liability) $0.204m

Using fair value hedge accounting, the change in fair value of the hedged item (the 6% bonds) is also recognised in profit or loss (as income as it is a reduction in a liability), any difference between the two elements (hedge instrument and hedged item) being the ineffectiveness of the hedge:

DR Bonds $0.2m

CR Profit or loss $0.2m

Difference without hedge accounting

The profit or loss would be distorted by showing the loss of $0.204m on the swap in profit or loss, without recognising the corresponding gain of $0.2m on the 6% bonds, given that the 6% bonds would continue to be recognised at the value of $5 million.

Cash flow hedge

The risk being hedged is the change in future cash flows.

A cash flow hedge is a hedge of the exposure to variability in cash flows that, both:

(i)   is attributable to a particular risk associated with a **recognised** asset or liability (such as all or some future interest payments on variable rate debt) or a **highly probable** forecast transaction, and

(ii) could affect profit or loss.

For example, in practice many companies hedge a percentage of forecast sales receipts for the next 12 month period e.g. if a company expects to receive USD 20 million in 6 months' time, it may decide to hedge, say, USD 15 million of this, being confident that the forecast will not be more than USD 5 million overstated and hence the hedge will remain effective.

Cash flow hedge rules

The gain or loss on the hedging instrument (or the portion of it that is deemed to be an effective hedge) is recognised in other comprehensive income (OCI).

Then, when the underlying transaction affects profit or loss, (e.g. invoice or delivery date), the cash flow hedge ends and the OCI entries are transferred ('recycled') into profit or loss. **N.B.** This is usually BEFORE the cash flow arises.

Illustration 4 (Integration question)

A Country X based trading company (functional currency X$) prepares accounts to 30 June each year.

In April 20X2, it receives an order from a Spanish customer, which it expects to fulfil in September 20X2. The customer will be invoiced in euro (EUR) on 1 September 20X2, and the company expects to receive EUR 300 million on 15 September 20X2.

The entity wishes to hedge the foreign exchange risk on this forecast transaction (which is highly probable) because there is a risk that the euro (EUR) to dollar (X$) exchange rate will change, reducing the X$ value of the sales.

On 15 April 20X2, the entity takes out a forward contract to sell EUR 300 million on 15 September 20X2 at an agreed exchange rate of X$ / EUR 2 (that is X$ 1 = EUR 2), designating the forecast cash flow as the hedged item and the currency contract as the hedging instrument.

Management prepares hedge documentation and assesses the hedge prospectively as almost 100% effective.

At 30 June 20X2, the exchange rate is X$ / EUR 2.5
(that is X$ 1 = EUR 2.5).

At 1 September 20X2, the exchange rate is X$ / EUR 2.9
(that is X$ 1 = EUR 2.9).

At 15 September 20X2, the exchange rate is X$ / EUR 3
(that is X$ 1 = EUR 3).

Required:

Show the impact of the cash flow hedge on the financial statements of the entity at 30 June 20X2 and 30 June 20X3, ignoring the time value of money throughout.

Solution:

Year ended 30 June 20X2

At 30 June 20X2, the hedging instrument i.e. the forward contract will be measured at fair value with the gain or loss being recognised in other comprehensive income (OCI):

Dr	Forward contract	USD30m
Cr	OCI – gain	USD30m
	(EUR300m ÷ 2) – (EUR300m ÷ 2.5)	

Note: The fair value of the forward contract should really be the present value of the difference here, but we are told to ignore the time value of money in this example.

Year ended 30 June 20X3

On 1 September 20X2, when the customer is invoiced, the exchange rate is X$ / EUR 2.9 (that is X$1 = 2.9 EUR).

Therefore, the fair value of the forward contract (ignoring time value of money) has risen by another X$ 16.6 million (being [300m / 2.5] - [300m / 2.9m]) and the value of the EUR 300 million transaction is now X$ 103.4 million (300m / 2.9).

Therefore the accounting entries on 1 September 20X2 are:

Record movement in fair value of hedging instrument

A X$ 30m gain has already been recognised at 30 June 20X2, so now an additional X$ 16.6m gain needs to be recognised in OCI.

Dr	Forward contract	X$ 16.6m
Cr	OCI – gain	X$ 16.6m

Record the sale (now invoiced)

Dr	Receivables (300m / 2.9)	X$ 103.4m
Cr	Sales	X$ 103.4m

Recycle OCI entries into profit or loss

Dr	OCI (total 30m + 16.6m)	X$ 46.6m
Cr	Profit or loss	X$ 46.6m

Finally, on 15 September 20X2 when the customer pays, the existence of the forward contract means that the EUR 300 million receipt will be translated at X$ / EUR 2, so will give a net receipt of X$ 150 million.

Therefore, the final accounting entry will be:

Dr	Cash	X$ 150m
Cr	Receivables	X$ 103.4m
Cr	Forward contract	X$ 46.6m

The overall effect on profit is a credit (gain) of X$ 150m (sales X$ 103.4m + recycled OCI of X$ 46.6m) which reflects sales made of EUR 300m at the contracted exchange rate of X$ / EUR 2 (that is X$ 1 = EUR 2).

Difference without hedge accounting

The above journal entries show the impact on the financial statements of using hedge accounting in this case. If hedge accounting had not been used, the profit or loss entries would have been split between two accounting periods.

Hedge accounting for this cash flow hedge ensured that all the profit or loss entries relating to the sale were recorded in the same accounting period.

Illustration 5 (Integration question)

Assume that it is now 31 December 20X9.

Fire Co borrowed $2 million on 1 January 20X7 at a floating rate of LIBOR, with annual interest payments over three years. Repayment of the borrowing is at par.

The variable interest rate payments have been hedged by an interest rate swap.

The interest rate swap is a three-year variable-to-fixed interest rate swap to hedge the interest rate risk of the borrowing. The swap was entered into on 1 January 20X7 and it satisfied the IAS 39 criteria so cash flow hedge accounting has been applied throughout.

The terms of the swap are:

- $2 million notional amount

- Pay 7% fixed, receive variable at LIBOR

- Annual payments over three years, with interest fixing dates on 1 January each year

The fair value of the swap at 31 December 20X7, based on current LIBOR rates, was $22,000, the fair value at 31 December 20X8 was $16,000 and the fair value at 31 December 20X9 is zero.

LIBOR was 7% at 1 January 20X7, 7.5% at 1 January 20X8, and 7.75% at 1 January 20X9.

Required:

Prepare the journal entries in respect of the cash flow hedge in the years 20X7, 20X8 and 20X9.

Solution:

The interest rate swap (IRS) provides a cash flow hedge against the interest payments on the borrowing.

Preparatory calculations

The following table shows a summary of relevant figures for the three year period, in preparation for the journal entries:

Year	LIBOR (1 Jan rate)	y/e interest paid on borrowing ($)	y/e swap settlement ($)	y/e FV of swap ($)	FV movement ($)
20X7	7%	140,000 (7%)	NIL	22,000	22,000
20X8	7.5%	150,000 (7.5%)	10,000 (0.5%)	16,000	(6,000)
20X9	7.75%	155,000 (7.75%)	15,000 (0.75%)	NIL	(16,000)

Cash flow hedge accounting journal entries

At 31 December 20X7

Dr Profit or loss – Interest expense $140,000

Cr Cash $140,000

to record the interest payment at 7% on the borrowing

Dr Interest rate swap (Asset in SOFP) $22,000

Cr Other comprehensive income (OCI) $22,000

to record the change in the fair value of the swap.

At 31 December 20X8

Dr Profit or loss – Interest expense $150,000

Cr Cash $150,000

to record the interest payment at 7.5% on the borrowing

Dr Cash $10,000

Cr OCI $10,000

to record the cash received on the swap settlement (0.5%, being the difference between the 7% fixed rate and the 7.5% LIBOR rate in 20X8)

Dr OCI $10,000

Cr Profit or loss – Interest expense $10,000

to reclassify to profit or loss the amount from OCI on account of the hedge - required to change the total interest expense for the year to a net figure of $140,000

Dr Other comprehensive income (OCI) $6,000

Cr Interest rate swap (Asset in SOFP) $6,000

to record the change in the fair value of the swap.

At 31 December 20X9

Dr Profit or loss – Interest expense $155,000

Cr Cash $155,000

to record the interest payment at 7.75% on the borrowing

Dr Cash $15,000

Cr OCI $15,000

to record the cash received on the swap settlement (0.75%, being the difference between the 7% fixed rate and the 7.75% LIBOR rate in 20X9)

Dr OCI $15,000

Cr Profit or loss – Interest expense $15,000

to reclassify to profit or loss the amount from OCI on account of the hedge - required to change the total interest expense for the year to a net figure of $140,000

Dr Other comprehensive income (OCI) $16,000

Cr Interest rate swap (Asset in SOFP) $16,000

to record the change in the fair value of the swap.

Key observations

As a result of entering into the hedging relationship, Fire Co has locked into a 7% fixed rate for the three year term of the borrowing i.e. there is no volatility in the figures recorded each year in the profit or loss as interest expense – each year the charge is $140,000, being 7% regardless of the actual LIBOR figures for the year. Note that each year of the swap, as interest is settled for that year, the changes in value for that year are recognised in profit or loss.

From a statement of financial position perspective though, the requirement to report the derivative hedging instrument in the statement of financial position at fair value results in volatility in Fire Co's OCI, as shown below:

	20X7	20X8	20X9
OCI opening balance	-	22,000	16,000
Swap cash settlement	-	10,000	15,000
Gain / (loss) on swap FV	22,000	(6,000)	(16,000)
Reclassification to P+L	-	(10,000)	(15,000)
OCI closing balance	22,000	16,000	-

Difference without hedge accounting

The impact of hedge accounting was that the profit or loss charge each year was the same ($140,000).

Without hedge accounting the profit or loss charge each year would have varied as LIBOR varied.

More on fair value and cash flow hedges

Two of the examples above (Illustrations 3 and 5) both looked at a borrowing and a swap.

However, the first of these illustrations was an example of a fair value hedge and the second was an example of a cash flow hedge. This is because:

- Illustration 3 showed the impact of hedge accounting where the borrowing was at a fixed rate and the swap was a fixed to floating rate swap. This is a fair value hedge because it is being used to hedge the change in value of the LIABILITY as a result of changes in market interest rates.

- Illustration 5 showed the impact of hedge accounting where the borrowing was at a floating rate and the swap was a floating to fixed rate swap. This is a cash flow hedge because it is being used to hedge the change in future CASH FLOWS arising from possible movements in interest rates.

Test your understanding 1 (Integration question)

AB entered into a forward contract on 31 January 20X1 to purchase B$1 million at a contracted rate of A$ / B$ 0.75 (that is A$1=B$0.75) on 31 May 20X1, because it expects to receive an invoice from its supplier for this amount on 1 May 20X1 and make the payment on 31 May 20X1.

AB prepares its financial statements to 31 March each year.

At 31 March 20X1, the exchange rate was A$ / B$ 0.80 (that is A$1=B$0.80).

Required:

(a) Prepare journal entries to show how this derivative contract would be recorded in the financial statements of AB in the year ended 31 March 20X1.

(b) Assume now that the instrument described above was designated as a hedging instrument in a cash flow hedge, and that the hedge was 100% effective. Explain how the gain or loss on the instrument for the year ended 31 March 20X1 should now be recorded and why different treatment is necessary.

Note: For simplicity, ignore the time value of money.

Net investment in a foreign operation

A net investment hedge is a hedge of the net investment in a foreign operation (that is the amount of the reporting entity's interest in the net assets of that operation).

The hedged item is the investment in a foreign operation and the risk being hedged is the change in the value of the investment due to movements in exchange rates. The hedging instrument is a foreign currency borrowing (a non-derivative financial instrument).

Net investment hedges only apply to groups of companies since they only apply to investments in foreign operations (i.e. foreign subsidiaries).

Normal accounting rules

When subsidiaries are consolidated into the group accounts, both the assets and liabilities are translated at the closing exchange rate.

Any foreign exchange profit or loss on retranslation of the net worth of a subsidiary is posted to other comprehensive income (OCI) on consolidation, whereas the foreign exchange profit or loss on retranslation of any borrowing taken out at group level to hedge that exposure is posted to profit or loss.

This mismatch can be eliminated by net investment hedge accounting.

Hedge accounting (net investment hedge) rules

Under hedge accounting, both the investment and the borrowing will be translated at closing rate at each year end and gains or losses on **both** items should be offset in other comprehensive income (OCI).

Any remaining gain or loss from the ineffective part of the hedge should be recognised in profit or loss.

Illustration 6 (Integration question)

Perry Co, whose functional currency is the Country P dollar (P$), has partly financed an investment in a foreign company via the use of a borrowing of JPY 700 million.

The value of the foreign subsidiary was JPY 750 million at 1 January 20X1 and JPY 740 million at 31 December 20X1, as it incurred a loss of JPY 10 million during 20X1.

Exchange rates were as follows:

1 January 20X1	P$ / JPY 0.90 (that is P$1 = JPY 0.90)
31 December 20X1	P$ / JPY 0.80 (that is P$1 = JPY 0.80)

The above hedging arrangement satisfies the requirements for offset per IAS 39.

Required:

Show the impact of the net investment hedge on the financial statements of Perry Co at 31 December 20X1.

Solution:

Under hedge accounting rules, both the investment and the borrowing will be re-translated each year end and the gains / losses offset in OCI (assuming that the hedge is effective).

Investment			Borrowing		
1 Jan	750m / 0.9	P$833m	1 Jan	700m / 0.9	P$778m
31 Dec	750m* / 0.8	P$938m	31 Dec	700m / 0.8	P$875m
Gain		P$105m	Loss		P$97m

* On 31 December, we revalue the opening investment of JPY 750 million at the closing rate on that date. The loss of JPY 10 million would be posted to profit or loss and to the statement of financial position, so that the net asset value of JPY 740 million is shown in the statement of financial position.

The hedge would be considered 108% (105/97) effective. If it had not been considered effective, the loss on retranslation of the borrowing would have been posted to profit or loss rather than to OCI.

Hedging a portion of the risk

Alternatively, in this example, the hedge could have been set up so that the JPY 700 million borrowing was used to hedge just JPY 700 million of the net investment, with any remaining part excluded and revalued directly to OCI in the normal way.

If the hedge had been set up in this way, the gain or loss on the retranslation of the excess over JPY 700 million of the foreign investment's value would have been posted to OCI, and the gains / losses on the hedged item and hedging instrument would have been offset against each other in OCI.

Effectiveness of the hedge

Hedge accounting can be applied if the effectiveness of the hedge is expected to be between 80% and 125% throughout its life.

In some cases, after a hedge has been set up and hedge accounting has been applied, expectations of effectiveness change and the hedge effectiveness may fall outside these limits i.e. the hedge fails the effectiveness test.

If the hedge fails the effectiveness test then the entity has to stop hedge accounting and revert back to normal accounting treatment for the financial instrument and the hedged item. This means recycling any other comprehensive income (OCI) entries back into profit or loss straight away.

The examples throughout this chapter have shown how to use hedge accounting for the effective portion of the hedge for each of the three types of hedging arrangement. In all cases if a portion is assessed to be ineffective, this ineffective portion of the gain or loss should be recognised in the statement of profit or loss.

Examples

If the hedge is a **cash flow hedge** and it fails the effectiveness test, any further gains or losses on the hedging (derivative) instrument will then have to go through profit or loss (rather than other comprehensive income).

If the hedge is a **fair value hedge** then the treatment of the derivative won't change (as FVPL is the normal treatment of a derivative) but the hedged item will no longer be FVPL and will revert back to normal accounting treatment. Note that this depends on what the hedged item is. For example, if it is inventory then it will go back to being measured at lower of cost and NRV.

How to improve the effectiveness of a hedge

It is in an entity's interests to try to maintain and improve the effectiveness of a hedge, so that hedge accounting can be continually applied.

This means ensuring that the calculated effectiveness stays within the 80% - 125% boundary.

Some specific examples of how entities aim to improve the effectiveness of a hedge are:

- only hedge a set value which is a proportion of forecast future cash flows so that the hedge is more likely to remain effective even if forecast future cash flows prove to be less than expected

- for forward contracts, only designate the spot component of the forward price as the hedging instrument (remember that the forward price is the spot price plus adjustment for interest differentials), so that the hedge of future cash flows is guaranteed to be 100% effective as they would also change in value according to the spot price.

6 Adoption of hedge accounting

Hedge accounting in practice

Hedge accounting can be adopted for any items for which cash flows are highly probable. So for example an entity might decide to use cash flow hedging to cover probable foreign currency sales over the next few years.

If covering sales over the next two years say, the entity would be 'adopting hedge accounting two years out'.

The normal hedging timespan for most entities is up to 12 months out. Entities generally hedge a proportion of forecast future foreign currency cash receipts / payments, reducing the proportion as time increases to ensure that the hedged amount is always less than the actual amount (to make sure that the entity doesn't over-hedge and fail the effectiveness test straight away).

Reduced volatility

Hedge accounting should reduce volatility by the matching mechanism.

This is because in the absence of hedge accounting, earnings figures include changes in values of derivatives even if the hedged position has not yet been recognised in profit or loss.

Hedge accounting enables an entity to offset these gains / losses on derivatives against losses / gains on another financial asset or liability.

Link to financial strategy

Hedge accounting can be used on a short term basis to reduce volatility of earnings.

However, an entity might decide to set up hedges over long term periods as part of its overall financial strategy (it might be considered to be the best strategy from an entity value perspective).

(**N.B.** Over long term periods, hedge accounting cannot be used indefinitely – an end date always needs to be set.)

Where an entity wishes to hedge future cash flows beyond the time period when they would be regarded as 'highly probable' and therefore quality for hedge accounting under IAS 39, the entity must decide to either:

(a) Hedge economic entity value, knowing that reported earnings are likely to be more volatile, or

(b) Limit the period of the hedge to that permitted for hedge accounting purposes.

That is, such an entity must decide whether economics or accounting should take priority.

7 Disclosure of financial instruments

IFRS 7 **Financial Instruments: Disclosures** provides the disclosure requirements for financial instruments. A summary of the requirements is detailed below.

Objective of IFRS 7

The objective of the IFRS is to require entities to provide disclosures in their financial statements that enable users to evaluate:

(a) the **significance** of financial instruments for the entity's financial position and performance; and

(b) the **nature and extent of risks** arising from financial instruments to which the entity is exposed during the period and at the end of the reporting period, and how the entity manages those risks.

Disclosures should be made by each class of financial instrument, so for example financial assets and financial liabilities.

General quantitative and qualitative risk disclosures

The **qualitative disclosures** describe management's objectives, policies and processes for managing those risks.

The **quantitative disclosures** provide information about the extent to which the entity is exposed to risk, based on information provided internally to the entity's key management personnel.

Together, the disclosures provide an overview of the entity's use of financial instruments and the exposures to risks they create.

Categories of risks

Three categories of risks are identified in IFRS 7 i.e. there are three specific risks that need to be considered:

- credit risk
- liquidity risk
- market risk

Credit risk

This is the risk that one party to a financial instrument will cause a financial loss for the other party by failing to discharge an obligation e.g. the risk that a customer might go into liquidation before it can pay an amount owing.

Disclosures relating to credit risk include:

- maximum exposure to credit risk without taking into account collateral (e.g. fixed or floating charges)
- details of collateral held as security and other credit enhancements, such as letters of credit
- information of financial assets that are either past due (when a counterparty has failed to make a payment when contractually due) or impaired.

For example, an entity would need to disclose the detail of any investments, for example money market instruments such as certificates of deposit (CDs) and commercial paper. For each material investment, information regarding the credit rating of the counterparty would have to be disclosed.

Liquidity risk

This is the risk that an entity will encounter difficulty in meeting obligations associated with financial liabilities.

Disclosures relating to liquidity risk include:

- a maturity analysis for financial liabilities that shows the maturity dates for all financial liabilities
- an explanation of how liquidity risk is managed.

Market risk

This is the risk that the fair value of (or future cash flows from) a financial instrument will fluctuate due to changes in market prices.

Market risk comprises three types of risk: currency risk, interest rate risk and other price risks.

Disclosures relating to market risk include:

- a sensitivity analysis (including methods and assumptions used) for each type of market risk exposed, showing impact on profit or loss and equity.

For example, an analysis of the sensitivity of financial results to reasonably probable market price changes would need to be disclosed (e.g. what would the revenue figure have been for a company with USA exposure if the USD had been worth 5% less in the year?)

IFRS 7 Disclosures: More detail

Information about the significance of financial instruments

(a) **Statement of financial position**

An entity must disclose the **significance** of financial instruments for their financial position and performance. The disclosures must be made for each class of financial instruments, namely:

- financial assets measured at fair value through profit and loss, showing separately those held for trading and those designated at initial recognition
- held-to-maturity investments
- loans and receivables
- available-for-sale assets
- financial liabilities at fair value through profit and loss, showing separately those held for trading and those designated at initial recognition
- financial liabilities measured at amortised cost

Additionally, IFRS 7 requires additional disclosures for items such as reclassifications or derecognition of financial instruments, information about financial instruments to be measured at fair value through profit and loss, reconciliation of the allowance for credit losses (irrecoverable debts) and breaches of loan agreements.

(b) **Statement of comprehensive income / Statement of profit or loss**

An entity must disclose items of income, expense, gains and losses, with separate disclosure of gains and losses from each class of financial instrument.

For financial instruments that are not measured at fair value through profit or loss, the interest income and interest expense must be disclosed.

The amount of impairment losses on financial assets and interest income on impaired financial assets must also be disclosed.

(c) **Other disclosures**

Additionally, the following must be disclosed:

- Accounting policies for financial instruments.

- Detailed information about hedge accounting, including a description of each hedge, hedging instrument, and fair values of those instruments, and nature of risks being hedged.

- For cash flow hedges, the periods in which the cash flows are expected to occur, when they are expected to enter into the determination of profit or loss, and a description of any forecast transaction for which hedge accounting had previously been used but which is no longer expected to occur.

- For cash flow hedges, the amounts recognised in other comprehensive income or reclassified from equity into profit or loss, or transfers into the carrying value of a non-financial asset or non-financial liability.

- For fair value hedges, information about the fair value changes of the hedging instrument and the hedged item. Cash flow hedge ineffectiveness recognised in profit or loss.

- Information about the fair values of each class of financial asset and financial liability, along with the comparable carrying amounts, a description of how fair value was determined and detailed information if fair value cannot be reliably measured.

Nature and extent of exposure to risks arising from financial instruments

(a) **Qualitative disclosures**

The qualitative disclosures describe:

- Risk exposures for each type of financial instrument.

- Management's objectives, policies, and processes for managing those risks.

- Changes from the prior period.

(b) Quantitative disclosures

The quantitative disclosures provide information about the extent to which the entity is exposed to risk, based on information provided internally to the entity's key management personnel. These disclosures include:

- Summary quantitative data about exposure to each risk at the reporting date.
- Disclosures about credit risk, liquidity risk, and market risk as further described below.
- Concentrations of risk.

Illustration 7: Example of IFRS 7 Disclosures

Real world example: Marks and Spencer's annual report and financial statements 2014

The disclosures made by Marks and Spencer in its annual report and financial statements 2014 are typical of those made by entities under IFRS 7.

Note 21 to the accounts contains the following disclosures:

- General information on treasury policy and financial risk management
- Risks disclosed under the headings of 'liquidity / funding risk', 'counterparty risk' (i.e. credit risk) and 'foreign currency risk' and 'interest rate risk' (two elements of market risk).

Specifically, the disclosures by risk category comprise:

Liquidity / funding risk

Details of outstanding borrowings and covenants

Maturity dates for outstanding borrowings, split between under 1 year, 1-2 years, 2-5 years and over 5 years.

Counterparty risk (i.e. credit risk)

Explanation of group treasury policy towards counterparties (i.e. details of how counterparties are credit checked and how much can be invested with counterparties of different credit ratings)

Analysis of investments and derivatives held, split by credit rating of counterparty.

Foreign currency risk

Details of hedging policies (i.e. use "forward foreign exchange contracts progressively covering up to 100% out to 18 months")

Details of foreign currency receivables and payables, and of borrowings (split by currency and by fixed or floating rate).

Interest rate risk

Details of exposure, and of the different types of derivatives used to manage the risk.

Market risk: Sensitivity analysis

The disclosure here covers the following scenario, which is judged to be reasonably probable by the management:

"the estimated impact on the income statement and equity as a result of market movements in foreign exchange and interest rates in relation to the Group's financial instruments. The Directors consider that a 2% +/– (last year 2%) movement in interest rates and a 20% +/– (last year 20%) weakening in sterling represents a reasonable possible change."

8 End of chapter objective test questions

Test your understanding 2 (Objective test question)

If a company has a fixed rate borrowing, it might be worried about an interest rate fall affecting the market value of its borrowing and hence its share price and competitiveness.

To hedge this the company could enter into an interest rate swap, swapping the fixed rate on the borrowing for a floating rate.

Which of the following describes the correct treatment under hedge accounting rules (IAS 39)?

A The borrowing would be at cost on the statement of financial position and the swap would be at fair value on the statement of financial position, with any gain or loss going to profit or loss

B The borrowing would be at fair value on the statement of financial position with any gain or loss going to profit or loss, and the swap would be at fair value on the statement of financial position with any gain or loss going to profit or loss

C The borrowing would be at cost on the statement of financial position and the swap would be at cost on the statement of financial position with any gain or loss going to profit or loss

D The borrowing would be at fair value on the statement of financial position and the swap would be at fair value on the statement of financial position with any gain or loss being recorded in other comprehensive income

Test your understanding 3 (Objective test question)

During its financial year ended 31 March 20X6, CDO acquired 100% of the issued share capital of DEP for EUR 750,000.

The purchase was partially financed by a EUR 600,000 borrowing. The borrowing is designated by CDO as a hedging instrument.

CDO's functional currency is the USD.

Which of the following describes the accounting treatment required for gains and losses on the investment and its hedging instrument?

A Gains or losses on both the investment and the hedging instrument are all recognised separately in the statement of profit or loss each year

B Gains or losses on the matched investment and the hedging instrument are recorded in other comprehensive income. Gains or losses on the unmatched amount are recognised in the statement of profit or loss each year

C Gains or losses on both the investment and the hedging instrument are all recognised separately in other comprehensive income each year

D Gains or losses on the matched investment and the hedging instrument are netted off. Gains or losses on the unmatched amount are recognised in other comprehensive income each year

Test your understanding 4 (Objective test question)

Under IAS 39 Financial Instruments: Recognition and Measurement, what is the correct treatment of a fair value hedge?

A When the underlying transaction affects profit or loss, the hedge ends and the OCI entries are recycled into profit or loss

B The gain or loss on the hedging instrument (or the portion of it that is deemed to be an effective hedge) is recognised in other comprehensive income (OCI)

C Both the investment and the borrowing will be translated at closing rate at each year end and gains or losses on both items should be offset in other comprehensive income (OCI)

D The changes in fair value of both the hedged item and the hedging instrument are recognised in profit or loss and will offset each other

Test your understanding 5 (Objective test question)

Which of the following disclosures are required by IFRS 7 Financial Instruments: Disclosures?

A Specific Standard Disclosures and General Standard Disclosures

B Economic, environmental and social disclosures

C Quantitative disclosures only

D Qualitative disclosures and quantitative disclosures

Test your understanding 6 (Objective test question)

Which TWO of the following are conditions which must exist in order for hedge accounting to be permitted under IAS 39 Financial Instruments: Recognition and Measurement?

A   There is formal designation and documentation of the hedging relationship at the inception of the hedge.

B   The hedge is expected to be at least 95% effective.

C   The effectiveness of the hedge has to be verified by the entity's auditors.

D   The hedge is assessed on an ongoing basis and has actually been highly effective throughout the financial reporting periods for which it was designated.

Test your understanding 7 (Objective test question)

Belle Co has been using hedge accounting to record the movement in value of some foreign currency denominated inventory (the hedged item) and an associated futures contract (the hedging instrument).

In the last accounting period the fair value of the inventory increased in from $80,500 to $82,000, and the fair value of the futures contract changed from $81,100 to $79,900.

What is the effectiveness of this hedge?

A   80.0%

B   97.4%

C   99.3%

D   101.5%

Test your understanding 8 (Objective test question)

Lau Co is a UK based company, which is funded by a combination of ordinary shares and fixed rate bank borrowings denominated in British pounds (GBP). It has no surplus cash.

The company manufactures electrical switches and sells them to retail outlets in the UK, allowing credit of 60 days. Most of Lau Co's raw materials are sourced locally, but some are imported from the eurozone, where the currency is the euro (EUR).

Which THREE of the following should Lau Co consider disclosing in its financial statements according to IFRS 7 Financial Instruments: Disclosures?

A   Credit risk management policy

B   Aged debtor analysis

C   The impact of adverse exchange rate movements on reported profit

D   Proportion of spending on infrastructure projects

E   Emissions of greenhouse gases

Test your understanding 9 (Objective test question)

A derivative is a financial instrument or certain other contract which has which THREE of the following characteristics?

A   it requires little or no initial investment

B   it is a highly probable forecast transaction

C   it gives the right, but not the obligation, to trade

D   it is settled at a future date

E   its value changes in response to the change in a specified rate or index

Test your understanding 10 (Objective test question)

Which of the following is NOT a type of hedge recognised by IAS 39?

A   A fair value hedge

B   A cash flow hedge

C   A net investment hedge

D   A money market hedge

Test your understanding 11 (Objective test question)

An entity, Thompson Co, reports in US dollars (USD) and decided in January 20X1 that it will need to buy an item of plant in one year's time for EUR 400,000.

As a result of being risk averse it wishes to hedge the risk that the cost of buying euros will rise and so enters into a forward contract to buy EUR 400,000 in one year for the fixed sum of USD 200,000. The fair value of this contract at inception is zero.

At the year-end of 31 July 20X1 the euro has depreciated and the present value of EUR 400,000 is USD 180,000.

How should this be dealt with in the financial statements of Thompson for the year ended 31 July 20X1, assuming that the conditions for hedge accounting are satisfied?

A   No entries yet, because the plant hasn't yet been purchased

B   Recognise a loss of USD 20,000 in the statement of profit or loss for the year

C   Recognise a loss of USD 20,000 in other comprehensive income

D   Record the value of the forward as USD 200,000 and wait until the plant is purchased before making any further entries to reflect any movement in its value.

9 End of chapter case style question

Test your understanding 12 (Case style question)

Nut Co owns inventories of 50,000 barrels of oil which cost $600,000 on 1 September 20X8.

To minimise the risk of losing out if the oil price falls, Nut Co enters into a futures contract to sell 50,000 barrels of oil for $620,000 on 1 December 20X8.

At the year end of 30 September 20X8, the market value of the oil is $13.00 per barrel and the futures price for delivery on 1 December 20X8 is $13.40 per ton.

Required:

Prepare journal entries to show the impact of the fair value hedge on the financial statements of Nut Co at 30 September 20X8, assuming that the conditions for hedge accounting are satisfied.

(15 minutes)

Test your understanding answers

Test your understanding 1 (Integration question)

(a) Derivative contracts should be accounted for as financial instruments held at fair value through profit or loss.

The value of the derivative will be the present value of the difference between the value of the contract when settled compared with the cost of B$1 million being purchased at the spot rate at the year-end date.

Cost of B$1 million at the contracted rate of B$0.75 = 1m/0.75 = A$1,333,333

Cost of B$1 million at the year end rate of B$0.80 = 1m/0.8 = A$1,250,000

Therefore , the derivative results in a liability at the year-end date of A$83,333 (1,333,333 – 1,250,000 - ignoring the time value of money) as the contract has unfavourable terms when compared to the year end rate. The loss on the derivative would be charged to the statement of profit or loss in the year to 31 March 20X1.

The journal entry to record the derivative would be:

Dr   Profit or loss (loss)   A$83,333

Cr   Derivative liability   A$83,333

(b) If the derivative was designated as a hedging instrument in a cash flow hedge then the loss of A$83,333 would be recognised in other comprehensive income until the invoice was received from the supplier (the hedged item is the payable). This ensures that the movements in the hedged item and the hedging instrument can be offset in the same accounting period.

Test your understanding 2 (Objective test question)

The answer is (B).

(A) is under normal accounting rules.

(C) and (D) are incorrect.

Test your understanding 3 (Objective test question)

The answer is (B).

According to IAS 39 gains and losses on designated hedging instruments (the borrowing) and hedged items (the net investment in DEP) are recorded in OCI.

Any gain or loss on the unhedged element of the investment (the EUR150,000 not covered by the borrowing) is recognised in the statement of profit or loss.

Test your understanding 4 (Objective test question)

The answer is (D).

The other treatments relate to cash flow hedges and net investment hedges.

Test your understanding 5 (Objective test question)

The answer is (D).

Specific Standard Disclosures and General Standard Disclosures are required under the provisions of the GRI's G4 Guidelines (NOT IFRS 7).

Economic, environmental and social disclosures are the GRI's Specific Standard Disclosures categories (under the general heading of 'Indicators').

IFRS 7 requires both qualitative disclosures and quantitative disclosures.

Test your understanding 6 (Objective test question)

The answer is (A) and (D).

Conditions for hedge accounting to be permitted are:

- There is formal designation and documentation of the hedging relationship at the inception of the hedge.

- The hedge is expected to be highly effective.

- The effectiveness of the hedge can be reliably measured.

- The hedge is assessed on an ongoing basis and has actually been highly effective throughout the financial reporting periods for which it was designated.

- (Cash flow hedges only) The forecast transaction that is the subject of the hedge must be highly probable and must present an exposure to variations in cash flows that could ultimately affect profit or loss.

Test your understanding 7 (Objective test question)

The answer is (A).

The effectiveness of the hedge is calculated by comparing the **movement** in the value of the hedged item and the **movement** in the value of the hedging instrument.

i.e. a movement of (82,000 - 80,500 =) $1,500 in the fair value of the hedged item and a movement of ($81,100 - $79,900 =) $1,200 in the fair value of the hedging instrument.

Therefore effectiveness is 1,200 / 1,500 = 80.0% (or alternatively 1,500 / 1,200 = 125%).

Test your understanding 8 (Objective test question)

The answer is (A), (B) and (C).

(D) and (E) would be disclosed in a sustainability report following the GRI G4 guidelines. They are not required by IFRS 7.

Test your understanding 9 (Objective test question)

The answer is (A), (D) and (E).

A highly probable transaction (B) is a hedged item not a derivative.

Point (C) relates to an option, which admittedly is a type of derivative, but all derivatives don't have to have this characteristic.

Test your understanding 10 (Objective test question)

The answer is (D).

Only three hedge types are mentioned in IAS 39 – fair value, cash flow and net investment.

Test your understanding 11 (Objective test question)

The answer is (C).

This transaction is a cash flow hedge. Because the forward contract has no fair value at its inception, the need to account for the derivative first arises at the end of the reporting period when it has a value and the change in value has to be recorded. Because it has been designated a cash flow hedge, the change in value is recognised in other comprehensive income to be carried forward at 31 July to match against the future cash flow. The value of this contract is in showing a loss of USD 20,000 at the end of the reporting period because Thompson is locked into buying EUR 400,000 for USD 200,000 when everyone else can buy for USD 180,000, hence Thompson is USD 20,000 worse off because it hedged the position.

To recognise the loss:

DR Other comprehensive income USD 20,000
CR Liability – derivative USD 20,000

Note that if this transaction had not been designated a hedging instrument then the loss would be recognised immediately in profit or loss.

Test your understanding 12 (Case style question)

The hedged item is the oil. The hedging instrument is the futures contract (a derivative).

At the year end **both** the hedged item and hedging instrument will be measured at fair value and gains or losses recorded in the statement of profit or loss.

Hedged item (oil)	
50,000 barrels × £13 per barrel	$650,000
Dr Inventory	$50,000
Cr P&L (gain)	$50,000
Hedging instrument (futures contract)	
50,000 × (12.40 (W1) –13.40)	$50,000
Cr Derivative (financial liability)	$50,000
Dr P&L (loss)	$50,000

The overall effect on profit is nil (loss of $50,000 on derivative and gain of $50,000 on inventory).

(W1) The opening price associated with the futures contract is $620,000 for 50,000 barrels, which corresponds to a price of $12.40 per barrel.

Financing – Equity finance

Chapter learning objectives

Lead	Component
B1: Evaluate the financing requirements of an entity and recommend a strategy for meeting those requirements	(c) Evaluate and compare alternative methods of raising equity finance.

Indicative syllabus content

- Methods of flotation (Initial Public Offering (IPO), introduction) and implications for the management of the entity and for its stakeholders.

- Use of rights issues, including choice of discount rate, impact on shareholder wealth and calculation of TERP (the theoretical ex rights price) and yield-adjusted TERP.

1 Overview of chapter

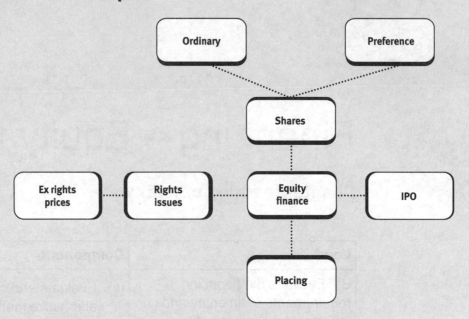

Introduction

In Chapter 3: 'Development of financial strategy', the financing decision was identified as one of the three key decisions of financial strategy (along with the investment decision and the dividend decision).

This chapter and the next two look at the financing decision of an entity in more detail.

First, this chapter introduces the factors to consider when making the fundamental financing decision i.e. should equity finance or debt finance be used?

Then, this chapter covers the main sources of equity finance and the next chapter looks at debt finance.

Finally, Chapter 7: 'Financing – Capital structure' considers the theoretical and practical implications of changing the entity's capital structure (i.e. the mix of long-term debt and equity finance).

2 General introduction to financing

Sources of finance

If a company has a large cash surplus, it may be able to afford to undertake new investment projects without having to resort to external sources of finance.

However, if external funds are required, the company might raise finance from the following sources:

(1) The capital markets:
- new share issues, for example by companies acquiring a stock market listing for the first time;
- rights issues;
- issues of marketable debt (e.g. bonds).

A company must be quoted / listed on a recognised stock exchange in order to be able to raise finance from the capital markets.

(2) Bank borrowings – long-term loans or short-term loans, including bank facilities such as revolving credit facilities (RCFs) and money market lines.

(3) Venture capital funds.

This is high risk finance provided by specialist organisations. The main problem is that the providers of venture capital funding tend to demand significant equity participation in a company and will also want to influence the policy of the company.

(4) Government and similar sources.

In general, finance can be raised from Equity or Debt sources.

Criteria for selecting sources of finance

To decide whether debt or equity should be used to fund a new investment, the following factors will be considered:

- cost of the different sources of finance
- duration – for how long is finance required?
- lending restrictions – for example security and debt covenants
- gearing level (also called capital structure – covered in detail in the next chapter).

- liquidity implications – the ability of the business to service the new debt, allocating sufficient cash resources to meet interest and capital repayment obligations

- the currency of the cash flows associated with the new project

- impact of different financing options on the financial statements, tax position and financial stakeholders of the entity

- availability – availability of finance depends on the creditworthiness of the borrower and also the willingness of lenders to extend credit (for bank borrowings) or liquidity of the capital markets (for equity and bonds).

In an exam, you will need to identify how these general factors apply to the specific circumstances of the entity in the question, in order to identify the preferred choice of finance in a particular situation.

More details on financing criteria

Cost

Each source of finance has a different cost. With debt capital, a company must pay interest on the debt, and to raise new debt finance it must pay a current rate of interest to persuade investors to provide capital. The cost of interest is an allowable expense for tax purposes, so the cost of debt capital to a company is the interest cost less the tax relief on the interest. This fact, and the fact that the providers of debt finance have lower risk than the providers of equity finance tend to make debt finance cheaper than equity.

The cost of equity capital is the return that ordinary shareholders expect on their investment, in the form of current dividends and expectations of dividend and share price growth in the future. Although a company does not have a legal obligation to pay dividends to its shareholders, it must provide a satisfactory return to support the share price. Without the prospect of good returns, investors will not subscribe for new equity when the company needs to raise new capital.

It is important here to appreciate that debt finance tends to be cheaper than equity. This is because providers of debt take lower risks than providers of equity and therefore earn less return. Interest on debt finance is also normally corporation tax deductible, returns to equity are not. The period of the finance will also affect the cost as long-term finance tends to be more expensive than short-term finance.

Duration

Equity capital is long-term 'permanent' capital. Most debt capital, on the other hand, is obtained for a fixed term. The length of borrowing can range from very short term (overdraft facility) to long-term. Bank loans are generally for no longer than the medium term (say, five to seven years) whereas debt finance raised by issuing bonds can be for a much longer term.

When a company is deciding whether to obtain long-term or short-term capital, it should apply the rule: 'Long-term assets should be financed by long-term funds'. Short-term assets, such as inventories and receivables, should normally be financed by a mixture of short-term and long-term funds.

Thus we would expect to see working capital financed partly by short-term facilities such as trade payables and a bank overdraft, whilst non-current assets should be funded by long-term sources of finance. This rule might be broken to gain access to cheap short-term funds, particularly short-term trade payables (which have no obvious cost) but the risks involved should be appreciated.

Lending restrictions

Security is often required for debt finance. This could be derived from existing assets or new assets to be acquired. Assets such as land and buildings hold their value better and are easier for a lender to sell than, say, plant and machinery.

Debt covenants are clauses written into existing debt agreements which protect the lender's interests by requiring the borrower to satisfy certain criteria.

Examples of debt covenants are:

- the interest cover must not fall below 5, and
- the ratio of non-current liabilities to equity must not increase beyond 0.75:1.

The lender will be reassured that the risk associated with the borrower will not change dramatically as long as such covenants are not breached.

Gearing

Gearing is the ratio of debt to equity finance. A high gearing ratio can be very risky. Although high gearing involves the use of cheap debt finance, high levels of debt also create an obligation to meet interest payments and debt principal repayment schedules. If these are not met the company could end up in liquidation. A company should try to achieve a satisfactory balance between equity finance and medium- and long-term debt for its long-term funding, to benefit from the lower cost of debt finance without exposing itself to the risks arising from excessive debt obligations.

The currency of the cash flows associated with the new project

If the cash flows from the investment project are expected to be denominated in a foreign currency, the entity may decide to raise finance denominated in the same foreign currency, to reduce the risk of exchange rate movements by matching the receipts from the project with the servicing costs of the finance.

The impact of different financing options on the financial statements, tax position and financial stakeholders of the entity

Investors (both debt holders and shareholders) will use ratio analysis to assess the performance of the business. It is therefore important that management consider the impact of any new financing on the financial statements of the business. For example, raising debt finance will affect the Return on Equity of the business, as well as the interest cover and gearing ratios.

Also, raising debt finance will give rise to interest payments which are tax deductible, so impacting the tax position of the business.

The existing financial stakeholders of the business (debt holders and shareholders) will be constantly monitoring the business's performance, so it will be important for management to clearly explain the rationale for any new financing method which impacts the financial statements or the tax position.

Availability

Not all companies have access to all sources of finance. Small companies traditionally have problems in raising both equity and long-term debt finance. Remember that many firms do not have an unlimited choice of funding arrangements.

The availability of debt finance is enhanced if an entity has a good credit rating. The more creditworthy a borrower is assessed as being, the more likely it is that funds will be relatively easy to raise.

3 Equity finance

Equity is another name for shares or ownership rights in a business.

Important terminology

Share – a fixed identifiable unit of capital in an entity which normally has a fixed nominal value, which may be quite different from its market value. (CIMA Official Terminology, 2005)

Shareholders receive returns from their investment in shares in the form of dividends, and also capital growth in the share price.

Ordinary shares

Ordinary shares pay dividends at the discretion of the entity's directors. The ordinary shareholders of a company are the owners of the company and they have the right to attend meetings and vote on any important matters.

On a winding-up of a company, the ordinary shareholders are subordinate to all other finance providers (i.e. they receive their money last, if there is any left after all other finance providers have been paid).

Preference shares

Preference shares are a form of equity that pays a fixed dividend, which is paid in preference to (before) ordinary share dividends, hence the name.

Also, on a winding-up of a company, the preference shareholders are subordinate to all the debt holders and creditors, but receive their payout before ordinary shareholders.

More details on preference shares

Comparison of preference shares with debt and with ordinary shares

Preference shares pay a fixed proportion of the share's nominal value each year as a dividend. This is why they are often considered to behave in a way which is more similar to debt finance (fixed annual returns) rather than ordinary shares (variable dividend at the discretion of the directors).

However, unlike interest on debt finance, preference share dividends are paid out of post-tax profits, so there is no tax benefit to a company of paying preference share dividends.

Also, there are certain circumstances (e.g. where a company has insufficient distributable profits) when the company will be allowed to skip its preference share dividends in a year. This is not the case with debt interest, which is an obligation every year, whether or not the company can afford to make the payment.

The lack of tax relief on dividends mentioned above explains why preference shares are relatively unattractive to companies compared with bank borrowings and other forms of fixed rate security such as bonds.

However, they do have some appeal to risk-averse investors looking for a relatively reliable income stream.

Different types of preference shares

There are four types of preference shares:

- cumulative preference shares, for which dividends must be paid including skipped dividends i.e. if a dividend is skipped one year, the skipped dividend has to be paid the following year along with the 'normal' dividend;

- non-cumulative preference shares, for which skipped dividends do not have to be paid later;

- participating preference shares, which give the holder fixed dividends plus extra earnings based on certain conditions (in a similar way to ordinary shares); and

- convertible preference shares, which can be exchanged for a specified number of ordinary shares on some given future date.

Also, note that some preference shares are redeemable, meaning that holders will be repaid their capital (usually at par) on some future date.

Example of convertible preference shares

Convertible preference shares are fixed-income securities that the investor can choose to turn into a certain number of ordinary shares after a predetermined time span or on a specific date.

The fixed-income component offers a steady income stream and some protection of the investor's capital. However, the option to convert these securities into ordinary shares gives the investor the opportunity to gain from a rise in the share price.

Convertibles are particularly attractive to those investors who want to participate in the rise of hot growth companies while being insulated from a drop in price should the ordinary share price growth not live up to expectations.

If a company were to issue some 5% $10 nominal value preference shares, convertible to ordinary shares in five years' time, the investor would receive a fixed amount of $5 each year for the first five years.

In five years' time though, the investor would have the choice to keep the preference shares or convert to a number of ordinary shares. The conversion ratio would have been set when the preference shares were first issued. For example it could be 3, i.e. each preference share could be converted into 3 ordinary shares.

In this example, the investor would be keen to convert if the ordinary shares on the conversion date were worth more than ($10 / 3 =) $3.33.

For example, if the ordinary share price growth has been impressive and the shares are actually worth $4.50 each on the conversion date, and investor could trade a single preference share (value $10) for 3 ordinary shares worth $13.50 in total.

Preference shares, especially convertible preference shares, are often used in the context of Management Buyouts (MBOs) – see details in the later chapter on 'Financial and strategic implications of mergers and acquisitions'.

The shares in a listed, or quoted, company will be traded on a capital market.

Capital markets

Capital markets (or stock markets) must fulfil both primary and secondary functions.

Primary function:

The primary function of a stock market is to enable companies to raise new finance (either equity or debt). Through the stock market, a company can communicate with a large pool of potential investors, so it is much easier for a company to raise finance in this way, rather than contacting investors individually.

Note that in the UK, a company must be a plc before it is allowed to raise finance from the public on the stock market.

Secondary function:

The secondary function of a stock market is to enable investors to sell their investments to other investors. A listed company's shares are therefore more marketable than an unlisted company's, which means that they tend to be more attractive to investors.

Listed v private companies

Private limited company (Ltd in UK terminology)

A private company limited by shares, usually called a private limited company, has shareholders with limited liability and its shares may not be offered to the general public, unlike those of a public limited company (see details below).

'Limited by shares' means that the company has shareholders, and that the liability of the shareholders to creditors of the company is limited to the capital originally invested, i.e. the nominal value of the shares and any premium paid in return for the issue of the shares by the company. A shareholder's personal assets are thereby protected in the event of the company's insolvency, but money invested in the company will be lost.

A limited company may be 'private' or 'public'. A private limited company's disclosure requirements are lighter, but for this reason its shares may not be offered to the general public (and therefore cannot be traded on a public stock exchange). This is the major distinguishing feature between a private limited company and a public limited company. Most companies, particularly small companies, are private.

Public limited company (plc in UK terminology)

A public limited company is a limited liability company that may sell shares to the public. It can be either an unlisted company, or a listed company on the stock exchange.

A stock exchange listing

When an entity obtains a listing (or quotation) for its shares on a stock exchange this is referred to as a flotation or an Initial Public Offering (IPO).

Advantages of a listing

- Once listed, the market will provide a more accurate valuation of the entity than had been previously possible.

- Realisation of paper profits, and mechanism for buying and selling shares in the future at will.

- Raise profile of entity, which may have an impact on revenues, credibility with suppliers and long-term providers of finance.

- Raise capital for future investment.

- Makes employee share schemes more accessible.

Disadvantages of a listing

- Costly for a small entity (flotation, underwriting costs, etc.)

- Making enough shares available to allow a market, and hence loss of at least some control of the original owners.

- Reporting requirements are more onerous.

- Stock exchange rules for obtaining a quotation can be stringent.

Impact of a listing on key stakeholders

Shareholders will normally benefit from a listing, in that their shares become more marketable. The listing can have a positive impact on the reputation of the company, so consequently the share price may rise.

The improvement in the company's reputation and profile that results from a listing can also benefit the managers and the employees of a company. Listed companies tend to be larger and less likely to fail, so can afford to offer better pay and career progression opportunities.

The better reputation of a listed company also impacts its credit rating and therefore reduces the risk of non-payment to suppliers and lenders. Listed companies are more likely to be viewed favourably by lenders, and to be granted generous credit terms by suppliers.

UK capital markets

There are two important capital markets in the UK:

- the full Stock Exchange – a market for larger companies. Entry costs are high and scrutiny is very high for companies listed on the 'full list', but the profile of a Stock Exchange listed company's shares is very high, so the shares are extremely marketable.

- the Alternative Investment Market (AIM) – a market for smaller companies, with lower associated costs and less stringent entry criteria.

The operation of stock exchanges

Prices of shares on the stock exchange are determined by the forces of supply and demand in the market. For example, if a company performs well, its shares become attractive to investors. This creates demand which drives up the price of the shares.

Conversely, investors who hold shares in an underperforming company will try to sell those shares, creating supply in the market. This drives down the price of the shares.

Methods of issuing new shares

The three most commonly used methods of issuing shares are:

A   IPO (initial public offering), or flotation

B   Placing

C   Rights issue

If a company already has a listing on a stock market then the company will either raise new funds by means of a rights issue, or by means of a placing. An IPO is more suitable when a company seeks a listing on the stock exchange for the first time.

These three methods will now be covered in turn below.

A   An IPO (or flotation)

Shares are offered for sale to investors, through an issuing house. The offer could be made at a fixed price set by the company, or in a tender offer investors are invited to tender for new shares issued at their own suggested price. All shares being offered are subsequently sold at the best price at which they would be taken up.

B   Placing

Shares are placed directly with certain investors (normally institutions) on a pre-arranged basis.

More details on IPOs and placings

Initial Public Offerings (IPOs)

These offers may be of completely new shares or they may derive from the transfer to the public of some or all of the shares already held privately. An issuing house, normally a merchant bank, acquires the shares and then offers them to the public at a fixed price.

The offers are usually made in the form of a prospectus detailed in newspapers, sometimes in an abbreviated form. Buying new issues through the prospectus in the newspaper avoids dealing charges.

Other examples of such issues include:

- government privatisations; and

- privately held shares transferred to the public.

It is easier for prospective purchasers to form a judgement about such entities where there is some track record, rather than with offers for a completely new entity.

Stagging

Some investors apply for new issues in the hope of selling immediately and reaping a quick profit. For this to succeed the number of shares purchased must be sufficiently high to cover selling charges. For oversubscribed issues, the allocation may be scaled down and the applicant may receive only a small number of shares. The strategy of selling immediately is called stagging (and investors who do it are called stags).

There have been some notable successes for stags, particularly in some of the privatisation issues, but there have also been cases where the initial dealing price has been substantially below the offer price.

An IPO lock-up period

An IPO lock-up period is a contractual restriction that prevents insiders who are holding a company's shares, before it goes public, from selling the shares for a period usually lasting 90 to 180 days after the company goes public. Insiders include company founders, owners, managers, employees and venture capitalists.

The purpose of an IPO lock-up period is to prevent the market from being flooded with a large number of shares, which would depress the share price.

Insiders' selling activities can have a particularly strong impact on a company's share price when the company has recently gone public because these shareholders typically own a relatively large percentage of the company's shares, while only a small percentage of shares are sold to the public.

Tender offers

A tender offer is an alternative to a fixed price offer.

Under a tender offer, subscribers tender for the shares at, or above, a minimum fixed price. Once all offers have been received from prospective investors, the company sets a 'strike price' and allocates shares to all bidders who have offered the strike price or more.

The strike price is set to make sure that the company raises the required amount of finance from the share issue.

Once the strike price has been set, all bidders who offered the strike price or more are allocated shares, and they all pay the strike price irrespective of what their original bid was.

Example of a tender offer

Bragg Co needs to raise $20 million to invest in a new project. The company has asked investors for tender offers and the following offers have been received:

Maximum price offered ($ per share)	No. of shares requested at this price (million)
2.00	5.0
2.20	4.1
2.40	1.9
2.60	3.2

The strike will be set at the highest possible level that generates the required amount of finance. This is to make sure that the company does not issue more shares than it has to, so that the dilution of the existing shareholders' holdings is kept to a minimum.

If Bragg Co sets the strike price at $2.60, only 3.2 million shares will be issued, raising $8.32 million in total ($2.60 × 3.2 million). This is not acceptable, since $20 million is needed.

If Bragg Co sets the strike price at $2.40, 5.1 million shares will be issued (being 1.9 million to the people who bid $2.40 and 3.2 million to the people who bid $2.60). Therefore, the total finance raised will be $2.40 × 5.1 million = $12.24 million, which again is not sufficient.

If Bragg Co sets the strike price at $2.20, 9.2 million shares will be issued (being 4.1 million to the people who bid $2.20, 1.9 million to the people who bid $2.40 and 3.2 million to the people who bid $2.60).

Therefore, the total finance raised will be $2.20 × 9.2 million = $20.24 million, which now is sufficient.

Hence, to ensure that $20 million is raised from the tender offer, the strike price would be set at $2.20, and any investor who bid $2.20 or more would be allocated shares at the strike price of $2.20.

Placings

A placing (sometimes called a 'placement' or 'private placement') is the sale of securities to a relatively small number of select investors as a way of raising capital.

Investors involved in private placements are usually large banks, mutual funds, insurance companies and pension funds.

Private placement is the opposite of a public issue, in which securities are made available for sale on the open market. Since a private placement is offered to a few, select individuals, the placement does not have to be registered or publicly announced. In many cases, detailed financial information is not disclosed and a the need for a prospectus is waived. Finally, since the placements are private rather than public, the average investor is only made aware of the placement after it has occurred.

This method is very popular, being cheaper and quicker to arrange than most other methods. However, it does not normally lead to a very active market for the shares after flotation.

Private equity

Private equity firms are taking an increasingly important role as equity investors.

Private equity is equity capital that is not quoted on a public exchange. It consists of investors and funds that make investments directly into private companies or conduct buyouts of public companies that result in a delisting of public equity.

Capital for private equity is raised from retail and institutional investors, and can be used to fund new technologies, expand working capital within an owned company, make acquisitions, or to strengthen a balance sheet.

The majority of private equity consists of institutional investors and accredited investors who can commit large sums of money for long periods of time. Private equity investments often demand long holding periods to allow for a turnaround of a distressed company or a liquidity event such as an IPO or sale to a public company.

The size of the private equity market has grown steadily since the 1970s. Private equity firms will sometimes pool funds together to take very large public companies private. Many private equity firms conduct leveraged buyouts (LBOs), where large amounts of debt are issued to fund a large purchase.

Private equity firms will then try to improve the financial results and prospects of the company in the hope of reselling the company to another firm or cashing out via an IPO.

Advisors to an IPO

Investment banks usually take the lead role in an IPO and will advise on:

- the appointment of other specialists (e.g. lawyers);
- stock exchange requirements;
- forms of any new capital to be made available;
- the number of shares to be issued and the issue price;
- arrangements for underwriting;
- publishing the offer.

Stockbrokers provide advice on the various methods of obtaining a listing. They may work with investment banks on identifying institutional investors, but usually they are involved with smaller issues and placings.

Institutional investors have little direct involvement other than as investors, agreeing to buy a certain number of shares. They may also be used by the entity and its advisors to provide an indication of the likely take up and acceptable offer price for the shares. Once the shares are in issue institutional investors have a major influence on the evaluation and the market for the shares.

C   Rights issue

A rights issue is where new shares are offered for sale to existing shareholders, in proportion to the size of their shareholding.

The right to buy new shares ahead of outside investors is known as the 'pre-emption rights' of shareholders. Note that the purpose of pre-emption rights is to ensure that shareholders have an opportunity to prevent their stake being diluted by new issues. Pre-emption rights are protected by law, and can only be waived with the consent of shareholders.

Rights issues are far cheaper to organise than a public share issue, but may be more expensive than a placing.

An issue price must be set which is:

- low enough to secure acceptance of shareholders; but
- not too low, so as to avoid excessive dilution of the earnings per share.

More details on rights issues

Definition

A rights issue may be defined as: "Raising of new capital by giving existing shareholders the right to subscribe to new shares in proportion to their current holdings. These shares are usually issued at a discount to market price." (CIMA Official Terminology, 2005)

Explanation

In a rights issue, the entity sets out to raise additional funds from its existing shareholders.

It does this by giving them the opportunity to purchase additional shares. These shares are normally offered at a price lower than the current share price quoted, otherwise shareholders will not be prepared to buy, since they could have purchased more shares at the existing price anyway. The entity cannot offer an unlimited supply at this lower price, otherwise the market price would fall to this value. Accordingly the offer they make to the existing shareholders is limited. For example they may offer one new share for every four held.

Selection of an issue price

In theory, there is no upper limit to an issue price but in practice it would never be set higher than the prevailing market price (MPS) of the shares, otherwise shareholders will not be prepared to buy as they could have purchased more shares at the existing market price anyway. Indeed, the issue price is normally set at a discount on MPS. This discount is usually in the region of 20%. In theory, there is no lower limit to an issue price but in practice it can never be lower than the nominal value of the shares. Subject to these practical limitations, any price may be selected within these values. However, as the issue price selected is reduced, the quantity of shares that has to be issued to raise a required sum will be increased.

Underwriting

Underwriting avoids the possibility that the entity will not sell all of the shares it is issuing, and so receive less funds than it expects. Underwriters are normally financial institutions such as merchant banks. In return for a fee, they agree to buy any shares that are not subscribed for in the issue. Underwriters receive their fee whether or not they are required to take up any unsubscribed shares.

The underwriting costs could potentially be avoided through a deep-discounted rights issue. In such an issue, the issue price is set at a large discount to the current market price so reducing the possibility of shareholders not taking up their rights.

Selection of an issue quantity

It is normal for the issue price to be selected first and then the quantity of shares to be issued becomes a passive decision. The effect of the additional shares on earnings per share, dividend per share and dividend cover should be considered. The selected additional issue quantity will then be related to the existing share quantity for the issue terms to be calculated. The proportion is normally stated in its simplest form, for example, 1 for 4, meaning that shareholders may subscribe to purchase one new share for every four they currently hold

Terms of a rights issue

The issue price for a rights issue can be set by the company.

For example, if Lauchlan Co wanted to raise $2m for a new investment project, it could issue 1m shares at $2 each, or 500,000 shares at $4 each, or 250,000 shares at $8 each, etc.

To decide on the final terms of the issue, the current share price needs to be considered.

Assume that in this example, Lauchlan Co currently has 2m $1 ordinary shares in issue, with a current market price of $5 per share.

Issuing new shares at anything greater than the existing share price of $5 per share would not help to encourage investors to take up their rights. In order to attract investors, a discount on current market value is usually offered.

However, note that if the new shares were issued at (say) $2 each, this would require 1m new shares to be issued, and so many new shares would have a big impact on the company's earnings per share.

In this case, it would seem sensible to balance the various requirements by offering the new shares to investors at $4 per share. This is sufficiently below current market price to give an incentive to the shareholders to take up their rights, while at the same time only requiring 500,000 new shares to be issued, so restricting the impact on earnings per share.

If the new shares were offered to existing shareholders at $4 per share, 500,000 new shares would need to be issued. Given that there are 2m shares currently in issue, the new issue would be announced as a '1 for 4 rights issue at $4 per share'. (2m / 500,000 = 4)

Market price after issue

- After the announcement of a rights issue there is a tendency for share prices to fall.
- The temporary fall is due to uncertainty about:
    - consequences of the issue;
    - future profits; and
    - future dividends.
- After the actual issue the market price will normally fall again because:
    - there are more shares in issue (adverse effect on earnings per share); and
    - new shares were issued at market price discount.

'Cum rights'

When rights issue is announced, all existing shareholders have the right to subscribe for new shares, and so there are rights ('cum rights') attached to the shares, and the shares are traded 'cum rights'.

'Ex rights'

On the first day of dealings in the newly issued shares, the rights no longer exist and the old shares are now traded 'ex rights' (without rights attached).

Theoretical prices/values

(a) Theoretical 'ex rights' price is the theoretical price that the class of shares will trade at on the first trading day after issue. It is calculated as follows:

$$\frac{(N \times \text{cum rights price}) + \text{Issue price}}{N + 1}$$

(b) Theoretical 'value of rights' per share is calculated as:

$$(\text{Theoretical ex rights price} - \text{issue price})/N$$

where N = no of rights required to buy 1 share

Rights issue illustration

TERP

Using the figures for Lauchlan Co (in the section 'Terms of a rights issue' above), where:

Cum rights price = $5

Issue price = $4

N = 4

Therefore, TERP = [(4 × $5) + $4] / 5 = $4.80

Value of the rights

Also, the value of the rights = (4.80 – 4) = $0.80 per new share, or 0.80 / 4 = $0.20 per old share.

Test your understanding 1 (Integration question)

(a) Plover Co has 1 million GBP1 ordinary shares quoted at GBP4.50 ex div. It is considering a 1 for 5 rights issue at GBP4.20 per share.

Required:

Calculate the theoretical ex rights share price.

(b) Assume that Plover Co intends to use the funds raised to finance a project with an NPV of GBP300,000.

Note: The NPV method has been covered earlier in the CIMA syllabus.

Required:

Calculate the theoretical ex rights share price if the project is undertaken.

Yield adjusted ex-rights price

The calculations of theoretical ex-rights price above assume that the additional funds raised will generate a return at the same rate as existing funds. If an entity expects (and the market agrees) that the new funds will earn a different return than is currently being earned on the existing capital then a 'yield-adjusted' TERP should be calculated.

Yield adjusted TERP

$$= [\text{Cum rights price} \times N/(N + 1)] + [(\text{Issue price}/N + 1) \times (Y_n/Y_0)]$$

where

Y_0 = Yield on 'old' capital

Y_n = Yield on 'new' capital

Using the figures for Lauchlan Co (in the section 'Terms of a rights issue' above), where:

Cum rights price = $5

Issue price = $4

and the rights issue was a 1 for 4 issue,

and also assuming:

*   the rate of return (yield) on the new funds = 15%
*   the rate of return on the existing funds = 12%

The yield-adjusted ex-rights price becomes:

Yield adjusted TERP = $(5 \times 4 / 5) + [(4 / 5) \times (15/12)] = \$5$

Alternatively, this is 1 new share at $4 × (15/12), plus 4 old shares at $5 each i.e. $25 in total, or $5 per share.

Notice that if the new funds are expected to earn a return above the rate generated by existing funds, there will be less dilution of the market price than suggested by the original TERP calculation.

Note: If you are given the NPV of the new project which the rights issue has funded (as in the Test your understanding question above), the yield adjusted TERP is calculated as:

(Original company market capitalisation + NPV of project + rights issue proceeds) / New total number of shares

Courses of action open to a shareholder

Possible actions for a shareholder are:

- do nothing. (Shareholders may be protected from the consequences of inaction by the company selling the rights on behalf of inactive shareholders);

- renounce the rights and sell them on the market;

- exercise the rights (that is buy all the shares at the rights price);

- renounce part of the rights and take up the remainder.

Illustration of actions open to a shareholder

A shareholder receiving notification of a rights issue from an entity has a number of options available.

Consider the position of a shareholder in Lauchlan Co (from the above example in the 'Terms of a rights issue' section.

If the shareholder owns 1,200 shares (worth $5 each), in the 1 for 4 rights issue he will be offered 300 new shares at $4 each.

Option 1 – Do nothing.

In this situation, the market value of the investment could be expected to fall by $240 from $6,000 to $5,760 (1,200 shares at $4.80).

The company would normally reserve the right to sell any 'unaccepted' shares for the best price available in the market. After having deducted any expenses and, of course, $4 per share, the balance would be sent to the shareholder. This cash balance could fully or partially compensate the shareholder for the reduction in market value. The shareholder's percentage share of the entity would reduce.

Option 2 – Sell the rights.

In this situation, the shareholder decides to sell the right to buy the shares at $4 each to another investor. A rational investor would not be expected to pay more than 80 cents per share (TERP – $4) for such a right. The existing shareholder might receive $240 (300 at 80 cents) less any dealing costs incurred. The shareholder's percentage share of the entity would be reduced.

Option 3 – Fully subscribe for the new shares.

In this situation, the shareholder will have to increase the value of the shareholding by paying the entity $1,200 for the 300 new shares. The shareholder will then own 1,500 shares which, using TERP, will be valued at $7,200. The shareholder's percentage share of the entity will be maintained.

Option 4 – Sell some rights to buy some new shares.

In this situation, the shareholder may be unable or unwilling to invest more funds in the entity. Since the rights can normally be sold in the market, the shareholder could sell sufficient of the rights to purchase the balance. In the Lauchlan Co example, each block of 5 rights sold at 80 cents raises sufficient cash to purchase one new share at $4. The shareholder could sell 250 at 80 cents to raise $200 which would be sufficient to purchase 50 at $4. The value of the investment will be maintained at $6,000 but the shareholder's percentage share of the entity will be reduced.

Implications of a rights issue

(a) From the viewpoint of the shareholders:

– they have the option of buying shares at preferential price;

– they have the option of withdrawing cash by selling their rights;

– they are able to maintain their existing relative voting position (by exercising the rights).

(b) From the viewpoint of the company:

– it is simple and cheap to implement;

– it is usually successful ('fully subscribed');

– it often provides favourable publicity.

Test your understanding 2 (Integration question)

Molson Co has a paid-up ordinary share capital of EUR2,000,000 represented by 4 m shares of 50 cents each.

Earnings after tax in the most recent year were EUR750,000 of which EUR250,000 was distributed as dividend. The current price/earnings ratio of these shares, as reported in the financial press, is 8.

The entity is planning a major investment that will cost EUR2,025,000 and is expected to produce a positive NPV of EUR402,400.

The necessary finance is to be raised by a rights issue to the existing shareholders at a price 25% below the current market price of the entity's shares.

Required:

(a) Calculate:

    (i)   the current market price of the shares already in issue;

    (ii) the price at which the rights issue will be made;

    (iii) the number of new shares that will be issued;

    (iv) the price at which the shares of the entity should theoretically be quoted on completion of the rights issue (i.e. the 'ex-rights price'), ignoring incidental costs and assuming that the market accepts the entity's forecast of project NPV.

(b) It has been said that, provided the required amount of money is raised and that the market is made aware of the earning power of the new investment, the financial position of existing shareholders should be the same whether or not they decide to subscribe for the rights they are offered.

Required:

Illustrate and comment on this statement.

4 End of chapter objective test questions

Test your understanding 3 (Objective test question)

A company, whose shares currently sell at $75 each, plans to make a rights issue of one share at $60 for every four existing shares.

What is the theoretical ex-rights price of the shares after the issue?

A $75.00

B $72.00

C $67.50

D $63.00

Test your understanding 4 (Objective test question)

Park Co is hoping to raise $460,000 through a rights issue to fund a new project.

Currently it has 1 million $1 shares in issue, trading at $1.45. The directors think that a discount of 20% will be required to encourage investors to take up their rights.

What should the terms of the rights issue be?

A   1 for 2

B   2 for 5

C   1 for 1

D   2 for 3

Test your understanding 5 (Objective test question)

Lambchop Co has 1 million shares in issue and it wants to raise some new finance by undertaking a 1 for 5 rights issue at $4.40 per share.

The theoretical ex rights price is $4.90.

What was the share price before the rights issue (to two decimal places)?

A $4.40

B $4.82

C $4.90

D $5.00

Test your understanding 6 (Objective test question)

Which of the following statements regarding preference shares are true?

A   Preference shares pay a dividend each year, being a fixed percentage of market value

B   Preference share dividends are tax deductible, just like debt interest

C   The cost of preference shares is generally higher than the cost of debt, but lower than the cost of ordinary shares

D   Preference shares are sometimes convertible and sometimes cumulative, but they are never redeemable

Test your understanding 7 (Objective test question)

DCD is a manufacturer of heavy construction equipment. It has manufacturing facilities around the world.

DCD's Ordinary Share Capital has a nominal value of $70 million ($0.50 shares) and the current market price per share is $6.00.

Proposed new manufacturing facility

The Board is planning to build a new manufacturing facility and has already identified a suitable site and prepared a schedule of forecast cash flows arising from the project.

It is expected that the proposed new facility would be fully operational within a year of the initial investment and that the project would generate a rate of return on funds invested of 20%. This is greater than the return on existing funds of 15% due to the greater efficiency of the new manufacturing facility.

Rights issue

The Board has decided to use a rights issue to finance the initial investment of $250 million. The new shares will be issued at a discount of 40% on current market price.

What is the approximate yield adjusted theoretical ex-rights price of the DCD shares?

A $4.90

B $5.20

C $5.60

D $6.93

Test your understanding 8 (Objective test question)

Alan Jones owns 2,000 shares in Bifold Co, a listed company with an issued share capital of 10m ordinary $1 shares with a current market price of $1.80 per share.

The company has just publicly announced its intention to pursue a 1-for-2 rights issue at $1.00 per share to raise funds for a new project with a net present value of £2m.

What will be the change in the overall wealth of Alan Jones (compared to his current wealth) if he chooses to subscribe for his rights?

A $267 loss

B   No change

C $200 gain

D $400 gain

Test your understanding 9 (Objective test question)

Audrey Co needs to raise $4 million to invest in a new project. The company has asked investors for tender offers and the following offers have been received:

Maximum price offered ($ per share)	No. of shares requested at this price (million)
1.00	4.2
1.10	3.7
1.20	2.2
1.30	1.2

At what price would the strike price be set, and how much finance would be raised in total?

A   Strike price: $1.00, Total funds raised $4.20 million

B   Strike price: $1.10, Total funds raised $4.07 million

C   Strike price: $1.20, Total funds raised $4.08 million

D   Strike price: $1.20, Total funds raised $4.20 million

Test your understanding 10 (Objective test question)

Maximo Co has some $1, 8% preference shares in issue. The shares are currently trading at $1.10.

The preference shares are redeemable at a 4% premium in three years' time, or alternatively they will be convertible into two ordinary shares on that date.

Maximo Co's ordinary shares have a nominal value of $0.25 and they are trading at $0.48. The ordinary share values have grown at 3% per year in recent years, and this level of growth is expected to continue.

What value (per preference share) is the rational investor likely to receive in three years' time if he chooses the better of the conversion or the redemption option?

A $0.99

B $1.04

C $1.05

D $1.14

Test your understanding 11 (Objective test question)

JJ Co has in issue 1.2 million shares, currently valued at $3 each, and a rights issue is being considered.

The rights issue will be either:

- 1 for 4 at $2.50 per share, or
- 1 for 3 at $1.875 per share.

Assuming that all shareholders take up their rights, and that there are no issue costs, what will be the effect of the rights issue on each shareholder's total wealth before taking account of any positive NPV generated by investing the new capital?

A   Total wealth increases more under the 1 for 4 scheme

B   Total wealth increases more under the 1 for 3 scheme

C   Total wealth is unchanged under both schemes

D   Total wealth decreases under both schemes

Test your understanding 12 (Objective test question)

MNO is planning a rights issue at a 30% discount to the current share price, in order to raise $7 million.

It currently has 10 million shares in issue, trading at $2.00 per share.

The directors are trying to calculate the theoretical value of a right per existing share, so that they can inform shareholders what the likely proceeds will be if shareholders decide to sell their rights rather than take them up.

What is the theoretical value of a right per existing share in these circumstances? Enter your answer in the box below, in $ and to two decimal places.

$ [   ]

5 End of chapter case style question

Test your understanding 13 (Case style question)

KB has a paid-up ordinary share capital of $1,500,000 represented by 6m shares of 25 cents each. It has no debt finance. Earnings after tax in the most recent year were $1,200,000. The P/E ratio of the entity is 12.

The company is planning to make a large new investment which will cost $5,040,000 and is considering raising the necessary finance through a rights issue at 192 cents.

Required:

(i)   Calculate the current market price of KB's ordinary shares.

(ii) Calculate the theoretical ex-rights price, and state what factors in practice might invalidate your calculation.

(iii) Briefly explain what is meant by a deep-discounted rights issue, identifying the main reasons why an entity might raise finance by this method.

(30 minutes)

Test your understanding answers

Test your understanding 1 (Integration question)

(a) The theoretical ex rights price (TERP) is:

$$\frac{(N \times \text{cum rights price}) + \text{Issue price}}{N + 1}$$

$$= [(5 \times 4.50) + 4.20]/6 = \text{GBP4.45}$$

Alternatively, TERP can be calculated by looking at the total value of all the shares as follows:

$$= \frac{\left((1m \times £4.50) + (\frac{1}{5} \times 1m \times £4.20) \right)}{\left(1m + \frac{1}{5} \times 1m \right)}$$

$$= \text{GBP4.45}$$

(b) The NPV of the project is GBP300,000, so in an efficient market, this will be the gain in wealth of the shareholders if the project is undertaken.

The total number of shares in issue is now

1 million + (1/5 × 1 million) = 1.2 million

Thus, the theoretical share price after the rights issue, and after undertaking the project is

4.45 + (300,000/1.2 million) = GBP4.70

Test your understanding 2 (Integration question)

(a) (i) Current market price of shares already in issue:

EPS = 750,000 / 4m = EUR 0.1875

Therefore, since the P/E ratio is 8, the price per share is 8 × 0.1875 = EUR 1.50

(ii) Price at which rights issue will be made:

£1.50 × 75% = £1.125

(iii) Number of new shares that will be issued:

EUR2,025,000 / EUR 1.125 = 1.8 million

(iv) 1.8m new shares are being issued at EUR1.125 per share, 4m existing shares are in issue with a market price of EUR 1.50 per share, and the new project will have an NPV of EUR 402,400.

Hence, the TERP is

[(4m × 1.50) + (1.8m × 1.125) + 402,400] / 5.8m = EUR 1.453

Alternatively: Ignoring the project initially, and using the formula from the formula sheet,

$$TERP = \frac{(N \times \text{cum rights price}) + \text{Issue price}}{N + 1}$$

= [(4m/1.8m) × 1.50 + 1.125] / (4m/1.8m) + 1 = EUR 1.384

and with the new project worth NPV = EUR402,400, this increases to

1.384 + (402,400 / 5.8m) = EUR 1.453 as before

(b) This statement can be illustrated as follows:

For every 20 shares held, the rights issue means another 9 shares.

At least in theory, the selling price of the right to purchase one share will be £1.453 less £1.125, that is, £0.328.

A shareholder with 20 shares taking up the rights will have wealth of

	EUR
Market value of 29 shares at EUR1.453 each	42.137
Less: Cost of taking up rights of nine new shares at EUR1.125 each	(10.125)
	32.012

A shareholder with 20 shares selling the rights will have wealth of:

	EUR
Market value of 20 shares at EUR1.453 each	29.060
Add: Sale of nine rights at EUR0.328 each	2.952
	32.012

The above calculations, however, assume no transaction costs.

Furthermore, the market may read a particular message into the rights issue that would affect the calculations.

Test your understanding 3 (Objective test question)

The answer is (B).

[(4 × $75) + $60] / 5 = $72

Test your understanding 4 (Objective test question)

The answer is (B).

A discount of 20% on the shares that are trading at $1.45 means an issue price of $1.16.

To raise $460,000 by issuing shares at $1.16 means that (460,000 / 1.16=) 396,552 shares need to be issued (i.e. approximately 400,000).

400,000 new shares compared to 1 million existing shares is a ratio of 2 to 5.

Test your understanding 5 (Objective test question)

The answer is (D).

The TERP is:

$$\frac{(N \times \text{cum rights share price}) + \text{Issue price}}{N + 1}$$

Therefore:

4.90 = [(5 × share price) + $4.40] / (5 + 1)

So the share price was $5.00 before the rights issue.

Test your understanding 6 (Objective test question)

The answer is (C) only.

Preference share dividends are a fixed percentage of NOMINAL value (A) and they are NOT tax deductible (B). Preference shares are sometimes redeemable (D).

Because the risk to a preference share investor is lower than that of an ordinary shareholder but higher than that of a debt holder, the cost of preference shares does tend to lie between the costs of the other two types of finance (C).

Test your understanding 7 (Objective test question)

The answer is (C).

A 40% discount to current market price is 60% × $6 = $3.60

Therefore, to raise $250m, 69.44 million shares will have to be issued ($250m / $3.60). With 140m shares currently in issue, this amounts to (approximately) a 1 for 2 rights issue.

Yield adjusted TERP

= [Cum rights price × N/(N + 1)] + [(Issue price/N + 1) × (Y_n / Y_0)]

= [$6 × 2/3] + [($3.60/3) × (20/15)]

=$5.60

Test your understanding 8 (Objective test question)

The answer is (D).

Current wealth is 2,000 × $1.80 = $3,600

Ex rights price incorporating the $2m NPV project will be

[(10m × $1.80) + (5m × $1.00) + $2m] / 15m shares = $1.6667

Therefore, if he subscribes for his rights (1,000 extra shares) his total share value will increase to (3,000 × $1.6667) = $5,000

The cost of taking the rights was 1,000 × $1.00 = $1,000

Hence his total wealth will be $5,000 – $1,000 = $4,000 (a gain of $400)

Test your understanding 9 (Objective test question)

The answer is (C).

The strike will be set at the highest possible level that generates the required amount of finance. This is to make sure that the company does not issue more shares than it has to, so that the dilution of the existing shareholders' holdings is kept to a minimum.

If Audrey Co sets the strike price at $1.20, 3.4 million shares will be issued (being 1.2 million to the people who bid $1.30 and 2.2 million to the people who bid $1.20).

Therefore, the total finance raised will be $1.20 × 3.4 million = $4.08 million

Test your understanding 10 (Objective test question)

The answer is (C).

The redemption option will be worth $1 × 1.04 = $1.04

The conversion option will be worth (assuming 3% per year growth continues):

(1.03) 3 × $0.48 × 2 = $1.05

The rational investor would choose the higher amount.

Test your understanding 11 (Objective test question)

The answer is (C).

Total wealth is always unaffected by the rights issue itself. Wealth only changes as a consequence of the NPV generated by any project invested in.

Test your understanding 12 (Objective test question)

The answer is $0.20.

An issue price at a 30% discount means $2.00 × (1 − 0.30) = $1.40

To raise $7 million using an issue price of $1.40, we need to issue 5 million shares (i.e. $7m / $1.40). Therefore this rights issue is a 1 for 2 issue (5 million new shares being issued and 10 million existing shares).

TERP is:

$$\frac{(N \times \text{cum rights price}) + \text{Issue price}}{N + 1}$$

i.e. [(2 × $2.00) + $1.40] / (2 + 1) = $1.80

and so the value of a right per existing share is

(Theoretical ex-rights price − issue price)/N

($1.80 − $1.40) / 2 = $0.20

Test your understanding 13 (Case style question)

(i) Earnings per share (EPS) = Profit after taxation / No of shares = 1,200,000 / 6m = $0.20

Market price = EPS × P/E = 0.20 × 12 = $2.40

(ii) Number of shares issued in rights issue = 5,040,000 / $1.92 = 2,625,000

Therefore, TERP = [(6m × $2.40) + (2.625m × $1.92)] / (6m + 2.625m) = $2.254

Factors that may invalidate this calculation in practice include:

– adverse factors affecting the value of KB's shares between setting the terms of the rights issue and the issue date (e.g. a market crash);

– whether the market considers the forecast return from the new funds to be realistic;

– the increased number of shares in issue may affect their marketability, causing a further reduction in the ex-rights share price;

– if shareholders do not take up their rights, shares will be left with the underwriters, which will depress the share price;

– the new project may be seen by investors as more risky than existing projects, with no corresponding increase in return;

– investors' expectations of future dividends per share may change as a consequence of the increase in the share capital.

(iii) A deep-discounted rights issue is an issue where the issue price is set well below the current market price of the shares. In some cases, the discount has been as much as 40% on the pre-issue price. The issue price must still, however, be above the nominal value to comply with company law. If share prices are volatile, there is a risk that the market price will fall below the rights issue price, which would lead to undersubscription. A deep-discounted rights issue should avoid this potential problem.

The lower issue price does mean that more shares will need to be issued to raise the same level of finance, with a consequent impact on future dividends per share and earnings per share.

6

Financing – Debt finance

Chapter learning objectives

Lead	Component
B1: Evaluate the financing requirements of an entity and recommend a strategy for meeting those requirements	(b) Evaluate and compare alternative methods of raising long- term debt finance.

Indicative syllabus content

- Criteria for selecting appropriate debt instruments (e.g. bank borrowings, bonds, convertible bonds, commercial paper).

- Target debt profile (e.g. interest, currency and maturity profile) to manage interest, currency and refinancing risk.

- Use of cross-currency swaps and interest rate swaps to change the currency or interest rate profile of debt.

- Tax considerations in the selection of debt instruments.

- Procedures for issuing debt securities (private placement and capital market issues, role of advisers and underwriters).

- Debt covenants (e.g. interest cover, net debt/EBITDA, debt/debt+equity).

- The lease or buy decision (for both operating and finance leases).

1 Overview of chapter

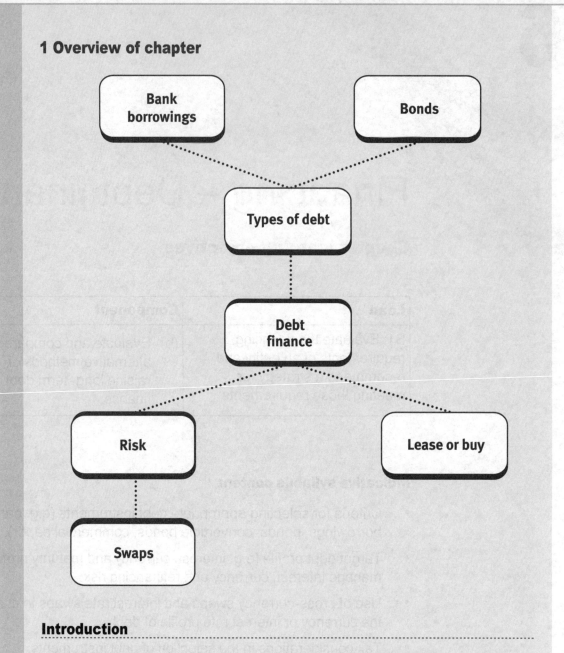

Introduction

The previous chapter considered different sources of equity finance. Now we move on to look at the different sources of debt finance.

This chapter looks at the different sources of debt finance, and the criteria to consider when trying to manage the risk associated with an entity's debt finance.

It concludes by introducing the important 'lease v buy' decision.

2 Debt finance

Debt finance is the loan of funds to a business without conferring ownership rights. The key features of debt financing arise from this 'arm's length relationship' are:

- Interest is paid out of pre-tax profits as an expense of the business. Therefore, paying interest reduces the taxable profits of the business and hence the tax payable.

- Debt finance carries a risk of default if interest and principal payments are not met.

Security – charges

The lender of funds will normally require some form of security against which the funds are advanced. This means that, in the event of default, the lender will be able to take assets in exchange of the amounts owing. There are two types of 'charge' or security that may be offered/required:

(1) **Fixed charge** – The debt is secured against a specific asset, normally land or buildings. This form of security is preferred because, in the event of liquidation, it puts the lender at the 'front of the queue' of creditors.

(2) **Floating charge** – The debt is secured against the general assets of the business. This form of security is not as strong; again it confers a measure of security on liquidation as a 'preferred creditor', meaning the lender is higher in the list of creditors than otherwise.

Covenants

A further means of limiting the risk to the lender is to restrict the actions of the directors through the means of covenants. These are specific requirements or limitations laid down as a condition of taking on debt financing. They may include:

(1) **Dividend restrictions** – Limitations on the level of dividends a company is permitted to pay. This is designed to prevent excessive dividend payments which may seriously weaken the company's future cash flows and thereby place the lender at greater risk.

(2) **Financial ratios** – Specified levels below which certain ratios may not fall, e.g. interest cover, gearing ratio, debt / EBITDA

(3) **Financial reports** – Regular accounts and financial reports to be provided to the lender to monitor progress.

(4) **Issue of further debt** – The amount and type of debt that can be issued may be restricted. Subordinated debt (i.e. debt ranking below the existing unsecured debt) can usually still be issued.

More details on covenants

Introduction

Covenants are put in place by lenders to protect themselves from borrowers defaulting on their obligations due to financial actions detrimental to themselves or the business.

Covenants are most often represented in terms of financial ratios which must be maintained for businesses which lend, such as a maximum debt-to-asset ratio or other such ratios. Covenants can cover everything from minimum dividend payments to levels that must be maintained in working capital to key employees remaining with the firm. Once a covenant is broken, the lender will typically have the right to call back the obligation from the borrower.

Impact on lender and borrower

Debt covenants benefit both the lender and the borrower:

*   debt restrictions could protect the lender by requiring or prohibiting certain activities of the lender: in other words, debt covenants should restrict the borrower from making decisions that would be detrimental to the lender; and

*   debt restrictions could benefit the borrower by reducing the cost of borrowing (e.g., through lower interest rates and higher credit ratings).

Debt covenants do not aim to place a burden on the borrower. Debt covenants are used to solve the agency problems among the management (i.e., of the borrowing company), debt holders, and shareholders that arise due to the differences in the objectives of the borrower and the lender.

Positive and negative debt covenants

Debt covenants can be either positive or negative.

Negative debt covenants state what the borrower cannot do and may include the following:

*   Incur additional long-term debt (or require that additional borrowing be subordinated to the original borrowing)

*   Pay cash dividends exceeding certain threshold

*   Sell certain assets (e.g., sell accounts receivable)

*   Enter into certain types of leases

- Combine in any way with another firm (e.g. takeover, merger)
- Compensate or increase salaries of certain employees

Positive debt covenants state what the borrower must do and may include the following:

- Maintain certain minimum financial ratios
- Maintain accounting records in accordance with generally accepted accounting principles
- Provide audited financial statements (normally within a specified amount of time after the year-end)
- Perform regular maintenance of assets used as security
- Maintain all facilities in good working condition
- Maintain life insurance policies on certain key employees
- Pay taxes and other liabilities when due

Examples of covenants

The most common financial ratios used in debt covenants include the following: net debt to cash flow, net debt to EBITDA, interest cover, tangible net worth, net worth, gearing ratio, current ratio, cash interest cover, debt to equity, etc.

In the above listed ratios, the same term can have different meanings in different debt agreements. For example:

Debt: total debt, funded debt, funded debt less cash, etc.

Cash flow: cash from operations, EBIT, EBITDA, etc.

According to research, covenants that most commonly lead to technical default include net worth (or tangible net worth) and current ratio.

Breach of a covenant

When a debt covenant is breached by the borrower, the lender has a range of alternative responses, including the following (non-exhaustive list):

- Waive the breach and continue the loan
- Waive the breach and impose additional constraints
- Require penalty payment
- Increase interest rate
- Demand immediate repayment of the loan

- Increase security needed
- Terminate debt agreement

A debt covenant breach represents a breach of contract. Lender's response to the breach of contract usually depends on the severity of the breach as well as the terms of the debt agreement. When a debt covenant breach is not severe, usually lenders either waive the breach or impose additional constraints on the borrower.

Types of debt finance

Debt may be raised from two general sources – banks or capital markets.

Bank finance

For companies that are unlisted, and for many listed companies, the first port of call for borrowing money would be the banks.

These could be the high street banks or, more likely for larger companies, merchant banks.

Terms and conditions are negotiable dependent on the term of the borrowing, the amount borrowed, and the credit rating of the company wishing to make the borrowing.

Capital markets

As an alternative to borrowing funds from a bank the company, if listed on the stock exchange, may issue long term bonds to investors in the capital markets.

Criteria for selecting debt instruments

Most companies can borrow from banks, but view direct borrowing from a bank as more restrictive and expensive than selling bonds on the capital market.

Entities deciding whether issue a bond or borrow from a bank to finance a particular investment should consider

- liquidity,
- timescale and
- cost

as determining factors.

Detailed considerations: Criteria to consider

Entities use bonds and bank borrowings to finance investment projects. These range from short-term to long-term investments and cover a variety of reasons including infrastructure development and corporate expansions. Generally speaking, a bond is meant to finance a long-term investment, whereas a bank borrowing is more suitable for short-term needs. But that is not always the case. In recent years, financial managers have shifted their attention to the bond market as it offers liquidity, lower overall costs and the flexibility entities need to run their businesses.

Accessibility to the market is a key feature that differentiates the bond market from bank borrowings. While the latter is open for most corporate entities, the bond market implies costly and cumbersome hurdles for the aspiring company. Only those that have overcome the process can operate in the bond market.

There is a tendency for small and medium sized enterprises (SMEs) to use bank borrowings. Clearly, local banks provide financial support, satisfy liquidity needs and a range of other banking services on a daily basis. Eventually, banks engage in a long relationship with SMEs that benefits the entity whenever the need for capital arises. This relationship provides flexibility when it comes to agree on the terms and conditions of the lending. A bank borrowing often allows borrowers to pay off the borrowing partly or totally, at any time, with little or no warning. A downside, however, is that repayment charges are typically linked to regional interest rates and other admin fees subject to the whim of the bank. Lenders are also capable of substantially changing the terms of the deal, but borrowers can take their accounts elsewhere assuming there is another lender available.

On the bond market, entities need to build up a reputation. They need to communicate their credit quality, which should determine the interest rate on the bond. Bonds have highly standardised terms and conditions. Standardisation plays an important role for entities. It enables the entity to reach a wider range of investors and creates liquidity.

Both types of funding entail operational costs, but there are differences between them. Entering the bond market might be rather difficult and expensive, but once in, the costs reduce significantly. This is because the lending agreement is based on the standardised terms defined by the issuer.

Borrowing from a bank, as discussed earlier, implies submission to the terms set out by the bank as well as dealing with sometimes uncertain conditions.

Examples of long-term debt finance: Terminology

Bank finance

Money market borrowings

The money market consists of financial institutions and dealers in money or credit who wish to either borrow or lend.

The money market is used by participants as a means for borrowing and lending in the short-term, from several days to just under a year. This contrasts with the capital market for longer-term funding, for example bonds and equity.

The core of the money market consists of interbank lending – banks borrowing from, and lending to, each other. However, large profit-making entities will also borrow and lend on the money market.

Revolving credit facilities (RCFs)

Under a RCF the borrower may use or withdraw funds up to a pre-approved credit limit. The amount of available credit decreases and increases as funds are borrowed and then repaid.

The borrower makes payments based only on the amount they've actually used or withdrawn, plus interest and the borrower may repay the borrowing over time or in full at any time.

RCFs are very flexible debt financing options, and they enable a company to minimise interest payments because the amount of funds borrowed fluctuates over time and is never more than the company needs.

Often the RCF will be offered by a single bank, or in the case of a large amount of finance required, a syndicate (group) of banks may offer the RCF to reduce the risk to any one lender.

Capital markets

Bonds

A bond is a debt security, in which the issuer owes the holders a debt and, depending on the terms of the bond, is obliged to pay interest (the coupon) and/or to repay the principal at a later date. i.e. a bond is a formal contract to repay borrowed money with interest at fixed intervals.

Thus a bond is like a loan: the issuer is the borrower (debtor), the holder is the lender (creditor) and more commonly referred to as the investor, and the coupon is the interest. Bonds provide the borrower with external funds to satisfy long-term funding requirements.

Bonds and shares are both securities which can be traded in the capital markets, but the major difference between the two is that shareholders have an equity stake in the company (i.e., they are owners), whereas bondholders have a creditor stake in the company (i.e., they are lenders). Another difference is that bonds usually have a defined term, or maturity, after which the bond is redeemed, whereas shares may be outstanding indefinitely.

Commercial paper

Large profit-making entities may issue unsecured short-term loan notes in the capital market, referred to as commercial paper.

These loan notes will generally mature within 9 months, typically between a week and 3 months. The notes can be traded at any time before their maturity date.

More details on the capital market (bond market)

Issuing debt finance (bonds) in the capital markets enables an entity to borrow a large amount of finance from (potentially) a wide range of potential investors.

The bond market can essentially be broken down into three main groups: issuers, underwriters and purchasers.

Issuers

The issuers sell bonds in the capital markets to fund the operations of their organisations. This area of the market is mostly made up of governments, banks and corporations.

The biggest of these issuers is the government, which uses the bond market to help fund a country's operations. Banks are also key issuers in the bond market, and they can range from local banks up to supranational banks such as the European Investment Bank. The final major issuer is corporates, which issue bonds to finance operations.

Underwriters

The underwriting segment of the bond market is traditionally made up of investment banks and other financial institutions that help the issuer to sell the bonds in the market.

In most cases, huge amounts of finance are transacted in one offering. As a result, a lot of work needs to be done to prepare for the offering, such as creating a prospectus and other legal documents. In general, the need for underwriters is greatest for the corporate debt market because there are more risks associated with this type of debt.

The underwriters sometimes place the bonds with specific investors ('bond placement'), or they can attempt to sell the bonds more widely in the market. Alternatively, under a medium term note (MTN) programme, the issuer (via the underwriter) can issue debt securities on a regular and/or continuous basis.

Purchasers

The final players in the bond market are those who buy the bonds. Buyers basically include every group mentioned as well as any other type of investor, including the individual.

Governments play one of the largest roles in the market because they borrow and lend money to other governments and banks. Furthermore, governments often invest in bonds issued by other countries if they have excess reserves of that country's money as a result of trade between countries. For example, Japan is a major holder of U.S. government debt, such as U.S. gilts.

How to issue bonds on the market

Listing and admission to the London stock exchange

The admission process in the UK is made up of two stages; listing and admission to trading.

Listing

If the bond issuer is not already a listed company, it must first apply to become listed on the London stock exchange.

Admission of companies to the Official List is controlled by the UK Listing Authority (UKLA), a division of the Financial Conduct Authority (FCA). The FCA retains responsibility for the approval of prospectuses, however issuers seeking admission to the Official List will also need to submit listing particulars to the UKLA.

A debt issuer seeking a London listing for its securities must apply for admission to the Official List (a 'listing') through the UKLA. The listing is dependent on the securities gaining admission to trading on the Main Market through satisfying the Exchange's admission and disclosure standards.

The listing process can take as little as three days depending on the complexity of the transaction and the completeness of the listing document submitted for approval. Appointing advisers with extensive experience of listing and agreeing the timetable well in advance should help shorten the process.

Admission to trading

In February 2010 London Stock Exchange launched an electronic, order-driven trading service for UK government, corporate and supranational bonds, called the Order book for Retail Bonds (ORB). This aims to offer retail investors efficient access to an on-screen secondary market in retail denominated London listed debt instruments. This new trading service was introduced in response to demand from private investors in the UK for a cost effective and transparent mechanism for gaining access to fixed income securities and to develop the market for retail denominated bonds in the UK.

For admission to the ORB, the Admissions team at London Stock Exchange require documentation to be submitted at least 11 days prior to the admission date. This documentation should include an electronic copy of the base prospectus and the relevant pricing supplement/final terms document, a copy of the relevant board minutes relating to the issue, confirmation of the market maker who will be supporting the security, and an indicative opening price for the security.

Market making

To ensure that all instruments available on the ORB are tradable and have prices available throughout the day it is a requirement for all bonds admitted to the ORB to have at least one registered market maker.

The issuer can act as market maker to their own securities or can engage the services of a third party broker, however the market maker must be a member firm of London Stock Exchange and be authorised to deal.

The market maker will be required to quote two-way prices (buy and sell) in the security throughout the continuous trading period.

The prices must be within a maximum spread requirement which is determined by the trading segment and trading sector of the security. There is also a minimum volume (equivalent to nominal value) of securities which must be quoted on either side.

To register in a security the market maker must complete and submit a registration information form. The market maker has no obligation to quote in more than one security and there is no fee payable to register in ORB securities.

International debt finance

Large companies can borrow money in foreign currencies as well as their own domestic currency from banks at home or abroad.

The main reason for wanting to borrow in a foreign currency is to fund a foreign investment project or foreign subsidiary.

The foreign currency borrowing provides a hedge of the value of the project or subsidiary to protect against changes in value due to currency movements. The foreign currency borrowing can be serviced from cash flows arising from the foreign currency investment.

More detail on foreign currency borrowings

The choice of currency for debt finance

In the developed countries of the world, companies can choose which currency they prefer for both bank borrowings and bonds. In most developing countries, companies will need to raise finance in an international currency such as US dollars.

Eurobond markets

Eurobonds are bonds issued on the international capital markets.

They can be denominated in any major international currency (i.e. not necessarily denominated in euro). Eurocurrency bonds may be listed on the domestic currency stock exchange but cannot be traded through that exchange. They are usually bearer instruments and pay interest annually, gross of tax.

This is in contrast to domestic bonds which are both listed and traded on the local stock exchange, and are usually registered bonds, that is, registered to a named holder.

The eurobond market is a self-regulated off-shore market. Self-regulation is promoted by the International Capital Market Association (ICMA) who set rules for members to follow in areas such as processing transactions and payment of commission.

3 Target debt profile

The next chapter ('Financing – Capital structure') discusses the factors an entity will have to consider when choosing what its overall capital structure (mix of debt and equity finance) should be.

Once an entity has decided how much debt finance is needed, several issues need to be considered as the entity aims to achieve its target debt profile. In particular, the following questions need to be answered:

- Should the entity borrow at a fixed or a floating (variable) rate?
- Should the debt have a short-term or a long-term repayment date?
- Should domestic currency or foreign currency borrowings be used?

The answers to these questions will determine the level of interest rate, refinancing and currency risk that the entity will face.

Interest rate risk

Interest rate risk is the risk of gains or losses on assets and liabilities due to changes in interest rates. It will occur for any organisation which has assets or liabilities on which interest is payable or receivable.

Interest rates and LIBOR

Non-financial organisations normally have many more interest-bearing liabilities than interest-bearing assets. These include bank borrowings and overdrafts, and issues of bonds or debentures. As a general rule:

- interest on bank borrowings and overdrafts is payable at a **variable rate** or **floating rate**, with the interest set at a margin above a benchmark rate such as the base rate or the London Inter Bank Offer Rate (LIBOR)

- interest on most bonds, debentures or loan stock is at a **fixed rate**.

When interest is at a floating rate, the amount of interest payable in each period is set by reference to the benchmark interest rate on a specific date, such as the starting date for the interest period. For example, suppose that a company has a bank borrowing on which it pays interest every six months at 50 basis points above LIBOR. (100 basis points = 1%, therefore 50 basis points = 0.50%.) At the start of an interest period, the six-month LIBOR rate might be, say, 4.75%: if so, the company would pay interest at the end of the six months at 5.25% for the six-month period. If LIBOR moves up or down, the interest rate payable every six months will go up or down accordingly.

> (**Note:** LIBOR is the London Interbank Offer Rate. It is a money market rate at which top-rated banks are able to borrow short-term in the London sterling or eurocurrency markets. There are LIBOR rates for major traded currencies, including the US dollar, euro and yen, as well as sterling (British pounds).)

The exposure to interest risk will depend on the amount of interest bearing assets or liabilities that an entity holds and the type that these are (floating or fixed rate).

Types of interest rate risk exposure

- **Floating rate borrowings:** If a company has floating rate borrowings, changes in interest rates alter the amount of interest payable or receivable. This directly affects cash flows and profits and the risk therefore is quite obvious.

- **Fixed rate borrowings:** If a company has fixed rate borrowings interest rate risk still exists. Even though interest charges themselves will not change, a fixed rate can make a company uncompetitive if its costs are higher than those with a floating rate and interest rates fall. (Remember interest rate risk can be about assets or liabilities – an asset that pays a fixed rate of interest will be worth less if interest rates rise.)

More on fixed rate exposure

Companies with fixed rate borrowings are also exposed to interest rate risk, because by paying a fixed rate of interest on its liabilities, a company runs the risk that:

- if interest rates fall, it will be unable to benefit from the lower rates available in the market, because it is committed to paying fixed rates, and

- competitor organisations might have floating rate liabilities, and so will benefit from lower interest costs, and so improve their profitability and competitive strength.

The same, of course, is true in reverse for a company that has fixed or floating rate deposits/investments.

Refinancing risk

Refinancing risk is associated with interest rate risk because it looks at the risk that borrowings will not be refinanced or will not be refinanced at the same rates.

The reasons for this could include:

- Lenders are unwilling to lend or only prepared to lend at higher rates.
- The credit rating of the company has reduced making it a more unattractive lending option.
- The company may need to refinance quickly and therefore have difficulty in obtaining the best rates.

The use of longer-term debt finance reduces the refinancing risk. Short-term debt finance has to be regularly repaid and then renegotiated if additional finance is needed, so the refinancing risk is higher.

Currency risk

Currency risk is the risk that arises from possible future movements in an exchange rate. It is a two-way risk, since exchange rates can move either adversely or favourably.

Currency risk affects any organisation with:

- assets and/or liabilities in a foreign currency
- regular income and/or expenditures in a foreign currency
- no assets, liabilities or transactions that are denominated in a foreign currency. Even if a company does not deal in any currencies, it will still face a risk since its competitors may be faring better due to favourable exchange rates on their transactions.

4 Interest rate and cross currency swaps

Introduction to swaps

Swap – a contract to exchange payments of some sort in the future. (CIMA Official Terminology, 2005)

In order to manage the interest rate risk and currency risk identified above, entities often use swap arrangements.

Swaps can be used to change the interest rate or currency profile of borrowings (e.g. fixed to floating and EUR to GBP borrowings) in line with capital structure targets and to manage risk.

When considering what kind of debt finance should be used, risk, cost and practicality will be key considerations.

Examples

- **Interest rate swap**
  - It might be cheaper for a company to issue a bond plus enter a swap to change the interest profile than raise floating rate bank borrowings directly. In this case an interest rate swap is being used to alter the interest rate profile of the borrowings from fixed to floating rates.

- **Cross currency swap**
  - In some cases where a company requires foreign currency borrowings, it may be easier and cheaper to raise funds in its own local currency and, at the same time, enter into a swap to change the currency profile to the required currency. In this case, the entity could use a borrowing in its own currency and a cross currency swap to access the foreign currency funds.

  - In other cases, it may be cheaper for a company to borrow in a global currency such as USD or EUR and then use a cross currency swap to change the currency profile to the home currency or a second foreign currency.

  - A common example of a cross currency swap is that of a parent company raising finance in a popular global currency (e.g. USD or EUR) and then swapping that into different currencies to lend on to foreign subsidiaries which require borrowings denominated in their own currencies. Even GBP companies may find it cheaper to issue bonds in EUR and then swap back into GBP.

Interest rate swaps

An interest rate swap is an agreement whereby two parties agree to swap a floating stream of interest payments for a fixed stream of interest payments and vice versa. There is no exchange of principal.

Features and operation

- In practice interest rate swaps are probably the most common form of interest rate hedge used by companies because they can hedge borrowings of anywhere between a year and 30 years and therefore can be used for long-term borrowings.

- In our syllabus we only consider the 'plain vanilla' swap of fixed or floating rate (or vice versa) without any complications that can occur in practice.

- Banks act as swap counterparties.

- There is a large and liquid market in swaps in major currencies and banks will quote bid/offer rates against a reference rate such as 6 month LIBOR or 12 month LIBOR.

Note: LIBOR (the London Interbank Offered Rate) is the most widely used benchmark or reference rate for short-term interest rates worldwide, although the swap could relate to Euribor, say.

Calculations involving the bank's quoted swap rates

In practice a bank normally arranges the swap and will quote the following:

- The 'offer rate' at which the bank is willing to receive a fixed interest cash flow stream in exchange for paying LIBOR.

- The 'bid rate' that they are willing to pay in exchange for receiving LIBOR.

- The difference between these gives the bank's profit margin and is usually at least 2 basis points.

Alternatively, in an exam question you might be given the two rates (without any reference to the bid/offer terminology) as follows:

XX Bank's swap rates are 3.00% – 3.10% against 12 month LIBOR.

In order to decide which is the appropriate rate to use in a given situation, always remember that the bank will have set the swap rates to ensure that it makes a profit margin.

So in this example, if a company wanted to pay a fixed rate to the bank in exchange for a receipt of the LIBOR rate (to swap a floating rate into a fixed rate), 3.10% would be paid by the company to the bank.

Alternatively, if a company wanted to pay LIBOR rate in exchange for a fixed receipt (to swap a fixed rate into a floating rate), only 3.00% would be paid by the bank to the company.

Diagrammatic example

So, considering the numerical example above in the context of the diagram:

- Company D wants to swap a fixed rate to a floating rate, so would pay LIBOR to the bank in exchange for 3.00%

- Company E wants to swap a floating rate to a fixed rate, so would pay 3.10% to the bank in exchange for LIBOR

- The bank would make a profit by setting up swaps with both Company D and Company E, because the LIBOR payments net off, and the fixed rate received by the bank is bigger than the fixed rate paid.

Illustration 1 (Integration question)

Co A currently has a 12-month borrowing at a fixed rate of 5% but would like to swap to variable. It can currently borrow at a variable rate of LIBOR + 12 basis points.

The bank is currently quoting 12-month swap rates of 4.90% - 4.95% for LIBOR.

Show Co A's financial position if it enters the swap.

Solution:

Actual borrowing	(5.00%)
Payment to bank	(LIBOR)
Receipt from bank (lower rate)	4.90%
Net interest rate after swap	**(LIBOR + 0.10%)**
Open market cost – no swap	(LIBOR + 0.12%)
Saving	2 basis points

The interest fixing date and the interest cash flows in an interest rate swap

In the above Illustration, we showed the net interest rate that would be paid by Company A in the swap arrangement, but exam questions might also ask you to calculate the interest cash flows.

In the case of Company A in the Illustration above, the net interest rate was LIBOR + 0.10%, so clearly the overall interest cash flow would be calculated by applying the actual LIBOR rate plus 0.10% to the value of Company A's borrowing.

However, it is important to note that the LIBOR rate will fluctuate daily, so in order to work out the interest cash flows in a swap, an 'interest fixing date' is agreed when the swap is set up, and it is the LIBOR on this fixing date that is used in the calculation.

Generally the interest fixing date is the start date of the swap period.

Test your understanding 1 (Objective test question)

Spray Co has a $10 million fixed rate borrowing. It has entered an interest rate swap to swap the interest to a floating rate for a three year period.

The bank has quoted a swap rate of 4.10% for LIBOR, with interest fixing dates on the start date of each year of the swap agreement.

Spray Co's fixed rate of interest is 4.40%.

LIBOR on the start date of year 2 of the three year swap agreement was 4.25%, but this had risen to 4.58% by the end of year 2 (12 months later).

What is the difference in Spray Co's overall net interest paid in the year (year 2 of the swap agreement) as a consequence of using the swap?

A $15,000 saving

B $15,000 extra cost

C $18,000 extra cost

D $48,000 extra cost

Advantages of using interest rate swaps

- To manage fixed and floating rate debt profiles without having to change underlying borrowing.

- To hedge against variations in interest on floating rate debt, or conversely to protect the fair value of fixed rate debt instruments.

- A swap can be used to obtain cheaper finance. For example, it may be cheaper to obtain floating rate finance by, say, issuing a bond and swapping into a floating rate rather than borrowing at floating rate directly from a bank.

Disadvantages of using interest rate swaps

- Interest rates may change in the future and the company might be locked into an unfavourable rate.

- Creditworthiness of the bank – the company and the bank arrange to make payments to each other for a fixed period. The company must therefore be confident about the creditworthiness of the bank before signing up to the swap.

Test your understanding 2 (Objective test question)

Ocean Co has a $5 million floating rate borrowing at a rate of LIBOR + 0.50%.

The directors have set up a swap, to fix the company's interest rate for a period of three years, from 1 January 20X0 to 31 December 20X2.

The bank's quoted swap rates are 3.80% – 4.00% for LIBOR, with interest fixing dates on the start date of each year of the swap agreement.

LIBOR information:

- LIBOR on 1 January 20X1 was 4.10%

- LIBOR on 1 July 20X1 was 4.05%

- LIBOR on 31 December 20X1 was 3.75%

What was the difference in Ocean Co's overall net interest paid in the year 20X1 as a consequence of using the swap?

A $15,000 saving

B $5,000 saving

C $2,500 extra cost

D $12,500 extra cost

Cross currency swaps

A cross currency swap allows a company to swap a currency it currently holds for a different currency for a fixed period, and then swap back at the same rate at the end of the period.

The company's counterparty in a cross currency swap would generally be a bank.

Characteristics of a cross currency swap

- In effect a cross currency swap has two elements:
    - An exchange of principal in different currencies, which are swapped back at the original spot rate.
    - An exchange of interest rates – the timing of these depends on the individual contract.
- The swap of interest rates could be 'fixed for fixed', 'floating for floating' or 'fixed for floating'
- The company entering the cross currency swap will end up with the currency it needs and also the type of interest rate it prefers (fixed or floating).

Illustration 2 (Integration question)

ABC Co is a US company that has issued a 100 million Swiss Francs (CHF) Eurobond on which it pays interest six-monthly at an annual fixed rate of 6%.

ABC Co has many operations in the USA, so wants to swap its CHF into US dollars (USD) using a fixed for fixed cross currency swap.

ABC Co's bank has quoted a cross currency swap exchange rate of CHF/USD 1.10 (that is, CHF 1 = USD 1.10), and fixed interest rates of 5.5% on USD in exchange for 6% on CHF, with interest payable semi-annually (that is, every six months).

Required:

Show how the fixed for fixed cross currency swap would work in the circumstances described, assuming the swap is only for one year and that interest is paid every six months.

Solution:

Timing	Explanation	Cash flows
Now	Exchange principals (at swap rate of CHF1 = USD 1.10)	Pay CHF 100m to the bank and receive USD 110m
6 mths' time	Pay swap interest to bank (5.5% × USD110m × 6/12)	Pay USD 3.025m
	Receive swap interest from bank (6% × CHF100m × 6/12)	Receive CHF 3m
	Pay Eurobond interest	Pay CHF 3m

End of year	Pay swap interest to bank (5.5% × USD110m × 6/12)	Pay USD 3.025m
	Receive swap interest from bank (6% × CHF100m × 6/12)	Receive CHF 3m
	Pay Eurobond interest (6% × CHF100m × 6/12)	Pay CHF 3m
	Swap back principals (at swap rate of CHF1 = USD 1.10)	Pay USD 110m to the bank and receive CHF 100m

The net result is that ABC Co has the use of the USD 110 million for the year, and effectively pays interest on this amount (in USD) at 5.5%.

Test your understanding 3 (Integration question)

Smiths Co is a UK based company that has borrowed 10 million British pounds (GBP) at a fixed interest rate of 5.25% per year, with interest paid annually.

The company is planning to expand into Europe so wants to swap GBP 10 million for Euros (EUR), and its fixed interest rate for a floating rate.

The bank has quoted a cross currency swap exchange rate of GBP/EUR 1.30 (that is, GBP 1 = EUR 1.30) and interest rates of LIBOR + 0.50% on EUR in exchange for 5.25% on GBP, with interest paid annually.

Assume that LIBOR is 5% at the start date of the swap.

Required:

Show how the fixed for floating cross currency swap would work in the circumstances described, assuming the swap is only for one year and that interest is paid at the end of the year.

Advantages of using cross currency swaps

- A cross currency swap is a useful tool for changing the currency profile of debt.

- This may help reduce interest costs where debt can be raised more easily or at a competitive rate in a second currency and it proves to be cheaper or easier overall to borrow in one currency and simultaneously enter into a swap to change the currency profile into another currency or several different currencies as required.

- Cross currency swaps may also be used as part of a broader strategy for managing currency risk. For example, by obtaining foreign currency borrowings to on-lend to foreign subsidiaries denominated in their local currencies.

Disadvantages of using cross currency swaps

- The main disadvantage is that, as in an interest rate swap , there is a risk that the other party to the contract might default on the arrangement. This is an even greater risk for cross currency swaps because:
    - the cash flows are in different currencies (and hence there can be no agreement to net them as there could be for interest rate swaps), AND
    - final principals are exchanged (again, unlike interest rate swaps).

5 Other sources of finance

Retained earnings / existing cash balances

There is a common misconception that a company with a large amount of retained earnings in its balance sheet (statement of financial position) can fund its new investment projects using these retained earnings. This is not the case.

A company can only use internal sources of finance to fund new projects if it has enough cash in hand.

The level of retained earnings reflects the amount of profit accumulated over the company's life. It is not the same as cash.

Sale and leaseback

This means selling good quality fixed assets such as high street buildings and leasing them back over many years (25+). Funds are released without any loss of use of assets.

Any potential capital gain on assets is forgone.

Sale and leaseback is a popular means of funding for retail organisations with substantial high street property e.g. Tesco, Marks and Spencer.

Grants

These are often related to technology, job creation or regional policy. They are of particular importance to small and medium-sized businesses (i.e. unlisted). Their key advantage is that they do not need to be paid back.

Grants can be provided by local governments, national governments, and other larger bodies such as the European Union.

Debt with warrants attached

A warrant is an option to buy shares at a specified point in the future for a specified (exercise) price. Warrants are often issued with a bond as a sweetener to encourage investors to purchase the bonds.

The warrant offers a potential capital gain where the share price may rise above the exercise price.

The holder has the option to buy the share on the exercise date but can also choose to sell the warrant before that date.

Convertible debt

This is similar in effect to attaching a warrant to a debt instrument except that the warrant cannot be detached and traded separately. The convertible debt is where the debt itself can be converted into shares at a predetermined price at a date or range of dates in the future.

This has the effect of giving the debt holder a potential capital gain over and above the return from the debt interest. If the value of the shares is greater than that of the debt on the exercise date, then conversion will be made by the investor. If, however, the share value is lower than the debt value, the investor may retain the debt to maturity.

Venture capital

This is finance provided to young, unquoted profit-making entities to help them to expand. It is usually provided in the form of equity finance, but may be a mix of equity and debt.

Venture capitalists generally accept low levels of dividends and expect to make most of their returns as capital gains on exit. A typical exit route is an IPO or flotation, which enables the venture capitalist to sell his stake in the entity on the stock market.

Venture capital is covered in more detail in the later chapter on 'Financial and strategic implications of mergers and acquisitions'.

Business angels

Business angels are similar to venture capitalists. Venture capitalists are rarely interested in investing in very small businesses, on the grounds that monitoring progress is uneconomic.

Business angels are wealthy investors who provide equity finance to small businesses.

Government assistance

Governments will often have a number of schemes, aimed at providing assistance to:

- small- and medium-sized profit-making entities;
- entities wanting to expand or relocate in particular regions;
- promote innovation and technology;
- projects that will create new jobs or protect existing ones.

You do not need to have knowledge of any specific scheme, but relevant discussion of methods of government assistance in your own country will earn credit in the examination.

6 The lease v buy decision

If a new project requires the use of an asset, such as a machine, a business often has the choice of whether to buy the asset outright, or whether to lease it.

Terminology

Lease

A lease is a commercial arrangement where an equipment owner (the lessor) conveys the right to use the equipment in return for payment by the equipment user (the lessee) of a specified rental over a pre-agreed period of time.

Finance lease

A lease is classified as a finance lease if it transfers substantially all the risks and rewards incidental to ownership (IAS 17).

Operating lease

A lease is classified as an operating lease if it does not transfer substantially all the risks and rewards incidental to ownership (IAS 17).

Reasons for leasing

- It is a readily available form of finance, especially for plant and equipment or motor vehicles. It is therefore very convenient for companies to enter into such arrangements.
- It removes the need for a significant capital outlay at the beginning of a project's life i.e. it avoids the need to find the capital at the outset.

- It may be cheaper in financial terms than conventional debt financing i.e. the effective interest rate on leasing may be less than the interest payable on a loan. This is because a lease is asset-backed finance and so is less risky for the lender. Consequently, lenders may therefore be prepared to offer a lower rate of interest than on a standard borrowing.

More details on operating and finance leases

The classification of leases adopted in IAS 17 Leases is based on the extent to which risks and rewards incidental to ownership of a leased asset lie with the lessor or the lessee.

Finance leases

Under a finance lease the risk and rewards of ownership lie with the lessee. Therefore, by applying substance over form the lessee should recognise the item being leased as an asset in its statement of financial position. A liability is also recognised for the amounts payable under the terms of the lease.

The term of the lease normally extends over the full useful life of the asset. The lessor therefore receives lease payments that will fully cover the cost of the asset. The agreement will usually not be cancellable and will not provide for any maintenance of the asset. The lessee effectively holds all the risks of asset ownership without being the legal owner. The leasing entity is not normally involved in dealing with the assets themselves, being a bank or finance entity. The asset is selected by the firm that will use it, who negotiates price, delivery, etc. The leasing entity simply buys the asset and arranges a lease contract with the lessee. At the end of the lease period there will usually be an agreement where the sale proceeds from the asset are shared between the lessor and lessee, or if the lessee desires it can carry on using the asset for payment of a nominal amount each year, called a peppercorn rent.

Sale and leaseback

Entities can use what is known as a sale and leaseback arrangement in order to convert certain assets that the entity owns into funds yet still continue to use the assets. For example if a building is sold to an insurance entity or some other financial intermediary and then leased back from the purchaser, the entity has secured an immediate cash inflow. The only cash outflow is the rental payments that it now has to make. These rental payments are usually allowed as a tax-deductible expense. However, the entity may be subject to capital gains tax, which will arise if the sale price is in excess of the written-down value as agreed by the tax authorities.

It must be remembered, however, that the leased asset no longer belongs to the entity; the lease may one day come to an end and then alternative assets will have to be obtained.

This financing possibility is particularly applicable to assets that appreciate in value, such as land, buildings or some other forms of property. It is particularly appropriate to entities owning the properties freehold, and to institutions such as insurance entities or pension funds that are interested in holding long-term secure assets. The property is leased back at a negotiated annual rental, although with long leasebacks there will need to be a provision for the revision of the rental at certain intervals of time.

Operating leases

Under an operating lease the risks and rewards of ownership lie with the lessor, not the lessee. Therefore, by applying substance over form it can be concluded that the lessee should not record the item being leased as an asset.

Instead lease payments should be recognised as an expense in the income statement on a systematic basis (using straight line) over the term of the lease. The expense will be included under the appropriate operating expense heading. Any difference between the amounts charged to the income statement and amounts paid will be treated as prepayments and accruals on the statement of financial position.

These agreements will usually not last for the full life of an asset. They are offered by entities who manufacture or deal in the particular product, often incorporating maintenance and other services. The lease can be cancelled and the equipment returned. Operating leases are common for office and business equipment, for example typewriters, photocopiers, computers and motor vehicles. The lessor will not recover his/her full investment on any one lease but will hope to lease a particular asset several times over its life.

Operating leases are particularly useful for industries where there is a rapid change in technology that makes it necessary to have the latest equipment, for example computers.

Hire purchase

Hire purchase is similar to leasing, except that the legal title to the asset passes to the hire purchase customer on payment of the final instalment payment. In a lease agreement ownership of the asset does not transfer to the lease.

Lease-or-buy decisions

The evaluation of the lease-or-buy decision is not a pure financing decision as it also involves interactions with the investment decision.

Operating leases

The evaluation of an operating lease is relatively straight forward. The process is as follows:

- Identify the lease payments payable over the life of the agreement.

- Adjust the lease payments for tax.

- Discount the after tax lease payments at a discount rate reflecting the asset's systematic risk.

Finance leases

The decision to lease or buy an asset is a financing decision that will be made only once the decision to invest in the asset has been taken. The decision to invest in the asset would be determined by discounting the operational costs and benefits from using the asset at the cost of capital normally used by the entity to evaluate projects, typically its weighted average cost of capital. Investing in the asset would be justified if a positive NPV is obtained.

The financing decision is then concerned with identifying the least-cost financing option. In evaluating the financing decision, it is usually assumed that the entity would have to borrow funds in order to purchase the asset.

Lease v buy evaluation

If an asset is needed for a major new investment, and the asset can be leased under a finance lease then a critical decision is:

- should the asset be leased?; or

- should the asset be purchased and the purchase cost financed by debt issue?

In the exam you may need to evaluate the lease against the borrowing to buy option to determine which would be better in financial terms.

The traditional approach to the evaluation is to use the NPV method i.e. determine the present value cost of leasing and compare this to the present value cost of borrowing to buy.

Note: The NPV method (Net Present Value) was covered earlier in the CIMA syllabus.

Note on discount rate

In the lease v buy evaluation, it is considered that the risk associated with the lease option is comparable to the risk associated with the borrow to buy option. Hence the same discount rate should be used for both NPV calculations.

The discount rate to use is the **post-tax cost of debt finance** – clearly this rate applies to the borrow to buy option, and it is considered to be appropriate to the leasing option too, since the post-tax cost of debt is effectively the opportunity cost of leasing.

Test your understanding 4 (Integration question)

Penny Co wishes to invest in new equipment costing $130,000. The equipment has a life of four years and no scrap proceeds are expected to be available after this period. Tax allowable depreciation is available at 25% on a reducing balance basis. The company can borrow at 12% pre-tax.

The equipment could alternatively be leased for a cost of $40,000 per annum payable in arrears over four years. Assume that the full lease payment is a tax deductible expense. Corporation tax is 33% payable one year in arrears.

Required:

Determine whether the company should lease or purchase the asset.

Further calculations on lease interest

In the above example, to simplify the calculations, we were told specifically that the full lease payment was to be treated as a tax deductible expense.

In reality, it will usually be just the interest element of the lease payment which is tax deductible. In this case, the first step is to calculate the interest element, using either the actuarial method, or the sum of digits method.

The following illustration shows how both methods work.

Illustration 3

Assume that KL Co has the option to buy an asset for USD100,000, or to lease it under a finance lease by paying USD29,500 per year in arrears for 4 years.

Clearly, the interest element in the lease amounts to (4 × USD29,500) – USD100,000 = USD18,000 in total. This interest can be allocated to years using either the actuarial method, or the sum of digits method.

Actuarial method

Here the implied interest rate is found by using an IRR approach.

As a short cut, the 4 year annuity factor at the IRR can be found by dividing the cost of the asset by the annual interest payment (i.e. 100,000/29,500). This gives a 4 year annuity factor of 3.390, which (from tables) is very close to the 7% factor. Hence, the implied interest rate in the lease is (approximately) 7%.

Now, the interest can be allocated to individual years using the following table:

£	Year 1	Year 2	Year 3	Year 4
Opening balance	100,000	77,500	53,425	27,665
+ Interest (7% × Op Bal)	7,000	5,425	3,740	1,937
– Lease payment	(29,500)	(29,500)	(29,500)	(29,500)
Closing balance	77,500	53,425	27,665	102

Note: The closing balance at the end of year 4 should be zero. The difference is due to rounding.

The lease interest payments have now been allocated to years, so can be used to calculate the tax relief each year.

Sum of digits method

This is a simpler way of allocating interest, based on the sum of digits formula:

$$n(n+1)/2$$

In this example, the lease payments are to be made over 4 periods, so the sum of digits is 10 (working: 4 × 5 /2 = 10)

Hence, the interest allocation is:

Year 1	4/10 × 18,000	USD7,200
Year 2	3/10 × 18,000	USD5,400
Year 3	2/10 × 18,000	USD3,600
Year 4	1/10 × 18,000	USD1,800

Once again, the tax relief on the lease interest can now be calculated easily.

Test your understanding 5 (Integration question)

Following on from the information in the Illustration above:

Assume that KL Co has the option to buy an asset immediately for USD100,000, or to lease it under a finance lease by paying USD29,500 per year in arrears for 4 years.

Other information

- KL Co is liable to corporate tax at a marginal rate of 30% which is settled at the end of the year in which it arises.

- KL Co accounts for depreciation on a straight-line basis at the end of each year

- Under the buy option, tax depreciation allowances on the full capital cost are available in equal instalments over the first four years of operation.

- Under the lease option, both the accounting depreciation and the interest element of the finance lease payments are tax deductible.

Required:

Advise KL Co whether the asset should be leased or bought, assuming that the interest on the lease should be allocated using the actuarial method. Use a discount rate of 5% in your evaluation.

7 End of chapter objective test questions

Test your understanding 6 (Objective test question)

A company is evaluating the decision whether to lease an asset or to buy it outright using newly borrowed funds.

Which of the following is the BEST discount rate to use for the evaluation, assuming that the decision has already been taken to acquire the asset?

A   Post tax cost of debt

B   WACC

C   Cost of equity

D   Pre-tax cost of debt

Test your understanding 7 (Objective test question)

Brasil Co has a $10 million borrowing, on which it is currently paying a floating rate of LIBOR+0.55%. The directors are concerned that interest rates are going to rise, so they are considering an interest rate swap to manage the company's exposure to risk.

The bank has quoted Brasil Co a swap rate of 2.86% against LIBOR.

What is Brasil Co's net payment if it enters the swap?

A   LIBOR + 2.86%

B   2.31%

C   2.86%

D   3.41%

Test your understanding 8 (Objective test question)

Mouse Co has a $10 million borrowing on which it pays interest at a fixed rate of 4.35%.

The company's directors predict that interest rates will fall over the next 12 months, so they want to use an interest rate swap to enable them to benefit from this predicted movement.

The bank is quoting swap rates of 4.19% – 4.29% against 12 month LIBOR. 12 month LIBOR is currently 4.04%.

What will be Mouse Co's interest payment at the end of the year, assuming that the company uses the swap and that LIBOR has fallen to 3.90% by the year end?

A $396,000

B $406,000

C $410,000

D $420,000

Test your understanding 9 (Objective test question)

Statement 1:

Under a finance lease, an unprofitable lessee can benefit from tax depreciation allowances passed on by the lessor.

Statement 2:

A lease is classified as a finance lease if it does not transfer substantially all the risks and rewards incidental to ownership.

Which of these statements in respect of finance leases are true?

A   Both statements

B   Just statement 1

C   Just statement 2

D   Neither statement

Test your understanding 10 (Objective test question)

Which THREE of the following statements about eurobonds are correct?

A   Entities that issue eurobonds keep a register of their eurobond holders

B   Eurobonds are traded on the international capital markets

C   They are sometimes denominated in euros

D   They are sometimes denominated in US dollars

E   Eurobond interest is normally paid semi-annually (every six months)

Test your understanding 11 (Objective test question)

The following information relates to an asset which a company is considering leasing or buying.

- Life of asset 10 years

- Cost if purchased $28,000

- Residual value $3,000

- Lease details: Ten annual repayments of $3,800 to begin at start of lease

The shareholders view the adoption of the lease as being an equivalent risk to borrowing at an after-tax cost of 10% per annum.

The first lease payment (or the purchase price) would be due on 1 January 20X2. The purchase price would not be eligible for tax depreciation allowances but lease payments would be allowed as a deduction from profit for tax purposes.

The firm has a 31 December year end and pays corporation tax at 35% one year after the year end in which profits are earned.

It makes sufficient profits to obtain tax relief on lease payments as soon as they arise.

What (to the nearest $100) is the net after-tax benefit of leasing the asset as opposed to buying it?

A $1,200

B $4,200

C $8,600

D $18,300

Test your understanding 12 (Objective test question)

Reef Co needs to raise some debt finance and the directors want to limit the entity's exposure to refinancing risk and interest rate risk.

Although the overall debt profile of an entity should be considered to fully assess the overall risk, as a general rule

- refinancing risk is likely to be greater with _____ **(long term / short term)** debt, and

- interest rate risk is likely to be greater with _____ **(fixed rate / floating rate)** debt

(Enter the correct phrase from the choice given.)

Test your understanding 13 (Objective test question)

An entity may issue convertible unsecured loan stock because

A   it is cheaper to service than ordinary debt

B   sales and earnings are expected to fall over the next few years

C   if conversion takes place, it will not disturb the firm's gearing ratio

D   if conversion takes place, it will generate additional capital funds for the firm

8 End of chapter case style question

Test your understanding 14 (Case style question)

XTA plc is the parent entity of a transport and distribution group based in the United Kingdom. The group owns and operates a network of distribution centres and a fleet of trucks (large delivery vehicles) in the United Kingdom. It is currently planning to expand into Continental Europe, operating through a new subsidiary entity in Germany. The subsidiary will purchase distribution centres in Germany and invest in a new fleet of trucks to be based at those centres. The German subsidiary will be operationally independent of the UK parent.

Alternative proposals have been put forward by Messrs A, B and C, Board members of XTA plc on how best to structure the financing of the new German operation as follows:

- **Mr A**: 'I would feel much more comfortable if we were to borrow in our base currency, British pounds (GBP), where we already have long-standing banking relationships and a good reputation in the capital markets. Surely it would be much more complicated for us to borrow in euros (EUR)?'

- **Mr B:** 'I am concerned about the exposure of our consolidated statement of financial position and investor ratios to GBP/EUR exchange rate movements. How will we be able to explain large fluctuations to our shareholders? If we were to raise long-term euro borrowings, wouldn't this avoid exchange rate risk altogether? We would also benefit from euro interest rates which have been historically lower than UK rates.'

- **Mr C**: We know from our market research that we will be facing stiff competition in Germany from local distribution companies. This is a high-risk project with a lot of capital at stake and we should finance this new venture by XTA plc raising new equity finance to reflect this high risk.'

Assume that today is Saturday 1 October 20X5. A summary of the latest forecast consolidated statement of financial position (balance sheet) for the XTA Group at 31 December 20X5 is given below. It has been prepared BEFORE taking into account the proposed German investment:

	GBP million
Assets	
Total assets	450
Equity and liabilities	
Equity	250
Long term borrowings	150
(there were no other non-current liabilities)	
Current liabilities	50
	———
Total equity and liabilities	450
	———

The proposed investment in Germany is scheduled for the final quarter of 20X5 at a cost of GBP 60m for the distribution centres, and GBP 20m for the fleet of trucks when translated from euros at today's exchange rate of GBP/EUR1.50 (that is GBP1 = EUR 1.50). There is a possibility that the euro could weaken against GBP to GBP/EUR 2.00 by 31 December 20X5, but it can be assumed that this will not occur until after the investment has been made. The subsidiary's statement of financial position at 31 December 20X5 will only contain the new distribution centres and fleet of trucks matched by an equal equity investment by XTA plc and will only become operationally active from 1 January 20X6.

Required:

(a) Write a memorandum to the Board of XTA plc to explain the advantages and disadvantages of using each of the following sources of finance:

   – a rights issue versus a placing (assuming UK equity finance is chosen to fund the new German subsidiary); and

   – a euro bank borrowing versus a euro-denominated eurobond (assuming euro borrowings are chosen).

(15 minutes)

(b) Evaluate EACH of the alternative proposals of Messrs A, B and C for financing the new German subsidiary and recommend the most appropriate form of financing for the group. Support your discussion of each proposal with

- a summary forecast consolidated statement of financial position for the XTA group at 31 December 20X5 incorporating the new investment; and

- calculations of gearing using book values

using year end exchange rates of both GBP/EUR 1.50 and GBP/EUR 2.00.

(30 minutes)

Test your understanding answers

Test your understanding 1 (Objective test question)

The answer is (B).

Solution:

Actual borrowing	(4.40%)
Payment to bank	(LIBOR)
Receipt from bank	4.10%
	————————
Net interest rate after swap	**(LIBOR + 0.30%)**
	————————

The interest fixing date is the start date of the year, so this overall net rate of LIBOR + 0.30% can be calculated as 4.25% (LIBOR on the year 2 start date) + 0.30% = 4.55%.

Hence, Spray Co pays 4.55% interest on its $10 million borrowing ($455,000 in the year) rather than the 4.40% fixed rate it would have paid without the swap ($440,000 in the year).

This is an extra cost of $15,000.

Test your understanding 2 (Objective test question)

The answer is (B).

Solution:

Actual borrowing	(LIBOR + 0.50%)
Payment to bank (higher rate)	(4.00%)
Receipt from bank	LIBOR
	————————
Net interest rate after swap	**(4.50%)**
	————————

The interest fixing date is the start date of the year (1 January 20X1), so the relevant LIBOR rate is 4.10%.

Hence, Ocean Co paid 4.50% overall net interest on its $5 million borrowing ($225,000 in the year) rather than the (4.10% + 0.50% =) 4.60% rate it would have paid without the swap ($230,000 in the year).

This is a saving of $5,000.

Test your understanding 3 (Integration question)

Timing	Explanation	Cash flows
Now	Exchange principals (at swap rate of GBP1 = EUR 1.30)	Pay GBP 10m to the bank and receive EUR 13m
End of year	Pay swap interest to bank ((LIBOR +0.50%) × EUR 13m)	Pay EUR 0.715m (on the assumption that the start date of the swap is the interest rate fixing date and hence LIBOR is 5%)
	Receive swap interest from bank (5.25% × GBP 10m)	Receive GBP 0.525m
	Pay interest on original borrowing (5.25% × GBP 10m)	Pay GBP 0.525m
	Swap back principals (at swap rate of GBP1 = EUR 1.30)	Pay EUR 13m to the bank and receive GBP 10m

The net result is that Smiths Co has the use of the EUR 13 million for the year, and effectively pays floating rate interest on this amount (in EUR) at LIBOR + 0.50%.

Test your understanding 4 (Integration question)

The discount rate is the post-tax cost of debt ∴ 12% (1 – 0.33) = 8.04% ≈ 8%.

Assumptions:

(1) Asset is purchased on first day of year 1.

(2) Tax is delayed by 1 year.

Buy asset

Tax allowable depreciation

		Tax @ 33%	Date
0	130,000		
1 TAD	32,500/97,500	10,725	2
2 TAD	24,375/73,125	8,044	3
3 TAD	18,281/54,844	6,033	4
4 SCRAP	0		
Balancing allowance	54,844	18,099	5

Year	Cash flow	PVF @ 8%	PV
0	(130,000)	1	(130,000)
1	–	–	–
2	10,725	0.857	9,191
3	8,044	0.794	6,387
4	6,033	0.735	4,434
5	18,099	0.681	12,325
			(97,663)

Lease asset

Year	Lease	Tax	Net	PVF @ 8%	PV
1	(40,000)		(40,000)	(0.926)	(37,040)
2	(40,000)	13,200	(26,800)	0.857	(22,968)
3	(40,000)	13,200	(26,800)	0.794	(21,279)
4	(40,000)	13,200	(26,800)	0.735	(19,698)
5		13,200	13,200	0.681	8,989
					(91,996)

Decision:

On purely financial grounds it is better to lease rather than buy the asset.

Test your understanding 5 (Integration question)

Buy option

	T_0	T_{1-4}
Purchase cost	(100,000)	
Tax relief on tax depreciation (30% × 100,000/4)		7,500
Discount factor (5%)	1	3.546
Present value	(100,000)	26,595
Net present value	(73,405)	

i.e. Buying the asset to undertake the project will cost USD 73,405 in present value terms.

Lease option

	T$_1$	T$_2$	T$_3$	T$_4$
Lease payment	(29,500)	(29,500)	(29,500)	(29,500)
Tax relief on depreciation and lease interest (W1)	9,600	9,128	8,622	8,081
	(19,900)	(20,372)	(20,878)	(21,419)
Discount factors (5%)	0.952	0.907	0.864	0.823
Present value	(18,945)	(18,477)	(18,039)	(17,627)
Net present value	(73,088)			

i.e. Leasing the asset to undertake the project will cost USD 73,088 in present value terms.

(W1) Tax relief calculation

	T$_1$	T$_2$	T$_3$	T$_4$
Implied interest (from Illustration 1 earlier in the chapter)	7,000	5,425	3,740	1,937
Depreciation	25,000	25,000	25,000	25,000
	32,000	30,425	28,740	26,937
Tax relief (30%)	9,600	9,128	8,622	8,081

Note: The tax relief on the lease interest is included in the evaluation as a relevant cash flow, but the lease interest itself is not a cash flow, so is not included.

Conclusion:

The lease option is cheaper so should be undertaken on financial grounds. However, the difference is so marginal that it will be important to undertake sensitivity analysis, and to consider other non-financial factors before a final decision is made.

Note that we are assuming that the positive NPV of any cash flows arising from the new project must exceed the negative NPV associated with the cost of the asset, to give an overall positive NPV.

Test your understanding 6 (Objective test question)

The answer is (A).

Test your understanding 7 (Objective test question)

The answer is (D).

Brasil Co is currently paying LIBOR + 0.55%.

A swap rate of 2.86% for LIBOR means that Brasil Co will pay the bank 2.86% in the swap in exchange for LIBOR.

Therefore, Brasil Co's net payment is (LIBOR + 0.55%) + 2.86% – LIBOR = 3.41%

Test your understanding 8 (Objective test question)

The answer is (D).

Actual borrowing	(4.35%)
Payment to bank	(LIBOR)
Receipt from bank (lower rate)	4.19%
Net interest rate after swap	**(LIBOR + 0.16%)**

The interest rate fixing date is normally the start date of the swap agreement, so LIBOR of 4.04% is the relevant value here.

Hence, interest payable at LIBOR + 0.16% amounts to (4.04% + 0.16% =) 4.20%.

Overall net interest is therefore 4.20% × $10 million = $420,000.

Test your understanding 9 (Objective test question)

The answer is (D).

Both statements are false.

Test your understanding 10 (Objective test question)

The answer is (B), (C) and (D).

Eurobonds are bearer instruments, so no register of bond holders is kept (A). Interest is normally paid annually (E).

They are traded on international capital markets (B) and can be denominated in any major global currency – (C) and (D).

Test your understanding 11 (Objective test question)

The answer is (C).

PV of buying = $28,000 – ($3,000 × 0.386) = $26,842

PV of lease payments (years 0-9) = $3,800 × (1 + 5.759) = $25,684

PV of lease tax relief (years 2-11) = $3,800 × 0.35 × 5.586 = $7,429

So the benefit of leasing is 26,842 – 25,684 + 7,429 = $8,587

Test your understanding 12 (Objective test question)

As a general rule

- refinancing risk is likely to be greater with **short term** debt, and
- interest rate risk is likely to be greater with **floating rate** debt.

Test your understanding 13 (Objective test question)

The answer is (A).

One of the main advantages of issuing CULS is the lower return that it demands due to the attraction of the option of conversion to equity, i.e. it is cheaper to service than ordinary debt.

If sales and earnings are expected to rise (not fall), it may be beneficial to issue CULS rather than to issue effectively underpriced equity (B).

If conversion takes place the firm's gearing ratio will change (C).

No extra capital is generated on conversion (D).

Test your understanding 14 (Case style question)

(a) **Rights issue versus placing**

Advantages of a rights issue

- no dilution of ownership by current shareholders
- reliable (can be underwritten)

Disadvantages of a rights issue

- limits potential investors to current shareholder base (placements can be marketed to a wider selection of institutional investors)
- more complex and more expensive than a placing
- takes longer to arrange than a placing

Euro bank borrowing versus euro-denominated eurobond

Advantages of a euro bank borrowing

- direct contact with lender
- flexible terms
- promotes good bank relationship
- access to a wider source of funds via syndicated credit from a panel of banks
- not dependent on a good rating
- relatively quick and cheap to arrange

Disadvantages of a euro bank borrowing

- does not give access to large, deep international capital markets which may support larger issues
- better rates possible from Eurobonds
- longer maturities may be harder to obtain from a bank (for example 20 years)

Examiner's note:

The answer to (a) above has been given in list form as a study aid, but in a case study examination, candidates would be expected to provide a memorandum, with short paragraphs (which could be in bullet point form) for each point.

(b) Revised statements of financial position (balance sheets)

The balance sheet of the German subsidiary is translated at closing rate since the company is operationally independent of the UK parent.

Table A: Mr A's proposal – long term borrowings in GBP

	Ex rate GBP/EUR1.50 GBP million	Ex rate GBP/EUR2.00 GBP million
Total assets	530	510
	(450 + 120/1.50)	(450 + 120/2.00)
Equity and liabilities		
Equity (balancing figure)	250	230
Long term borrowings	230	230
Current liabilities	50	50
Total equity and liabilities	530	510

Table B: Mr B's proposal – long term EUR borrowings

	Ex rate GBP/EUR1.50 GBP million	Ex rate GBP/EUR2.00 GBP million
Total assets	530	510
	(450 + 120/1.50)	(450 + 120/2.00)
Equity and liabilities		
Equity (balancing figure)	250	250
Long term borrowings	230	210
	(150 + 120/1.50)	(150 + 120/2.00)
Current liabilities	50	50
Total equity and liabilities	530	510

Table C: Mr C's proposal – UK (GBP) equity funding

	Ex rate GBP/EUR1.50	Ex rate GBP/EUR2.00
	GBP million	GBP million
Total assets	530	510
	(450 + 120/1.50)	(450 + 120/2.00)
Equity and liabilities		
Equity (balancing figure)	330	310
Long term borrowings	150	150
Current liabilities	50	50
Total equity and liabilities	530	510

Table D: Gearing levels

Current position (debt to debt plus equity) = 150 / (150 + 250) = 37.5%

Scenario:	Ex rate GBP/EUR1.50	Ex rate GBP/EUR2.00
Mr A	48%	50%
Mr B	48%	46%
Mr C	31%	33%

Evaluation of Board members' comments

Mr A: GBP-denominated borrowings

Reputation in the UK markets: Mr A's comment on the advantage of GBP borrowings due to reputation in the UK capital markets is not valid since banks providing GBP loans should be equally willing to provide euro loans and a good reputation in the capital markets will extend beyond the United Kingdom.

Foreign exchange risk: There is, however, a major exchange risk arising from funding euro-based assets with GBP borrowings, arising mainly from the retranslation of the net investment in the subsidiary at the year end and the effect this has on equity values and gearing levels. This is illustrated in Table A, where the value of equity has fallen from GBP 250m to GBP 230m as a result of the weakening of the euro against GBP from a rate of GBP/EUR 1.50 to GBP/EUR 2.00. The effect on gearing is seen in Table D where a fall in the value of the euro leads to deterioration in gearing levels from 48% to 50%.

Impact on gearing: The use of borrowings has a major impact on gearing level, with debt/equity deteriorating from 37.5% to 48% (at GBP/EUR 1.50). Euro-denominated borrowings have a similar impact at current exchange rates.

Other exchange risk: There is also an exchange risk on the GBP value of the repatriation of euro profits to the United Kingdom via dividends, interest and management charges.

Mr B: euro-denominated borrowings

Lower euro interest rates: This is not a valid argument since, under interest rate parity, spot rates are expected to move to compensate for lower euro interest rates and so any gain on interest payments is likely to be offset by a loss on the capital value of the borrowing when it is repaid.

Exchange risk and equity values: Euro borrowings provide a natural hedge by matching the currency of the assets with that of the funding used to finance those assets. At the statement of financial position date, the exchange gain or loss on retranslating the net investment in the German subsidiary will be substantially matched by an equal and opposite gain or loss on retranslating the euro borrowings. This is illustrated in Table B, where a weakening of the euro borrowings against GBP is seen to have no impact on the value of equity.

Note: It could be noted that the hedge accounting provisions of IAS 39 can be applied to avoid volatility in reported profit figures. Without hedge accounting, gains and losses on the borrowing would be recognised in profit for the year whereas gains and losses on the investment in the German subsidiary would be recognised as part of equity under IAS 21. If hedge accounting is permitted, the hedge provided by the borrowing can be designated as such and exchange rate movements on both the investment and the borrowing recognised as changes in the value of equity.

Exchange risk and gearing levels: The gearing ratio has again deteriorated markedly as a result of increased borrowing. In addition, gearing levels are exposed to exchange rate changes. In this case, gearing has improved from 48% to 46% as a result of a fall in the value of the euro, but a negative impact would have resulted from a strengthening of the euro against GBP.

Mr C: UK equity

Risk profile: Mr C is correct in his assertion that equity finance is more suitable than long-term borrowings for a high risk project, since dividends can be cut or reduced if profits are lower than expected, whereas the interest on borrowings always has to be paid in full at each due date.

Exchange risk: However, with equity finance denominated in GBP and the investment being linked to the value of the euro, there is no natural hedge of exchange rate risk arising on the revaluation of the net investment in Germany. Table C shows that the value of equity would fall from GBP 330m to GBP 310m as a result of a fall in the value of the euro from GBP/EUR 1.50 to GBP/EUR 2.00 and there would be a deterioration in gearing from 31% to 33%.

Gearing levels: These are at a much more acceptable level of around 31%. Indeed, additional long-term borrowings may not be practical if lenders are concerned about the already high gearing levels in the group and/or if the new venture has a high risk profile. In this case, the company may have no choice but to raise new equity finance.

Recommendation

The German distribution centre and transport fleet should be financed by long-term euro borrowings (which would be designated as a hedge under IAS 39 and hedge accounting provisions applied, as noted above) in order to match the currency and maturity of the assets to be funded and remove exposure of equity and reported profit to exchange rate gains and losses.

It would be preferable for such euro borrowings to be raised by the German subsidiary so that the euro borrowing interest can be paid out of euro earnings. This also provides the opportunity for reducing the cost of funding by securing the borrowings on the euro assets.

The proportion of new long-term borrowings may be restricted by the following:

* German tax authority regulations on minimum capitalisation levels.
* Value of assets in the German subsidiary that can be used for security.
* Level of parent company loan guarantees offered (where additional security is required).
* Debt capacity of the group (that is acceptable gearing level).

To the extent that long-term borrowings are not possible, the group should consider a rights issue or placing to raise additional equity finance.

Financing – Capital structure

Chapter learning objectives

Lead	Component
B1: Evaluate the financing requirements of an entity and recommend a strategy for meeting those requirements	(a) Evaluate the impact of changes in capital structure for an incorporated entity on shareholders and other stakeholders.

Indicative syllabus content

- Capital structure theories (traditional theory, Modigliani and Miller (MM)'s theories with and without tax and practical considerations and calculations using MM formulae).

- Calculation of cost of equity or weighted average cost of capital (WACC) to reflect a change in capital structure.

- Modelling impact of choice of capital structure on financial statements and key performance measures (e.g. ratios of interest to investors and lenders and compliance with debt covenants).

- Structuring the debt/equity profile of group companies, including tax implications and thin capitalisation rules.

1 Overview of chapter

Introduction to capital structure

An analysis of capital structure, using the gearing ratio and interest cover, is important when trying to assess the risk associated with a business.

This chapter looks at capital structure in detail. In particular we shall consider the implications for the business of a change in capital structure.

When a business changes its capital structure, there will be an impact on its financial ratios and an impact on its weighted average cost of capital (WACC).

The impact on financial ratios is covered later in the chapter, but we start with a detailed analysis of the impact on WACC of a change in capital structure.

2 The impact on WACC of a change in capital structure

The WACC formula was introduced earlier in the CIMA syllabus:

$$k_o = k_{eg}\left[\frac{V_E}{V_E + V_D}\right] + k_d\,(1-t)\left[\frac{V_D}{V_E + V_D}\right]$$

It is clear that if a company changes its capital structure (gearing level), the WACC will change, since the ratio of debt to equity is a key variable in the formula.

Also, since the value of an entire company (debt plus equity) can be calculated as the present value of its post-tax operating cash flows (before financing) discounted at the WACC, when the WACC changes so does the value. (See the later chapter: 'Business valuation' for more details on this.)

Several studies have focused on this link between capital structure and company value. The key question is:

> "What capital structure should the company aim for in order to maximise the company's value?"

The main studies are:

- the traditional view;

- the Modigliani-Miller view, ignoring taxation;

- the Modigliani-Miller view, taking into account the tax relief on debt interest payments.

These studies are based on different assumptions and come to different conclusions. They are covered below.

In order to understand the different views, it is vital to understand the two opposing forces which impact on the WACC as capital structure changes.

The two opposing forces which impact WACC

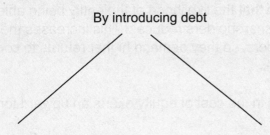

By introducing debt

Downward force on WACC

- Debt is cheaper than equity and would cause the WACC to fall

Upward force on WACC

- K_e increases because of financial risk and would cause the WACC to rise

Impact on WACC of an increase in gearing

As an entity increases the amount of debt in its capital structure, two opposing forces impact on the weighted average cost of capital:

Downward force on the WACC

In general, the entity's cost of debt finance is cheaper than its cost of equity finance, for two reasons:

- Interest is an obligation which has to be paid out each year, whereas dividends are paid only if the company can afford them. This means that debt holders face less risk, so accept lower returns.

- Interest is a tax deductible expense, whereas dividends are paid out of post-tax profits. This further reduces the cost of debt for the company.

Therefore, as the entity increases its gearing by raising more debt finance, the greater proportion of (cheaper) debt in the capital structure exerts a downward force on the WACC.

Upward force on the WACC

As the gearing level increases, the extra interest payments to debt holders mean that the likelihood of the entity being able to afford to pay dividends to shareholders reduces. This increases the risk perception of the shareholders, so they demand higher returns to compensate for the increased risk.

This increase in the cost of equity exerts an upward force on the WACC.

Net effect

Clearly, the two factors identified have opposing impacts on the weighted average cost of capital. The key questions are:

Which of the two forces is stronger?

What is the net effect of these two factors?

There is no simple answer to these questions. In fact, the different gearing theories propose different answers to the questions, based on different assumptions.

However, an understanding of these two factors, and these key questions, is crucial to a sound understanding of the capital structure theories covered in this chapter.

Impact of capital structure on the equity investor

High gearing exists when an entity has a large proportion of prior charge capital in relation to equity and low gearing exists when there is a small proportion of prior charge capital. High gearing increases the financial risk of the equity investor but the reward can be in the form of increased dividends when profits rise. If, however, profits falter, the equity investor can expect to be the first to feel the effect of the reduction in profits.

Low gearing or no gearing may not necessarily be in the equity investor's best interests because the entity might then be failing to exploit the benefits which borrowing can bring.

Provided that the return generated from borrowed funds is greater than the cost of those funds, capital gearing could be increased. The extent to which it is prudent for an entity to increase its capital gearing will depend upon many variables such as the type of industry within which the entity operates, the cost of funds in the market, the availability of investment opportunities and the extent to which the company can continue to benefit from the 'tax shield'.

The ordinary share price of highly geared entities will tend to be depressed in times of rising interest rates.

3 Traditional view

According to the 'traditional' view of gearing and the cost of capital, as an organisation introduces debt into its capital structure the weighted average cost of capital will fall because initially the benefit of cheap debt finance more than outweighs any increases in the cost of equity required to compensate equity holders for higher financial risk.

As gearing continues to increase the equity holders will ask for increasingly higher returns. The cost of equity therefore rises as gearing increases. Eventually this increase in the cost of equity will start to outweigh the benefit of cheap debt finance, and the weighted average cost of capital will rise. At extreme levels of gearing the cost of debt will also start to rise (as debt holders become worried about the security of their loans) and this will also contribute to an increasing weighted average cost of capital.

The diagram below demonstrates this position in which:

- k_e is the cost of equity;
- k_d is the cost of debt;
- k_o is the overall or weighted average cost of capital.

Traditional view of gearing and the cost of capital

X = optimal level of gearing, where k_o is at a minimum.

The traditional view therefore claims that there is an optimal capital structure where the weighted average cost of capital is at a minimum. This is at point X in the above diagram.

At point X the overall return required by investors (debt and equity) is minimised.

It follows that at this point the combined market value of the entity's debt and equity securities will also be maximised (because the value of the entity's debt and equity and the WACC are inversely related – discounting the future operating cash flows at a lower cost of capital will give a higher value.)

Optimal capital structure

4 Capital structure: Modigliani and Miller's view

In 1958, the two American economists, Professors Modigliani and Miller, challenged the traditional view of gearing and the cost of capital. Over a 20-year period they put forward a number of propositions as to why the traditional view of gearing might be wrong.

They began by assuming that the effect of tax relief on debt interest could be ignored.

Modigliani and Miller without tax (1958)

The 1958 proposition was that companies which operate in the same type of business and which have similar operating risks must have the same total value, irrespective of their capital structures.

Their view is based on the belief that the value of a company depends solely upon the future post tax (pre financing) operating income generated by its assets.

The way in which the funding is split between debt and equity should make no difference to the total value of the company (equity plus debt). In fact, one of M & M's assumptions is that the investors are indifferent between personal and corporate gearing.

Thus, the total value of the company will not change with gearing. This means that its weighted average cost of capital will not change with gearing, and will be the same at all levels of gearing.

Their view is represented in the following diagrams.

Modigliani and Miller view (no taxation)

If the weighted average cost of capital is to remain constant at all levels of gearing, it follows that any benefit from the increased proportion of cheaper debt finance (downward force on the WACC) must be exactly offset by the increase in the cost of equity (upward force on the WACC).

The essential point made by M & M is that, ignoring taxation, a company should be indifferent between all possible capital structures. This is at odds with the beliefs of the traditionalists.

M & M support their case by demonstrating that market pressures will ensure that two companies identical in every aspect apart from their gearing level will have the same overall market value.

Modigliani and Miller with tax (1963)

In 1963, M & M amended their model to include the impact of corporation tax. This alteration changes the results of their analysis significantly.

Previously they argued that companies that differ only in their capital structure should have the same total value of debt plus equity. This was because it was the size of a firm's operating earnings stream that determines its value, not the way funding was split between debt and equity.

However, the corporation tax system carries a distortion under which returns to debt holders (interest) are tax deductible for the company, whereas returns to equity holders are not. M & M, therefore, conclude that geared companies have an advantage over ungeared companies, i.e. they pay less tax and will, therefore, have a greater market value and a lower weighted average cost of capital.

Graph of M & M model with tax

As gearing increases, the WACC steadily decreases, and hence the value of the company (debt plus equity) increases.

In the presence of tax, the downward force on the WACC (the impact of the greater proportion of debt finance) is stronger than the upward force (the increase in cost of equity).

If the other implications of the M & M view are accepted, the introduction of taxation suggests that the higher the level of taxation, the lower the combined cost of capital.

Modigliani and Miller (M & M) formulae

M & M developed the following formulae that can be applied to finding the value, cost of equity or WACC of companies that have a given level of business risk, but changing capital structure.

With tax

Value of the company (debt+equity)

$$V_g = V_u + TB$$

Cost of equity

$$k_{eg} = k_{eu} + (k_{eu} - k_d) V_D (1 - t) / V_E$$

WACC

$$k_{adj} = k_{eu} [1 - (V_D t / (V_E + V_D)]$$

where V = Value of company (V_g = value of geared company, V_u = value of ungeared company)

k_e = Cost of equity (k_{eg} = cost of equity in geared co, k_{eu} = cost of equity in ungeared co)

k_d = Cost of debt (must be gross of tax)

k_{adj} = the weighted average cost of capital in a geared company

B, V_D = MV of debt

V_E = MV of geared company's equity

T, t = Corporation tax rate

WACC = weighted average cost of capital

TB is often referred to as the present value of the tax shield

The without-tax formulae are simply a special case of the with-tax formulae, where t = 0.

Interpreting the M & M graphs and formulae

Without tax

Company value ($V_g = V_u$)

The graph showed a horizontal line for company value in the M & M without tax theory.

This is backed up by the formula, which shows that if T=0, the values of an ungeared company and an equivalent ungeared company are the same.

WACC ($k_{adj} = k_{eu}$)

The graph also showed a horizontal line for WACC in the M & M without tax theory.

Again, the formula backs this up. If t=0, the formula reduces to $k_{adj} = k_{eu}$. This shows that the WACC of the geared company is always the same as the WACC of an equivalent ungeared company, irrespective of the level of gearing.

With tax

Company value ($V_g = V_u + TB$)

The graph showed an upward sloping line for company value in the M & M with tax theory.

This is backed up by the formula, which shows that the higher the value of B (value of debt), the greater the value of the entire company should be.

As the company increases its gearing, the value of the entire company (debt plus equity) increases.

Cost of equity ($k_{eg} = k_{eu} + (k_{eu} - k_d) V_D(1 - t) / V_E$)

The cost of equity slopes upwards as gearing increases under M & M's assumptions, because shareholders face higher risk so demand higher returns.

We can see from the formula that the k_{eg} increases as the amount of debt (V_D) increases relative to the value of equity (V_E).

Note that the inclusion of (1-t) in the formula has the impact of reducing the slope of the line if the tax rate increases. Most importantly, this means that the cost of equity in the M & M with tax theory will always increase less steeply than in the without tax theory. This helps to explain why the upward force on WACC is smaller in the with tax theory, and hence why the downward force on the WACC caused by the (net of tax) cheap debt finance is the net stronger force in the with tax theory.

WACC ($k_{adj} = k_{eu} [1 - (V_D t / (V_E + V_D)]$)

The formula shows that WACC will reduce as gearing (measured by debt divided by (debt + equity)) increases. This is seen on the graph as a downward sloping line.

Test your understanding 1 (Integration question) – no tax

X Co is identical in all operating and risk characteristics to Y Co, except that X Co is all equity financed and Y Co is financed by equity valued at $2.1m and debt valued at $0.9m based on market values. **X Co and Y Co-operate in a country where no tax is payable.**

The interest paid on Y Co's debt is $72,000 per annum, and it pays a dividend to shareholders of $378,000 per annum. X Co pays an annual dividend of $450,000.

Required:

(a) Calculate the value of X Co.

(b) Calculate the cost of capital for X Co.

(c) Calculate the cost of equity for Y Co, and the cost of debt for Y Co.

(d) Calculate the weighted average cost of capital for Y Co.

Test your understanding 2 (Integration question) – with tax

X Co is identical in all operating and risk characteristics to Y Co, except that X Co is financed only by equity valued at $3m whereas Y Co has debt valued at $0.9m (based on market value) as part of its capital structure. **X Co and Y Co-operate in a country where tax is payable at 33%.**

The interest paid on Y Co's debt is $72,000 per annum, and it pays a dividend to shareholders of $401,760 per annum. X Co pays an annual dividend of $450,000.

Required:

(a) Calculate the value of the equity of Y Co.

(b) Calculate the cost of capital for X Co.

(c) Calculate the cost of equity for Y Co, and the cost of debt for Y Co.

(d) Calculate the weighted average cost of capital for Y Co.

M & M's key assumptions

- There exists a perfect capital market in which there are no information costs or transaction costs.

- Debt is risk free and k_d remains constant at all levels of gearing.

- Investors are indifferent between personal and corporate gearing.

- Investors and companies can borrow at the same rate of interest.

5 Capital structure in the real world

Introduction

We need to adjust M & M 's theories to also take into account real life factors.

The most unrealistic of M & M's key assumptions is that debt is risk free.

In reality, there is a greater risk to both the lenders and shareholders with very high levels of gearing. This is the risk that the company is unable to service the debt and end up in financial distress or even insolvent.

In reality, lenders will ask for higher interest if they perceive that there is a greater risk of default.

Practical considerations

This then leaves the problem of how companies determine their capital structures in the real world.

The main practical considerations are:

- The company's ability to borrow money (the company's 'debt capacity')
- Existing debt covenants
- Increasing costs of debt finance as gearing rises
- Views of other stakeholders and rating agencies
- Tax exhaustion

More detail on practical considerations

The company's ability to borrow money (the company's 'debt capacity')

- The maximum level of borrowing that a company can comfortably support is referred to as its debt capacity. (**Definition** of debt capacity from CIMA Official Terminology, 2005 is the "extent to which an entity can support and / or obtain loan finance.")

- A company can only increase its gearing if it can find a lender who will provide it with debt finance. In recessionary times, this should not be taken for granted.

- A company's capacity to borrow is increased if it is able to offer good quality, valuable assets as collateral.

- Debt capacity is function of a company's credit-worthiness (introduced in an earlier chapter) and credit scoring. (**Definition** of credit scoring from CIMA Official Terminology, 2005 is the "assessment of the credit-worthiness of an individual or company by rating numerically a number of both financial and non-financial aspects of the target's present position and performance.")

Existing debt covenants

- Debt covenants reduce the flexibility of management. Existing debt covenants may even prevent the company from borrowing more.

- Management must keep the company well within the terms of the existing covenants (keeping plenty of 'leeway' or 'headroom') to ensure that the flexibility of the company is maximised.

Increasing costs of debt finance as gearing rises

- M & M assumed that debt was risk free, and that k_d would be constant at all levels of gearing. In reality, an increased level of gearing is likely to be perceived as risky by lenders, so the interest rates on borrowings generally increase as gearing increases.

Views of other stakeholders and rating agencies

- The gearing theories focus on the position of the shareholders and the lenders at different levels of gearing. In reality, the views of other stakeholders should also be considered. In particular, many stakeholders perceive high levels of gearing to be risky. This could impact on the credit score or credit worthiness of the company. A reduction in credit worthiness may be evidenced by a credit rating downgrade by one of the credit rating agencies.

- For example,
    - customers may be concerned about buying goods from companies that have poor credit worthiness (due to concerns about warranties and guarantees being honoured)

    - suppliers might not want to supply, or advance credit (due to the risk of default)

    - employees and managers might choose to leave if they fear for their job security.

- All these factors will damage the company's prospects and reputation.

Tax exhaustion

- M & M's with tax theory suggests that the benefits of tax relief on debt interest will help to reduce the company's cost of capital at all levels of gearing. This is not the case in practice.

- At some level of gearing the interest payable will be so high that taxable profit will be reduced to zero. Beyond this point, there will be no further benefit of raising debt finance.

- However, in order for tax exhaustion to apply, the company must be making a loss and will have breached any interest cover covenants. The company is therefore likely to have much greater problems to contend with than the loss of tax relief.

6 The impact on financial ratios of a change in capital structure

When an entity changes its financing (capital structure), there will be an impact on ratio analysis (especially the gearing ratio).

The impact of a change in financing on ratio analysis - the gearing ratio

The two key measures of gearing are:

$$\text{Capital gearing} = \frac{\text{Debt}}{\text{Debt + Equity}} \times 100$$

$$\text{OR} \quad \frac{\text{Debt}}{\text{Equity}} \times 100$$

Note: Both of these measures are used in practice, but the first one is more commonly used.

Clearly if an entity changes its capital structure by raising new finance as either debt or equity, these gearing ratios will change.

Exam questions often test the calculation of gearing ratios before and after a change in capital structure.

Test your understanding 3 (Objective test question)	
Statement of financial position for X Co	
	USDm
Non-current assets (total)	23.0
Current assets (total)	15.0
TOTAL ASSETS	**38.0**
Equity and Liabilities	
Ordinary share capital	10.0
Ordinary share premium	4.0
Preference share capital (irredeemable)	1.5
Reserves	1.5
Non-current liabilities	
10% bonds	8.0
Current liabilities	
Trade creditors	8.0
Bank overdraft	5.0
TOTAL EQUITY & LIABILITIES	**38.0**

X Co statement of profit or loss extract

	USDm
Operating profit (PBIT)	4.0
Finance Charges	(1.0)
Profit before tax (PBT)	3.0
Tax @ 30%	(0.9)
Net profit	2.1

X Co is considering raising additional debt finance of USD 6m. The interest rate on the new debt will be 12% per annum. Operating profit is expected to stay constant after the new finance has been raised.

What will be the interest cover and the capital gearing ratio (measured as debt / (debt + equity) at book value, and including the bank overdraft as part of debt) for X Co after the new finance has been raised?

A   Interest cover 2.33, gearing 52.8%

B   Interest cover 2.33, gearing 56.9%

C   Interest cover 1.22, gearing 52.8%

D   Interest cover 1.22, gearing 56.9%

Illustration 1: More complex gearing ratio calculation

PPP is considering raising $250 million new finance to fund the acquisition of QQQ. QQQ is considered to have a value to PPP of $270 million.

Extracts from PPP's statement of financial position show:

	$m
Long term borrowings	950
Share capital ($1 shares)	500
Retained reserves	400

The directors of PPP haven't yet decided whether debt or equity finance should be used to fund the takeover. However, if equity is to be used, the new shares will be issued at a price of $2.60 per share. The current market share price is $2.90 per share.

Required:

Calculate the gearing ratio measured as (debt/(debt + equity)):

(a) before the acquisition of QQQ,

(b) after the acquisition, assuming that debt finance is used to fund the takeover,

(c) after the acquisition, assuming that equity finance is used to fund the takeover.

In all cases, present your calculations using both book values and market values.

Solution:

Gearing based on book values

Pre-acquisition	950 / [950 + (500 + 400)] = **51.4%**
Post-acquisition – using debt	(950+250) / [(950+250)+(500+400+20 **(W1)**)] = **56.6%**
Post-acquisition – using equity	950 / [950 + (500 + 400 + 250 + 20 **(W1)**)] = **44.8%**

(W1) Since QQQ is worth $270m to PPP but the purchase price is $250m, the value of PPP's equity will increase by $20m irrespective of how the purchase is financed.

Gearing based on market values (W2)

Pre-acquisition	950 / [950 + 1,450] = **39.6%**
Post-acquisition – using debt	(950+250) / [(950+250) + (1,450+20)] = **44.9%**
Post-acquisition – using equity	950 / [950 + (1,450 + 250 + 20)] = **35.6%**

(W2) Market value of existing shares = $2.90 × 500m = $1,450m

Note: The issue price of the new shares ($2.60) is irrelevant when calculating the gearing ratios. Of course the issue price does affect the number of shares issued and therefore other ratios such as EPS (see further examples below), but gearing ratios are calculated based on total values of equity and debt so the issue price is not relevant here.

Debt covenants

A useful application of the impact of financing decisions on ratio analysis is in the context of debt covenants.

For example, the gearing ratio is often used in debt covenants - an entity might have to keep its gearing ratio below a given percentage to comply with its debt covenants.

If you are asked in the exam to assess the impact of a decision on a given debt covenant, you should calculate the necessary ratio assuming the decision has been made and then compare the result to the given target.

For example, if the covenant requires that gearing should not exceed 30% (measured as (debt / (debt + equity)) you should calculate the ratio (assuming the decision has been made) using the formula given, and see if the result remains below 30%.

Test your understanding 4 (Objective test question)

Grass Co has a debt covenant that requires its gearing ratio (measured as debt / (debt + equity) using market values) to be less than 40%, and its interest cover to be greater than 2.

Extracts from its recent financial statements show that it has 100,000 $1 shares in issue and it has a 10% interest bank borrowing of $60,000. It made a profit before interest and tax last year of $15,000.

The current share price is $1.40 per share.

The directors of Grass Co are considering borrowing an extra $20,000 from the bank as a secured borrowing at an interest rate of 6% per annum.

Annual profits are expected to stay constant, but the share price is expected to fall to $1.35 per share to reflect the shareholders' perception of increased financial risk.

Assuming the new finance is raised, which of the following shows Grass Co's position with regard to its debt covenant:

A   Gearing: MET, Interest cover: MET

B   Gearing: FAILED, Interest cover: MET

C   Gearing: FAILED, Interest cover: FAILED

D   Gearing: MET, Interest cover: FAILED

7 Structuring the debt / equity profile of group companies

Introduction

Individual companies and groups of companies both have to decide on an appropriate capital structure by considering the various theoretical and practical points covered earlier in this chapter.

However, there are additional considerations for groups of companies.

General considerations for groups of companies

Tax issues

Within a group of companies, it makes sense to maximise borrowings in regimes with the highest tax rate, to increase the amount of tax relief available. Tax relief can be limited though, by transfer pricing issues and by thin capitalisation rules – see below for details.

Country risk

There will be less exposure to risk if an entity borrows funds in the country where it generates its net income. Any servicing costs for the finance can then be paid out of the income generated without worrying about exchange rate movements.

Type of finance provided by the parent

Note that if debt and equity are both supplied by the parent company, the choice between debt and equity finance for a subsidiary has no cash implications in the context of groups, unlike the situation for a single company.

This is because both are financed in cash by the parent and therefore can be funded by the parent by either debt or equity.

The choice of capital structure for a subsidiary is therefore independent of the decision regarding the appropriate group capital structure.

Transfer pricing

Transfer pricing adjustments may be necessary for transactions between connected companies, to ensure that companies cannot reduce their tax liabilities by using a transfer price that is below or above an arm's length price.

In the context of capital structure, this means that if one company in a group has borrowed money from another company in a group, an adjustment will be necessary if it is deemed that the interest rate charged is not set at a market rate.

Illustration 2 (Objective test question)

Vulture Co is a wholly owned subsidiary of Red Co.

It has borrowed $100,000 from Red Co, at an annual interest rate of 2%. The market rate of interest is 5% per annum.

What is the annual interest payment from Vulture Co to Red Co, and what is the adjustment needed for tax purposes?

A   Interest $5,000, tax purposes adjustment $3,000

B   Interest $2,000, tax purposes adjustment $3,000

C   Interest $5,000, tax purposes adjustment $2,000

D   Interest $2,000, tax purposes adjustment $5,000

Solution:

The answer is (B).

Annual interest payment = $100,000 × 2% = $2,000

However, at market rate of interest (5%) the interest paid would have been $100,000 × 5% = $5,000.

Therefore an adjustment of $3,000 (5,000 - 2,000) will be made to Vulture Co and Red Co's accounts for tax purposes. Vulture Co will reduce its profits for tax purposes and Red Co will increase its profits by the same amount.

Thin capitalisation rules

When a company pays a dividend, there is no tax relief for the payment.

When it pays interest on borrowings, the interest is tax allowable. This means that companies would prefer to be financed through borrowings (debt) rather than through shares (equity).

The thin capitalisation rules aim to stop companies from getting excessive tax relief on interest.

This occurs (usually) because they have entered into a borrowing with a related party that exceeds the amount a third party lender would be prepared to lend. (Note that the additional borrowing is most likely to be provided by the parent company within a group structure.)

The rules ensure that

- interest on the part of the borrowing that an independent third party would be prepared to lend the company is allowable

- the excess is disallowed

- the borrowing capacity of the individual company and its subsidiaries is considered (but not the rest of the group).

Factors determining thin capitalisation

The tax authorities will usually look at two areas to determine whether they believe a company is thinly capitalised:

- Gearing
    - This is measured as the ratio of debt to equity.
    - A higher proportion of debt could cause thin capitalisation problems.
    - In the UK a limit of around 50:50 is considered by the tax authorities to be reasonable.

- Interest cover
    - This is the ratio of earnings before tax and interest to interest on borrowings.
    - It measures how risky the loan is for the lender.
    - Many commercial lenders will look for a ratio of around 3, so this is the figure considered by the tax authorities to be reasonable.

Illustration 3 (Integration question)

Archer plc is UK company, which is a wholly owned subsidiary of Berry Inc, a company resident in Babylonia.

Archer borrows GBP100,000 from Berry Inc paying a market rate of interest of 8%. Archer had to borrow from Berry Inc as its UK bankers were not prepared to lend it more than GBP60,000.

Required:

Advise Archer plc of how much interest on borrowings it is likely to have relieved for tax purposes.

Solution:

A third party was only prepared to lend Archer plc GBP60,000.

As it has borrowed GBP100,000 from its parent company, it is likely that interest on the excess GBP40,000 will be disallowed for tax purposes.

Therefore, of the GBP8,000 interest Archer plc pays to Berry Inc, only GBP4,800 is likely to be allowed for tax.

Test your understanding 5 (Integration question)

Eagle Co is a wholly owned subsidiary of White Co.

Extracts from Eagle Co's financial statements for the last accounting period are shown below:

	$m
Share capital	10.0
Reserves	15.6
Bank borrowing	8.5
Borrowing from parent company	20.0

The annual interest rate payable on both the bank borrowing and the borrowing from the parent company is 4%. The borrowing from the parent company was 25% more than Eagle Co could have raised from the bank at that time.

The tax authorities consider a company to be thinly capitalised if its gearing ratio (debt : equity) is above 50:50.

Required:

Calculate the amount of Eagle Co's interest payable on the parent company borrowing that will be allowable for tax relief.

8 End of chapter objective test questions

Test your understanding 6 (Objective test question)

Modigliani and Miller's 1958 'without tax' gearing theory concludes that:

A   There is an optimum gearing level at which the value of the company is minimised

B   There is an optimum gearing level at which the value of the company is maximised

C   The value of the company is unaffected by the gearing level

D   The value of the company reduces as the gearing level increases

E   The value of the company increases as the gearing level increases

Test your understanding 7 (Objective test question)

A company has:

- Current cost of equity of 12%

- Ungeared cost of equity of 10%

- WACC of 9.25%

- Market value of equity of $210 million

- Market value of debt of $70 million

- Tax rate of 30%

The company plans to raise $20 million of debt and use these funds to repurchase shares.

According to Modigliani and Miller's theory with tax, WACC would move to:

A   8.62%

B   10.35%

C   9.06%

D   10.87%

Test your understanding 8 (Objective test question)

The traditional view of gearing concludes that:

A   There is an optimum gearing level at which the cost of capital is minimised

B   There is an optimum gearing level at which the cost of capital is maximised

C   The cost of capital continually reduces as the gearing level increases

D   The cost of capital continually increases as the gearing level increases

E   The cost of capital is unaffected by the gearing level

Test your understanding 9 (Objective test question)

Ghost Co's most recent statement of financial position shows long term borrowings of $12.4 million, share capital ($1 shares) of $6.8 million and accumulated reserves of $5.2 million.

Ghost Co is considering raising $4 million of new long term debt finance to fund the acquisition of Face Co.

Face Co is considered to have a value to Ghost Co of $4.5 million.

The current market share price for Ghost Co is $2.90 per share.

What will be the gearing ratio – measured as (debt/(debt + equity)) at book value – after the acquisition?

A   69.2%

B   59.2%

C   56.7%

D   49.8%

Test your understanding 10 (Objective test question)

Until recently, VV was an ungeared company with a cost of equity of 13%. It recently issued some debt finance and its cost of equity increased to 14%.

If VV pays tax at a rate of 20%, and if the yield required by VV's lenders is 8%, what is the gearing level (measured as (debt/equity)) of VV according to Modigliani and Miller's theory with tax:

A   0.25

B   0.20

C   0.33

D   0.30

Test your understanding 11 (Objective test question)

BB is an all-equity financed company with a cost of equity of 10%.

The directors of BB are proposing to raise $200 million to invest in a new project. This investment will carry similar risk to BB's current business. It is proposed that the investment will be financed by either

- a rights issue of shares, or

- an issue of an undated bond carrying 5% interest pre-tax (this rate is deemed to reflect the returns required by the market for the risk and duration of the bond).

Earnings for BB are forecast to be $100 million in the first year after the new investment. Subsequently, earnings are expected to remain at a constant level each year. The corporate income tax rate is 20%. This is not expected to change.

According to Modigliani and Miller's theory with tax, BB's value if it issues the bond and undertakes this project will be:

A $1,200 million

B $1,040 million

C $1,000 million

D $ 960 million

Test your understanding 12 (Objective test question)

Which THREE of the following are key assumptions of Modigliani and Miller's 1963 gearing theory?

A   The capital market is strongly efficient

B   Debt is risk free

C   Cost of equity stays constant at all levels of gearing

D   Companies do not pay tax

E   Investors and companies can borrow at the same rate of interest

Test your understanding 13 (Objective test question)

The following information relates to Present Co, a geared company that pays tax at 25%:

- Current cost of equity 14%

- Ungeared cost of equity 12%

- WACC 11.4%

Market value of equity is $400 million and market value of debt is $100 million. Present Co plans to raise $50 million of debt and use these funds to repurchase shares.

According to Modigliani and Miller's theory with tax, WACC would move to:

A   12.55%

B   10.76%

C   12.98%

D   11.12%

Test your understanding 14 (Objective test question)

Modigliani and Miller's 1963 Theory of Capital Structure with Tax assumes that

A   The cost of equity remains constant regardless of gearing level

B   A company is liable to tax, but not its shareholders

C   Companies can borrow at zero cost

D   Financial distress does not carry any cost

Test your understanding 15 (Objective test question)

Which THREE of the following reasons are most likely to result in an entity using equity (rather than debt) finance to fund a new investment project?

A   the project is a short-term project

B   the entity has a very low level of gearing

C   the banks are unwilling to lend, having just downgraded the entity's credit rating

D   the project's cash flows are likely to be variable, and might even be negative in the first year

E   the entity is a service business with very few tangible assets

9 End of chapter case style questions

Test your understanding 16 (Case style question)

The finance director of Netra plc, a company listed on the UK's AIM (Alternative Investment Market), wishes to estimate what impact the introduction of debt finance is likely to have on the company's overall cost of capital. The company is currently financed only by equity.

Netra plc Summarised capital structure

	£000
Ordinary shares (25 pence par value)	500
Reserves	1,100
	1,600

The company's current share price is 420 pence, and up to £4 million of fixed rate irredeemable debt could be raised at an interest rate of 10% per annum. The corporate tax rate is 33%.

Netra's current earnings before interest and tax are £2.5 million. These earnings are not expected to change significantly for the foreseeable future.

The company is considering raising either:

(i)   £2 million in debt finance;

(ii) £4 million in debt finance

In either case the debt finance will be used to repurchase ordinary shares.

Required:

(a) Using Miller and Modigliani's model in a world with corporate tax, estimate the impact on Netra's cost of capital of raising:

  (i) £2 million; and

  (ii) £4 million in debt finance.

  State clearly any assumptions that you make.

(b) Briefly discuss whether or not the estimates produced in part (a) are likely to be accurate.

(30 minutes)

Test your understanding 17 (Case style question)

Canalot Co is an all equity company with an equilibrium market value of GBP32.5 million and a cost of capital of 18% per year.

The company proposes to re-purchase GBP5 million of equity and to replace it with 13% irredeemable bonds.

Canalot's earnings before interest and tax are expected to be constant for the foreseeable future. Corporate tax is at the rate of 35%. All profits are paid out as dividends.

Required:

Explain and demonstrate how this change in capital structure will affect:

1 the market value;
2 the cost of equity; and
3 the cost of capital

of Canalot Co, using the assumptions of Modigliani and Miller.

(15 minutes)

Explain any weaknesses of both the traditional and Modigliani and Miller theories and discuss how useful they might be in the determination of the appropriate capital structure for a company.

(15 minutes)

Test your understanding answers

Test your understanding 1 (Integration question) – no tax

(a) $V_g = V_u + TB$

so given that $T = 0$,

$V_g = V_u$

so the value of X Co is the same as the value of Y Co, ($2.1m + $0.9m) $3m

(b) Assuming no growth in dividends, using the dividend valuation model,

k_{eu} = Dividend / V_E = 450,000 / 3,000,000 = 15%

(c) **Cost of debt for Y Co** (assuming debt is irredeemable)

k_d = Interest / V_D = 72,000 / 900,000 = 8%

Cost of equity for Y Co:

Using M & M's formula:

$k_{eg} = k_{eu} + (k_{eu} - k_d) V_D(1 - t) / V_E$

k_{eg} = 15% + (15%–8%)×0.9/2.1 = 18%

(Alternatively, using the dividend valuation model,

k_{eg} = Dividend / V_E = 378,000 / 2,100,000 = 18%)

As shown on the graphs, the geared company has a higher cost of equity.

(d) Weighted average cost of capital:

WACC = (18% × 2.1 / 3) + (8% × 0.9 /3) = 15%

Again, notice that this corresponds to the graphs seen above. In the no tax case, the WACC is constant irrespective of capital structure.

Test your understanding 2 (Integration question) – with tax

(a) $V_g = V_u + TB$

so given that T = 0.33,

V_g = 3,000,000 + (33% × 900,000) = $3,297,000

so the value of the equity = 3,297,000 – 900,000 (value of debt) = $2,397,000

(b) Assuming no growth in dividends, using the dividend valuation model,

k_{eu} = Dividend / V_E = 450,000 / 3,000,000 = 15%

(c) **Cost of debt for Y Co** (assuming debt is irredeemable)

k_d = Interest / V_D = 72,000 / 900,000 = 8%

Cost of equity for Y Co:

Using M & M's formula:

$k_{eg} = k_{eu} + (k_{eu} - k_d) V_D(1 - t) / V_E$

k_{eg} = 15% + (15%–8%)×900,000×(1 – 0.33)/2,397,000 = 16.76%

As shown on the graphs, the geared company has a higher cost of equity.

(d) Weighted average cost of capital:

WACC = (16.76% × 2,397 / 3,297) + (8% × (1 – 0.33) 900 /3,297) = 13.65%

Alternatively, using M & M's formula:

$k_{adj} = k_{eu} (1 - tL)$ = 15% (1 – 33% × 900 / 3,297) = 13.65%

Again, notice that this corresponds to the graphs seen above. In the with tax case, the WACC reduces as the level of debt in the capital structure increases.

Test your understanding 3 (Objective test question)

The answer is (A).

Interest cover = 4m/(1m + (12% × 6m)) = 2.33 times

Capital gearing ratio

Debt	=	5m + 8m + 6m	= USD19m
Equity	=	10m + 4m + 1.5m + 1.5m	= USD17m
D / (D+E)	=	19m/(19m + 17m) × 100	= 52.8%

Test your understanding 4 (Objective test question)

The answer is (A). Both covenant terms will still be met after the finance is raised.

Before the finance is raised:

Gearing = 60,000 / (60,000 + (100,000 × $1.40)) = 30%

Interest cover = 15,000 / (10% × 60,000) = 2.5

After the finance is raised:

Gearing = (60,000 + 20,000) / (60,000 + 20,000 + (100,000 × $1.35)) = 37%

Interest cover = 15,000 / [(10% × 60,000) + (6% × 20,000)] = 2.1

Test your understanding 5 (Integration question)

Interest payable on the parent company borrowing and charged through the accounts is ($20m × 4%) = $0.8m

Current gearing (debt : equity) is (20m + 8.5m) / (10.0m + 15.6m) i.e. $28.5m / $25.6m

Accordingly the company is considered to be too thinly capitalised by the tax authorities, and the thin capitalisation rules apply.

The amount of interest on the parent company borrowing disallowed for tax purposes will be ($20m × 25/125 × 4%) = $0.16m

Therefore the amount of interest on the parent company borrowing that is tax allowable is (0.8m − 0.16m) = $0.64m

Test your understanding 6 (Objective test question)

The answer is (C).

Modigliani and Miller's 1958 gearing theory is the 'no tax' theory. It concludes that the value of the company is unaffected by the gearing level.

Test your understanding 7 (Objective test question)

The answer is (C)

$WACC = k_{eu} (1 - tL)$

where k_{eu} is given as 10%, t is 30% and L is the gearing level measured as (debt/debt+equity)).

Gearing working:

The value of the company was $280 million (210 equity and 70 debt).

Therefore, using the equation $V_g = V_u + TB$,

$280 = V_u + (30\% \times 70)$

so V_u = $259 million

Hence, with the new gearing level,

Vg = 259 + (30% × 90) = $286 million

and therefore, WACC = 0.10 × [1–(30% × 90/286)] = 9.06%

Test your understanding 8 (Objective test question)

The answer is (A).

The traditional view of gearing concludes that the cost of capital follows a U shaped curve, and therefore that there is an optimum gearing level at which the cost of capital is minimised.

Test your understanding 9 (Objective test question)

The answer is (C).

Debt will rise to $12.4m + $4m = $16.4m.

Equity will rise (because of the extra value generated by the takeover) to

$6.8m + $5.2m + $0.5m = $12.5m

Therefore, [D/(D+E)] = 16.4 / (16.4 + 12.5) = 56.7%

Test your understanding 10 (Objective test question)

The answer is (A).

M & M's formula is:

$$k_{eg} = k_{eu} + (k_{eu} - k_d) \, V_D(1 - t) / V_E$$

where kd is the yield to the debt holders.

Plugging the given numbers in shows:

$$0.14 = 0.13 + [(0.13\text{-}0.08) \, V_D(1 - 0.20) / V_E \,]$$

So rearranging the equation gives $V_D / V_E = 0.25$

Test your understanding 11 (Objective test question)

The answer is (B).

Modigliani and Miller's formula is:

$$V_g = V_u + TB$$

Therefore, the value of the company if it funds the project using the bond is Vu (the value if the company continued to be all equity financed) plus 20% × $200 million (i.e. $40 million).

Vu can be found by discounting the earnings figure as a perpetuity. So

Vu = $100m / 0.10 = $1,000 million

Therefore, Vg = $1,000 million + $40 million = $1,040 million

Test your understanding 12 (Objective test question)

The answer is (A), (B) and (E).

The key assumptions of Modigliani and Miller's 1963 gearing theory are:

- Companies do pay tax
- The capital market is strongly efficient
- There are no transaction costs
- Debt is risk free
- Cost of debt stays constant at all levels of gearing
- Investors are indifferent between personal and corporate gearing
- Investors and companies can borrow at the same rate of interest

So the correct three points were (A), (B) and (E) (i.e. the capital market is strongly efficient, debt is risk free and investors and companies can borrow at the same rate of interest).

Test your understanding 13 (Objective test question)

The answer is (D)

$$WACC = k_{eu} (1 - tL)$$

where k_{eu} is given as 12%, t is 25% and L is the gearing level measured as (debt/debt+equity)).

Gearing working:

The value of the company was $500 million (400 equity and 100 debt).

Therefore, using the equation $V_g = V_u + TB$,

$500 = V_u + (25\% \times 100)$

so V_u = $475 million

Hence, with the new gearing level,

Vg = 475 + (25% × 150) = $512.5 million

and therefore, WACC = 0.12 × [1–(25% × 150/512.5)] = 11.12%

Test your understanding 14 (Objective test question)

The answer is (D).

Under M & M's theory, the cost of equity rises as gearing increases (A) and the risk of debt is nil so companies can borrow at low cost (but not zero cost) (C).

Both shareholders and companies are assumed to pay tax in the 1963 theory (B).

In their 1963 theory, M & M assumed that there were no costs to financial distress and liquidation (D).

Test your understanding 15 (Objective test question)

The answer is (C), (D) and (E).

Short term projects (A) should not be funded by long term equity finance.

A low level of gearing would generally mean that the entity is not fully benefitting from the tax advantages of debt finance (B).

Few tangible assets (E) and a poor credit rating (C) would make raising debt finance more difficult. For a project with variable cash flows (D), the necessity of making interest payments each year could cause financial distress.

Test your understanding 16 (Case style question)

(a) Assuming that all earnings are paid out as dividends, the current cost of equity (and overall cost of capital) is total earnings divided by the market value of the company's shares:

	£000
Earnings before finance charges and tax	2,500
Taxation	825
Earnings = dividends	1,675

The market value of equity is two million shares × 420 pence per share = £8.4 million.

$$K_e = \frac{£1,675,000}{£8,400,000} = 19.94\%$$

If equity is replaced by debt the value of the company will increase.

V geared = V ungeared + TB (tax rate × amount of debt)

With £2 million debt

V geared = 8,400 + (2,000 × 0.33) = 9,060.

	£000
Total value of the company	9,060
Market value of debt	2,000
Value of equity	7,060

With £4 million debt

V geared = 8,400 + (4,000 × 0.33) = 9,720

	£000
Total value of the company	9,720
Market value of debt	4,000
Value of equity	5,720

Cost of equity	£2 million debt	£4 million debt
	£000	£000
Earnings before f.charges and tax	2,500	2,500
Finance charges	(200)	(400)
	2,300	2,100
Taxation (33%)	(759)	(693)
Earnings/dividends	1,541	1,407
Cost of equity Ke =	1,541/7,060 = 21.83%	1,407/5,720 = 24.60%

WACC

£2 million debt:

$$WACC = 21.83 \times \frac{7,060}{9,060} + 10\,(1 - 0.33)\,\frac{2,000}{9,060} = 18.49\%$$

£4 million debt:

$$WACC = 24.60 \times \frac{5,720}{9,720} + 10\,(1 - 0.33)\,\frac{4,000}{9,720} = 17.23\%$$

Alternative method of calculation

Or alternatively using WACC $= K_{eu}\left(1 - \dfrac{Dt}{E + D}\right)$

£2 million debt:

$$\text{WACC} = 19.94 \left(1 - \frac{2,000 \times 0.33}{7,060 + 2,000}\right) = 18.49\%$$

£4 million debt:

$$\text{WACC} = 19.94 \left(1 - \frac{4,000 \times 0.33}{5,720 + 4,000}\right) = 17.23\%$$

The higher the level of gearing, the lower the cost of capital becomes, due to the benefit from tax relief on finance charges.

(b) As debt is introduced into the capital structure it is likely that the cost of capital will initially fall. However, the estimates produced in (a) may not be accurate because:

(i) They rely on the assumptions of the Modigliani and Miller (M & M) model, many of which are unrealistic such as the capital market is perfectly efficient, debt is risk free, information is costless and readily available, there are no transaction costs, investors are rational and make the same forecasts about the performance of companies, and investors and companies can borrow at the risk-free rate.

(ii) Only corporate taxation is considered and not the impact of other forms of taxation including personal taxation.

(iii) M & M assumed that debt is permanent.

(iv) The estimates ignore possible costs that might be incurred as gearing increases, which would reduce share price and increase the cost of equity (and possibly debt). These include bankruptcy costs, agency costs and tax exhaustion.

(v) Inaccuracies exist in the measurement of the data required for the model.

Answer to the first task:

Market value

Modigliani and Miller's hypothesis including the effects of corporation tax suggests that:

$$V_g = V_u + TB$$

Where V_g is the value of the geared company

V_u is the value of an equivalent ungeared company

B is the market value of debt

T is the rate of corporation tax

In the case of Canalot:

V_u = GBP32.5 million

B = GBP5 million

T = 35%

$\therefore V_g$ = 32.5m + 5m × 35% = GBP34.25m

The original value was GBP32.5 million.

This therefore represents an increase of GBP1.75 million.

Cost of equity

Modigliani and Miller propose the following formula for calculating the cost of equity of a geared company:

$$K_{eg} = K_{eu} + (K_{eu} - K_d) \times \frac{V_d}{V_e} \times (1-t)$$

where K_{eg} is the cost of equity of the geared company

K_{eu} is the cost of equity of an equivalent ungeared company

K_d is the cost of debt before tax

V_d is the market value of debt

V_e is the market value of equity

t is the rate of corporation tax

K_{eu} = 18% (given)

K_d = 13%

V_d = 5m

$V_e = V_g - D$ = 34.25m – 5m = 29.25m

$$\therefore K_e = 18\% + (18\% - 13\%)\ \frac{5}{29.25} \times (1 - 0.35)$$

= 18.56%.

The cost of equity has increased by 0.56%, reflecting the increase in financial risk as a result of gearing.

Cost of capital

Using Modigliani and Miller's formula:

$$WACC = K_{eu} \left[1 - \frac{Dt}{D + V_e} \right]$$

$$= 18\% \left[1 - \frac{5 \times 0.35}{34.25} \right]$$

$$= 17.08\%$$

Alternatively the traditional weighted average cost of capital formula may be used, i.e.

$$WACC = 18.56\% \times \frac{29.25}{34.25} + 13\%(1 - 0.35) \times \frac{5}{34.25}$$

$$= 17.08\%$$

The previous WACC was equal to K_{eu}, i.e. 18%. It has therefore decreased by 0.92%, reflecting the tax benefits of increased gearing.

Answer to the second task:

The traditional view of capital structure theory is intuitive only; it is not based on any empirical evidence or computation and therein lies its major weakness.

It argues that there exists an optimal capital structure where the overall cost of capital is minimised and thus the company value is maximised. This is based on the following propositions:

- as gearing increases the cost of equity rises due to the increase in financial risk, but this is outweighed by the lower cost of debt and so the overall cost of capital decreases;

- as gearing continues to increase the cost of equity rises more sharply, such that this effect is greater than the effect of the lower cost of debt and the cost of capital rises;

- therefore there exists a minimum optimal cost of capital

The theory is useful in as much as it highlights the fact that financing and capital structure may affect a company's value but it gives no suggestion as to where that optimal level lies.

Modigliani and Miller's theory, however, was initially based on empirical evidence and followed by quantification. Their hypothesis which includes the effects of corporate taxes (an adjustment to their original model) suggests that the optimal capital structure comprises 99.9% debt. Since this policy is not adopted by companies there must be certain flaws in this theory, the most important of which was later corrected by Miller himself, i.e. the effect of personal taxes.

Other common criticisms of the model include the following:

- the use of unrealistic assumptions, for instance:
  - there are no transaction costs;
  - information is freely available;
  - individuals can borrow on the same terms as companies;
  - individuals are prepared to exchange personal gearing for corporate gearing;

- costs associated with high levels of gearing are not considered. These may include the following:

(1) Bankruptcy costs

As gearing reaches high levels the probability of bankruptcy increases and if bankruptcy occurs there will be associated costs. These include the liquidation fees and the loss on the disposal of assets in a forced sales situation.

(2) Tax exhaustion

The benefit derived from increasing the level of gearing relates to the tax relief obtained by companies on returns paid to debt, i.e. interest. However, at very high levels of gearing there is the possibility that the company will not have sufficient taxable profits from which to deduct the debt interest. In this situation the advantage of gearing up will be lost.

(3) Agency costs

These relate to constraints imposed on the company by providers of finance through restrictive covenants contained within terms of agreement. Such constraints are aimed to protect the interest of (primarily) the debt holders when a company finds itself in a potentially difficult situation close to bankruptcy.

As a result of the above and the effect of personal taxes, it is clear that benefits related to increased gearing do not continue indefinitely. The final position is not well defined, but it may be possible that there exists a point where the cost of capital is minimised before the additional costs of high gearing outweigh the benefits. Thus, if managers are able to quantify such costs and benefits, this adapted theory may be of use to them in identifying an appropriate level of gearing to adopt.

Dividend policy

Chapter learning objectives

Lead	Component
B2: Evaluate dividend policies for an incorporated entity that meet the needs and expectations of shareholders.	(a) Evaluate alternatives to cash dividends and their impact on shareholder wealth and entity performance measures. (b) Recommend appropriate dividend policies, including consideration of shareholder expectations and the cash needs of the entity.

Indicative syllabus content

- Impact of scrip dividends on shareholder value and entity value/financial statements/performance measures.

- Impact of share repurchase programmes on shareholder value and entity value/financial statements/performance measures.

- Implications for shareholder value of alternative dividend policies including MM's theory of dividend irrelevancy.

- Development of appropriate dividend policy, taking into account the interests of shareholders and the cash needs of the entity.

1 Overview of chapter

2 Dividend policy

One long-standing question in corporate finance is: Is shareholders' wealth affected by a company's dividend policy?

Notice that the question is not asking whether *dividends* matter – of course they do (as we know from the dividend valuation model) – what the question asks is whether the chosen *policy* matters. Examples of such policies may include:

(i) paying a constant annual dividend;

(ii) paying out a constant proportion of annual earnings;

(iii) increasing dividends in line with the annual rate of inflation, etc;

(iv) paying out what's left after financing all future investment – the residual policy.

The key factors to consider in relation to the payment of dividends are:

(1) Modigliani and Miller's (M & M) dividend irrelevancy argument

(2) The interests of shareholders (the clientele effect and the bird-in-the-hand argument)

(3) The signalling effect or information content of dividends

(4) The cash needs of the entity

Dividend irrelevancy: Modigliani and Miller's theory

M & M's dividend irrelevancy theory says that the pattern of dividend payout should be irrelevant. As long as companies continue to invest in positive NPV projects, the wealth of the shareholders should increase whether or not the company makes a dividend payment this year.

M & M's Dividend Irrelevancy Theory

M & M's argument here is built up as follows:

(i)   The return on a share is determined by the share's (systematic) risk.

(ii) The return itself is delivered to shareholders in two parts: one part is the dividend paid and the other is the capital gain/loss in the share price.

(iii) The dividend decision that a company makes is a decision as to how the return is delivered: how much of the annual earnings should be paid out as dividends and how much of the annual earnings should be retained and re-invested within the company – and so flow through to shareholders in the form of a capital gain on the share price.

(iv) As the dividend decision does not affect the *risk* of the shares, it does not affect their *return*. All the dividend decision therefore does is to determine *how* the return is to be split up between dividends and capital gains.

(v)   Do shareholders mind how their returns are split between dividends and capital gains? The answer according to M & M is: no, they do not *if* we assume:

    (a) There are no taxes (really, there are no differences between the taxation on dividends and on capital gains).

    (b) Shares can be bought and sold free of any transaction costs (such as stock-brokers' commission).

M & M argue that shareholders can 'manufacture' a dividend policy irrespective of the company policy. For instance, if a person is holding shares for income but the company withholds a dividend, the shareholder can sell some of the shares to replace the lost income.

The assumptions that M & M make play a key role. Obviously, if dividends were taxed and capital gains were tax free, shareholders *would* mind how their return was delivered – they would strongly prefer it to be delivered in the form of capital gains rather than dividends.

Similarly, investors who were holding shares for the income they generated *would* mind how their return was delivered if they had to incur transaction costs when realising their capital gains so as to turn them into income – such investors would strongly prefer if the return were delivered in the form of dividends, rather than capital gains.

However, given their assumptions hold good, M & M could claim that shareholders are indifferent between dividends and capital gains and so the dividend decision / the dividend policy that the company pursues is irrelevant.

The interests of shareholders

It is critical that a business satisfies the needs of its shareholders with its dividend policy. If the shareholders don't feel that the business's dividend policy meets their expectations, they will sell their shares, perhaps causing the share price to fall.

Two important considerations in the context of shareholders' interests are the clientele effect and the bird-in-the-hand argument:

Clientele effect

In the real world, there are differential tax treatments of dividends and capital gains, and there are transaction costs on share dealings.

As a result, shareholders *are* concerned as to how their return is delivered to them by the company. Thus companies should follow a *consistent* dividend policy so as to ensure that they gather to them a clientele of shareholders who like that particular policy.

Thus the argument here is that the *actual* dividend policy that a company follows is unimportant but, having decided on a particular policy, it should then keep to it.

The bird-in-the-hand argument

This analysis puts forward a very simple argument.

Some investors may find capital gains more tax-efficient than dividends, and some investors will avoid transaction costs if their returns are delivered in the form of capital gains rather than dividends; despite all this, investors generally have a strong preference for dividends.

The reason given is that a dividend is *certain* and investors prefer a certain dividend *now*, to the promise of uncertain *future* dividends (arising out of retaining and re-investing earnings).

The signalling effect

Investors read 'signals' into the company's dividend decision and that these signals say as much about the company's *future* financial performance as they say about its *past* financial performance.

Thus management will not necessarily reduce the dividend per share just because last year's performance was poor, if they believe that *next* year's performance will be good.

If this analysis is correct, and investors do indeed read signals into the dividend decision, then the dividend decision becomes important: it becomes important for the company *not* to give the *wrong* signal.

More details on signalling

It is widely believed that there are two very strong dividend signals:

(1) a *reduction in the dividend* per share signals that the company is in financial difficulties;

(2) a *failure to pay out any dividend* at all signals that the company is very close to receivership.

Thus a company must take great care when settings dividend levels and ensure that the market is kept fully informed of future prospects.

These ideas are very widely held in practice and this view is supported by Lintner who discovered that dividend growth lagged two to three years behind earnings growth. This evidence can be interpreted to mean that managers are reluctant to increase the dividend per share until they are *confident* that they will be able to maintain that new level of dividends in the future (and will not be subsequently obliged to reduce the dividend per share).

However, there are exceptions to this interpretation. For many years, Apple Computers paid no dividends to its investors, preferring instead to reinvest the profits back into the business to fund new investments and to reduce the requirement to raise finance externally. Despite the absence of a dividend, the market responded positively to Apple throughout, and the share price rose strongly.

In conclusion, although paying dividends (or not paying dividends) can give investors a signal as to how successful the company is likely to be in future, it is not the only important indicator to investors. Other factors such as investment plans, gearing levels, strategy and quality of management are also important as investors assess the likely success of a business.

The cash needs of the entity

We saw in the earlier Chapter 3: 'Development of financial strategy' that the investment, financing and dividend decisions are all inter-linked.

Therefore, it is important to also consider the impact of investment and financing when considering dividend policy. Different types of business will have very different cash needs and will therefore have to set their dividend, investment and financing policies accordingly.

For example:

- A small company, or a company with a poor credit rating, will often struggle to raise finance from external sources, so its cash needs might have to be met by restricting the amount of dividends it pays out.

- A growing company will have many potential investment opportunities. The cash needs for these new investments will have to be met by balancing dividend policy alongside external finance sources.

- A well-established, stable company might well be cash rich, in which case it might be able to afford to pay out large dividends without compromising its internal cash needs.

How to reconcile these differing views of dividend policy in the real world

Given these contrasting views, how are managers to decide on the dividend policy that they should pursue?

The answer is that, in the real world, like so much else in corporate finance, managers have to make a *judgement* after taking many varying factors into account.

In this process they will consider:

(1) What dividends are the shareholders expecting (e.g. the clientele effect)?

(2) What are the cash needs of the company?

(3) What dividend did the company pay last year? Consider the signal that a dividend announcement will give.

However they will also take into account a range of other factors, such as:

(1) Is it legal to pay out a dividend?

(2) Is the cash available to pay out a dividend?

(3) Do we have a minimum gearing ratio imposed on the company as a financial covenant in a debt agreement?

(4) What is the tax impact for shareholders of paying dividends?

(5) What investment opportunities does the company face?

(6) How difficult/expensive is it to raise external finance?

(7) What has been the rate of inflation (and so what dividend increase is needed to maintain the purchasing power of last year's dividends)?

(8) What has been the capital gain/loss in the share price over the last year?

3 Dividend policy in practice

In practice, there are a number of commonly adopted dividend policies:

- stable dividend policy

- constant payout ratio

- zero dividend policy

- residual approach to dividends.

Stable dividend policy

Paying a constant or constantly growing dividend each year:

- offers investors a predictable cash flow

- reduces management opportunities to divert funds to non-profitable activities

- works well for mature firms with stable cash flows.

However, there is a risk that reduced earnings would force a dividend cut with all the associated difficulties.

Constant payout ratio

Paying out a constant proportion of equity earnings:

- maintains a link between earnings, reinvestment rate and dividend flow but
- cash flow is unpredictable for the investor
- gives no indication of management intention or expectation.

Zero dividend policy

All surplus earnings are invested back into the business. Such a policy:

- is common during the growth phase
- should be reflected in increased share price.

When growth opportunities are exhausted (no further positive NPV projects are available):

- cash will start to accumulate
- a new distribution policy will be required.

Residual dividend policy

A dividend is paid only if no further positive NPV projects available. This may be popular for firms:

- in the growth phase
- without easy access to alternative sources of funds.

However:

- cash flow is unpredictable for the investor
- gives constantly changing signals regarding management expectations.

Ratchet patterns

Most firms adopt a variant on the stable dividend policy – a **ratchet pattern** of payments. This involves paying out a stable, but rising dividend per share:

- Dividends lag behind earnings, but can then be maintained even when earnings fall below the dividend level.
- Avoids 'bad news' signals.
- Does not disturb the tax position of investors.

4 Scrip / bonus dividends and share repurchase

Scrip dividends

A scrip dividend (or bonus / scrip issue) is where shareholders are offered bonus shares free of charge as an alternative to a cash dividend.

They are useful where the company wishes to retain cash in the business or where shareholders wish to reinvest dividends in the company but avoid brokerage costs of buying shares. There may also be tax advantages of receiving shares rather than cash in some jurisdictions.

If all shareholders opt for bonus shares, the scrip issue has the effect of capitalising reserves. Reserves reduce and share capital increases.

The disadvantage to shareholders is that, unlike reserves, share capital is non-distributable in the future. In addition, both share price and earnings per share are likely to fall due to the greater number of shares in issue, although the overall value of each shareholder's shares and share in future earnings should, theoretically, remain unchanged.

However, it has the important advantage to the issuer of retaining cash in the business while still achieving a distribution of reserves.

Example of a scrip dividend

A recent issue by Santander bank in February 2011 was set up in a similar manner to a rights issue except that the rights were issued without charge.

Shareholders were given rights to receive additional Santander shares and three options for their allotment of rights:

(1) Sell the rights off market to Santander and receive a fixed cash amount.

(2) Sell the rights on market and receive cash.

(3) Hold the rights and receive new Santander shares, 1 share for every 65 rights held.

Share repurchase

A share repurchase can be used to return surplus cash to shareholders.

It tends to be used when the company has no positive NPV projects to invest the cash in, so it returns the cash to shareholders so that they can make better use of it rather than it sitting idle (in cash investments) in the company.

Alternatively, a share repurchase can be used to privatise a company, by buying back a listed company's shares from a wide pool of investors. However, this is rare.

Share repurchase v one-off large dividend

As an alternative to a share repurchase, a company may decide to use a one-off large dividend to return surplus cash to shareholders.

If all shareholders agree to the repurchase, both a share repurchase and a one-off large dividend have the same impact on the cash, and the gearing of the company (they reduce the value of equity, so increase the gearing and hence financial risk and cost of equity). Although the impact on shareholder value is the same for any individual shareholder, the impact on the price per share will differ. A dividend results in a lower share price as the number of shares remains the same, but a share repurchase is unlikely to affect the individual share price but only the number of shares in issue.

The one-off dividend has the advantage of certainty of ultimate payout. However, a share repurchase has the following advantages:

- investors can choose whether or not to sell their shares back (they may prefer to keep the shares if they feel that future returns will be high)
- it avoids the risk of a false dividend signal – after a one-off large dividend, the shareholders may be disappointed when the higher level of dividend is not maintained in the future.

5 The impact of scrip dividends and share repurchase on financial ratios

Scrip dividends

The impact of a scrip dividend on shareholder wealth is nil. There are more shares in issue but the overall shareholder value stays the same, hence the share price decreases.

For example, if price per share is $11 and if a shareholder has 100 shares, then after the issue of a 10% scrip dividend, the number of shares increases to 110. Hence, price per share will decrease to $1100/110 = $10.

The impact of a scrip dividend on the entity's performance measures / ratios is:

- total shareholder's equity (in the statement of financial position) remains the same
- it doesn't change the capital structure (and gearing ratio) because the equity value stays the same.

Test your understanding 1 (Objective test question)

LL is a large listed company. Its $1 ordinary shares are quoted on the local stock exchange.

Equity comprises:

- Ordinary share capital ($1 shares) $1,500m
- Reserves $500m

LL's share price is $1.90 per share.

The Board of LL is aware that the market is expecting LL to pay a dividend of $200m to be paid at the year end, but in order to fund the investment in an important new project, the Board is considering offering a scrip dividend of 1 share for every 12 shares held instead of a cash dividend.

Profit after tax and interest is forecast to be $380 million in the current financial year.

What is the expected share price of LL after the scrip dividend has been issued? (to 2 decimal places)

A $0.16

B $1.75

C $1.90

D $2.03

Share repurchase

The impact of a share repurchase on shareholder wealth is the same as the impact of a cash dividend being paid.

The impact of a share repurchase on the entity's performance measures / ratios is different from the impact of a cash dividend though. After a share repurchase there will be fewer shares in issue, so the earnings per share of the entity will increase.

Illustration 1 (Integration question)

McGreggor Co has 10,000 share in issue, trading at $50 per share. The Board is considering returning cash of $50,000 to shareholders either as a cash dividend or as a share repurchase.

Required:

Calculate the wealth of a shareholder who currently owns 100 shares in each case.

Solution:

Cash dividend

Dividend per share = ($50,000 / 10,000 shares) = $5

Therefore, ex-dividend share price = $50 – $5 = $45

So the shareholder who owns 100 shares will have wealth of:

Dividend received + Share value

= (100 × $5) + (100 × $45) = $5,000

Share repurchase

Number of shares repurchased in total will be ($50,000 / $50) = 1,000 i.e. 10% of the total 10,000 shares.

Therefore there will now be (10,000 − 1,000 =) 9,000 shares in issue, with a value of

[(10,000 × $50) − $50,000] / [10,000 − 1,000] = $50 each

So the shareholder who owned 100 shares before the repurchase will now have wealth of:

Cash received in share repurchase + Share value

= (10 × $50) + (90 × $50) = $5,000

6 End of chapter objective test questions

Test your understanding 2 (Objective test question)

Mr Smith is an investor who is considering buying shares.

Mr Smith is retired, so does not receive a regular income from any source. He therefore pays little (if any) income tax. However, he does have several valuable assets that he could sell if he needed to.

Which TWO of the following companies have dividend policies that most closely match Mr Smith's requirements?

Company A – follows the residual dividend policy advocated by Modigliani and Miller

Company B – follows a zero dividend policy, preferring to reinvest all profits back into the business

Company C – follows a stable dividend policy where each year's dividend is 3% higher than the year before

Company D – pays out a dividend each year of 20% of earnings per share

Test your understanding 3 (Objective test question)

A company plans to return surplus cash to shareholders by paying a special dividend, making it clear to investors that this is a one-off event.

The company is funded by a mix of debt and equity and currently does not have any unused bank facilities available.

Which of the following is the MOST likely consequence of this plan?

A   The share price would rise due to the signalling effect of the special dividend

B   Shareholder wealth would decrease by the value of cash paid as a special dividend

C   The company would become less vulnerable to a hostile takeover bid

D   The company would become more able to respond promptly to new business opportunities

Test your understanding 4 (Objective test question)

A company has 10 million $0.50 shares in issue. The company is planning to repurchase 1 million of these shares at a price of $1.50 each.

Currently, the company's cash balance is $2 million and its earnings per share is $0.20.

What will be the cash balance and the earnings per share (EPS) after the share repurchase?

A   Cash: $1.5 million, EPS: $0.22

B   Cash: $0.5 million, EPS: $0.20

C   Cash: $1.5 million, EPS: $0.20

D   Cash: $0.5 million, EPS: $0.22

Test your understanding 5 (Objective test question)

Honeybear Co has 6 million shares in issue, trading at $5.20 per share.

The directors have decided to offer a 3 for 5 scrip dividend to shareholders.

What will be the company's share price after the scrip dividend has been issued?

A $1.95

B $3.12

C $3.25

D $8.67

Test your understanding 6 (Objective test question)

Redhead Co has 100 million $1 shares in issue, trading at $2.24. It also has $70 million of bonds in issue, trading at $106 per cent.

After several years of growth, the company has accumulated a cash pile of $20 million. The directors have decided to repurchase some of the company's shares at market value in order to return this cash pile to the shareholders.

What will be the gearing level of Redhead Co after the share repurchase? (measured as debt / (debt + equity) using market values)

A   24.9%

B   26.7%

C   41.2%

D   46.7%

Test your understanding 7 (Objective test question)

Which THREE of the following strategies are most likely to enhance shareholder wealth?

A   Increasing cash for bonuses

B   Increasing the dividend payout ratio

C   Increasing brand reputation and recognition

D   Investing in projects with a positive NPV

E   Moving profitable operations to low tax regimes

Test your understanding 8 (Objective test question)

P Co is considering paying out a large one-off special dividend to return a large amount of cash to its shareholders.

Which TWO of the following are valid arguments in favour of such a policy?

A   If P Co has no foreseeable use for the cash, it should be returned to investors so that they can put it to better use

B   It sends a positive signal to the market, unlike a share repurchase

C   A large payment in a single year reduces the risk of a misleading signalling effect

D   It is likely to increase shareholder wealth

E   Paying the cash out is likely to provide protection against hostile take-over

Test your understanding 9 (Objective test question)

Mr Jones is an investor who is considering buying shares.

Mr Jones is a chartered management accountant who works for a large listed company. He earns a large salary from his employment and pays income tax at the highest marginal rate. However, he has few valuable assets and has never previously made any taxable capital gains.

Which TWO of the following companies have dividend policies that most closely match Mr Jones's requirements?

Company A – follows the residual dividend policy advocated by Modigliani and Miller

Company B – follows a zero dividend policy, preferring to reinvest all profits back into the business

Company C – follows a stable dividend policy where each year's dividend is 3% higher than the year before

Company D – pays out a dividend each year of 20% of earnings per share

Test your understanding 10 (Objective test question)

Which of the following statements is consistent with Modigliani and Miller's dividend irrelevancy theory?

A   A policy of steady growth in dividends is preferable to a residual dividend policy

B   Shareholder wealth can be maximised by retaining a high percentage of earnings

C   The share price is NOT affected by a dividend payment

D   Shareholder return can be measured as the aggregate of dividends plus growth in share price

7 End of chapter case style questions

KK is a listed manufacturing company that is wholly equity financed. 25% of the shares are held by members of an extended family group. KK has adopted 31 December as its financial year end.

Dividend decision

In previous years, KK has maintained a dividend pay-out rate of 80% of earnings. However, some board members have recently questioned whether such a policy is appropriate. Some board members support the 80% pay-out but others have suggested that a lower dividend is necessary in order to help finance expansion in manufacturing capacity to take advantage of new markets that are opening up in Asia.

It is too late to change the dividend for the current financial year, 20X3, since the dividend for the year is about to be paid. The first time that a change in dividend policy could be adopted is in 20X4.

Additional financial information for KK:

*   It is standard practice for KK to pay dividends once a year based on forecast earnings for that year.

*   Dividends are paid at or shortly before the end of the year.

*   A dividend of $ 0.50 in respect of the current financial year (20X3) has already been declared. this was based on the historical pay-out rate of 80% of forecast earnings for 20X3 of $ 12.5 million.

*   Historically, KK has achieved a return on reinvested funds of 16%.

*   KK has a cost of equity of 14.7%.

*   There are currently 20 million shares in issue.

*   Today's share price is $ 5.00 (cum div).

Possible reduction in dividend pay-out

The board of KK is considering cutting the regular dividend pay-out rate from 80% to 50% of earnings with effect from 20X4. If agreed, this would be made public by an announcement on 1 January 20X4.

The board is aware that there would be a delay of 12 months between cutting the dividend pay-out rate and realising any benefit in terms of higher earnings as a result of the higher level of reinvested funds. Discussions regarding a possible change in the dividend pay-out rate have so far been internal and only known by the management team at KK. No announcement has yet been made about a possible change in dividend policy and the share price does not yet reflect the possibility of a cut in pay-out rate.

Growth formula

$g = r \times b$

- Where g = annual growth
- r = return on reinvested funds
- b = proportion of funds retained

Required:

Calculate the following performance measures for KK for both years 20X4 and 20X5 assuming a reduction in KK's dividend pay-out to 50% of earnings from 20X4 onwards:

- Growth rate using the growth formula provided.
- Earnings.
- Dividend per share.

(20 minutes)

Test your understanding 12 (Case style question)

DIVS plc is a large international company with widespread interests in advertising, media and various consultancy activities associated with sales promotion and marketing. In recent years the company's earnings and dividend payments, in real terms, have grown on average by 15% and 12% per year respectively. The company is likely to have substantial cash surpluses in the coming year, but a number of investment opportunities are being considered for the subsequent two years. The senior managers of the company are reviewing their likely funding requirements for the next two to three years and the possible consequences for dividend policy.

At present the company has a debt : equity ratio of 1 : 5, measured in market value terms. It does not want to increase this ratio at the present time but might need to borrow to pay a maintained dividend in the future.

The senior managers of the company are discussing a range of issues concerning financial strategy in general and dividend policy in particular.

Required:

Assume you are an independent financial advisor to the board of DIVS plc. Write a report to the board which discusses the following issues:

(i)   The re-purchase of some of the company's shares in the coming year using the forecast surplus cash, the aim being to reduce the amount of cash needed to pay dividends in subsequent years. Other implications of share repurchase for the company's financial strategy should also be considered.

(ii)   The advisability of borrowing money to pay dividends in years 2 and 3.

(iii) The likely effect on the company's cost of equity if the company decides on share repurchase and / or further borrowing.

(45 minutes)

Test your understanding 13 (Case style question)

STR is a well-established marketing consultancy in a country with a low interest rate. STR is a successful business which has experienced rapid growth in recent years. There are 20 million $1 ordinary shares in issue. These ordinary shares are quoted on a recognised stock exchange and 40% are owned by the founders of the business. Dividends were 40 cents per share in 20X3 and grew by 5% per annum between 20X3 and 20X6. This pattern is expected to continue beyond 20X6. Dividends are paid in the year in which they are declared.

Extracts from the financial statements for the past three years are as follows:

	20X4	20X5	20X6
	$million	$million	$million
Profit before tax	21.6	24.4	26.7
Tax expense	7.7	2.6	4.3
Net cash generated after deducting interest, tax and net capital expenditure, but excluding ordinary dividends	19.2	(7.1)	18.8

Additional information:

- The opening cash balance in 20X4 for cash and cash equivalents was $6 million;

- The opening book value of equity in 20X4 was $60 million;

- Long-term borrowings remained at $50 million throughout the three years and the annual gross interest cost on the borrowings was $1 million;

- There were a number of disposals of non-current assets in 20X4 and an exceptionally high level of capital expenditure in 20X5.

The directors have noticed the build-up of cash and cash equivalents. They are concerned that this might not be in the best interest of the shareholders and could have an adverse effect on the share price. Various proposals have been made to reduce the level of cash and cash equivalents.

Required:

(a) Calculate the following financial information for STR for each of the years 20X4 to 20X6:

– Closing cash balance;

– Closing book value of equity.

(10 minutes)

(b) Analyse and discuss the financial performance of the entity from the viewpoint of both the lenders and shareholders, referring to the information calculated in part (a) above and making appropriate additional calculations. Up to 6 marks are available for calculations.

(20 minutes)

(c)

(i) Discuss the comparative advantages and disadvantages of a share repurchase versus a one-off dividend payment.

(15 minutes)

(ii) Advise the directors of STR on alternative financial strategies that they could consider that would reduce the level of surplus cash.

(15 minutes)

Test your understanding answers

Test your understanding 1 (Objective test question)

The answer is (B).

In theory, shareholder wealth is unaffected by a scrip dividend.

Consider a typical shareholder with 120 shares. Under the terms of the scrip dividend, this shareholder would receive an entitlement to one new share for every 12 held. That is, the right to acquire 10 new shares (where 10 = 120/12).

This may give the shareholder the illusion of increased 'value' as he now holds 130 shares. However, the company itself has not changed in value and so the total value that those shares represent is unchanged.

Therefore, the value of each share after the scrip issue will be ($1.90 × 120) / 130 = $1.75

Test your understanding 2 (Objective test question)

The answer is (C) and (D).

Mr Smith has no other regular income, so he would prefer to invest in a company that pays out a dividend each year.

Company C would be his preferred choice - it gives a predictable payout.

Company D would be his second choice - a dividend will be paid each year, although the amounts could be variable.

Companies A and B would not give Mr Smith the income he needs. Selling shares to manufacture dividends would not be appealing to Mr Smith because he has capital gains already but pays very little income tax, so he would prefer dividends to capital gains.

Test your understanding 3 (Objective test question)

The answer is (C)

Having paid out a large amount of cash as a dividend there would be much less chance of a predator wanting to take over the company.

Test your understanding 4 (Objective test question)

The answer is (D)

The amount of cash required for the repurchase is 1 million shares at $1.50 each, so $1.5 million in total. Hence, cash will fall from $2 million to $0.5 million.

The new number of shares in issue will be (10 million – 1 million =) 9 million, so assuming that earnings stay constant, the EPS will be (total earnings / 9 million).

Currently, earnings are $0.20 × 10 million = $0.20 million.

Therefore, EPS will be $0.20 million / 9 million = $0.22 after the repurchase.

Test your understanding 5 (Objective test question)

The answer is (C).

A scrip dividend does not change the value of the overall company, therefore the total company value will still be:

6 million × $5.20 = $31.2 million.

After the 3 for 5 scrip issue, the number of shares in issue will be:

6 million + (6 million × 3/5) = 9.6 million.

Therefore, the share price will be $31.2 million / 9.6 million = $3.25.

Test your understanding 6 (Objective test question)

The answer is (B).

Market value of debt is $70m × 1.06 = $74.2m

Current market value of equity is 100m × $2.24 = $224m, so after the share repurchase it will be $204m.

Therefore (D / (D+E)) = 74.2 / (74.2 + 204) = 26.7%

Test your understanding 7 (Objective test question)

The answer is (C), (D), and (E)

Cash for bonuses (A) would cause more money to be paid out of the business, leaving less for reinvestment.

Increasing the dividend payout ratio (B) without any underlying increase in positive NPVs generated would make no difference to shareholder wealth.

Test your understanding 8 (Objective test question)

The answer is (A) and (E).

Paying a dividend of any sort should not impact shareholder wealth - only undertaking a positive NPV project can enhance shareholder wealth (D).

A large payment in a single year would increase the risk of a misleading signalling effect (C).

Both special dividends and share repurchases can send positive signals to the market (B).

Test your understanding 9 (Objective test question)

The answer is (A) and (B).

Mr Jones has a large regular income, so he would prefer to invest in a company that pays out as little as possible in dividends. If Mr Jones ever does need an income from his investments, selling shares to create capital gains would be the most tax efficient approach.

Test your understanding 10 (Objective test question)

The answer is (D)

M & M's theory said that the pattern of dividends is irrelevant. The key point is that any positive NPV projects should be undertaken. Hence (A) and (B) are incorrect.

Although shareholder wealth will not be affected by a dividend payment, the share price will be under M & M's theory. A large dividend will convert shareholder wealth from share value to cash, so the share price will fall even though overall shareholder wealth stays the same. Therefore (C) is incorrect.

Test your understanding 11 (Case style question)

Performance measure	20X3	20X4	Workings	20X5	Workings
Earnings growth (%)	3.2	3.2	No change as reinvestment of additional retained earnings not actioned until this year	8	g = r × b = 16% × 50% = 8%
Earnings ($m)	12.5	12.9	= $ 12.5 million × 1.032	13.932	= $ 12.9 million × 1.08
Dividend per share ($)		0.50 0.3225	= 12.9m × 50% / 20m	0.3483	= (13.932 × 50%)/20m

where 3.2% = r × b = 16% × 20%

Test your understanding 12 (Case style question)

Report

To: Board of Directors, DIVS plc

From: Independent financial advisor

Date: XX/XX/XX

Re: Dividend policy and other financing issues

You are currently considering the current and future position of the company as regards dividend payments and financing over the next two to three years, in the light of your current cash surplus and the investment opportunities available to you from next year.

This report addresses the following issues:

- the implications of share re-purchase to reduce future dividend payments;
- borrowing funds to finance dividends;
- the possible effects on cost of equity if either or both of the above actions are taken.

(i) *Share re-purchase*

You are likely to have substantial cash surpluses in the coming year. Your first decision is to decide how much to distribute, bearing in mind both your investment financing requirements in the future and the possible reactions of shareholders and other market players. In the current climate, it is expected that 'spare' cash, in excess of that required for specific profitable investment opportunities, should be returned to the shareholders to do with as they wish.

You have some investment opportunities open to you in the near future. Whether or not you have to retain some of the current surplus cash to fund these will depend upon the extent to which you expect there to be spare funds generated in the next two or three years.

Once the amount to be distributed (if any) has been decided upon, you then need to decide whether to return it to all the shareholders as a dividend, or to some of them in the form of a share re-purchase. The latter option will result in only a small number of shareholders – likely to be the large institutional investors – receiving cash, although their proportionate holding, and therefore entitlement to future dividends, will be reduced.

Other shareholders will have to sell shares, incurring transaction costs, to 'manufacture' dividends should they need them.

It should be noted that a share re-purchase is administratively more complex in that it requires prior approval from a general meeting of shareholders (assuming the Articles of Association provide that it can happen at all). It is also no longer possible for institutions to reclaim tax on the distribution in the UK.

The two types of distribution will also affect share prices differently. When a dividend is declared, the value of the shares falls from cum-div to ex-div, the shareholders having had some of their capital investment realised as cash.

In theory, if the share re-purchase is made at current market price, a share re-purchase should leave the individual share price unchanged – there has been a reduction in total market value in proportion to the total number of shares in issue.

It should also be noted that a share re-purchase would result in a higher future EPS figure than if a normal dividend had been paid. However this should not affect the market's perception of the health of the company, as it is purely a result of the same earnings being spread over a smaller number of shares.

Overall, it would appear that there is no particularly strong argument for a share re-purchase in preference to a dividend payment to all shareholders. Whilst you may see this as a means of reducing future dividend payments, it is likely that the remaining shareholders, who would be holding a greater proportion of shares than previously, would expect a higher dividend per share. If this expectation is not met, share prices may be affected adversely.

(ii) *Borrowing to pay dividends*

If it is decided to distribute an amount in the current year that cannot be maintained (with planned growth) in future years out of operational cash flows, then additional funds will need to be borrowed.

This will raise the company's gearing level above the current 1:5 debt:equity ratio, with two consequences. First, the company will be funded by a greater proportion of cheap finance, particularly as debt interest is tax deductible. Second, shareholders may perceive a greater risk as being attached to their dividends, as more of the earnings are attributed to fixed interest payments. It is a question of finding the optimum balance between these two effects.

(iii) *Effect on cost of equity*

The probable effect of increasing the gearing level will be, as discussed in (ii) above, to increase the required return by (cost of) equity. Borrowing will directly affect the gearing level, by increasing the debt element.

The payment of a dividend or a share repurchase will also increase the gearing level, by lowering the value of the equity (as discussed in (i) above, a dividend results in a lower share price with the number of shares being maintained; a share repurchase results in a maintained share price with a lower number of shares).

Thus both actions may result in a higher cost of equity.

Overall recommendations

It is advised that any surplus cash over and above the needs of all positive NPV investments should be paid out in the form of a dividend. This 'residual' dividend policy may lead to fluctuating dividends, however, and institutional investors generally prefer a steady dividend pattern; you will need to keep a careful eye on your share price to ensure it is not being adversely affected in the long term.

Should you need to borrow in the future, you should find this to your advantage, as your current gearing level is quite low, and the benefits of cheaper debt should outweigh any increase in cost of equity.

Key answer tips

In part (a) ensure that your workings are clearly set out. In part (b) it is vital that you discuss any ratios calculated rather than simply presenting the examiner with a set of numbers. Part (c) is bookwork and a good reminder that you need to be familiar with all aspects of the syllabus.

(a) **Cash balances**

	20X4	20X5	20X6
	$m	$m	$m
Net cash flow before dividends	19.2	(7.1)	18.8
Dividends (W1)	(8.4)	(8.8)	(9.3)
Net cash flow	10.8	(15.9)	9.5
Cash b/f	6	16.8	0.9
Cash c/f	16.8	0.9	10.4

Book value of equity

	20X4	20X5	20X6
	$m	$m	$m
Profit before interest and tax (bal)	22.6	25.4	27.7
Interest	(1.0)	(1.0)	(1.0)
Profit before tax	21.6	24.4	26.7
Tax expense	(7.7)	(2.6)	(4.3)
Profit after tax	13.9	21.8	22.4
Dividends (W1)	(8.4)	(8.8)	(9.3)
Retained profit	5.5	13.0	13.1
Book value of equity b/f	60	65.5	78.5
Book value of equity c/f	65.5	78.5	91.6

(W1) *Dividends*

20X4: dividend = 20 million × $0.40 × 1.05 = $8.4 million

20X5: dividend = $8.4 million × 1.05 = $8.82 million

20X6: dividend = $8.82 million × 1.05 = $9.261 million

(b) **Additional calculations**

	20X4	20X5	20X6
Interest cover	22.6×	25.4×	27.7×
Dividend cover	1.65×	2.48×	2.41×
Earnings per share (cents)	69.5	109	112

Gearing = debt net of cash / (debt + equity)

	20X4	20X5	20X6
Debt	50	50	50
Cash	16.8	0.9	10.4
Debt net of cash	33.2	49.1	39.6
Equity	65.5	78.5	91.6
Debt (net) + equity	98.7	127.6	131.2
Gearing	33.6%	38.5%	30.2%

Return on equity

	20X4	20X5	20X6
Profit after tax	13.9	21.8	22.4
Equity	65.5	78.5	91.6
Return on equity	21.2%	27.8%	24.5%

Return on capital employed, using net debt + equity

	20X4	20X5	20X6
Profit before interest and tax (bal)	22.6	25.4	27.7
Debt (net) + equity	98.7	127.6	131.2
Return on capital	22.9%	19.9%	21.1%

Comments

The financial performance from the shareholders' point of view has generally been encouraging:

- Both earnings per share and the book value of equity have been increasing.

- Dividends have increased.

- Return on equity has consistently been above 20%.

- Financial gearing has fallen in 20X6 and dividend cover is now over two, indicating lower risk attached to the dividends.

The only area of worry, however, is that return on equity fell from 20X5 to 20X6.

The financial performance from the lenders' point of view has been less convincing. On a positive note:

- Interest cover is very high and rising, suggesting a low default risk.

- Gearing fell in 20X6, again suggesting less risk for lenders.

However,

- STR had poor cash flow in 20X5. Lenders may wish to see more detailed analysis of cash flow to determine if any underlying problems persist.

(c)

   (i)   The relative advantages of a share repurchase verses a one-off dividend are as follows:

Share repurchase	One-off dividend
• A repurchase may be more tax efficient than a dividend for some shareholders.	• A dividend may be more tax advantageous for some shareholders.
• A reduction in the number of shares should boost EPS.	• All shareholders are treated fairly.
• Increased gearing as equity is reduced. This is only an advantage if STR is moved closer to its optimal gearing level.	• The amount of cash paid is more certain – with a repurchase it will not be known in advance how many shareholders will choose to sell.
• Does not create an expectation of higher future dividends. On the contrary, less cash will be needed for future dividends due to fewer shares.	

   (ii) Alternative strategies for reducing a cash surplus include the following:

- – increase the growth rate of dividends

- – long-term equity investments – e.g. acquire other firms and/or buy stakes in rivals, customers, etc

- – reduce debt by repaying borrowings

- – increase capital expenditure

- – increase investment in research and development – e.g. to enter new markets.

Financial and strategic implications of mergers and acquisitions

Chapter learning objectives

Lead	Component
C1: Evaluate opportunities for acquisition, merger and divestment.	(a) Evaluate the financial and strategic implications of proposals for an acquisition, merger or divestment, including taxation implications.

Indicative syllabus content

- Recognition of the interests of different stakeholder groups.

- Reasons for and against acquisitions, mergers and divestments (e.g. strategic position, synergistic benefits, big data opportunities, risks and tax implications).

- Taxation implications (group loss relief, differences in taxation rates, withholding tax, double tax treaties).

- Process and implications of a management buy-out, including potential conflicts of interest.

- Role/function/implications of acquisition by private equity or venture capitalist.

- Role and scope of competition authorities in relation to mergers and acquisitions.

1 Overview of chapter

Terminology

The term 'merger' is usually used to describe the joining together of two or more entities.

Strictly, if one entity acquires a majority shareholding in another, the second is said to have been acquired (or 'taken over') by the first. If the two entities join together to submerge their separate identities into a new entity, the process is described as a merger.

In fact, the term 'merger' is often used even when an acquisition / takeover has actually occurred, because of the cultural impact on the acquired entity – the word merger makes the arrangement sound like a partnership between equals.

> ### Types of merger / acquisition
>
> Mergers and acquisitions can be classified to reflect the nature of the enlarged group:
>
> - **Horizontal integration** results when two entities in the same line of business combine. For example, recent bank and building society mergers are a good example of this type of integration.
>
> - **Vertical integration** results from the acquisition of one entity by another which is at a different level in the 'chain of supply' – as an example, UK breweries have moved heavily into the distribution of their product via public houses.
>
> - **A conglomerate** results when two entities in unrelated businesses combine.

2 The reasons for growth by acquisition or merger

Specific reasons for merger / acquisition

The following reasons have been suggested as to why entities merge or acquire.

- **Increased market share / power**. In a market with limited product differentiation, price may be the main competitive weapon. In such a case, large market share may enable an entity to drive prices – for example reducing prices in the short term to eliminate competition before increasing prices later.

- **Economies of scale**. These result when expansion of the scale of productive capacity of an entity (or industry) causes total production costs to increase less than proportionately with output. It is clear that a merger which resulted in horizontal or vertical integration could give such economies since, at the very least, duplication would be avoided. But how could a conglomerate merger give economies? Possibly through central facilities such as offices, accounting departments and computer departments being rationalised. (Indeed, both sets of management are unlikely to be needed in their entirety.)

- **Combining complementary needs**. Many small entities have a unique product but lack the engineering and sales organisations necessary to produce and market it on a large scale. A natural course of action would be to merge with a larger entity. Both entities gain something – the small entity gets 'instant' engineering and marketing departments, and the large entity gains the revenue and other benefits which a unique product can bring. Also if, as is likely, the resources which each entity requires are complementary, the merger may well produce further opportunities that neither would see in isolation.

- **Improving efficiency**. A classic takeover target would be an entity operating in a potentially lucrative market but which, owing to poor management or inefficient operations, does not fully exploit its opportunities. Of course, being taken over would not be the only way of improving such a poor performer, but such an entity's managers may be unwilling to give themselves the sack.

- **A lack of profitable investment opportunities – surplus cash**. An entity may be generating a substantial volume of cash, but sees few profitable investment opportunities. If it does not wish to simply pay out the surplus cash as dividends (because of its long-term dividend policy, perhaps), it could use it to acquire other entities. A reason for doing so is that entities with excess cash are usually regarded as ideal targets for acquisition – a case of buy or be bought.

- **Tax relief**. An entity may be unable to claim tax relief because it does not generate sufficient profits. It may therefore wish to merge with another entity which does generate such profits.

- **Reduced competition**. It is often one benefit of merger activity – provided that it does not fall foul of the competition authorities.

- **Asset-stripping**. A predator acquires a target and sells the easily separable assets, perhaps closing down or disposing of some of its operations.

- **Big data opportunities.** When one entity takes over another, the knowledge and expertise of the target entity can increase the amount of big data available to the predator, to enable the combined firm to develop better competitive advantage.

More on big data opportunities

What is Big Data?

There are several definitions of Big Data, the most commonly used referring to large volumes of data beyond the normal processing, storage and analysis capacity of typical database application tools. Although Big Data does not refer to any specific quantity, the term is often used when speaking about petabytes and exabytes of data.

The definition can be extended to incorporate the types of data involved. Big Data will often include much more than simply financial information and can involve other organisational data which is operational in nature along with other internal and external data which is often unstructured in form.

One of the key challenges of dealing with Big Data is to identify repeatable business patterns in this unstructured data, significant quantities of which is in text format. Managing such data can lead to significant business benefits such as greater competitive advantage, improved productivity and increasing levels of innovation.

Why is Big Data so important?

Several major business benefits arise from the ability to manage Big Data successfully:

- Driving innovation by reducing time taken to answer key business questions and therefore make decisions
- Gaining competitive advantage
- Improving productivity

Risks associated with Big Data

Availability of skills to use Big Data systems which is compounded by the fact that many of the systems are rapidly developing and support is not always easily and readily available. There is also an increasing need to combine data analysis skills with deep understanding of industry being analysed and this need is not always recognised.

Security of data is a major concern in the majority of organisations and if the organisation lacks the resource to manage data then there is likely to be a greater risk of leaks and losses.

Data Protection issues as organisations collect a greater range of data from increasingly personal sources (e.g. Facebook).

It is important to recognise that just because something CAN be measured, this does not necessarily mean it should be. There is a risk that valuable time is spent measuring relationships that have no organisational value.

If organisations are to effectively utilise Big Data, this will require a change in perspective to ensure sense can be made of the information.

Examples of how Big Data is used

Consumer facing organisations monitor social media activity to gain insight into customer behaviour and preferences. This source can also be used to identify and engage brand advocates and detractors and assess responsiveness to advertising campaigns and promotions.

Financial Services organisations can use data on customer activity to carefully segment their customer base and therefore accurately target individuals with relevant offers.

Health organisations can monitor patient records and admissions to identify risk of recurring problems and intervene to avoid further hospital involvement.

Test your understanding 1 (Integration question)

MONEY is a company operating in the financial services industry offering high net worth clients private banking facilities and investment advice. It has recently been approached by the Board of CASH, a company providing business loans and other forms of borrowing to small businesses and start-up companies. The directors of CASH are looking to sell the company to raise the capital to start a new venture and believe the company would be a good strategic fit with MONEY.

Required:

Advise MONEY how the acquisition of CASH will give rise to Big Data opportunities.

The following reasons why entities merge are of questionable validity:

- **Diversification, to reduce risk**. While acquiring an entity in a different line of activity may diversify away risk for the entities involved, this is surely irrelevant to the shareholders. They could have performed exactly the same diversification simply by holding shares in both entities. The only real diversification produced is in the risk attaching to the managers' and employees' jobs, and this is likely to make them more complacent than before – to the detriment of shareholders' future returns.

- **Shares of the target entity are undervalued**. This may well be the case, although it would conflict with the efficient markets theory. However, the shareholders of the entity planning the takeover would derive as much benefit (at a lower administrative cost) from buying such undervalued shares themselves. This also assumes that the acquirer entity's management are better at valuing shares than professional investors in the market place.

Synergy

Definition

Synergy may be defined as two or more entities coming together to produce a result not independently obtainable.

For example, a merged entity will only need one marketing department, so there may be savings generated compared to two separate entities.

Importance of synergy in mergers and acquisitions

For a successful business combination we should be looking for a situation where:

MV of combined company (AB)   > MV of A + MV of B

Note: MV means Market Value here.

If this situation occurs we have experienced synergy, where the whole is worth more than the sum of the parts. This is often expressed as 2 + 2 = 5.

It is important to note that synergy is not automatic. In an efficient stock market A and B will be correctly valued before the combination, and we need to ask how synergy will be achieved, i.e. why any increase in value should occur.

Sources of synergy

There are several reasons why synergistic gains arise. These break down into the following:

- **operating economies**, such as economies of scale and elimination of inefficiency,
- **financial synergy**, such as the reduced risk caused by diversification,
- **other synergistic effects**, such as market power.

Detailed examples of synergy

Synergy from operating economies

Economies of scale – Horizontal combinations (acquisitions of a company in a similar line of business) are often claimed to reduce costs and therefore increase profits due to economies of scale. These can occur in the production, marketing or finance areas. Note that these gains are not automatic and diseconomies of scale may also be experienced. These benefits are sometimes also claimed for conglomerate combinations (acquisition of companies in unrelated areas of business) in financial and marketing costs.

Economies of vertical integration – Some acquisitions involve buying out other companies in the same production chain, e.g. a manufacturer buying out a raw material supplier or a retailer. This can increase profits by 'cutting out the middle man'.

Complementary resources – It is sometimes argued that by combining the strengths of two companies a synergistic result can be obtained. For example, combining a company specialising in research and development with a company strong in the marketing area could lead to gains.

Elimination of inefficiency – If the victim company is badly managed, its performance and hence its value can be improved by the elimination of inefficiencies. Improvements could be obtained particularly in the areas of production, marketing and finance.

Financial synergy

Several financial arguments are proposed in this area.

Diversification – The argument goes that diversification normally reduces risk. If the earnings of the merged companies simply stay the same (i.e. no operating economies are obtained), there could still be an increase in value of the company due to the lower risk.

Diversification and financing – If the future cash flow streams of the two companies are not perfectly positively correlated (i.e. if they are forecast to fluctuate in different ways) then, by combining the two companies, the variability of their operating cash flow may be reduced. A more stable cash flow is more attractive to creditors and this could lead to cheaper financing.

The 'boot strap' or P/E game – It is sometimes argued that companies with high P/E ratios are in a good position to acquire other companies as they can impose their high P/E ratio on the victim firm and increase its value.

Other synergistic effects

Surplus managerial talent – Companies with highly skilled managers can make use of this resource only if they have problems to solve. The acquisition of inefficient companies is sometimes the only way of fully utilising skilled managers.

Surplus cash – Companies with large amounts of surplus cash may see the acquisition of other companies as the only possible application for these funds. Of course, increased dividends could cure the problem of surplus cash, but this may be rejected for reasons of tax or dividend stability.

Market power – Horizontal combinations may enable the firm to obtain a degree of monopoly power that could increase its profitability. Removing competition from a market in this way could attract the attentions of the competition authorities, e.g. the Competition and Markets Authority in the UK, who could rule the acquisition unlawful.

Speed – Acquisition may be far faster than organic growth in obtaining a presence in a new and growing market.

By considering all the above sources of synergy, a company can work towards increasing the post-merger value of the newly formed joint company.

Test your understanding 2 (Case style question)

Williams Inc is the manufacturer of cosmetics, soaps and shower gels. It also markets its products using its own highly successful sales and marketing department. It is seen as an employer of choice and as such has a talented and loyal workforce with a history of developing new and exciting products which have sold well. It is now considering extending its range, however it has currently a build-up of unfulfilled orders due to a lack of capacity.

GSL is a well-known herbal remedy for skin problems. GSL Co was founded by three brothers in the 1950s and until the death of the remaining brother in 2007 has performed well – however the new Chairman has limited experience and the company has not performed well over recent years. GSL has a dedicated team of herbalists who have developed products, which would find a ready market – however, there is insufficient funds and expertise to correctly market these products and market share is low.

Williams' products and GSL's products are made using similar production technologies and their financial and administrative systems are similar and it is hoped savings can be made here.

Required:

Identify any potential synergy gains that would emerge from a merger of Williams and GSL.

(15 minutes)

The impact of mergers and acquisitions on stakeholders

Impact on acquiring company's shareholders

The existence of synergy has been discussed above as a key benefit to shareholders of an acquisition. All companies have a primary objective to maximise shareholder wealth, so it is clear that if synergy can be achieved, an acquisition should benefit the acquiring company's shareholders.

Impact on the target company's shareholders

The acquiring company will often pay a premium to the shareholders of the target company, to encourage them to sell their shares. Therefore there is also a financial benefit to them when a takeover happens.

Impact on lenders / debt holders

Debt will often be repayable in the event of a change in control. It all depends on whether the bank borrowings and bonds contain a change in control clause. With bank borrowings they almost certainly will. The risk profile of the acquirer may be quite different from that of the original borrower and the bank will not wish to become exposed to a higher credit risk. Bonds may be the same.

The acquirer is therefore likely to need to arrange new financing, debt and/or equity financing as appropriate in advance of the takeover.

Impact on managers and staff

In many acquisitions, an easy way to generate synergy is to make some staff redundant to avoid there being duplication of roles. Therefore, the managers and employees, particularly of the target company, often view a takeover with dread. However, the managers of the acquiring company often see takeovers as an opportunity, to demand higher salaries and bonuses now that they manage a larger company.

The acquirer may wish to retain many managers whose knowledge and skills may be essential to the successful continuation of the business, at least in the short term. In such a case, the acquirer may seek assurance and contractual tie-ins to ensure that such people remain with the business for a certain period of time.

Impact on society as a whole

Governments monitor takeovers carefully, and if they feel that a takeover will not be in the best interests of society as a whole, the takeover can be investigated and sometimes stopped. Competition law in most countries prevents monopolies being created which might be able to exploit their power to take advantage of customers.

Problems with acquisitions

If an acquisition generates the expected synergy, shareholders in both the acquiring company and the target should see an increase in wealth.

However, not all mergers and acquisitions are successful.

Synergy will not automatically arise. Unless the management of the two entities can work together effectively, there is a chance that any forecast benefits of the new arrangement might not be realised.

In many cases, the forecast synergy is not achieved, or is not as large as expected. It may be that the premium paid on acquisition by the acquirer was too high, so the shareholder value of the acquirer actually reduced as a result of the acquisition.

Also, cultural clashes between the two companies can make the integration of the two businesses very difficult.

Another reason for failure is that the opportunity cost of the investment could be too high. This means that the acquirer realises that the funds tied up in the acquisition could have been better used, to generate higher returns elsewhere.

Detailed reasons why mergers / acquisitions fail

The fit/lack of fit syndrome

There may be a good fit of products or services, but a serious lack of fit in terms of management styles or corporate structure.

Lack of industrial or commercial fit

Failure can result from a horizontal or vertical takeover where the acquired entity turns out not to have the product range or industrial position that the acquirer anticipated. Usually in the case where a customer or supplier is acquired, the acquirer knows a lot about the acquired entity; even so, there may be aspects of the acquired entity's operations which may cause unexpected problems for the acquirer, such that, even in these cases, a prospective acquisition should be planned very carefully and not be based solely on experience gained from a direct relationship with the acquired entity.

Lack of goal congruence

This may apply not only to the acquired entity but, more dangerously, to the acquirer, whereby disputes over the treatment of the acquired entity might well take away the benefits of an otherwise excellent acquisition.

'Cheap' purchases

The 'turn around' costs of an acquisition purchased at what seems to be a bargain price may well turn out to be a high multiple of that price. In these situations, the amount of resources in terms of cash and management time could well also damage the acquirer's core business. In preparing a bid, a would-be acquirer should always take into account the likely total cost of an acquisition, including the input of its own resources, before deciding on making an offer or setting an offer price.

Paying too much

The fact that a high premium is paid for an acquisition does not necessarily mean that it will fail. Failure would result only if the price paid is beyond that which the acquirer considers acceptable to increase satisfactorily the long-term wealth of its shareholders.

Failure to integrate effectively

An acquirer needs to have a workable and clear plan of the extent to which the acquired company is to be integrated, and the amount of autonomy to be granted. At best, the plan should be negotiated with the acquired entity's management and staff, but its essential requirements should be fairly but firmly carried out. The plan must address such problems as differences in management styles, incompatibilities in data information systems, and continued opposition to the acquisition by some of the acquired entity's staff. Failure to plan can – and often does – lead to failure of an acquisition, as it leads to drift and demotivation, not only within the acquired entity but also within the acquirer itself.

Every aspect of a prospective acquisition, as it will affect the would-be acquirer, should be weighed up before embarking on a bid. Problems of integration have a much better chance of being resolved before bidding action is taken than they do after the event, when many more complications can ensue.

Even if a product fit is satisfactory, the would-be acquirer should be satisfied that the aspects of its own operation affected by the bid will be properly adaptable to the new activities. Running the rule carefully over one's own operations may yield vital information as to areas which may need adaptation before a bid can be contemplated, and provide vital clues to appropriate areas for search when a bid has actually been launched. One factor of special importance is a clear assessment of the flexibility of one's own information systems.

Inability to manage change

Several of the above points stress the need for an acquirer to plan effectively before and after an acquisition if failure is to be avoided. But this in itself calls for the ability to accept change – perhaps even radical change – from established routines and practices. Indeed, many acquisitions fail mainly because the acquirer is unable – or unwilling – reasonably to adjust its own activities to help ensure a smooth takeover. One such situation is where the acquired company has a demonstrably better data information system than the acquirer, which it might be greatly in the acquirer's interest to adopt.

3 Tax implications of mergers and acquisitions

Introduction

There are several tax implications of mergers and acquisitions:

- differences in tax rates and double tax treaties
- group loss relief
- withholding tax.

Differences in tax rates and double tax treaties

Different countries around the world have different tax rates. Therefore, if one company acquires another company based in a different country, there are likely to be different tax rates for the two companies in the group.

The OECD (Organisation for Economic Cooperation and Development) is an organisation of developed countries whose main purpose is to maintain financial stability and the expansion of world trade.

In order to help avoid double taxation between countries, the OECD has published a model Double Taxation Convention with an accompanying commentary.

Significance of the OECD model double tax treaty

Whenever a double tax treaty is drawn up between two countries (or an old treaty is renegotiated) the OECD model is used as a guide.

Detailed knowledge of specific treaties is not required in your examination.

The main function of any treaty is to avoid double taxation and to decide which country shall have the right to tax income.

Group loss relief

Members of a group of companies may surrender losses to other profitable group members for corresponding accounting periods.

Losses surrendered must be set against the claimant company's taxable total profits of a 'corresponding' accounting period.

(Note that in this context, a corresponding accounting period = any accounting period falling wholly or partly within the surrendering company's accounting period.)

Key considerations for group loss relief

Tax planning primarily seeks to ensure losses are used within the group to save the most tax. Accordingly, losses are first set against profits taxed at the highest rate.

Group relief is only available for losses and profits generated after a company joins a group. It is not possible to have group relief for preacquisition losses or to relieve preacquisition profits.

Group relief ceases to be available once arrangements are in place to sell the shares of a company. This will usually occur sometime before the actual legal sale of the shares.

Withholding tax

A withholding tax, also called a retention tax, is a government requirement for the payer of an item of income to withhold or deduct tax from the payment, and pay that tax to the government.

In the context of groups of companies, withholding taxes need to be considered when one company makes payments to another within the group (for example as dividends, or interest on loans).

Typically the withholding tax is treated as a payment on account of the recipient's final tax liability.

It may be refunded if it is determined, when a tax return is filed, that the recipient's tax liability to the government which received the withholding tax is less than the tax withheld, or additional tax may be due if it is determined that the recipient's tax liability is more than the withholding tax.

4 The role and scope of competition authorities

Introduction to competition authorities

During a takeover, it is important that the companies comply with relevant legislation and regulations.

Competition authorities monitor takeovers and mergers on behalf of national governments.

General principles

The role of the competition authorities varies from country to country but as a general rule their aims are:

- to strengthen competition
- to prevent or reduce anti-competitive activities
- to consider the public interest.

If the competition authorities find that a proposed merger or takeover is ant-competitive, they have the power to block the takeover completely, or to allow it to proceed subject to certain conditions being met (for example the combined entity might be required to sell off some of its retail outlets after the acquisition).

More detail on competition authorities

Many bids, because of their size, will require review by the competition authorities, and a limited number will subsequently be investigated if the authorities think that a merger might be anti-competitive or against the public interest.

Anti-competitive

An anti-competitive merger or acquisition can be defined as one that leads to a substantial lessening of competition or one that would significantly impede effective competition.

In many countries, 'anti-competitive' is deemed to be the creation of a new entity that will have 25% or more of the share of a market.

Public interest

To assess whether a merger or acquisition is in the 'public interest', the competition authorities will consider factors such as:

- National security (including security of energy and food supplies)
- Media quality
- Financial stability (e.g. protecting the stability of banks and financial services)

Investigations

Investigations may take several months to complete during which time the merger is put on hold, thus giving the target company valuable time to organise its defence. The acquirer may abandon its bid as it may not wish to become involved in a time consuming investigation.

The authorities may simply accept or reject the proposals or accept them subject to certain conditions.

Examples

In recent years, the competition authorities in the UK have investigated the several UK banking mergers and also mergers in the UK airport industry. BAA was told by the authorities in 2009 that it had to sell off three of its existing airports in order to open up the market.

In addition, if the offer gives rises to a concentration (i.e. a potential monopoly) within the EU, the European Commission may initiate proceedings. This can result in considerable delay, and constitutes grounds for abandoning a bid.

5 Divestment

Definition

Divestment: Disposal of part of its activities by an entity. (CIMA Official Terminology, 2005).

Reasons for divestment

The reasons for divestment include:

The sum of the parts of the entity may be worth more than the whole

As identified earlier in this chapter, businesses which combine will attempt to find areas where resources can be combined to generate synergy. However, it may be that a business with many disparate parts actually ends up suffering from the opposite effect. For example, the company could be spending a lot of money trying to integrate business units together where there are no apparent benefits.

In such situations, the divestment of part of the business should be considered.

Divesting unwanted or less profitable parts

If there is an underperforming business unit which fails to meet general company performance targets, divestment should be considered. The opportunity cost of holding onto the underperforming business unit could be very high.

However, management should always consider the effect of the divestment on the other parts of the company. For example, if a division is sold off which previously performed some work for other business units within the company, disposing of that business unit will lead to the other parts of the business having to buy in goods and services from third parties.

Strategic change (e.g. to shift the strategic focus onto the core activities)

A part of the business which operates in a different market sector from the rest of the group may be considered for divestment. Increased focus on the company's core activities should help to develop the expertise of management and staff, and the strength of the company's brand.

A response to crisis

In a crisis, when cash is needed quickly, a part of the business might be divested if an attractive offer is received.

The most common examples of divestments are sell offs (trade sales), spin offs and management buyouts.

More on divestment: Sell-offs and spin-offs

Sell-off (or trade sale)

A sell-off is the sale of part of an entity to a third party, usually in return for cash.

The most common reasons for a sell-off are:

* to divest of a less profitable business unit if an acceptable offer is received – this could be through a management buyout – see below;

* to protect the rest of the business from takeover – a part of the business which is attractive to a purchaser may be sold off to avoid the whole company being taken over;

* to generate cash in a time of crisis.

A sell-off may disrupt the rest of the organisation if key staff or products from within the organisation are part of the business unit sold off.

Spin-off (or demerger)

In a spin-off (or demerger) a new entity is created, where the shares of that new entity are owned by the shareholders of the entity that made the transfer of assets into the new entity. There are now two entities, each owning some of the assets of the original single entity. The ownership has not changed, and in theory the value of the two individual entities should be the same as the value of the original single entity.

Reasons for spin-offs

Spin-offs may be justified as follows

- they allow investors to identify the true value of a business that was hidden within a large conglomerate;

- they should lead to a clearer management structure;

- they reduce the risk of a takeover bid for the core entity.

6 Management buyouts

Definition

Definition of a management buyout (MBO): Purchase of a business from its existing owners by members of the management team, generally in association with a financing institution. (CIMA Official Terminology, 2005)

Overview of an MBO

In an MBO, the purchaser of the business is not another company (like in a sell-off / trade sale), but the existing management.

Usually the management provide some of the capital for the buyout, but the majority is provided by other financiers such as venture capitalists and financial institutions.

MBOs: Considerations for the divesting company

Members of the buyout team may possess detailed and confidential knowledge of other parts of the vendor's business and the vendor will therefore require satisfactory warranties over such aspects which it will not be able to control.

More seriously, key members of the MBO team may have skills vital to the vendor's operation, especially in regard to information services and networking.

A vendor may be reluctant to allow key players to end their contracts of service to take part in an MBO, because losing vital operational skills can hardly be compensated by forms of warranty.

MBOs: Considerations for the management team

Considerations before an MBO

MBOs are not dissimilar to other acquisitions and many of the factors to be considered will be the same.

- **Do the current owners wish to sell?** – The whole process will be much easier (and cheaper) if the current owners wish to sell. However, some MBOs have been concluded despite initial resistance from the current owners.

- **Potential of the business** – The management team engaged in the buyout will be making the switch from a relatively safe salaried position to a risky ownership position. They must, therefore, ensure that the victim business will be a long-run profit generator. This will involve analysing the performance of the business and drawing up a business plan (products, markets, required new investment, sources of finance, etc.) for future operations. Research shows that MBOs are less likely to fail than other types of new ventures, but several have collapsed, and managers must appreciate the risks they are taking and attempt to reduce them as far as possible.

- **Loss of head office support** – On becoming an independent firm many of the services that are taken for granted in a large organisation may be lost. The importance of these services varies from one industry to another but provision will have to be made for support in the areas of finance, computing, research and development, etc. Although head office fees might be saved, after the buyout these support services can involve considerable expense when purchased in the outside market.

- **Quality of the management team** – The success of any MBO will be greatly influenced by the quality of the management team. It is important to ensure that all functional areas (marketing, sales, production, finance) are represented and that all managers are prepared to take the required risks. A united approach is important in all negotiations and a clear responsibility structure should be established within the team.

- **The price** – As in any takeover situation the price paid will be crucial in determining the long-term success of the acquisition. The usual valuation techniques may be employed, often with more confidence as managers are likely to have a clearer idea of the future prospects of the firm. Care must be taken to ensure that all relevant aspects of the business are included in the package. For example, trademarks and patents may be as important as the physical assets of the firm. In a similar way, responsibilities for redundancy costs, etc. must be clearly defined.

Financing the MBO

In an MBO, unlike a corporate-backed takeover, the acquiring group usually lacks the financial resources to fund the acquisition.

For small buyouts the price may be within the capabilities of the management team, but it is unlikely that many managers could raise the large amounts involved in some buyouts.

Several institutions specialise in providing funds for MBOs. These include the following:

* venture capitalists;
* banks;
* private equity firms;
* other financial institutions.

Terminology: Leveraged buyout

A leveraged buyout occurs when an investor, typically a private equity firm, acquires a controlling interest in a company's equity and where a significant percentage of the purchase price is financed through leverage (borrowing).

Leveraged buyouts involve institutional investors and financial sponsors (like private equity firms) making large acquisitions without committing all the capital required for the acquisition.

The role of venture capitalists

Venture capitalists

Typically venture capitalists will be prepared to advance funds for five to ten years, and will expect annual returns on their funds of 25% or more.

The types of finance and the conditions attached vary between the institutions. Points to be considered include the following.

The form of finance – The management team will always want to keep at least 50% of the equity for themselves (a controlling stake), so this limits the amount of equity finance that can be raised from the venture capitalist. However, raising too much from the venture capitalist as debt finance can lead to an unacceptable rise in the level of gearing in the business (perhaps for example if the company has debt covenants which limit the gearing level).

Therefore, venture capitalists often provide their funds as a mix of equity and debt, in order to give themselves security (the debt) while allowing them to participate if things go well (the equity).

As a compromise, convertible preference shares are often used. This ensures that the venture capitalist can benefit in the longer term if the company is successful (by converting to equity) but in the short term the control stays with the management team and the gearing level is not adversely affected.

Exit strategy – The most important fact that any investing institution will want to know is how and when they will get their money back. The exit strategy is an important part of the agreement to advance money in the first place. Exit strategies are explained more fully later in this chapter.

The involvement of the institution – Some institutions may require board representation as a condition of providing funds.

Ongoing support – The management team should also consider the institution's willingness to provide funds for later expansion plans. Some investors also offer other services such as management consultancy to their clients.

The role of private equity firms

Private equity is sometimes confused with venture capital because both terms refer to firms that invest in companies and exit through selling their investments (often using methods such as initial public offerings (IPOs)).

However, there are major differences between private equity and venture capital firms.

Private equity firms mostly buy mature companies that are already established. The companies may be deteriorating or not making the profits they should be due to inefficiency. Private equity firms buy these companies and streamline operations to increase revenues. Venture capital firms, on the other hand, mostly invest in start-ups with high growth potential.

Private equity firms often buy 100% ownership of the companies in which they invest. As a result, the private equity firms are in total control of the company after the buyout. Venture capital firms invest in 50% or less of the equity of the companies.

Most venture capital firms prefer to spread out their risk and invest in many different companies. If one start-up fails, the entire fund in the venture capital firm is not affected substantially. By contrast, private equity firms prefer to concentrate all their efforts in a single company. Since they invest in already established and mature companies, the chances of absolute losses from such investments are minimal.

Details on financing MBOs

Financiers tend to favour established businesses with reliable cash flows (to pay down the debt) and a clear exit route.

They like definitive plans, but say they prefer them brief and to the point.

The emphasis should be on the competences of the team, and the market opportunity to be exploited, with detailed financial numbers (focussing on cash flow) put into an appendix. How services previously supplied by group departments, or fellow subsidiaries, will be replaced is likely to be a key item.

Managers will be required to invest some of their own money and this will take the form of shares with special features, for example a high proportion of any disposal value.

Suggested financial structure

Capital structures are inevitably complex, with several levels of risk/reward:

- **Secured borrowings** are usually obtained from a bank, with a first charge on the assets taken over by the venture.

- The provider of **senior debt** will require a first-ranking security over all the assets involved in the MBO venture and, usually, over the capital of the MBO as evidenced by shares in the new entity. Security will also involve undertakings from the MBO team regarding the provision of financial information and the setting of restrictions on the MBO's capacity to raise other debt finance and to dispose of assets.

- **Junior debt** is usually called mezzanine finance, which is an intermediate stage between senior debt and equity finance in relation to both risk and return. The return on mezzanine finance can comprise a mixture of debt interest and the ability to convert part of the debt into equity, perhaps by the conversion of warrants. By this means the lender can in time have a share in the premium resulting from eventual exit from the venture. The debt interest will carry a risk premium, as it is subordinate to the senior debt and with less security: it may even be unsecured.

- **Venture capital** is a form of equity provided mainly by institutional investors, whose reward will usually be in some form of dividends, probably preferential, combined with appreciation of their MBO equity holding which will build up a capital gain for when the investment is realised.

- The last link in the structural chain is the **equity holding granted to the MBO team** itself which, if their activities are successful, will provide a substantial capital gain when the venture is exited, either through flotation or by other means. Meanwhile, the MBO management will draw salaries or fees for their services.

MBOs: Considerations for the financiers

Key points for investors – usually banks or other institutions – in deciding whether to support an MBO are as follows:

- What is actually for sale, and why? It may be a division or subsidiary of an entity which no longer fits that entity's strategy, or it may be separable assets such as a factory or group of retail outlets.

- Whether the activities are profitable and enjoy a satisfactory cash flow. The prospective returns must justify the operational and financial risks involved. Profits must be sustainable and cash flow adequate to sustain the level of activities proposed.

- Whether the management is sufficiently strong. This point is particularly significant if the MBO relates to loss-making activities, although sufficient allowance must be made for the possibility that its existing owners may be burdening it with excessive overheads. Financial competence and marketing skills in the MBO's sector are especially important.

- Whether the price is reasonable and a sufficient contribution is being made by the managers. The managers should have some financial involvement and the future prospects for the new entity should be demonstrable, especially in a 'turn-around' situation.

These points are important as the main risks associated with MBOs, and hence the reasons why they may fail are:

- the bid price offered by the MBO team might be too high;

- a lack of experience in key areas such as financial management;

- a loss of key staff who either perceive the buyout as too risky, or do not have capital to invest;

- a lack of finance;

- problems in convincing employees and fellow colleagues of the need to change working practices or to accept redundancy.

Investors, probably institutions, backing the MBO will initially hold a majority of the equity, with a relatively small minority of shares held by the managers.

Although the backers must be prepared to hold their investment for the long term, they and the managers will be looking to the entity growing successfully to the point where it can be launched on the stock exchange. At this stage, a market value can be obtained for the equity and, if desired, some portion of the investment can be realised.

Where the backers desire a lower-risk element in their investment, they can require that some part of it will be in the form of redeemable convertible preference shares. This can give them priority in obtaining income through a preference dividend and preferential rights of repayment if the entity should fail. There is also the prospect of redemption if the entity does not develop satisfactorily, or conversely, the convertible aspect will allow backers eventually to increase their equity holding if the entity should prove successful.

7 Exit strategies

Overview of exit strategies

The investors and financiers in an MBO will want to realise a profit from their investment in the medium term.

Debt finance will normally have a specified repayment date, so the debt providers will have a clear exit route (assuming the borrowing company has performed in line with expectations and can afford to repay the debt as planned).

Exit strategies for equity holders

For the providers of equity, the exit route is not as easy to identify.

The most common exit route for an equity investor is the sale of the shares to another investor. This could be through one of the following methods:

Trade sale

If the MBO company receives an offer for all its shares from another company, the financiers will be able to realise their investment. However, in a trade sale, all the shares are normally acquired by the bidding company, so the management would have to sell their shares in their own company too. They may not be happy to do this, because the appeal of an MBO to managers is that they will own their own company rather than have to report to other shareholders.

IPO (Initial Public Offering)

An IPO or flotation on the stock market was introduced in the earlier chapter on 'Financing – Equity finance'.

An IPO gives the financiers who want to sell their shares the chance to do so on the stock market. If the managers want to keep hold of their shares, they will be able to do so.

The problem with an IPO is that the company will have to satisfy certain stringent criteria in order to join the stock exchange, and there will be significant costs associated with the listing.

After an IPO, the shares will be freely traded, which should increase their marketability and hence their value. On the other hand, the company becomes much more susceptible to takeover when its shares are listed.

Independent sale to another shareholder

The managers could try to increase their shareholdings in the company by 'buying out' the other financiers.

This would be expensive, but if the managers could afford it, it would prevent other external shareholders buying the shares and having a say in the running of the business.

8 End of chapter objective test questions

Test your understanding 3 (Objective test question)

BB is a listed company located in Country B. It is a retail clothing business which operates a large number of branded retail stores throughout Country B. Its functional currency is the B$. BB currently has five distinct brands, each owned and managed by a separate business unit. Each business unit runs its own chain of retail stores. BB is seeking to sell QQ, one of these business units, in a management buyout.

A selling price of B$ 450 million has been agreed. It is anticipated that the effective date of the disposal will be 1 July 20X4.

The managers of QQ have been in discussions with a bank and a venture capitalist regarding the financing for the MBO. The proposal is that the managers will put in B$45 million of equity, and the venture capitalist B$180 million (for class B equity shares with limited voting rights). Then the venture capitalist and the bank will each invest B$112.5 million as debt finance.

The venture capitalist expects a return on the equity portion of its investment of at least 25% a year on a compound basis over the first 4 years of the MBO. No dividends are to be paid during this period.

What is the minimum total equity value of QQ on 30 June 20X8 required in order to satisfy the venture capitalist's expected return?

A   B$225.0 million

B   B$360.0 million

C   B$439.5 million

D   B$549.3 million

Test your understanding 4 (Objective test question)

The directors of a company are considering whether to dispose of one of its subsidiaries.

The directors of the subsidiary are interested in a management buy-out.

There is a potential conflict of interest if, during the negotiation phase of the management buy-out, the directors of the subsidiary company were to:

A   Lease some new vehicles to update the company's distribution facilities

B   Accept projects with high net present values

C   Perform a revaluation of assets

D   Employ more staff in the subsidiary's administration office

Test your understanding 5 (Objective test question)

Stan Co is a large multinational company. It has operations in several markets (including clothing, food and furniture) and geographical locations. Although Stan Co was originally a manufacturing company, it has expanded its operations into distribution and retailing in recent years.

The directors of Stan Co have decided to acquire the entire share capital of Ball Co, a small company that brews beer and sells it through its own network of bars.

What sort of business combination is this?

A   Vertical integration

B   Horizontal integration

C   A conglomerate

D   A management buyout

Test your understanding 6 (Objective test question)

NN sells electrical goods and operates a number of retail outlets in a particular region of the country. NN is in the process of acquiring the share capital of QQ, a company that sells the same type of products in the same region of the country through its own retail stores. Post-acquisition NN would be the largest retailer of electrical goods in that region. NN and QQ have perfectly positively correlated cash flow streams because they operate in the same market sector and location.

Which THREE of the following would be most likely to be synergistic benefits to NN of purchasing QQ?

A   Cash benefit by sale and leaseback of retail store property acquired

B   Increased sales due to owning a larger portfolio of retail outlets

C   Increased profit due to reduced competition in the region

D   Reduction in staff costs due to elimination of duplicated administrative roles

E   Cost savings due to economies of scale in purchasing activities

Test your understanding 7 (Objective test question)

The directors of GG Co have decided to sell off one of the company's subsidiaries, HH Co, for $100 million.

The managers of HH Co are keen to set up a management buyout in order to take control of their company.

They have proposed the following financing package, after lengthy discussions with bankers and venture capitalists:

	$ million
Equity invested by managers ($1 'A' shares carrying 1 vote each)	10
Equity invested by venture capitalist ($1 'B' shares carrying 1 vote for every 10 shares)	30
Borrowing from venture capitalist – unsecured, 10% interest rate, redeemable in five years	30
Borrowing from bank – secured, 6% interest rate, redeemable in five years	30
TOTAL	**100**

Which THREE of the following statements about the financing package are false?

A   The managers own enough of the equity to enable them to vote and carry decisions in a general meeting

B   The venture capitalists own enough of the equity to prevent the managers from voting and carrying decisions in a general meeting

C   If HH Co were to go into liquidation, the bank borrowing would take priority over all the other sources of finance

D   The bank borrowing interest rate is lower than that on the borrowing from the venture capitalists because the bank borrowing is a mezzanine loan

E   If HH Co were to go into liquidation, the borrowing from the venture capitalists would take priority over all the other sources of finance

Test your understanding 8 (Objective test question)

Which THREE of the following reasons are often stated as valid justification for an acquisition, in that they help to increase shareholder wealth?

A   Diversification of risk

B   Reduction of competition

C   Big data opportunities

D   Better career prospects for directors

E   Asset stripping

Test your understanding 9 (Objective test question)

The directors of Hood Group have decided to sell off a loss-making subsidiary, Tucker Co. A management team from Tucker Co has expressed an interest in buying the company.

For which one of the following reasons would the parent company be likely to agree to sell Tucker Co to the management team rather than an external buyer, if the MBO team and the external buyer have both offered the same price?

A   To avoid redundancy costs

B   To avoid non-cooperation from management and employees hostile to the divestment

C   Because the MBO team knows more about the company than the external buyer

D   To raise the cash more quickly

9 End of chapter case style questions

Country T and Country V are separated by sea but linked by a rail tunnel. They have different currencies (T$ and V$ respectively) but are part of the same Trade Group which promotes free trade between its members and has authority over membership countries in matters relating to competition.

TNL is a public listed company, based in Country T, which owns and operates the rail link between Country T and Country V. Trains that travel through the tunnel carry passengers, cars and other vehicles such as trucks.

TNL was first listed on 1 June 20X4 by offer for sale of 100 million ordinary shares to the public at a price of T$ 3.70. Today, 21 November 20Y3, the share price is just T$ 2.95. The fall in the share price since 20X4 is largely the result of disappointing growth and market concerns about TNL's ability to renegotiate bank borrowings that are shortly due for repayment. The ordinary shares are held by a large number of individual shareholders as well as by large institutions and pension funds. The number of shares in issue remains unchanged since 20X4.

Debt funding is in the form of bank borrowings from a consortium of 10 banks to a total principal value of T$ 190 million. The borrowings were taken out on 1 June 20X4 and have a 10 year term. New borrowings are currently being negotiated to finance the repayment of the original borrowings on 1 June 20Y4.

There is strong price competition between TNL and two independent ferry companies, TT and VV which are based in Countries T and V respectively. Prices are generally low for travel by ferry since ferries are less convenient as they operate less frequently and have longer journey times than the rail tunnel link. TT has incurred losses in the past two years.

The board of TNL has approached ferry company TT with a view to acquiring it. The directors of TT are opposed to the bid and have referred the bid to the regional competition authorities of both Country T and the Trade Group.

Required:

Discuss the possible reasons why TNL may wish to acquire TT, and explain:

- Why the competition authorities in Country T and in the Trade Group might be concerned about the proposed acquisition.

- The possible actions that the competition authorities could take and the implications of these for TNL.

(30 minutes)

Advise TNL on:

- The factors that the banks are likely to consider when deciding whether or not to renew the loans made to TNL.

- Other appropriate sources of finance that should be considered.

(30 minutes)

Test your understanding 11 (Case style question)

Country Y

Country Y is a large industrialised country with strong motor vehicle and construction industries. The glass industry supplies glass to these industries as well as to specialist users of glass such as contact lens manufacturers. There are five major glass manufacturing entities, each with market coverage in Country Y of between 5% and 40%.

Entity Q

Entity Q is a quoted entity and a major player in the glass industry. It has a market share in Country Y of approximately 35%. It is an old, well-established entity with a number of factories used to manufacture glass both locally and abroad. It has a stable, but unexciting, growth rate of 3% per annum and is facing increasing competition from new glass manufacturing entities setting up in its key markets. However, Q's high earnings levels of earlier years have resulted in relatively low levels of debt.

The head office building of Q is in the far north of Country Y in a remote geographical area. It is a considerable distance from the capital city and major centres of population in the south of the country. The building is much larger than the entity requires and several floors are unoccupied.

The management team of Q is highly experienced; the majority of the senior managers have worked for Q for the whole of their working lives.

The computer systems of Q were written especially for the entity, but are in need of replacement in favour of something more flexible and adaptable to changing circumstances.

Entity Z

Entity Z, with a market share in Country Y of 10%, is a comparatively new and small, but fast growing unquoted family-owned entity. It specialises in certain niche markets for high security and extra heat-resistant glass. The patents for this specialist glass were developed by the founder owner who now acts as Managing Director. The development of the business has largely been funded by high levels of borrowings at rates of interest well above standard market rates. In addition, the directors have often been required to provide personal guarantees against personal assets.

The management team of Z works in the capital city of Country Y, which is in the more prosperous southern part of the country. Z has a manufacturing base on the outskirts of the capital city.

The management team of Z is enthusiastic to grow the business, but is continually frustrated by a lack of financial and human resources and marketing network that would enable Z to expand into international markets. Also, on a personal level, many of the senior managers own a substantial number of shares in Z and are keen to realise some of their capital gains and become financially more secure.

The computer systems of Z consist of a basic accounting package and an internal network of PCs. Spreadsheet packages are widely used for budgeting and other financial reporting.

Takeover bid

The directors of Q have approached the directors of Z with a view to making a takeover bid for Z. A condition of the bid would be the retention of the current management team of Z, who have vital knowledge of the specialist manufacturing techniques required to manufacture the product range of Z. The directors of Z have been initially quite positive about the bid.

Both parties are concerned that the deal may be referred to Country Y's Competition Directorate, which regulates the country's competition policy, for approval and that conditions may be imposed that could make the takeover less attractive.

Required:

(a) Explain the role of competition authorities such as Country Y's Competition Directorate.

(15 minutes)

(b) Advise the directors of Q and Z on the potential problems of merging the management structure and systems of the two entities and how these could be minimised.

(15 minutes)

(c) Discuss whether the choice of capital structure for the new combined entity is likely to affect the overall value of the entity. Include references to Modigliani and Miller's (M & M's) theory of capital structure in your answer.

(30 minutes)

Test your understanding answers

Test your understanding 1 (Integration question)

Big Data management involves using sophisticated systems to gather, store and analyse large volumes of data in a variety of structured and unstructured formats. Companies are collecting increasing volumes of data through everyday transactions and marketing activity. If managed effectively this can lead to many business benefits although there are risks involved.

If MONEY acquires CASH it will get access to a significant amount of new data regarding a potentially brand new customer base. MONEY needs to consider whether this new data is going to be manageable and whether it will provide useful information.

If, following the acquisition, the two companies are going to continue to be managed as completely separate entities then it may be complicated to integrate the systems to be able to perform sophisticated analysis across the two sets of data. MONEY therefore need to be clear what the objective of such analysis may be and whether the business benefits make it worthwhile.

MONEY would need more information on the current customer base of CASH to identify if there are any likely cross-selling opportunities. Although CASH provides loans to small businesses and start-ups, it is quite possible that some of these companies will have entrepreneurs in control who will be high net worth individuals, if not now then at some point in the future. Having access to information about such individuals can allow MONEY to produce more targeted marketing activity and increase its client base relatively easily. This can work both ways as CASH can identify from MONEY's clients possible lending opportunities as some of these clients are likely to be business owners.

If the two companies are concerned that their individual clients may not like being targeted by other companies, another option is to use the data available to expand the product range for each entity. So MONEY could offer its clients an increased range of borrowing options and CASH could offer its clients investment advice.

Test your understanding 2 (Case style question)

- Operating efficiencies – the unused capacity at GSL can be used to produce Williams' products without adding to costs and capacity.

- Marketing synergies.

- If the cash flow streams of Williams and GSL are not perfectly positively correlated then by acquiring GSL – Williams may reduce the variability of their operating cash flow. This being more attractive to investors may lead to cheaper financing.

- The 'dedicated' herbalists of GSL and the R+D staff of Williams may be a complementary resource.

- Fixed operating and administrative costs savings.

- Consolidation of manufacturing capacity on fewer and larger sites.

- There may be bulk buying discounts.

- Possibility of joint advertising and distribution.

- GSL is badly managed – thus the elimination of inefficiency could allow for financial synergy.

Test your understanding 3 (Objective test question)

The answer is (D).

The VC is making a B$ 180 million equity investment. To generate a return of 25% a year on a compound basis this investment will need to grow to B$ 439.5 million (= B$ 180 million × $(1.25)^4$) at the end of 4 years.

The VC investment represents 80% (= 180/(180+45) × 100%) of the equity, therefore the total equity value will need to be B$ 549.3 million (= B$ 439.5 million / 0.80).

Test your understanding 4 (Objective test question)

The answer is (C)

All the other decisions are ones that would be perfectly acceptable in the normal course of business.

The value of the subsidiary's assets is likely to be a key issue when determining the consideration to be paid in the MBO, so revaluing assets could be contentious.

Test your understanding 5 (Objective test question)

The answer is (C).

The two businesses seem to have very little in common, so the combination would be referred to as a conglomerate.

Test your understanding 6 (Objective test question)

The answer is (C), (D) and (E).

The two businesses operate in the same region so combining them should lead to an opportunity to combine administrative roles (D), make more profit due to less competition (C) and wield greater purchasing power over suppliers (E).

Test your understanding 7 (Objective test question)

The answer is (B), (D) and (E).

The managers do own enough of the equity to enable them to vote and carry decisions in a general meeting; they have 10 million votes and the venture capitalists have 3 million votes (A).

If HH Co were to go into liquidation, the **secured** bank borrowing would take priority (C).

Test your understanding 8 (Objective test question)

The answer is (B), (C) and (E).

Diversification of risk (A) can be done more effectively by investors rather than companies.

Directors should only undertake acquisitions if there are benefits to shareholders, rather than considering their own career prospects (D).

Test your understanding 9 (Objective test question)

The answer is (B).

When an MBO team wants to buy a company, they will almost certainly be reluctant to co-operate with the sale to an outside buyer.

Although the MBO team will know more about the company than an outside buyer (C) this is not a matter of direct concern to the selling company.

Since the parent company has two potential buyers, avoiding redundancy costs (A) is not an issue either. Either purchaser would have to consider the need for redundancies after the takeover. There would be no cost to the parent.

There is no particular reason why a sale to an MBO team would be quicker than a sale to an external purchaser (D).

Test your understanding 10 (Case style question)

Answer to the first task

TNL may wish to acquire TT in order to:

- Gain economies of scale/synergistic benefits. For example, TNL and TT could share the same booking internet site.

- Increase market power. By offering ferry services as well as rail services, TNL will have increased influence over ferry prices in addition to rail prices. This increase in power could be used to its advantage.

- Increase customer loyalty. Marketing promotions (e.g. frequent traveller schemes) could be shared across TNL and TT, reducing marketing costs and increasing customer loyalty and convenience by offering a 'one-stop' shop for both rail and ferry tickets.

- Increase market share through cross subsidies or a price war. TNL could offer rail link passenger reduced cost ferry tickets or cross subsidise the ferry business by reducing fares for the ferries (financed by higher priced rail link tickets) in order to build its market share of the ferry business. TNL could use a price war in the ferry business to build market share and destroy competition, funding by profits from the rail link business.

- Obtain tax relief. TNL may be able to make use of tax losses incurred by TT by offsetting losses against any profits in TNL.

Competition authorities intervene where it is considered that the bid would have a serious effect on competition in the market by giving significant market power to a particular market participant or where the bid is contrary to public interest.

The competition authorities of the Trade Grouping would be particularly interested due to the reduction in competition that would arise in a key communication link between two countries in the Union. Country T's competition authorities may be less concerned as the move would give Country T a competitive advantage over Country V.

In this case, there is a high risk to TNL that the competition authorities find grounds to investigate the proposed acquisition further. If TNL were to own all ferry and rail links from Country T, it could be in a position to control prices and affect competition It already has a monopoly position in respect of the rail link and it may not be considered in the public interest to also allow TNL to acquire significant control over the ferry operation. For example, it could raise prices for rail link passengers and cross-subsidise the ferry business in an attempt to put VV out of business.

Whatever the final result, referring the bid to the regulatory authorities can be expected to significantly delay the bid and create uncertainty and costs for TNL at this key time when it needs to renegotiate bank borrowings. If they decide to intervene, the regulatory authorities would have the power to either prevent the acquisition going ahead or impose certain conditions on TNL. Such conditions might include, for example, price constraints or a requirement to operate the ferries from a port that is not so close to the rail link tunnel.

Answer to the second task

Issues that the banks are likely to consider:

- How will TNL pay back the original borrowings if the banks do not agree to renew the loans? Would the banks be likely to get any money back anyway?

- To what extent would the referral to the competition authorities affect TNL – for example, what price controls might be imposed and how would that affect TNL's profitability?

- What is the likely impact on TNL's future results of acquiring TT? Would it be likely, in practice, to realise synergistic benefits from the acquisition?

- Can TNL afford to buy TT; how would it be financed? Given that it is likely to be a hostile bid then TNL will need to pay a significant premium for TT.

- TNL's latest long term cash forecast and the sensitivity of cash flow to other possible government intervention (e.g. green taxes) or market prices (e.g. fuel and exchange rates, especially regarding V$ costs and V$ selling prices (regarding sales within Country V)).

- How do the credit ratings agencies view TNL? Have they put TNL on 'Negative outlook' to indicate the possibility of a downgrade in the next few months. How should this impact on the banks' willingness to lend and on the interest rate offered?

- Deterioration in gearing levels – and hence risk.

    - Gearing on 1 June 20X4: 34% (= 190/(190 + 370))

    - Current gearing: 39% (= 190/(295 + 190))

- Management reputation – has the original team left? What is the background and reputation of the current team?

- Impact of government assistance. If the tunnel is seen as strategically important for the Country might the Government step in and provide support to TNL. This would reduce the banks' risk.

Other sources of finance:

Rights issue

TNL may have to ask shareholders for cash by means of a rights issue if banks are unwilling to renew borrowings. However, investors may not be willing to invest additional sums of money in a company that has seen such a decline in the value of its shares in the last 10 years.

If the banks are unwilling or unable to rollover the borrowings, it is likely to be very difficult for TNL to be able to obtain finance from other sources such as, for example, bonds, because of its poor credit worthiness. Indeed, TNL may have no choice but to ask shareholders for cash by means of a rights issue if banks are unwilling to renew the bank borrowings.

Under a rights issue:

- Shareholders would be given the right to buy additional shares in proportion to their existing shareholding at a discount to the current share price.

- The share price is likely to fall, largely as a result of the discount.

However, a rights issue is a risky option in this case since the cash would be used to repay debt. Shareholders prefer to subscribe new capital to finance new projects and hence promote future growth and returns. Shareholders may not be willing to help finance the repayment of debt, especially since they have already seen their previous investment in TNL lose value.

The size of the rights issue could also be a problem – at a 20% discount shares would be issued at T$ 2.36 per share before taking issue costs into account. This equates to 80.5 million shares which is an 80.5% increase in the number of shares currently in issue. At this scale it is unlikely that any rights issue would be wholly successful.
Even if the company were highly successful, shareholders may not have the funds or may be unwilling to make the additional investment.

Equity is more costly to service than debt and could lead to a reduction in the value of the company due to the loss of the tax benefit on debt interest.

Government funding

If the business is seen as key to Country T's trade position, then the government may be prepared to step in and offer funding as a last resort rather than see the company fail and the rail link cease to operate. This would result in conditions being imposed on TNL which might restrict its operations and future development.

Test your understanding 11 (Case style question)

(a) The Competition Directorate is a government-run or funded body which aims to protect competition within the local marketplace. Its brief will vary from country to country, but a Competition Directorate should consider the following issues:

– Whether a merger or acquisition is in the public interest. For example, there may be a policy to prevent all reservoirs being under one body for security reasons;

– Whether there would be substantial lessening of competition, leading to the risk of price setting and less competitive pricing so that the consumer is forced to pay an inflated price for goods or services;

– The ability to measure whether competition is still operating and prices set fairly after the merger has taken place. For example, for public utilities, there needs to be a sufficiently large number of utility entities to enable the regulator to compare prices with other entities in the same market.

(b) **Potential problems in merging the management structures and how to minimise them**

Potential problems that could be raised include the following:

- The importance of retaining the current management team. This is key to the success of the merger and plans to develop the business of Z;

- Different locations (opposing ends of the country);

- Spare capacity in the office building in the north of the country, but the management team of Z may well not be willing to move out of the capital. On the other hand, moving the management of Q down to the capital would result in an expensive empty office block in the north that may stand empty and, cost aside, there may not be a suitable office building to house the combined entity in or near to the capital city.

Possible solutions:

- Offer the current management team an attractive salary package;

- Obtain guarantees backed by financial incentives for management to stay with the business;

- Determine which key employees and managers are willing to relocate and which operations need to be centralised and then identifies the lowest cost solution.

Potential problems in merging the systems and how to minimise them

Potential problems include:

- Completely different type of systems at present: PC network for Z and bespoke system for Q. It is unlikely that Q could operate on a network of PCs and the transition would, in any case, be very problematic. On the other hand, it is unlikely that the different nature of the business of Z would fit well into the bespoke system that Q operates.

Possible solution:

- The management may need to agree to run the systems independently and build an effective interface.

(c) Under M & M, capital structure is irrelevant if you ignore taxes. However, if tax is included, debt becomes cheaper because of the tax shield and the value of the entity therefore increases as the proportion of debt increases. After a certain point, the entity reaches its debt capacity. That is, the level of debt at which there is a high risk of financial distress and both lenders and shareholders demand increased returns to compensate for the higher levels of risk.

From the information provided in the question, it would appear that Q is currently borrowing at levels well below its debt capacity and would therefore increase the value of the entity by taking on a higher proportion of debt.

Similarly, Z could well be borrowing in excess of its debt capacity and so its value would be enhanced by reducing the proportion of debt on its statement of financial position.

It is therefore highly likely that both entities would benefit from the improved capital structure that would result from a merger or takeover if Q were to fund the takeover of Z using debt or were to acquire Z together with its high levels of debt.

Business valuation

Chapter learning objectives

Lead	Component
C2: Evaluate the value of entities.	(a) Calculate the value of a whole entity (quoted or unquoted), a subsidiary entity or division using a range of methods including taxation
	(b) Evaluate the validity of the valuation methods used and the results obtained in the context of a given scenario

Indicative syllabus content

- Asset valuation (e.g. historic cost, replacement cost and realisable value).

- Forms of intangible asset (including intellectual property rights, brands etc.) and methods of valuation.

- Share prices (quoted on stock market or private sale for non-quoted entities).

- Earnings valuation (e.g. price/earnings multiples and earnings yield).

- Dividend valuation (e.g. dividend growth model, including estimating growth from past or forecast figures and including non-constant growth assumptions).

- Discounted free cash flow valuation (including taxation, risk-adjusted discount rate, foreign currency cash flows and sensitivity analysis).

- Ideas of diversifiable risk (unsystematic risk) and systematic risk.

- Capital asset pricing model (CAPM), including the meaning and derivation of the component and, the ability to gear and un-gear betas.

- Calculation of an appropriate cost of capital for use in discounted cash flow analysis (e.g. cost of equity or WACC) by reference to the nature of the transaction (e.g. division or an entire entity), including use of CAPM, dividend valuation model and MM WACC formula.

- Efficient market hypothesis and its relevance for the valuation of quoted entities.

- Impact of government incentives on entity value (e.g. capital or revenue grants).

- Strengths and weaknesses of each valuation method.

- Validity of the results for use in decision making according to the nature of the target entity (e.g. a division, a whole entity, quoted or unquoted).

1 Overview of chapter

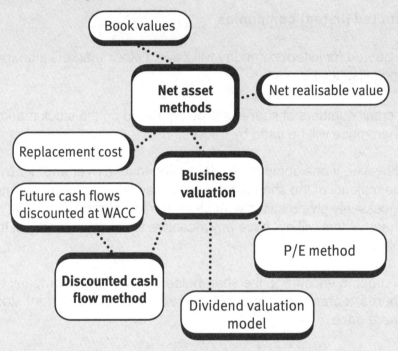

2 Introduction to business valuation

Business valuation is not a precise, scientific process. The value of a business is affected by:

- reported sales, profits and asset values
- forecast sales, profits and asset values
- type of industry
- level of competition
- range of products sold
- breadth of customer base
- perspective – the buyer and the seller will often have different expectations and hence may value the business differently.

The valuation methods covered in this chapter give suggested values of a business.

The final value is then agreed between buyer and seller after a process of negotiation.

Valuation of quoted and unquoted companies

Quoted (listed) companies

A quoted (or listed) company will have a stock market value (or market capitalisation).

If small numbers of shares are being traded on the stock market, this share price will be used by traders.

However, if one company is attempting to take over another by acquiring the majority of the shares, the market capitalisation value will not necessarily give a suitable value for the transaction, since the shareholders will not have any incentive to sell their shares at the current market price.

In order to encourage the shareholders in the target company to sell their shares, a premium is normally offered on top of the current stock market share price.

In conclusion, when valuing a listed company, the current stock market share price should be used as a starting point for the calculations rather than as a definitive final figure.

Unquoted (unlisted) companies

An unquoted (or unlisted) company has no stock market value. Also, there is likely to be less published information available which might help a purchaser to assess the value of an unlisted company. Unless there has been a recent private sale of the company's shares for a known value, the valuation process for an unlisted company is usually quite complex.

When valuing an unlisted company, estimates often have to be made, based on available information taken from similar listed companies ('proxy' companies).

The valuation methods shown below often value unlisted companies using data derived from proxy listed companies e.g. cost of equity, beta, dividend yield, P/E ratio.

In practice, it can be difficult to find a similar listed company.

The final answer may have to be discounted by 25% to 35% to account for:

- relative lack of marketability of unquoted shares – it is more difficult for investors to sell their shares if the company is not listed

- lower levels of scrutiny, therefore greater risk of poor quality financial information.

- higher risk of being a smaller, less well-regarded company with, possibly, a more volatile earnings record.

3 The different valuation methods

There are three basic ways of valuing a business:

Asset based valuation method

The business's assets form the basis for the valuation. Asset based valuation methods are difficult to apply to businesses with high levels of intangible assets, but this chapter covers methods of valuing intangible as well as tangible assets.

Earnings based valuation method

The projected earnings for a business will give an indication of the value of that business. For example, a business with high forecasted earnings will be attractive to a potential purchaser, and hence will be valued highly. In this chapter, we shall see how earnings can be used in business valuation.

Cash flow based methods

In theory, a business's value should be equal to the present value of its future cash flows, discounted at an appropriate cost of capital. This chapter explains how to identify and forecast future cash flows, and how to choose an appropriate discount rate.

Specifically, we shall see how the dividend valuation model can be used to value the business based on its expected dividend payments, and a discounted cash flow approach can be used to value the overall cash flows of the business.

When should each method be used?

Although the most important thing is to know how to use the various methods to calculate values, it is also necessary to understand the circumstances in which each is most appropriate.

For example asset-based valuations have very limited relevance for entities which are going concerns especially if they have substantial intangible assets.

In each of the following sections, the various valuation methods are explained together with the circumstances in which they might be most appropriate.

4 Asset based valuation

In this method the company is viewed as being worth the sum of the value of its assets.

Remember to deduct borrowings when arriving at an asset value if just the equity is being acquired, but not if only the physical assets and related liabilities are being purchased without acquiring any liability for the borrowings.

An asset based valuation is most useful when a company is being broken up, rather than purchased as a going concern. Since the method does not incorporate the valuation of intangible assets, it usually gives a low valuation figure, which helps the parties to set a minimum price in a takeover situation.

Asset valuations are therefore likely to be more useful for capital-intensive businesses, than for service businesses, where many of the assets are intangible.

Alternative asset valuation bases

The asset valuation can be calculated in various ways:

Book value

This method suffers from being largely a function of depreciation policy, for example, some assets may be written down prematurely and others carried at values well above their real worth. Original costs may be of little use if assets are very old, or if asset replacement has been irregular over time.

Thus, this method is of little use in practice.

Replacement value

This method calculates the cost of replacing the business's assets, which may be relevant if the assets are going to be used on an on-going basis, or if the bidder wants to estimate the minimum price that would have to be paid to buy the assets and set up a similar business from scratch (especially if an estimate of intangible value can be added on).

Break-up value / Net realisable value

Individual assets are valued at the best price obtainable, which will depend partly on the second-hand market and partly on the urgency of realising the asset.

This method can be used to set a minimum selling price for the vendors, as they could liquidate the business as an alternative to selling the shares.

The strengths and weaknesses of asset based valuations

The main strengths of asset-based valuations are:

*   the valuations are fairly readily available;
*   they provide a minimum value of the entity.

The main weaknesses of asset-based valuations are:

*   future profitability expectations are ignored;
*   statement of financial position valuations depend on accounting conventions, which may lead to valuations that are very different from market valuations;
*   it is difficult to allow for the value of intangible assets such as intellectual property rights.

More detail on asset based valuation

An asset based valuation method for a listed company will usually give a value considerably lower than the market value of all the company's shares (the market capitalisation value).

So it should be obvious that shareholders/the market does not value the company on the basis of the statement of financial position's assets.

Shareholders are not buying the company for its assets but for the income those assets can produce.

This future income is generated from the use of the statement of financial position assets together with the intangible assets like highly skilled workforce, strong management team and competitive positioning of the company's products.

Thus assets in the crude sense of statement of financial position values are only one dimension of a company's overall value (in a normal going concern situation).

Test your understanding 1 (Integration question)

The summarised balance sheet (statement of financial position) of Owen at 31 December 20X7 is as follows:

Assets	$000
Non-current assets	23,600
Current assets	8,400
	32,000

Equity and liabilities	
Capital and reserves	
$1 Ordinary shares	8,000
Retained earnings	11,200
	19,200
Non-current liabilities	
6% Unsecured bond	8,000
Current liabilities	4,800
	32,000

Required:

Calculate the value of one ordinary share in Owen, using an asset based valuation method.

Fowler is wanting to make a bid for Owen.

It has estimated that the replacement cost of Owen's non-current assets is $40 million.

Required:

Calculate the value of a share in Owen from Fowler's perspective.

Test your understanding 2 (Integration question)

Ray plc, a UK listed manufacturing company, is considering a takeover bid for Ribbon Ltd, a smaller, unlisted company in the same industry.

Ribbon Ltd has been making losses in the last 2 years, so it is considered that an asset based method should be used to value the business.

Extracts from Ribbon Ltd's Statement of Financial Position

Assets	GBP000
Non-current assets (Note 1)	1,207
Current assets (Note 2)	564
	1,771
Equity and liabilities	
Capital and reserves	
GBP1 Ordinary shares	100
Retained earnings	553
	653
Non-current liabilities	
5% bonds	600
Current liabilities	518
	1,771

Note 1: The non-current assets comprise specialised manufacturing equipment. To replace the equipment would cost GBP1.5m, but if Ribbon Ltd were to be closed down, the assets would sell for no more than GBP1m.

Note 2: Receivables contain an amount of GBP120,000 from a large customer which has just gone into liquidation. A contract for the same customer, included in work in progress (inventory) at a value of GBP30,000 will now have to be scrapped.

Required:

Calculate the expected valuation of Ribbon Ltd, from the perspective of Ray plc. Explain and justify your figures.

5 Valuation of intellectual capital / intangible assets

Definition of intellectual capital

The term 'intellectual capital' has many complex connotations and is often used synonymously with intellectual property, intellectual assets and knowledge assets.

Intellectual capital can be thought of as the total stock of capital or knowledge-based equity that the entity possesses. As such, intellectual capital can be both the end result of a knowledge transformation process or the knowledge itself that is transformed into intellectual property or intellectual assets of the firm.

Intellectual capital includes:

- Human resources – The collective skills, experience and knowledge of employees

- Intellectual assets – Knowledge which is defined and codified such as drawing, computer program or collection of data

- Intellectual property – Intellectual assets which can be legally protected such as patents and copyrights.

Brands

Intellectual property is legally defined and assigns property rights to such things as patents, trademarks and copyrights.

These assets are the only form of intellectual capital that is regularly recognised for accounting purposes.

However, accounting conventions based upon historical costs often understate their value.

Valuation of intellectual capital / intangible assets

It is recognised that goodwill, brands and other intellectual capital (intangible assets) often have a significant value. Indeed often intellectual capital is the main contributor of value to an entity.

The asset based methods covered above do not incorporate this value.

There are two ways of valuing the intangible assets of an entity:

(1) **Simple estimate:**

Value of intangibles =

Value of equity (either using a quoted market capitalisation or using one of the earnings based methods below i.e. DVM, P/E method, or PV of future cash flows)

minus

Value of the tangible assets (see Asset Valuation above)

(2) **Calculated Intangible Value (CIV) method:**

The Calculated Intangible Value (CIV) method of company valuation has been developed to estimate the value of a company's intellectual capital (in other words the value of the intangible assets that do not appear in a company's statement of financial position). Therefore it is an advance on the basic asset valuation.

The CIV method is based on a comparison of the total return that the company is producing against the return that would be expected based on industry average returns on tangible assets. Any additional return is assumed to be the return on intangible assets.

This additional return is assumed to continue in perpetuity and can be converted into a present day value for intangibles (the Calculated Intangible Value, or CIV) by discounting at the company's cost of capital.

The value of intangible assets thus calculated is then added to the value of the tangible assets of the business to generate a total value.

i.e. Total value of the entity = Value of tangible assets + CIV

CIV is an adaption of the asset valuation method and suffers from the same drawback as the basic asset valuation method, in that it is based on historical figures. unlike DCF valuations which look forward into the future and are based on forecast future outcomes when valuing a going concern.

Other drawbacks of CIV include:

- CIV assumes future growth in income from intangibles will be constant at the cost of capital.

- CIV is based on profit rather than cash flow.

- CIV is based on an industry average return which might not be representative of the company being valued.

Illustration of the CIV calculation (Objective test question)

UUU Co is a financial services company based in the USA.

It reported a profit before tax in the most recent financial year of USD 28.5 million, and the value of its tangible assets is USD 210 million.

The average return on tangible assets for firms in the financial services industry is 9%. The tax rate is 25% and UUU Co's cost of capital is 14%.

What is the value of UUU Co using the CIV approach?

A   USD 51.4 million

B   USD 217.2 million

C   USD 238.5 million

D   USD 261.4 million

Solution:

The answer is (D).

Workings:

		USDm
Current pre-tax profit		28.5
Less: Industry ROA × Tangible assets	9% × 210m	(18.9)
Excess annual return (pre-tax)		9.6
Post-tax excess annual return	9.6m × (1–0.25)	7.2
CIV (assuming constant perpetuity)	7.2m × 1/0.14	51.4

Therefore, the total value of UUU Co is estimated to be

210m + 51.4m = USD 261.4m

Test your understanding 3 (Objective test question)

Chapman Co has just reported a pre-tax profit of $24.29m, and the value of its tangible assets in its statement of financial position is $128.66m.

The average return on assets for companies in the same industry is 10%.

The tax rate is 30% and Chapman Co's cost of capital is 16%.

What is the value of Chapman Co using the CIV approach?

A $179m

B $153m

C $137m

D $50m

6 Earnings based valuations

Introduction

In an earnings based valuation, the earnings of the business are forecasted and then an 'earnings multiple' is applied.

This earnings multiple could simply be a number negotiated between buyer and seller (e.g. a business could be valued at 3 times earnings), or it could be a perpetuity factor based on a suitable cost of capital. In this latter case, the earnings forecast is being taken as an approximation of cash flow and effectively a discounted cash flow approach is being used (see more details later in the chapter).

The most commonly used approach is to take a suitable P/E ratio as the earnings multiple.

P/E valuation method

The P/E valuation method is a very simple method which values the equity of a business by applying a suitable P/E ratio to the business's earnings (profit after tax).

Value of company's equity = Total post-tax earnings × P/E ratio

Value per share = EPS × P/E ratio

Using the P/E valuation formula

The P/E ratio method is the simplest valuation method. It relies on just two figures (the post-tax earnings and the P/E ratio).

Post-tax earnings

The current post-tax earnings, or EPS, for a company can easily be found by looking at the most recent published accounts. However, these published figures will be historic, whereas the earnings figure needed for valuation purposes should be an expected, future earnings figure.

It is perfectly acceptable to use the published earnings figure as a starting point, but before performing the valuation, the historic earnings figure should be adjusted for factors such as:

- one-off items which will not recur in the coming year (e.g. debt write offs in the previous year);

- directors' salaries which might be adjusted after a takeover has been completed;

- any savings ('synergies') which might be made as part of a takeover.

P/E ratio

The P/E ratio for a listed company is a simple measure of the company's share price divided by its earnings per share.

The P/E indicates the market's perception of the company's current position and its future prospects. For example, if the P/E ratio is high, this indicates that the company has a relatively high share price compared to its current level of earnings, suggesting that the share price reflects good growth prospects of the company.

An unlisted company has no market share price, so has no readily available P/E ratio. Therefore, when valuing an unlisted company, a proxy P/E ratio from a similar listed company is often used.

Proxy P/E ratios

As explained above, an unlisted company will not have a market-driven P/E ratio, so an industry average P/E, or one for a similar company, will be used as a proxy.

However, proxy P/E ratios are also sometimes used when valuing a listed company – of course if a listed entity's own P/E ratio is applied to its own earnings figure, the calculation will just give the existing share price.

In particular, proxy P/E ratios are used in the context of bootstrapping, which is covered in the next chapter.

Test your understanding 4 (Objective test question)

Molier is an unquoted entity with a recently reported after-tax earnings of $3,840,000. It has issued 1 million ordinary shares with nominal value of $0.50 each. A similar listed entity has a P/E ratio of 9.

What is the current value of one ordinary share in Molier using the P/E basis of valuation?

A $34.56 million

B $69.12 million

C $34.56

D $69.12

The strengths and weaknesses of P/E method valuations

The main strengths of P/E method valuations are:

* they are commonly used and are well understood;
* they are relevant for valuing a controlling interest in an entity.

The main weaknesses of P/E method valuations are:

* they are based on accounting profits rather than cash flows;
* it is difficult to identify a suitable P/E ratio, particularly when valuing the shares of an unlisted entity;
* it is difficult to establish the relevant level of sustainable earnings.

Test your understanding 5 (Integration question)

Company X is considering a bid for Company Y.

X has earnings of $3m per annum, and Y has earnings of $1.5m per annum. The P/E ratio of X is 12 and that of Y is 8.

If the takeover proceeds, it is expected that synergies of $0.5m per annum will be generated, and that the combined company will have a P/E ratio of 11.

Required:

Calculate the maximum price that X should pay for Y, and the minimum price that Y should accept.

Earnings yield method

In some questions, you may not be given the P/E ratio, but you may be given the Earnings Yield instead.

The earnings yield is the reciprocal of the P/E ratio i.e. Earnings Yield = 1/ (P/E ratio).

Hence,

Value of company = Total earnings / Earnings Yield

Value per share = EPS / Earnings Yield

Understanding and interpretation of Earnings Yield

Some deeper analysis is desirable, for example examining the trend of share price over a number of quarters in the light of any events such as profits warnings and acquisitions (or rumours thereof), and the likely effect that they have had on earnings.

The stability of Earnings Yield is often as important as its growth, bearing in mind that in a general way the market is absorbing new information to try to assess a sustainable level of EPS on which to base growth for the future. Clearly, effective growth is dependent on a stable base, and the trend of Earnings Yield over time is to an extent a reflection of this factor.

A prospective acquirer would, of course, be concerned to assess the worth of a prospective biddee on the basis of its becoming part of the acquiring entity, and the valuation will especially need to take into account the expectations of the biddee's shareholders.

A further point relates to the acquirer's intentions regarding the biddee. If, for example the latter entity is to be partially demerged, that is certain parts disposed of to other entities in which they would provide a better fit, then the share price valuation may well be greater than if the whole biddee entity was to be retained. Nevertheless, any such break-up considerations will need to take into account all the stakeholders, including employees, suppliers and customers of the biddee, as any serious demotivation will take away from the goodwill value of the acquisition and quite possibly damage that of the acquiring entity itself.

7 Cash flow valuation: The dividend valuation model

Dividend Valuation Model (DVM) Theory

The theory states that the value of the company / share is the present value of the expected future dividends, discounted at the shareholders' required rate of return.

This links to the NPV method covered earlier in your studies, where the discounted cash flows from a project represented the gain in wealth to shareholders if the project were undertaken – wealth (share value) is linked to discounted future cash flows.

If we assume that all cash flows to equity are paid out as dividends, the DVM would therefore give the same result as valuing a company by discounting cash flows to equity at the cost of equity.

DVM formula

Either: $$P_0 = \frac{do}{k_e} \qquad\qquad P_0 = \frac{do(1+g)}{k_e - g}$$

Assuming: a constant dividend   **or**   constant growth

Note that:

g = forecast future growth rate in dividends, and:

P_0 = Value of company, when do = Total dividends

P_0 = Value per share, when do = Dividends per share

Also, note that the simple formula (when assuming a constant dividend) is just a rearrangement of the standard dividend yield formula:

Dividend yield = (Dividend / Share price) × 100%

In fact, the formulae presented here are just short-cuts which can be applied if there is no growth, or if there is constant growth in dividends into perpetuity.

The dividend valuation model in its most basic form is just a cash flow discounting model, which can be used for any set of discrete future dividend cash flows even if they don't grow at a constant rate in perpetuity.

i.e. Value = (Dividend in 1 year × 1 year discount factor) + (Dividend in 2 years × 2 year discount factor) +....etc

Test your understanding 6 (Integration question)

Target has just paid a dividend of EUR250,000. It has 2 million shares in issue.

The current return to shareholders in the same industry as Target is 12%, although it is expected that an additional risk premium of 2% will be applicable to Target, being a smaller and unlisted company.

Required:

Calculate the expected valuation of Target, if

(a) dividends are expected to be constant

(b) dividends are expected to grow at 4% per annum

Forecasting growth – Gordon's growth model

Background

Gordon's growth model was developed by the economist Myron Gordon. It attempts to derive a future growth rate, rather than simply extrapolating the historical growth rate.

Gordon argued that an increase in the level of investment by a company will give rise to an increase in future dividends. Therefore, the two key elements in determining future dividend growth will be the rate of reinvestment by the company and the return generated by the investments.

Formula

Gordon's growth model formula is:

g = r × b

where r = return on reinvested funds and b = proportion of funds retained.

Example

Bennett Co generates an average return on its investments of 10% per year. In recent years the company has paid out 40% of its earnings as a dividend.

Using Gordon's growth model, the expected future growth rate is:

g = r × b = 0.10 × (1 – 0.40) = 0.06 (6% per year)

Assumptions

There are a number of assumptions that underpin this model:

- the entity must be all equity financed;
- retained profits are the only source of additional investment;
- a constant proportion of each year's earnings is retained for reinvestment;
- projects financed from retained earnings earn a constant rate of return.

The strengths and weaknesses of dividend-based valuations

The strengths of dividend-based valuations are:

- value is based on the present value of the future dividend income stream (cash flow to an investor), so the method has a sound theoretical basis;
- they are useful for valuing minority shareholdings where the shareholder only receives dividends from the entity, over which he has no control.

The main weaknesses of using the dividend valuation model are:

- it is very difficult to forecast dividends and dividend growth, especially in perpetuity. For example, how can we predict whether there will be sufficient worthwhile projects to invest in over such a long term period? And what about the normal life cycle of a business – this could be the initial growth part of the cycle and not sustainable in the long term. Also, what about a new company that has yet to pay a dividend, that would be given a zero value under DVM but could actually be worth a considerable sum of money;

- particularly for unlisted companies, it can be difficult to estimate the cost of equity (note that in the exam, if you are not given the cost of equity, you should use CAPM to derive it, or use proxy company information). Also, for unlisted companies, a consistent dividend policy with constant growth rate is unlikely.

Uneven growth rates

The dividend valuation model formula cannot be used directly when the annual growth rate is expected to change.

In such cases, the entity's lifespan should be segmented into the periods for which the varying growth rates apply, and value each separately.

Illustration 1 (Integration question)

Target has just paid a dividend of EUR250,000. It has 2 million shares in issue.

The current return to shareholders in the same industry as Target is 12%, although it is expected that an additional risk premium of 2% will be applicable to Target, being a smaller and unquoted company.

Required:

Calculate the expected valuation of Target, if dividends are expected to stay constant for 3 years, then grow at 4% per annum thereafter.

Solution:

Separate the future dividend stream into two parts: first, the constant dividends for 3 years, then the growing perpetuity thereafter.

First 3 years

Present value of expected dividends = $250{,}000 \times AF_{1\text{-}3}$ (14%) = EUR 0.580m

Perpetuity from year 4:

Use the given DVM formula, then adjust for the fact that the dividend stream starts in year 4, not year 1 as normal:

$[(250{,}000 \times 1.04) / 0.14{-}0.04)] \times DF_3 (14\%) = EUR\ 1.755m$

Total value = 0.580m + 1.755m = EUR 2.335m

or 2.335 / 2 = EUR1.17 per share.

Test your understanding 7 (Integration question)

Western Co has paid out a steadily growing dividend over the last few years, where dividends have grown at 2% per year. The company's cost of equity is 10% and the dividend just paid (at the most recent year end) was $1.5 million in total.

Western Co has 10 million shares in issue and its shares are valued at $1.91.

Change of future plans

A new chief executive has just been appointed. He has expressed his intention to change the dividend policy of Western Co, as follows:

> The next dividend (in 1 year's time) will be half of what it would have been under the previous dividend policy. Then, the chief executive hopes to be able to increase the dividend by 10% per year for the next three years, before increasing the dividend at 5% per year in perpetuity.

Required:

Calculate the likely change in share value if the new policy is introduced, on the assumption that the dividend valuation model is used to value the shares and that the proposed changes have been publicly announced to the market.

Concluding thoughts on the dividend valuation model (DVM)

The DVM demonstrates the underlying principle that a company is worth the sum of its discounted future cash flows.

However, DVM is based on very simplistic model, but does provide a useful analytical tool for investors to use to evaluate different assumptions about growth and future prospects.

The challenge is to make the model as applicable to reality as possible, which means using the most reliable assumptions available.

8 Cash flow valuation: Discounted cash flow method

Overview of the method

Under the discounted cash flow (DCF) method, a value for the equity of the entity is derived by estimating the future annual after-tax cash flows of the entity, and discounting these cash flows at an appropriate cost of capital. This is theoretically the best way of valuing a business, since the discounted value of future cash flows represents the wealth of the shareholders.

The cost of capital used to discount the cash flows should reflect the systematic risk of the cash flows.

Test your understanding 8 (Objective test question)

The expected after-tax cash flows of Thomas, an all equity financed company with 2 million shares in issue , will be as follows:

Year	GBP
1	120,000
2	100,000
3	140,000
4	50,000
5 onwards	130,000

A suitable cost of capital for evaluating Thomas is 12%.

What is the value of Thomas's equity (in total) using the DCF basis of valuation?

A   GBP 392,050

B   GBP 1,006,300

C   GBP 1,083,333

D   GBP 1,475,383

More details on cash flows and cost of capital

Cash flows to equity

Ideally, cash flows to equity should be used in DCF valuations rather than post-tax post-financing cash flows.

Cash flows to equity are similar to post-tax post-financing cash flows, except that they include average sustainable levels of capital and working capital net cash flow investments over the longer term rather than this year's figures.

Post-tax cash flows (after financing charges) are often used as an approximation for cash flows to equity.

However, where sufficient information is provided in a question to enable cash flows to equity to be calculated, cash flows to equity should be used in the DCF valuation instead of post-tax post-financing cash flows.

Free cash flow

The concept of 'free cash flow'

Free cash flow is the cash generated by the business that is 'freely' available for distribution to investors after having met all the immediate obligations of the business and investment in working capital and in non-current assets that is necessary to sustain on-going operations.

There are many different ways of defining free cash flow.

In CIMA materials and F3 OTQs you will find the following terms being used:

Cash flow to equity refers to cash flow generated by the company after tax, reinvestment needs and debt-related cash flows. That is, cash flow attributable to equity investors.

Cash flow to all investors refers to cash flow generated by the company after tax and reinvestment needs but before debt-related cash flows. That is, cash flow attributable to all investors, both debt and equity investors.

Free cash flow to equity is sustainable cash flow to equity, and free cash flow to all investors is sustainable cash flow to all investors.

Use of cash flows to equity

The value of the shareholders' stake (equity) in an entity is the sum of the future cash flows to equity discounted at the cost of equity.

Note that if we assume that a company pays out all of its cash flow to equity as a dividend, the DCF company valuation method (where cash flows to equity are discounted at cost of equity) will give exactly the same result as the DVM valuation method introduced earlier in the chapter, where the cash flows to equity used in the DCF calculation are assumed to grow at a constant rate and the same growth rate is used in the DVM valuation.

The problem of lack of information

In a project appraisal, the cash flows generated from the project are easily identifiable, but in a business valuation they can be harder to identify and quantify.

This is because there are so many of them, and because the necessary information does not usually exist in the public domain.

Therefore, for business valuation, we often have to estimate cash flows using readily-available accounting information.

How to calculate cash flow data from profit data

Cash flow to equity	**Cash flow to all investors**
(1) Start with profit before interest and tax (PBIT).	(1) Start with PBIT.
(2) Deduct tax for the year (see note, below) and interest to give profit for the year.	(2) Deduct tax for the year, excluding tax relief on interest (see note, below).
(3) Adjust for non-cash items (e.g. add back depreciation).	(3) Adjust for non-cash items (e.g. add back depreciation).
(4) Adjust for cash items such as capex/disposal of non-current assets; changes in working capital; new debt raised/debt repaid.	(4) Adjust for cash items such as capex/disposal of non-current assets; changes in working capital.

Note: Tax can be calculated as (PBIT – interest) × tax rate. Or, if tax depreciation allowances differ from depreciation, tax is: (PBIT + depreciation – tax depreciation allowances – interest) × tax rate.

Note: Tax can be calculated as PBIT × tax rate. Or, if tax depreciation allowances differ from depreciation, tax is: (PBIT + depreciation – tax depreciation allowances) × tax rate

Example of free cash flow to all investors

The recently published accounts of Matty show the following figures:

	$ million
Profit before interest and tax	220
Interest	40
Profit after interest but before tax	180
Tax expense (tax rate 20%)	36
Depreciation	8
Capital expenditure	70
Increase in working capital	10
Debt repayment	15

Required:

Calculate the free cash flow to all investors in the year.

Solution:

	$ million
Profit before interest and tax	220
Less tax expense based on PBIT: 20% × $220m	(44)
Plus depreciation	8
Less capital expenditure	(70)
Less increase in working capital	(10)
Free cash flow to all investors	104

Example of free cash flow to equity

The recently published accounts of Matty show the following figures:

	$ million
Profit before interest and tax	220
Interest	40
Profit after interest but before tax	180
Tax expense (tax rate 20%)	36
Depreciation	8
Capital expenditure	70
Increase in working capital	10
Debt repayment	15

Required:

Calculate the free cash flow to equity in the year.

Solution:

	$ million
Profit for the year (220 – 40 – 36)	144
Plus depreciation	8
Less capital expenditure	(70)
Less increase in working capital	(10)
Less debt repayment	(15)
Free cash flow to equity	57

Another example of free cash flow to equity

The recently published accounts of Carey show the following figures:

Operating profit (after deducting depreciation of USD 3m) = USD 32m

Interest paid = USD 2m

Taxation = USD 9m

Capital expenditure = USD 4m, which is assumed to represent a sustainable level of investment in non-current assets.

Required:

Calculate the free cash flow to equity in the year.

Solution:

Free cash flow to equity = 32m + 3m – 2m – 9m – 4m = USD 20m

An appropriate cost of capital

The introductory paragraph above explained that 'an appropriate cost of capital' should be used for discounting. In some exam questions, you will be told directly which cost of capital to use. However, in other cases you will be expected to either calculate or select an appropriate cost of capital. It is then important to understand the following relationships:

Use of cost of equity as a discount rate

The cost of equity can be used to discount the cash flows TO EQUITY (i.e. post-tax cash flows AFTER financing charges) in order to value the equity in a company directly.

Use of WACC as a discount rate

WACC can be used to discount the cash flows TO ALL INVESTORS (i.e. post-tax cash flows BEFORE financing charges) when valuing a project or an entity (debt + equity value). To find the company's equity value, the value of debt would need to be deducted.

In summary:

ENTITY VALUE	EQUITY VALUE / SHAREHOLDER VALUE
= equity value plus debt value	= entity value minus debt value
Discount cash flows attributable to all investors (i.e. after tax but before interest) at WACC	Discount cash flows attributable to equity investors (i.e. cash flows after tax and interest) at the cost of equity
	DEBT VALUE

Note that the equity valuation method is likely to more appropriate for divisions since they commonly report on a pre-financing basis. They do not have their own capital structure and therefore the cost of financing that is required to calculate entity value.

Use of proxy company information

The cost of capital used must reflect the risk of the entity's cash flows.

For listed companies, it is normally quite easy to identify the cost of capital, using the huge amount of information which is publicly known about the listed company. However, for an unlisted company, or perhaps a division of a company, it is much more difficult (due to lack of available information) to identify an appropriate cost of capital.

If a cost of capital is not given, or if is difficult to derive one, a proxy cost of capital from a similar listed company could be used instead. Much more detail on deriving a suitable cost of capital is presented in the next section below.

Test your understanding 9 (Integration question)

Chassagne Co is considering making a bid for Butler Co, a rival company.

The following information should be used to value Butler Co.

Statement of profit or loss for the most recent accounting period

	GBP m
Revenue	285.1
Cost of sales	(120.9)
Gross profit	164.2
Operating expenses (inc depreciation GBP 12.3m)	(66.9)
Profit from operations	97.3
Finance costs	(10.0)
Profit before tax	87.3
Taxation	(21.6)
Profit after tax	65.7

Other information

- selling prices are expected to rise at 3% pa for the next 3 years and then stay constant thereafter.

- sales volumes are expected to rise at 5% pa for the next 3 years and then stay constant thereafter.

- assume that cost of sales is a completely variable cost, and that other operating expenses (including depreciation) are expected to stay constant.

- Butler Co invested £15m in non-current assets and £2m in working capital last year. These annual amounts are expected to stay constant in future.

- Butler Co's financing costs are expected to stay constant each year in the future.

- the marginal rate of tax is 28%, payable in the year in which the liability arises.

- assume that book depreciation equals tax depreciation.

- Butler Co has 500 million shares in issue.

- the WACC of Butler Co is 9% and its cost of equity is 12%.

> **Required:**
>
> Calculate the value of the equity in Butler Co (in total and per share) by forecasting future cash flows to equity and discounting them to present value using cost of equity.

The strengths and weaknesses of cash-based valuations

The strengths of this method of valuation are:

- theoretically this is the best method of valuation;
- it can be used to place a maximum value on the entity;
- it considers the time value of money.

The weaknesses of this method are:

- it is difficult to forecast cash flows accurately;
- it is difficult to determine an appropriate discount rate;
- what time period should we evaluate in detail and then how do you value the company's worth beyond this period? i.e. the realisable value at the end of the planning period;
- the basic NPV method does not evaluate further options that may exist. However, the approach can be modified, by adding decision trees and probabilities to the analysis, to enable us to assess the sensitivity of the results to potential variations in cash flows;
- the basic model assumes that the discount rate and tax rates are constant through the period, although again this problem can be overcome by using sensitivity analysis and other methods of analysing risk such as probabilities and decision trees.

9 Deriving a suitable cost of capital for discounting

Introduction

In some questions, you will be told what the cost of capital of the entity is, so it will be clear what cost of capital to use for discounting the forecast cash flows.

However, in some questions you may only be given information for a proxy entity (if information for your chosen entity is not available).

When using a proxy cost of capital, care must be taken to ensure that it reflects the business risk and the capital structure of the entity being valued.

If necessary, a risk adjusted cost of capital could be used.

Risk adjusted cost of capital

In the earlier chapter on 'Financing – Capital structure' we saw how to use Modigliani and Miller's (M & M's) equations to adjust an entity's cost of equity or cost of capital to reflect a different capital structure.

In this chapter we shall revisit the M & M equations and also cover the Capital Asset Pricing Model (CAPM), which can also be used to derive a risk adjusted cost of capital for discounting.

Modigliani and Miller's (M & M's) equations

M & M's equations relating to cost of equity and cost of capital were introduced in the earlier chapter on 'Financing – Capital structure'. They are shown again below:

Cost of equity $\quad\quad k_{eg} = k_{eu} + (k_{eu} - k_d) V_D (1 - t) / V_E$

WACC $\quad\quad\quad\quad k_{adj} = k_{eu} [1 - (V_D t / (V_E + V_D)]$

where $\quad V_E$ = value of equity, V_D = value of debt

$\quad\quad\quad k_e$ = Cost of equity (k_{eg} = cost of equity in geared co, k_{eu} = cost of equity in ungeared co)

$\quad\quad\quad k_d$ = Cost of debt (must be gross of tax)

$\quad\quad\quad k_{adj}$ = the weighted average cost of capital in a geared company

$\quad\quad\quad t$ = Corporation tax rate

$\quad\quad\quad$ WACC = weighted average cost of capital

Illustration 2 (Integration question)

Eamon Co is forecast to generate a constant stream of post-tax cash flows (after interest charges) of $10m per year.

The company is not listed, and no cost of equity has been calculated. However, a similar listed entity, Frank Co, which operates in the same business sector has a cost of equity of 10%.

Frank Co is all equity financed whereas Eamon Co has 20% debt and 80% equity by market values. The tax rate is 30%, and the yield on Eamon's debt is 4%.

Required:

Calculate the value of Eamon Co, using the discounted cash flow method.

Solution:

The given post-tax and post-interest cash flows need to be discounted using an appropriate cost of equity.

Although Frank Co operates in the same business sector, its gearing is different. Hence, a risk adjusted cost of equity (suitable to Eamon Co's circumstances) would be (using M & M's formula):

$$k_{eg} = k_{eu} + (k_{eu} - k_d)(1-t) V_D / V_E$$

$$= 10\% + (10\% - 4\%)(1-0.30)\ 20/80$$

$$= 11.05\%$$

Therefore, the value of Eamon Co's equity is $10m / 0.1105 = $90.5m

The Capital Asset Pricing Model (CAPM)

The CAPM enables us to calculate the required return from an investment given the level of risk associated with the investment (measured by its beta factor).

Before showing how the CAPM formula can be used to derive a suitable risk-adjusted cost of capital for discounting, we first need to introduce the model and explain the terminology surrounding it.

In order to explain how the CAPM works, it is first necessary to introduce the concepts of systematic and unsystematic risk.

Systematic and unsystematic risk

There are two elements that make up the risk associated with a company:

*   Unsystematic (or specific) risk is the risk of the company's cash flows being affected by specific factors like strikes, R&D successes, systems failures, etc.

*   Systematic (or market) risk is the risk of the company's cash flows being affected to some extent by general macro-economic factors such as tax rates, unemployment or interest rates.

TOTAL RISK

Unsystematic risk

Company specific factors
Can be eliminated by diversification

Systematic risk

General economic factors
Cannot be eliminated

The impact of diversification

By holding a portfolio of investments, the unsystematic risk is diversified away but the systematic risk is not, so will be present in all portfolios.

For example, the return from a single investment in an ice-cream entity will be subject to changes in the weather – sunny weather producing good returns, cold weather poor returns. By itself the investment could be considered a high risk. If a second investment were made in an umbrella entity, which is also subject to weather changes, but in the opposite way, then the return from the portfolio of the two investments will have a much-reduced risk level. This process is known as diversification, and when continued can reduce portfolio risk to a minimum.

If an investor enlarges his portfolio to include approximately 25 shares the unsystematic risk is reduced to close to zero, the implication being that we may eliminate the unsystematic portion of overall risk by spreading investment over a sufficiently diversified portfolio.

The capital asset pricing model (CAPM) enables us to calculate the required return for a well-diversified investor who is not subject to unsystematic risk.

If we can measure the systematic risk of a company or investment, the CAPM will enable us to calculate the level of required return.

ß (beta) factor

The method adopted by CAPM to measure systematic risk is an index, ß (beta). The ß factor is the measure of a share's volatility in terms of market risk.

The ß factor of the market as a whole is 1. Market risk makes market returns volatile and the ß factor is simply a yardstick against which the risk of other investments can be measured.

The ß factor is critical to applying the CAPM; it illustrates the relationship of an individual security to the market as a whole, or conversely the market return given the return on an individual security.

Beta values fall into four categories, with the following meanings:

(i) ß > 1   The shares have **more** systematic risk than the stock market average.

(ii) ß = 1   The shares have the **same** systematic risk as the stock market average.

(iii) ß < 1   The shares have **less** systematic risk than the stock market average.

(iv) ß = 0   The shares have **no** risk at all.

A share's beta value can be interpreted quite precisely:

ß = 1.25   :   The shares have 25% **more** systematic risk than the average level on the stock market.

ß = 0.80   :   The shares have 20% **less** systematic risks than the average. (i.e. they only have 80% of the average level).

The security market line (SML)

The security market line (SML) gives the relationship between systematic risk and return. We know two relationships:

(1) **The risk-free security**

This carries no risk and therefore no systematic risk and therefore has a **beta** of zero.

(2) **The market portfolio**

This represents the ultimate in diversification and therefore contains only systematic risk. It has a **beta** of 1.

The results may be plotted:

R_f is the point on the graph where the line intersects the axis, and then the higher the systematic risk, the higher the required rate of return.

The SML and the relationship between required return and risk can be shown using the formula shown below.

Formula – given in the exam

$$k_e = R_f + [R_m - R_f] \, \beta$$

where

k_e = required return from individual security

β = beta factor of individual security

R_f = risk-free rate of interest

R_m = return on market portfolio

Note: In exams, the question will sometimes refer to the market premium – this is the difference between R_m and R_f. It is the long term market premium that should be used in CAPM if this is different from current market rates.

Calculating beta factors

Beta factors for a company are calculated statistically from past observed returns; for example the London Business School 'Risk Measurement Service' is published quarterly, using monthly returns from the previous five years to calculate each quoted share's beta.

Such an analysis begs two questions:

- Is it reasonable to use a beta factor, calculated from the past, as the basis of decision-making about the future?

- Are beta values observed to be stable over time?

Beta values tend to be more stable for highly diversified shares such as investment trusts than for more focused companies. Naturally beta will only be stable if the company's systematic risk remains the same, i.e. the company carries on the same areas of business in the long term.

Since betas are calculated statistically, the calculated beta value will be more reliable the more separate data went into its calculation. Therefore the longer the period underlying the calculations the better.

However if the beta will be used to estimate a required rate of return for a future project, it is important that the company's risk class in future will be more or less unchanged by accepting the project. Many businesses deal with this apparent paradox by using a sector average beta rather than using their own calculated beta.

The CAPM gives a required return for a given level of risk (measured by the beta factor).

Therefore, if we can estimate the level of risk associated with an entity (the beta of the entity), we can use CAPM to give a required return to shareholders.

This required return to shareholders is essentially the cost of equity which can then be used to derive an appropriate WACC for the entity.

Alpha values

If the CAPM stated that we should expect, on average, an annual return of 16.5%, this does not mean that the shares will produce a return (dividend yield plus capital gain) of 16.5% each year. Remember, shares are a risky investment which produces an uncertain annual return.

Suppose in one particular year, Company A shares produce an actual return of 18%. The shares are said to have produced a positive 'abnormal' return of 1.5% – that is, 1.5% higher than the expected return.

The alpha value of a share is simply its average abnormal return. Suppose Company A shares have an alpha value of +2%, this implies that in the recent past the shares have, on average, produced a return of 16.5% + 2% = 18.5%.

Alpha values can be either positive or negative, and in a perfect world they should be zero. In other words the average return that the shares actually do produce **should** be the same as the return indicated by CAPM. However, the world isn't perfect and so that will not always happen. Hence we get positive and negative alpha values.

Criticisms of the CAPM

(1) CAPM is a single period model. This means that the values calculated are only valid for a finite period of time and will need to be recalculated or updated at regular intervals.

(2) CAPM assumes no transaction costs associated with trading securities.

(3) Any beta value calculated will be based on historic data which may not be appropriate currently. This is particularly so if the company has changed the capital structure of the business or the type of business it is trading in.

(4) The risk free rate may change considerably over short periods of time.

(5) CAPM assumes an efficient investment market where it is possible to diversify away risk. This is not necessarily the case, meaning that some unsystematic risk may remain.

(6) Additionally, the idea that all unsystematic risk is diversified away will not hold true if stocks change in terms of volatility. As stocks change over time it is very likely that the portfolio becomes less than optimal.

(7) CAPM assumes all stocks relate to going concerns, this may not be the case.

Asset betas, equity betas and debt betas

In order to calculate cost of equity and / or WACC for use in business valuation, we first need to expand our understanding of beta factors.

- The beta factor is a measure of the systematic risk of an entity relative to the market.

- This risk will be dependent on the level of business risk and the level of financial risk (gearing) associated with an entity.

- Hence, the beta factor for a geared company will be greater than the beta factor for an equivalent ungeared company.

The relationship between the beta factors for ungeared and geared companies is given by the following formula (given in the exam):

$$\beta_u = \beta_g \left[\frac{V_E}{V_E + V_D [1-t]} \right] + \beta_d \left[\frac{V_D [1-t]}{V_E + V_D [1-t]} \right]$$

where

β_g = the equity (geared) beta measures the systematic business risk and the systematic financial risk of a company's shares

β_u = the asset (ungeared) beta measures the systematic business risk *only*

β_d = the debt beta measures the risk associated with the debt finance. Usually we assume that debt is risk free and hence the debt beta is zero. If this is the case, the second term in the given formula disappears and the formula becomes:

$$\beta_u = \beta_g \left[\frac{V_E}{V_E + V_D [1-t]} \right]$$

More on systematic risk

The entity's systematic risk is important in the CAPM formula.

Remember:

- Shareholders are only interested in systematic risk because they hold well-diversified portfolios. Systematic risk of an entity is measured by its beta.

- Shareholders in a geared company suffer two types of systematic risk i.e. business and financial risk.

- The business risk of a company refers to the risk of the operating cash flows.

- Financial risk is the increased volatility of dividend payments to shareholders as gearing increases.

From the M & M analysis, we know that a share's systematic risk can be split up between the systematic *business* risk and the systematic *financial* risk.

Systematic business risk arises out of the risky nature of the company's business caused by:

- revenue sensitivity;

- proportion of fixed to variable production costs.

Systematic financial risk arises out of how the company has financed itself – its gearing or capital structure.

Use of the formula: Degearing and regearing beta factors

For example, suppose a question tells you that the ABC company has a gearing ratio (D : E) of 1 : 2; the shares have a beta value of 1.45 (the equity beta); and the corporation tax rate is 30%. Then:

$$ß_u = 1.45 \times \frac{2}{2 + 1 \times (1 - 0.30)} = 1.074$$

Note: If a question only states the beta, assume it is an equity beta. Also, if there is no mention of a debt beta, assume it is zero.

This indicates that shareholders in ABC have a beta value/systematic risk exposure of 1.45. Of this value, 1.074 arises out of the risky nature of the company's business (its business risk) and the rest (i.e. 1.45 – 1.074 = 0.376) arises out of the financial risk caused by the company's capital structure.

Notice four very important implications of this analysis:

(1) A company's equity beta will always be greater than its asset beta, except

(2) If it is all equity financed (and so has no financial risk), when its equity beta and asset beta will be the same.

(3) Companies in the same 'area of business' (i.e. same business risk) will have the same *asset* beta, but

(4) Companies in the same area of business will *not* have the same *equity* beta unless they also happen to have the same capital structure.

As we shall see, the *third* of these points is particularly important.

Application to business valuation

There are two ways in which the gearing / degearing formula above can be used in order to derive a cost of equity and / or a WACC that can be used in business valuation.

Both methods start from the assumption that you have been given an equity beta for a proxy company.

- **Method 1:** Use the formula to derive the proxy entity's ungeared beta factor. Assume that this beta factor also reflects the business risk of the entity being valued, so regear this ungeared beta to reflect the capital structure of the entity being valued. Then use CAPM to derive a cost of equity for the entity being valued and (if necessary) use this k_e in the standard WACC formula to find the entity's WACC.

- **Method 2:** Use the formula to derive the proxy entity's ungeared beta factor, then use CAPM to find an 'ungeared cost of equity' (k_{eu}) for the proxy entity. On the assumption that this k_{eu} is also a measure of the ungeared cost of equity of the entity being valued (same business risk), use M & M's WACC formula to calculate the WACC of the entity being valued.

(**Note:** Method 2 can only be used to calculate WACC, whereas Method 1 derives both cost of equity and WACC.)

Both methods will now be illustrated, to show that they give the same answer for WACC.

Illustration 3 (Integration question)

We are trying to value the company Garvey Co, an unlisted company with an estimated debt:equity ratio of 1:2. Post-tax cash flows before financing charges have been forecasted, so a suitable WACC is now needed for discounting. Since Garvey Co is an unlisted company, it has been difficult to derive a WACC for Garvey Co directly, because the necessary information is not readily available. Therefore, it has been decided to use proxy information as a starting point.

Information for Rocket Co, a listed company in the same business sector as Garvey Co is as follows:

	Rocket Co
Current geared (equity) beta	1.86
Current capital structure ratio (D:E by market value)	1:1

The tax rate is 30% and the return on the stock market has been 12% per annum in recent years. Debt is assumed to be risk free and has a pre-tax cost of 5% per annum.

Required:

Calculate a suitable WACC for Garvey Co.

Solution:

Method 1:

Step 1

Rocket Co's ungeared / asset beta is calculated and then used as an estimate of Garvey Co's asset beta (because Garvey Co and Rocket Co are in the same area of business and so will have the same *asset* beta). Since debt is risk free, use

$$\beta u = \beta g \times \frac{V_E}{V_E + V_D(1-t)}$$

$$\beta u = 1.86 \times \frac{1}{1 + 1(1-0.30)} = 1.09$$

Step 2

A geared / equity beta for Garvey Co is calculated next. As we know, an equity beta reflects both systematic business risk *and* systematic financial risk. Garvey Co's equity beta will reflect the business risk of Garvey Co and Rocket Co, and the capital structure of Garvey Co (1:2 D:E).

Using: $\beta_g = \beta_u [1 + (V_D (1-t)/ V_E)$

So: $\beta_g = 1.09 [1+ (1 \times (1-0.30) / 2)]$

So $\beta g = 1.47$

Step 3

This equity beta is then input into the CAPM to give a cost of equity capital for Garvey Co:

$$k_e = R_F + [R_M - R_F] \beta g$$

$$ke = 5\% + [12\% - 5\%] \times 1.47 = 15.3\%$$

Step 4

The WACC is now calculated using the standard WACC formula:

$$k_o = k_{eg} \left[\frac{V_E}{V_E + V_D} \right] + k_d (1-t) \left[\frac{V_D}{V_E + V_D} \right]$$

$$= 15.3\% \times (2/3) + 5\% \times (1-0.30) \times (1/3) = 11.4\%$$

Method 2:

Step 1

As above, the existing geared / equity beta of Rocket Co is degeared, to give an ungeared / asset beta of 1.09.

Step 2

Input this ungeared beta into the CAPM formula to give an ungeared cost of equity (k_{eu})

$$k_{eu} = 5\% + [12\% - 5\%] \times 1.09 = 12.6\%$$

Step 3

Use the M & M WACC formula:

$$k_{adj} = k_{eu} (1 - tL)$$

$$= 12.6\% (1 - 30\% \times (1/3)) = 11.4\% \text{ as before.}$$

Test your understanding 10 (Objective test question)

QQQ is planning a takeover bid for ABC, a telecoms company with a D : E ratio of 1 : 3.

The cash flows (after tax but before interest) for ABC have been forecasted, and now the directors of QQQ are trying to estimate a suitable WACC to use for discounting.

XYZ is a 'typical' listed telecoms company. It has an *equity* beta of 1.25 and a D : E ratio of 1 : 2.

Assume that R_F = 6%, R_M = 14%, and the tax rate is 30%. It is assumed that corporate debt is risk-free (and so the debt beta is zero).

Which of the following is a WACC that could be used in the valuation of ABC?

A   12.4%

B   14.8%

C   15.1%

D   18.3%

The EMH and business valuation

Implications of the Efficient Market Hypothesis (EMH) in business valuation

The level of efficiency in the market is very important when considering the value of a business.

In a strongly efficient market, the share price of a listed company will reflect all factors which are known (both publicly and privately) about that company. Hence it is less likely that a premium will be paid (above the existing share price) in a takeover.

In a semi strongly efficient market, the existing share price will reflect all that is publicly known about a company. Therefore, if we can identify or predict other factors which are not currently in the public domain, this might justify a higher value and hence the payment of a premium on acquisition.

The company's intentions and prospects may well have to be communicated to the market (unless the market is strongly efficient) in order for a purchaser to make a proper assessment of the company's value. This will be particularly important when using earnings or cash flow based valuation methods, which rely on accurate forecasts of future information.

Summary of valuation methods: When should each be used?

This chapter has covered the different valuation methods in turn, and has separately identified the strengths and weaknesses of each of the methods.

To conclude, we should consider the circumstances in which each valuation method is most useful.

Asset based methods

The asset based valuation methods are most appropriate when valuing capital intensive businesses with plenty of tangible assets.

For a service business, the asset based approach is likely to significantly undervalue the business, unless some effort is also made to value the intangible assets of the business.

Note however that in times of uncertainty, the asset based approach avoids the need to forecast future earnings or cash flows, so it may be favoured in these circumstances.

Dividend valuation model (DVM)

The DVM is a suitable valuation method when valuing a minority shareholding in a company, because if an investor purchases a minority stake, the dividends represent the forecast income from the investment, which will impact his wealth.

If the investor were to purchase a majority stake, it would be more relevant to consider overall company cash flows or asset values as a basis for the valuation.

P/E method and discounted cash flow method

Both these methods are based on forecasts of the future, and often use proxy information from proxy companies. These factors may be difficult to identify in practice.

Providing that the forecasts are accurate, these methods value the business based on its future prospects, so automatically include a measure of the goodwill / intangible assets associated with a business.

For service businesses, these methods are generally preferred to the asset based methods.

10 End of chapter objective test questions

Test your understanding 11 (Objective test question)

A company is planning to sell a wholly owned subsidiary (B) on 1 January 20X1 and is preparing a valuation for B as at that date using a discounted cash flow approach.

Additional information:

- The net operating cash flows of B are forecast to be $250 million in the year to 31 December 20X1 and are expected to remain at this level every year thereafter.

- New equipment at a cost of $200 million will need to be paid for on 1 January 20X1. Tax depreciation allowances can be claimed over 4 years on a straight line basis on this equipment.

- The corporate income tax rate is 30%. Tax is paid a year in arrears.

- Assume all cash flows arise at the end of the year unless stated otherwise.

- B has a financial year ending 31 December each year.

The trainee accountant has begun to produce an analysis of net cash flow for the valuation which is shown below. All figures are in $ million.

Select the TWO grid squares that contain an error.

Time (years)	0	1	2	3-5	6+
Net operating cash flow (NOCF)	-	250	250	250	250
Tax on NOCF	-	-	(75)	(75)	(75)
New equipment	(200)	-	-	-	-
Tax relief on new equipment	-	15	15	30	-

Test your understanding 12 (Objective test question)

Company XX is using the Calculated Intangible Value (CIV) company valuation method to value its intangible assets.

Key data:

- XX has a WACC of 12%, cost of debt of 7% and cost of equity of 14%

- Net profit before tax for XX is $50 million

- XX's tangible assets are $67 million

- Average industry return on tangible assets is 16%

- Corporate income tax is 20%

Complete the following CIV calculation:

CIV = [$50 million – ([UNKNOWN FIGURE 1] × $67 million)] × [UNKNOWN FIGURE 2] / 0.12

[UNKNOWN FIGURE 1] is

A   0.16

B   0.12

C   0.07

D   0.14

[UNKNOWN FIGURE 2] is

E   0.80

F   0.20

G   1.20

H   1.80

Test your understanding 13 (Objective test question)

You are a management accountant working for Mega Co.

The directors of Mega Co have asked you to prepare some business valuation calculations for a potential target company, Mini Co.

They are particularly keen for you to use an asset based valuation method.

Which THREE of the following are potential problems with valuing Mini Co using an asset based method?

A   The asset based method might under-value Mini Co if it has significant intangible assets

B   The asset based method might over-value Mini Co if it has recently revalued its non-current assets

C   The asset based method will not be useful if Mini Co has been making losses in recent years

D   The asset based method ignores the future prospects and earnings potential of Mini Co

E   Mega Co, as the acquiring company, will be interested in the replacement cost valuation of Mini Co's assets, but replacement costs might not be readily available.

Test your understanding 14 (Objective test question)

You have been asked to calculate the equity beta factor for VERA.

Introductory data:

- BLAIZE is a listed company in the same industry as VERA. It has an equity beta of 1.45.

- Gearing levels – (debt/equity) by market value:
  - VERA   45/55
  - BLAIZE   30/70

- Tax rate is 25%. The beta of debt is 0.10.

Which one of the following shows the correct formula for ungearing the proxy company's equity beta (which would be the first step in trying to calculate an equity beta for VERA):

A: $\beta u = 1.45 \times \dfrac{70}{100} + 0.10 \times \dfrac{30}{100}$

B: $\beta u = 1.45 \times \dfrac{55}{55 + 45\,(1 - 0.25)} + 0.10 \times \dfrac{45\,(1 - 0.25)}{55 + 45\,(1 - 0.25)}$

C: $\beta u = 1.45 \times \dfrac{40}{40 + 30\,(1 - 0.25)} + 0.10 \times \dfrac{30\,(1 - 0.25)}{40 + 30\,(1 - 0.25)}$

D: $\beta u = 1.45 \times \dfrac{70}{70 + 30\,(1 - 0.25)} + 0.10 \times \dfrac{30\,(1 - 0.25)}{70 + 30\,(1 - 0.25)}$

Test your understanding 15 (Objective test question)

The systematic risk of an project's return is the result of uncertainties in the return caused by

A   factors unique to the project

B   factors unique to the entity undertaking the project

C   factors unique to the industry to which the project belongs

D   nationwide economic factors

11 End of chapter case style questions

Test your understanding 16 (Case style question)

The board of directors of Predator plc, a UK company, is considering making an offer to purchase Target Ltd, a private limited company in the same industry. If Target Ltd is purchased it is proposed to continue operating the company as a going concern in the same line of business.

Summarised details from the most recent financial statements (statements of financial position and statements of profit or loss) of Predator and Target are shown below:

	Predator plc as at 31 March		Target Ltd as at 31 March	
	£m	£m	£000	£000
Freehold property		33		460
Plant and equipment		58		1,310
Inventory	29		330	
Receivables	24		290	
Cash	3		20	
less current liabilities	(31)	25	(518)	122
		116		1,892
Financed by: Ordinary shares		35		160
Reserves		43		964
Shareholders funds		78		1,124
Medium term bank borrowings		38		768
		116		1,892

Predator plc, 50 pence ordinary shares, Target Ltd, 25 pence ordinary.

| Year | Predator plc | | Target Ltd | |
	PAT £m	Dividend £m	PAT £000	Dividend £000
T5	14.30	9.01	143	85.0
T4	15.56	9.80	162	93.5
T3	16.93	10.67	151	93.5
T2	18.42	11.60	175	102.8
T1	20.04	12.62	183	113.1

NB: T5 is five years ago and T1 is the most recent year.

Target's shares are owned by a small number of private individuals. Its managing director, who receives an annual salary of £120,000, dominates the company. This is £40,000 more than the average salary received by managing directors of similar companies. The managing director would be replaced if Predator purchases Target.

The freehold property has not been revalued for several years and is believed to have a market value of £800,000.

The value of plant and equipment in the statement of financial position is thought to reflect its replacement cost fairly, but its value if sold is not likely to exceed £800,000. Approximately £55,000 of inventory is obsolete and could only be sold as scrap for £5,000.

The ordinary shares of Predator are currently trading at 430 pence ex-div. A suitable cost of equity for Target has been estimated at 15%.

Both companies are subject to corporation tax at 33%.

Required:

Estimate the value of Target Ltd using the different methods of valuation and advise the board of Predator as to how much it should offer for Target's shares.

(30 minutes)

Test your understanding 17 (Case style question)

AB is a telecommunications consultancy based in Europe that trades globally. It was established 15 years ago. The four founding shareholders own 25% of the issued share capital each and are also executive directors of the entity.

The shareholders are considering a flotation of AB on a European stock exchange and have started discussing the process and a value for the entity with financial advisors. The four founding shareholders, and many of the entity's employees, are technical experts in their field, but have little idea how entities such as theirs are valued.

Assume you are one of AB's financial advisors. You have been asked to estimate a value for the entity and explain your calculations and approach to the directors. You have obtained the following information.

Summary financial data for the past three years and forecast revenue and costs for the next two years is as follows:

Statements of profit or loss for the years ended 31 March

	20X4 (actual) EURm	20X5 (actual) EURm	20X6 (actual) EURm	20X7 (forecast) EURm	20X8 (forecast) EURm
Revenue	125.0	137.5	149.9	172.0	198.0
Cash operating costs	37.5	41.3	45.0	52.0	59.0
Depreciation	20.0	22.0	48.0	48.0	48.0
Pre-tax earnings	67.5	74.2	56.9	72.0	91.0
Taxation	20.3	22.3	17.1	22.0	27.0

Statements of financial position at 31 March

	20X4 EURm	20X5 EURm	20X6 EURm
Assets			
Non-current assets			
Property, plant and equipment	150	175	201
Current assets	48	54	62
	198	229	263
Equity and liabilities			
Equity			
Share capital (EUR 1 shares)	30	30	30
Retained earnings	148	179	203
	178	209	233
Current liabilities	20	20	30
	198	229	263

Note: The book valuations of non-current assets are considered to reflect current realisable values.

Other information/assumptions

- Growth in after tax cash flows for 20X9 and beyond (assume indefinitely) is expected to be 3% per annum. Cash operating costs can be assumed to remain at the same percentage of revenue as in previous years. Depreciation will fluctuate but, for purposes of evaluation, assume the 20X8 charge will continue indefinitely. Tax has been payable at 30% per annum for the last three years. This rate is expected to continue for the foreseeable future and tax will be payable in the year in which the liability arises.

- The average P/E ratio for telecommunication entities' shares quoted on European stock exchanges has been 12.5 over the past 12 months. However, there is a wide variation around this average and AB might be able to command a rating up to 30% higher than this;

- An estimated cost of equity capital for the industry is 10% after tax;

- The average pre-tax return on total assets for the industry over the past 3 years has been 15%.

Required:

(a) Calculate a range of values for AB, in total and per share, using methods of valuation that you consider appropriate. Where relevant, include an estimate of value for intellectual capital.

(30 minutes)

(b) Discuss the methods of valuation you have used, explaining the relevance of each method to an entity such as AB. Conclude with a recommendation of an approximate flotation value for AB, in total and per share.

(30 minutes)

Note: A report format is not required for this question.

Test your understanding answers

Test your understanding 1 (Integration question)

Assuming the statement of financial position values are realistic, the valuation is:

	$000
Non-current assets	23,600
Current assets	8,400
Less: 6% Unsecured bond	(8,000)
Less: Current liabilities	(4,800)
	19,200

So the value per share is $19,200,000 / 8,000,000 = $2.40

(Note that the asset value of $19,200,000 is equal to the value of the ordinary share capital plus reserves.)

Fowler's perspective

Value per share = ($19,200,000 + $40,000,000 – $23,600,000) / 8,000,000

= $4.45

Test your understanding 2 (Integration question)

GBP000		Explanation / justification
Non-current assets	1,500	Ray plc is buying the business, so would have to buy the machinery from scratch if it decided on the alternative of organic growth. The realisable value will be a useful minimum value from Ribbon Ltd's perspective, but it is not relevant to Ray plc.
Current assets (564–120–30)	414	The inventory and receivables relating to the bankrupt customer will not be acquired by Ray plc. They are therefore excluded from the valuation.
Less: 5% bonds	(600)	
Less: Current liabilities	(518)	In order for Ray plc to takeover Ribbon Ltd, it needs to buy the equity of the business. After the takeover, Ray plc will be responsible for meeting these liabilities, so they should be included in the valuation of Ribbon Ltd.
	796	

Value per share = GBP 796,000 / 100,000 = GBP 7.96

Test your understanding 3 (Objective test question)

The answer is (A).

Workings:

		$m
Current pre-tax profit		24.29
Less: Industry ROA × Tangible assets	10% × 128.66m	(12.87)
Excess annual return		11.42
Post-tax excess annual return	11.42m × (1–0.30)	7.99
CIV (assuming constant perpetuity)	7.99m × 1/0.16	49.94

Therefore, the total value of Chapman Co is estimated to be

128.66m + 49.94m = $178.60m (approx $179m)

Test your understanding 4 (Objective test question)

The answer is (C).

Workings:

EPS = 3,840,000 / 1,000,000 shares = $3.84

Value per share = P/E × EPS = 9 × $3.84 = $34.56

Test your understanding 5 (Integration question)

The maximum that X should be prepared to pay for Y is the total increase in value generated by taking over Y, i.e.

Value of combined	= 11 × (3m +1.5m +0.5m)	= $55m
Less value of X	= 12 × 3m	= $36m
Max. price to pay		= $19m.

However, the shareholders of Y will value their company at 8 × 1.5m = $12m since they will not have enough information to enable them to value the expected synergies.

The price paid by X to take over Y is then likely to fall somewhere between these two valuations, depending upon the negotiating skills of the buyer and seller.

Test your understanding 6 (Integration question)

(a) $\quad Po = \dfrac{250{,}000}{0.14}$

$\quad$ = EUR 1.786 million, or 1.786/2 = EUR 0.893 per share.

(b) $\quad Po = \dfrac{250{,}000 \times 1.04}{0.14 - 0.04}$

$\quad$ = EUR 2.6 million, or 2.6/2 = EUR 1.30 per share.

Test your understanding 7 (Integration question)

Dividend in 1 year would have been $1.5 million × 1.02 = $1.53 million.

Therefore under the new policy it will be half of this i.e. $0.765 million.

So the present value of dividends for the next four years, discounted at 10%, will be:

$(0.765 \times 0.909) + (0.765 \times 1.10 \times 0.826) + (0.765 \times 1.10^2 \times 0.751) + (0.765 \times 1.10^3 \times 0.683)$

= $2.780 million

After the first four years, the dividends will settle into a growing perpetuity, whose present value is:

$[(0.765 \times 1.10^3 \times 1.05) / 0.10 - 0.05] \times 0.683 = \$14.604$ million

Therefore, the total value is $2.780 million + $14.604 million = $17.384 million, or approximately $1.74 per share for each of the 10 million shares.

This is a fall of $0.17 per share.

Test your understanding 8 (Objective test question)

The answer is (B).

Workings:

Year	GBP	DF (12%)	PV
1	120,000	0.893	107,160
2	100,000	0.797	79,700
3	140,000	0.712	99,680
4	50,000	0.636	31,800
5	130,000	0.567	73,710
		NPV	392,050

However, this ignores cash flows after year 5. Assuming the year 5 cash flow continues to infinity, this has a present value of:

130,000 / 0.12 = GBP 1,083,333

This has a present value today of:

GBP 1,083,333 × 0.567 = GBP 614,250

This gives a total present value (value of equity) of:

614,250 + 392,050 = GBP 1,006,300

Test your understanding 9 (Integration question)

GBPm	Year 1	Year 2	Year 3 etc
Sales (×1.03×1.05)	308.3	333.5	360.6
Cost of sales (×1.05)	(126.9)	(133.3)	(140.0)
Gross profit	181.4	200.2	220.6
Operating expenses	(66.9)	(66.9)	(66.9)
Financing costs	(10.0)	(10.0)	(10.0)
Forecast profit before tax	104.5	123.3	143.7
Less Taxation (28%)	(29.3)	(34.5)	(40.2)
Add back depreciation	12.3	12.3	12.3
Less Capital expenditure	(15.0)	(15.0)	(15.0)
Less Working capital investment	(2.0)	(2.0)	(2.0)
Forecast cash flows to equity	70.5	84.1	98.8
DF 12%	0.893	0.797	0.797/0.12
Present value	63.0	67.0	656.2

So the net present value = GBP786.2m

This is the total value of the equity in Butler Co.

With 500 million shares in issue, this corresponds to a value of

786.2 / 500 = GBP 1.57 per share.

Test your understanding 10 (Objective test question)

The answer is (A).

Workings:

Method 1:

Step 1

XYZ's asset beta is calculated and then used as an estimate of ABC's asset beta (because ABC and XYZ are in the same area of business and so will have the same *asset* beta).

Using: $\text{ßu} = \text{ßg} \times \dfrac{E}{E + D(1 - t)}$

$\text{ßu} = 1.25 \times \dfrac{2}{2 + 1(1 - 0.30)} = 0.926$

Step 2

An equity beta for ABC is calculated next. As we know, an equity beta reflects both systematic business risk *and* systematic financial risk. ABC's equity beta will reflect ABC's business risk and ABC's gearing of 1:3.

Using: $\text{ßu} = \text{ßg} \times \dfrac{E}{E + D(1 - t)}$

$0.926 = \text{ßg} \times \dfrac{3}{3 + 1 \times (1 - 0.30)}$

$0.926 = \text{ßg} \times 0.811$

$\dfrac{0.926}{0.811} = \text{ßg} = 1.14$

Step 3

This equity beta is then input into CAPM to give a cost of equity capital for ABC:

$$k_e = R_F + [R_M - R_F]\, \beta g$$

$$Ke = 6\% + [14\% - 6\%] \times 1.14 = 15.12\%$$

Step 4

ABC's WACC is now calculated.

However, before we can do this calculation, we need to identify ABC's after-tax cost of debt capital. In many questions this information is given, but here it is not.

If you need a cost of debt in order to answer a question, but are not given one, then you can make use of the fact that we are allowed to assume 'corporate debt is risk-free'. In these circumstances:

$$k_d = R_F$$

$$\text{and } kd(1 - t) = R_F (1 - T)$$

Therefore: $kd(1 - t) = 6\% (1 - 0.3) = 4.2\%$

Hence the WACC can be calculated using:

$$WACC = k_e \times \frac{E}{V} + kd(1{-}t) \times \frac{D}{V} = 15.12\% \times \frac{3}{4} + 4.2\% \times \frac{1}{4} = 12.4\%$$

Alternatively: Method 2:

Step 1

As above, the existing geared / equity beta of XYZ is degeared, to give an ungeared / asset beta of 0.926.

Step 2

Input this ungeared beta into the CAPM formula to give an ungeared cost of equity (k_{eu})

k_{eu}= 6% + [14% – 6%] × 0.926 = 13.4%

Step 3

Use the M & M WACC formula

$k_{adj} = k_{eu} (1 – tL)$

=13.4% (1 – 30% × (1/4)) = 12.4% as before.

Test your understanding 11 (Objective test question)

The two cells containing errors are highlighted in bold below:

Time (years)	0	1	2	3-5	6+
Net operating cash flow (NOCF)	-	250	250	250	250
Tax on NOCF	-	-	(75)	(75)	(75)
New equipment	(200)	-	-	-	-
Tax relief on new equipment	-	**15**	15	**30**	-

The new machine is bought on 1 January 20X1, so the first tax depreciation allowance will be claimed at the end of 20X1. However, because tax is paid a year in arrears in this scenario, the tax relief on this first allowance would only be received one year later, at the end of 20X2 (corresponding to year 2 in the table).

The 30 in the 'year 3-5' column implies that $30m of tax relief would be received each year in year 3, 4 and 5. This is not the case. The figures should be split into separate columns for years 3, 4 and 5.

The tax relief figures should appear as $15m each year in years 2, 3, 4 and 5.

Test your understanding 12 (Objective test question)

[UNKNOWN FIGURE 1] is (A) 0.16 and [UNKNOWN FIGURE 2] is (E) 0.80

The missing figures were industry return on assets as [UNKNOWN FIGURE 1] and (1-tax rate) as [UNKNOWN FIGURE 2].

Test your understanding 13 (Objective test question)

The answer is (A), (D) and (E).

If Mini Co has recently revalued its assets, arguably the asset based method will be more accurate (B).

If Mini Co has been making losses recently, asset based valuations are unaffected (C). Admittedly earnings based valuations might be more problematic.

Test your understanding 14 (Objective test question)

The answer is (D)

Use the given formula, and make sure that Ve and Vd are the equity and debt values for the proxy company (BLAIZE in this case).

Test your understanding 15 (Objective test question)

The answer is (D).

Systematic risk reflects variations in the return of a security due to general market factors.

Test your understanding 16 (Case style question)

The approaches to use for valuation are:

(1) Asset valuation

(2) Dividend valuation model

(3) P/E ratio / Earnings valuation.

(1) **Asset valuation**

Target is being purchased as a going concern, so realisable values are irrelevant.

	£000
Net assets per accounts (1,892 – 768)	1,124
Adjustments to freehold property (800 – 460)	340
Adjustment to inventory	(50)
Valuation	**1,414**
	Say £1.4m

(2) **Dividend valuation model**

The average rate of growth in Target's dividends over the last four years is 7.4% on a compound basis.

Growth working: $(113.1/85.0)^{(1/4)} - 1 = 0.074$

The estimated value of Target using the dividend valuation model is therefore:

Valuation $\dfrac{£113,100 \times 1.074}{0.15 - 0.074}$ = **£1,598,281 Say £1.6m**

(3) **P/E ratio/Earnings valuation**

A suitable P/E ratio for Target will be based on the P/E ratio of Predator as both companies are in the same industry.

P/E of Predator: $\dfrac{70m \times £4.30}{£20.04}$ = or $\dfrac{430}{28.63}$ **= 15**

Target's maintainable earnings are:

£183,000 + (£40,000 × 67%) = £209,800 after adjusting for the savings in the director's remuneration.

The estimated value is therefore £209,800 × 15 = £3,147,000, **say £3.1m.**

Advice to the board

On the basis of its tangible assets the value of Target is £1.4m, which excludes any value for intangibles.

The dividend valuation gives a value of around £1.6m.

The earnings based valuation indicates a value of around £3.1m, which is based on the assumption that not only will the current earnings be maintained, but that they will increase by the savings in the director's remuneration. It is also based on a proxy P/E ratio of 15 which was taken from a much larger listed company with a higher level of historic growth. Arguably this P/E ratio is too high for the circumstances of Target.

On the basis of these valuations an offer of around £2m would appear to be most suitable. The directors should, however, be prepared to increase the offer to:

Maximum price:

It is worth noting that the maximum price Predator should be prepared to offer is:

The NPV of the combined group after the acquisition	X
The NPV of the acquiring company before the acquisition	(X)
Maximum price	**X**

If **synergy** occurs this could justify a higher price than shown by the valuation methods illustrated.

The comment on the maximum price is particularly appropriate in this question as this an example of horizontal integration where considerable synergies normally exist.

Test your understanding 17 (Case style question)

(a) **Calculations**

Methods that could be considered are:

- Asset value
- Market capitalisation
- Dividend/earnings valuation model
- NPV

Each method is calculated as follows:

Asset value

The statement of financial position for 20X6 shows net assets of EUR233m (€233m). However, this entity clearly has substantial intellectual capital, which the value of tangible assets in the statement of financial position does not reflect. An estimate of the value of an intangible asset can be attempted as follows.

This method involves taking the excess returns on tangible assets and uses this figure as a basis for determining the proportion of return attributable to intangible assets.

(1) Calculation of average pre-tax earnings for three years:

(€67.5m + €74.2m + €56.9m)/3 = €66.2m

(2) From the statement of financial position the average year end tangible assets over the last three years is calculated as:

(€198m + €229m + €263m)/3 = €230m

(3) The return on assets is calculated by dividing earnings by average assets as follows:

(€66.2m/€230m) × 100 = 28.8%

(4) The industry's return on assets for this same three years is 15% (as per the scenario).

(5) Multiply the industry average pre-tax return on assets by the entity's average tangible assets to show what the average telecoms entity would earn from that amount of tangible assets:

€230m × 15% = €34.5m

Subtract this from the entity's pre-tax earnings:

€66.2m – €34.5m = €31.7m This figure shows how much more AB earns from its assets than the average telecommunications company.

(6) The after tax premium attributable to intangible assets is calculated as follows:
  (a) Three-year average income tax rate = 30%
  (b) Excess return = €31.7m
  (c) Multiply (i) by (ii) = €9.5m
  (d) (ii)–(iii) = €22.2m

(7) The NPV of the premium is calculated by dividing the premium by the entity's cost of capital as follows:

€22.2m/0.08 = €277m

If the NPV of the estimated value of intellectual capital is added to the value of net tangible assets we get €263m + €277m = €540m, less current liabilities gives a net figure of €510m.

Tutorial Note: Candidates would have gained credit for any valid attempt to place a value on intellectual capital.

Market capitalisation / PE method

If we use the industry average P/E of 12.5 the potential value is €497.5m. If AB can command a rating up to 30% higher, this value rises to €646.7m.

Note: €497.5m is calculated as €56.9m (20X6 pre-tax earnings) less €17.1m (taxation) multiplied by 12.5 (industry average P/E)

Dividend/earnings model

There is insufficient information to use the DVM, although earnings could be used as a proxy. However, as the future growth rate is not constant the simplified model cannot be used. The NPV approach would give broadly similar results.

NPV

	20X7 EURm	20X8 EURm
After tax profit	50	64
Add: Depreciation	48	48
Cash flow	98	112
DF 10%	0.909	0.826
PV	89	93

DCF of cash flows for 20X9 and beyond are

€112m × 1.03 × 0.826/(0.10 − 0.03) = €1.361m

NPV = €89m + €93m + €1,361m = €1,543m

Tutorial Note: The calculations here use the industry average cost of capital. An acceptable alternative would use 8%, the earnings yield (reciprocal of P/E ratio of 12.5). In this case the NPV would be €2,164m.

Summary of valuations

	Total EURm	Per share EUR
Asset value	233	7.70
Asset value including intellectual capital	455	15.17
PE method	497–647	16.57–21.57
NPV	1,543	51.43

(b) **Discussion of methods and recommendation**

Asset value

Asset value has little relevance except in specific circumstances such as a liquidation or disposal of parts of a business. Asset value is of even more limited usefulness in an entity such as AB, which earns a substantial proportion of its income from intellectual capital that generally does not feature in the statement of financial position.

Market capitalisation / PE method

The P/E basis of valuation has the advantage that it bases value on the future earnings of the entity. In a listed entity, the P/E ratio is used to describe the relationship between the share price (or market capitalisation) and earnings per share (or total earnings). It is calculated by dividing the price per share by the earnings per share. Market capitalisation is the share price multiplied by the number of shares in issue. Market capitalisation is not necessarily the true value of an entity as it can be affected by a variety of extraneous factors but for a listed entity it provides a benchmark that cannot be ignored in, say, a take-over situation.

In the case of an unlisted entity, a P/E ratio that is representative of similar quoted entities might be used as a starting point for arriving at an estimated market value, based upon the present earnings of the unlisted entity. The potential market capitalisation would be the entity's latest earnings multiplied by the benchmark P/E ratio.

AB is an unlisted entity so it does not have a market capitalisation or a quoted P/E ratio. Applying the industry average P/E provides a benchmark but not a very good one. As noted in the scenario, there is a wide variation around this average. Also, although not stated, the definition of the industry is likely to be very broad. A better approach might be to find an entity similar to AB and apply its P/E. Again, this is very rough and ready. As AB is unlisted there are arguments for both lowering and raising the P/E as compared with either a proxy entity or the industry average. The Financial Advisor's estimate is that AB could command a rating 30% higher than the industry average. It is not clear how this estimate was made, as an argument could be made for lowering the P/E ratio to reflect the higher risk and lower liquidity of such entities. It would be more appropriate to use the NPV method and adjust the discount rate – as discussed below.

NPV/Earnings method

Forecasting cash flows and discounting at a specific risk adjusted discount rate is the theoretically correct valuation method. The valuation here uses the industry average cost of equity. Using an industry average suffers from the problems noted above. Also, the cost of equity will include an element of return for financial risk if entities have debt in their capital structure. Many entities included in the industry average will have substantial debt finance.

What is needed here is an exercise to calculate a more accurate cost of capital. As with using the P/E ratio approach, discussed above, finding a proxy entity may be more reliable than using an industry average.

Recommendation

As shown in the summary table in part (a), the likely market value ranges from €233m (net tangible assets) to €1,543m (NPV). The NPV valuation is substantially higher than any of the others. While this method is theoretically correct, the reliability of the results does of course depend on the accuracy of the forecast cash flows and the discount rate used. Using growth in perpetuity (although a sensible simplification for examination purposes) is unrealistic.

None of the figures produced by this exercise is wholly reliable, neither is it expected to be, as this is simply an estimate based on incomplete information. The main recommendation must be to conduct a more detailed evaluation involving other advisors such as the entity that will be responsible for the flotation. It needs also to be established what percentage of their shareholding each director wishes to sell on flotation and how many new shares will need to be reissued. The calculations have been made on the current number of shares in issue to the directors/founding shareholders.

However, if a recommendation has to be made, a flotation value in the region of €600m or €20 per share would be conservative.

(Tutorial Note: Any sensible recommendation, or argument for not making one on the evidence available, would gain credit.)

A secondary recommendation would be to split the shares in readiness for a flotation. The share prices produced by all valuation methods, except asset value, are 'heavy' – that is buyers would not get many shares for their money. More shares would need to be in issue to allow a reasonably liquid market in them.

Pricing issues and post-transaction issues

Chapter learning objectives

Lead	Component
C3: Evaluate pricing issues and post-transaction issues.	(a) Evaluate alternative pricing structures and bid process including taxation implications.
	(b) Evaluate post-transaction issues.

Indicative syllabus content

- Forms of consideration and terms for acquisitions (e.g. cash, shares, convertibles and earn-out arrangements), and their impact on shareholders, including taxation impact.

- Treatment of target entity debt (settlement, refinancing).

- Methods/implications of financing a cash offer and refinancing target entity debt.

- Bid negotiation (e.g. managing a hostile bid) including agency issues.

- Potential post-transaction value for both acquirer and seller (e.g. taking into account synergistic benefits, forecast performance and market response).

- Integration of management/systems and effective realisation of synergistic benefits.

- Types of exit strategies and their implications.

1 Overview of chapter

The last two chapters have covered business valuation and strategic issues associated with acquisitions and mergers.

This chapter continues to look at acquisitions and mergers, but we now move on to look at practical matters such as what form of consideration should be used in an acquisition (for example cash or a share exchange) and the negotiation process that surrounds a bid.

2 Defences against hostile takeover bids

Any listed company needs to be aware that a bid might be received at any time.

The directors of a company subject to a hostile takeover bid should act in the best interests of their shareholders. However, in practice they will also consider the views of other stakeholders (such as employees, and themselves).

If the board of directors of a target company decides to fight a bid that appears to be financially attractive to their shareholders, then they should consider one of the following defences:

- Pre bid defences
  - Communicate effectively with shareholders
  - Revalue non-current assets
  - Poison pill
  - Change the Articles of Association to require 'super majority' approval for a takeover

- Post bid defences
  - Appeal to their own shareholders
  - Attack the bidder
  - White Knight
  - Counterbid – sometimes called a 'Pacman' defence
  - Refer the bid to the Competition authorities

Details of takeover defences

Pre-bid defences

Communicate effectively with shareholders

This includes having a public relations officer specialising in financial matters liaising constantly with the entity's stockbrokers, keeping analysts fully informed, and speaking to journalists.

Revalue non-current assets

Non-current assets are revalued to current values to ensure that shareholders are aware of true asset value per share.

Poison pill strategy

Here a target company takes steps before a bid has been made to make itself less attractive to a potential bidder. The most common method is for existing shareholders to be given rights to buy future bonds or preference shares. If a bid is made before the date of exercise of the rights, then the rights will automatically be converted into full ordinary shares.

Super majority

The Articles of Association are altered to require that a higher percentage (say 80%) of shareholders have to vote for the takeover.

Post-bid defences

Appeal to their own shareholders

For example, by declaring that the value placed on the target company's shares is too low in relation to the real value and earning power of the company's assets, or alternatively that the market price of the bidder's shares is unjustifiably high and is not sustainable.

A well-managed defensive campaign would include:

(i)   Aggressive publicity on behalf of the company preferably before a bid is received. Investors may be told of any good research ideas within the company and of the management potential or merely be made more aware of the company's achievements.

(ii) Direct communication with the shareholders in writing stressing the financial and strategic reasons for remaining independent.

Note: Under the City Code in the UK, any forecasts must be examined and reported on by the auditors or consultant accountants.

Attack the bidder

Typically concentrating on the bidder's management style, overall strategy, methods of increasing earnings per share, dubious accounting policies and lack of capital investment.

White Knight strategy

This is where the directors of the target company offer themselves to a more friendly outside interest. This tactic should only be adopted in the last resort as it means that the company will lose its independence. This tactic is acceptable provided that any information given to a preferred bidder is also given to a hostile bidder. The alternative company's management will be considered to be sympathetic to the target company's management.

Counterbid, or Pacman defence

Where the bidding company is itself the subject of a takeover bid by the target company.

Competition authorities

The target entity could seek government intervention by bringing in the Competition authorities. For this to be effective it would have to be proved that the takeover was against the public interest.

3 The form of consideration for a takeover

Introduction

When one firm acquires another, two questions must be addressed regarding the form of consideration for the takeover:

(1) what form of consideration should be offered? Cash offer, or share exchange, or earn-out are the three main choices.

(2) if a cash offer is to be made, how should the cash be raised? The choice is generally debt finance or a rights issue to generate the cash (if the entity does not have enough cash already).

The key considerations regarding these two questions are outlined below.

Form of consideration

Cash

In a cash offer, the target company shareholders are offered a fixed cash sum per share.

This method is likely to be suitable only for relatively small acquisitions, unless the bidding entity has an accumulation of cash.

Advantages:

*   When the bidder has sufficient cash the takeover can be achieved quickly and at low cost.

*   Target company shareholders have certainty about the bid's value i.e. there is less risk compared to accepting shares in the bidding company.

*   There is increased liquidity to target company shareholders, i.e. accepting cash in a takeover, is a good way of realising an investment.

*   The acceptable consideration is likely to be less than with a share exchange, as there is less risk to target company shareholders. This reduces the overall cost of the bid to the bidding company.

Disadvantages:

*   With larger acquisitions the bidder must often borrow in the capital markets or issue new shares in order to raise the cash. This may have an adverse effect on gearing, and also cost of capital due to the increased financial risk.

*   For target company shareholders, in some jurisdictions a taxable chargeable gain will arise if shares are sold for cash, but the gain may not be immediately chargeable to tax under a share exchange.

- Target company shareholders may be unhappy with a cash offer, since they are 'bought out' and do not participate in the new group. Of course, this could be seen as an advantage of a cash offer by the bidding company shareholders if they want to keep full control of the bidding company.

Share exchange

In a share exchange, the bidding company issues some new shares and then exchanges them with the target company shareholders. The target company shareholders therefore end up with shares in the bidding company, and the target company's shares all end up in the possession of the bidding company.

Large acquisitions almost always involve an exchange of shares, in whole or in part.

Advantages:

- The bidding company does not have to raise cash to make the payment.

- The bidding company can 'boot strap' earnings per share if it has a higher P/E ratio than the acquired entity (terminology explained later in this chapter).

- Shareholder capital is increased – and gearing similarly improved – as the shareholders of the acquired company become shareholders in the post-acquisition company.

- A share exchange can be used to finance very large acquisitions.

Disadvantages:

- The bidding company's shareholders have to share future gains with the acquired entity, and the current shareholders will have a lower proportionate control and share in profits of the combined entity than before.

- Price risk – there is a risk that the market price of the bidding company's shares will fall during the bidding process, which may result in the bid failing. For example, if a 1 for 2 share exchange is offered based on the fact that the bidding company's shares are worth approximately double the value of the target company's shares, the bid might fail if the value of the bidding company's shares falls before the acceptance date.

Earn-out

Definition of an earn-out arrangement: A procedure whereby owners/managers selling an entity receive a portion of their consideration linked to the financial performance of the business during a specified period after the sale. The arrangement gives a measure of security to the new owners, who pass some of the financial risk associated with the purchase of a new entity to the sellers. (CIMA Official Terminology, 2005)

The purchase consideration is sometimes structured so that there is an initial amount paid at the time of acquisition, and the balance deferred.

Some of the deferred balance will usually only become payable if the target entity achieves specified performance targets.

More details on earn-out arrangements

Earn-out arrangements are often employed when the buyers and sellers disagree about the expected growth and future performance of the target company.

A typical earn-out takes place over a three to five year period after the acquisition and may involve 10% - 50% of the purchase price being deferred and paid across during that period.

Earn-outs are popular among private equity investors, who do not necessarily have the expertise to run a target business after acquiring it, as a way of keeping the previous owners involved following the acquisition.

Example:

An entrepreneur selling a business is asking $2 million based on projected earnings, but the buyer is willing to pay only $1 million based on historical performance.

An earn-out provision might structure the deal so that the entrepreneur receives more than the buyer's offer only if the business achieves certain targets. For example the earnout might set the purchase price at $1 million plus 10% of gross sales over the next three years.

Earn-out targets

The financial targets used in an earn-out calculation may include revenue, net income, EBITDA or EBIT targets.

Sellers tend to prefer revenue as the simplest measurement, but revenue can be boosted through business activities that hurt the bottom line of the company. On the other hand, buyers tend to prefer net income as the most accurate reflection of overall economic performance, but this number can be manipulated downward through extensive capital expenditures and other front-loaded business expenses.

Some earn-outs may be based on entirely non-financial targets such as the development of a product or the execution of a contract.

Limitations of earn-outs

Earn-outs have several fundamental limitations.

They generally work best when the business is operated as envisioned at the time of the transaction, rather than in circumstances where the business plan changes, often in response to a change in the business environment.

In some transactions, the buyer may have the ability to block the earn-out targets from being met. Outside factors may also impact the company's ability to achieve earn-out targets.

Sellers need to negotiate earn-out terms very carefully, taking into account all these issues.

Summary of the key issues relating to forms of consideration

Considerations of different stakeholders

In order to evaluate which form of consideration is appropriate in a particular case, it is important to assess the positions of both the target company's shareholders, and the bidding company and its shareholders.

Position of the target company's shareholders

The target company's shareholders may want to retain an interest in the business, in which case a cash offer would not be welcomed. However, there is a greater certainty of value with a cash offer (share prices fluctuate, so in a share exchange the target company's shareholders cannot be completely sure whether they are receiving an appropriate valuation for their shares).

Position of the bidding company and its shareholders

The bidding company will have to issue new shares if it is to undertake a share exchange. This may require the consent of shareholders in a general meeting. The shareholders may be concerned in a share exchange that their control of the bidding company will be diluted by the issue and exchange of shares.

Another key consideration is the impact of the takeover on the bidding company's financial statements. An issue of new shares could reduce the level of earnings per share (a measure which is often used as a key performance measure by market analysts). However, if a cash offer is made, the raising of the necessary cash could have a significant impact on the gearing of the bidding company.

Methods of financing a cash offer

If the bidding company has a large cash surplus, it might be able to make a cash offer without raising any new finance.

However, in most cases, this will not be the case, so various financing options will have to be considered by the bidding company. The main two options are debt or a rights issue.

Note that the amount of finance needed might be higher than expected if there is a plan to repay the target entity debt at the time of the takeover. This can sometimes be a requirement of the target entity's lenders, as stipulated in a debt covenant.

If target entity debt has to be repaid, the bidding company's total cash requirement will need to cover the cost of purchasing the equity shares and the value of the target entity debt.

Debt

The bidding company could borrow the required cash from the bank, or issue bonds in the market.

The advantage of using debt in this situation is the low cost of servicing the debt. However, raising new debt finance will increase the bidding company's gearing. This will increase the risk to the bidding company's shareholders, so might not be acceptable to the shareholders.

Rights issue

If the bidding company shareholders do not want to suffer the increased risk which debt finance would bring, the alternative would be for the bidding company to offer a rights issue to its existing shareholders. The funds raised can then be used to buy the shares in the company being acquired. Gearing levels are thereby protected.

From the shareholders' point of view, the problem with this financing option is that it is the shareholders themselves who have to find the money to invest.

Evaluating a share for share exchange

One popular question is to comment on the likely acceptance of a share for share offer. The procedure is as follows:

- Value the predator company as an independent entity and hence calculate the value of a share in that company.

- Repeat the procedure for the victim company.

- Calculate the value of the combined company post integration. This is calculated as:

Value of predator company as independent company	X
Value of victim company as independent company	X
Value of any synergy	X
Total value of combined company	X

- Calculate the number of shares post integration:

Number of shares originally in the predator company	X
Number of shares issued to victim company	X
Total shares post integration	X

- Calculate the value of a share in the combined company, and use this to assess the change in wealth of the shareholders after the takeover.

Illustration 1 (Integration question)

Company A has 200m shares with a current market value of GBP4 per share. Company B has 90m shares with a current market value of GBP2 per share.

A makes an offer of 3 new shares for every 5 currently held in B. A has worked out that the present value of synergies will be GBP40m.

Required:

Calculate the expected value of a share in the combined company (assuming that the given share prices have not yet moved to anticipate the takeover), and advise the shareholders in company B whether the offer should be accepted.

Solution:

MV of A = GBP800m

MV of B = GBP180m

PV of synergies = GBP40m

TOTAL = GBP1,020m

No. of new shares = 200m + (3/5) × 90m = 254m

New share price = 1,020m / 254m = GBP4.02

	Shares	MV	Old wealth	Change
A	200m	GBP804m	GBP800m	GBP4m
B	(3/5) × 90m = 54m	GBP216m	GBP180m	GBP36m

The wealth of the shareholders in company B will increase by GBP36m as a consequence of the takeover. This is a (36/180) 20% increase in wealth.

Company B's shareholders should be advised to accept the 3 for 5 share for share offer.

Further numerical illustration (Integration question)

Initial example – cash offer

Summary of information regarding Entity A and Entity B, two UK companies (currency GBP, or £):

	Entity A	Entity B
Market price per share (£)	75	15
Number of shares	100,000	60,000
Market value (£)	7,500,000	900,000

Required:

If A intends to pay £1.2m cash for B, what is the cost premium if:

(a) the share price does not anticipate the takeover;

(b) the share price of Entity B includes a 'speculation' element of £2 per share?

Solution:

(a) The share price accurately reflects the true value of the entity (in theory).

Therefore, the cost to the bidder is simply £1,200,000 – £900,000, that is, £300,000.

Entity A is paying £300,000 for the identified benefits of the takeover.

(b) The cost is £300,000 + (60,000 × £2), or £420,000.

Follow up example – share exchange

Suppose A offers 16,000 shares (£1.2m / £75) instead of £1.2m cash. The cost appears to be £300,000 as before, but because B's shareholders will own part of A, they will benefit from any future gains of the combined entity. Their share will be (16,000/(16,000 + 100,000)), or 13.8%.

Further, suppose that the benefits of the combination have been identified by A to have a present value of £400,000 (i.e. A thinks that B is really worth £900,000 + £400,000, or £1.3m). Therefore, the combined entity of A and B is worth £7.5m + £1.3m, or £8.8m.

Required:

Calculate the true cost of the takeover to the acquirer's shareholders.

Solution:

Estimate of post-acquisition prices

	A	**B**
Proportion of ownership	86.2%	13.8%
Market value: £8.8m × proportion	£7.586m	£1.214m
Number of shares currently in issue	100,000	60,000
Price per share (£)	75.86	20.23

What we are attempting to do here is to value the shares in the entity before the takeover is completed, based on estimates of what the entity will be worth after the merger. The valuation of each entity also recognises the split of the expected benefits which will accrue to the combined form once the merger has taken place.

The true cost to A can now be calculated as follows:

	£
60,000 B shares at £20.23	1,213,800
Less: Current market value	(900,000)
	————
Benefits being paid to B's shareholders	313,800
	————

Test your understanding 1 (Case style question)

Mavers Co and Power Co are listed on the Stock Exchange.

Relevant information is as follows:

	Mavers Co	**Power Co**
Share price today	$3.05	$6.80
Shares in issue	48 million	13 million

Mavers Co wants to acquire 100% of the shares of Power Co.

The directors are considering offering 2 new Mavers Co shares for every 1 Power Co share.

Required:

Evaluate whether the 2 for 1 share for share exchange will be likely to succeed.

If necessary, recommend revised terms for the offer which would be likely to succeed.

(30 minutes)

Bootstrapping and post-acquisition values

In the previous examples, we were told specifically what the values of the separate companies were before the takeover, and the synergy generated by the takeover was also given.

Sometimes we might have to derive these figures, using the bootstrapping method as in the following illustration.

Illustration 2 (Case style question)

	Post-tax profit	P/E ratio	Pre-acquisition value
Company C	$10m	16	$160m
Company D	$1m	8	$8m

If Company C takes over Company D, the post-acquisition value of the combined company can be estimated by applying Company C's P/E ratio to the combined post-tax profit.

This is known as **bootstrapping,** and it is based on the assumption that the market will assume that the management of the larger company will be able to apply common approach to both companies after the takeover, thus improving the performance of the acquired company by using the methods that they have been using on their own company before the takeover.

Value of (C+D) post-acquisition = 16 × ($10m + $1m) = $176m

Thus, the value of the synergy is this combined value, less the values of the individual companies pre-acquisition, i.e.

$176m – $160m – $8m = $8m

4 Treatment of target entity debt

Introduction

In looking at forms of consideration above, we have assumed that the takeover bid will need to be sufficient to attract the target entity shareholders to want to sell their shares.

However, in many takeovers, the consideration needs to be greater than this, to deal with any 'material adverse change clauses' attached to the target entity's borrowings.

Treatment of debt in the target entity

A material adverse change clause is often used to make the target entity's borrowings repayable if the company is sold.

Therefore, when considering how to fund a takeover, the bidding company will have to ensure that sufficient funds are available to purchase the shares from the target entity's shareholders, and to repay the debt in the target entity.

> ### Illustration 3
>
> **Example:**
>
> Company P is considering a takeover bid for Company H.
>
> The $2.2 million borrowings in Company H are repayable if Company H is acquired.
>
> Therefore, Company P is considering one of the following offers:
>
> - P to pay $ 4.9 million in cash ($ 2.7 million cash to H's shareholders PLUS $ 2.2 million to finance the repayment of H's borrowings).
>
> - Exchange two P $ 0.50 ordinary shares for each H ordinary share held PLUS P to pay H $ 2.2 million in cash to finance the repayment of H's borrowings.
>
> **Comments:**
>
> - Note that the bids look very similar to the ones seen earlier in the chapter, but they now contain a reference to the extra payment required to repay the debt

- We need to be careful with business valuation here. For example, in the previous chapter: 'Business valuation' we saw that:
  - applying an appropriate P/E ratio to the company's earnings, or discounting forecast cash flows to equity using cost of equity gives the value of the EQUITY, whereas:
  - discounting forecast cash flows to all investors using WACC gives the value of the WHOLE ENTITY (equity plus debt), and:
  - an asset valuation could be either an EQUITY valuation or an ENTITY valuation, depending what is included in the valuation calculation.

- Therefore, when deciding what size of offer should be made, it is critical to assess whether the valuation figure already includes the value of both debt and equity or whether it is just an equity valuation.

- Note that in the circumstances described in the offer above, P would need to consider how to finance the cash offer of $4.9 million (e.g. by borrowing), but it would also have to consider the possibility of borrowing under the share for share exchange offer.

Test your understanding 2 (Objective test question)

BB is considering a takeover bid for QQ.

BB has prepared a valuation of QQ based on a forecast of cash flows before financing charges, discounted at an appropriate weighted average cost of capital. The valuation is $130 million.

If BB does acquire QQ, QQ's debt of $20 million will become repayable.

If BB wants to make a cash offer, what should the value of the cash offer be in total?

A $20 million

B $110 million

C $130 million

D $150 million

5 The post-merger or post-acquisition integration process

Introduction to the post-merger or post-acquisition process

Mergers and acquisitions often fail to deliver the anticipated benefits as a result of failing to effectively integrate the newly acquired entity into the parent.

Poor planning and a lack of information to guide the integration plans ahead of the acquisition will lead to post-acquisition integration problems.

Druker's Golden Rules

P. F. Druker (1981) identified five Golden Rules to apply to post-acquisition integration.

(1) Ensure a 'common core of unity' is shared by the acquired entity and acquirer. Shared technologies or markets are an essential element.

(2) The acquirer should not just think 'What is in it for us?', but also 'What can we offer them?'.

(3) The acquirer must treat the products, markets and customers of the acquired entity with respect.

(4) Within 1 year, the acquirer should provide appropriately skilled top management for the acquired company.

(5) Within 1 year, the acquirer should make several cross-entity promotions of staff.

Post-acquisition value enhancing strategies

The following are key points to consider when determining strategy for the combined entity:

- The integration strategy must be in place before the acquisition is finalised.

- Review each of the business units for potential cost cuttings/synergies or potential asset disposals. It is possible there are outlets more valuable to another entity, but it is important they are in good shape before they are sold. However, more than this is needed for a full effective enhancement programme and a position audit could be carried out.

- Consider the effect on the workforce and determine how many, if any redundancies are likely and what the cost will be.

- Risk diversification may well lower the cost of capital and therefore increase the value of the entity.

- The entity's cost of capital should be re-evaluated.

- Make a positive effort to communicate the post-acquisition intentions within the entity to prevent de-motivation and avoid adverse post-acquisition effects on staff morale.

- There may be economies of scale to identify and evaluate.

- Undertake a review of assets, or resource audit, and consider selling non-core elements or redundant assets.

- There may well be a need to pursue a more aggressive marketing strategy.

- The risks of the acquisition need to be evaluated.

- There needs to be harmonisation of corporate objectives.

Impact on ratios or performance measures

Following the completion of an acquisition the purchaser will need to examine thoroughly the financial and management accounting records of each business unit of the acquired entity.

Thus, the directors of the acquirer will be particularly interested in the financial condition of those units which they might plan to dispose of.

From a strategic point of view these are likely to be of more use to another entity with whom they would form a better fit. However, it is still essential that financially and operationally they should be in as good shape as possible to ensure that a good price can be obtained for them.

Illustration 4

Hall Co has just acquired a subsidiary called Wodgits as part of a larger acquisition.

Hall Co has no other subsidiaries in the same business sector as Wodgits, so management are considering disposing of Wodgits.

A small listed company called Bigwodge, whose core business is similar to Wodgits, has been identified, and by using all published and any other information reasonably available, the following analysis has been prepared:

	Wodgits	Bigwodge
Return on Capital Employed (ROCE)	14.9%	25.0%
Asset turnover	1.3 times	1.8 times
Net profit margin	11.5%	13.9%
Current ratio	1.5 times	2.2 times
Inventory holding period	68 days	57 days
Receivables collection period	54 days	43 days
Payables payment period	49 days	37 days

Other key information:

- Bigwodge has a P/E ratio of 18.
- Wodgits made an operating profit of $860,000 last year.
- Wodgits has total non-current assets of $4.87m, out of which land and buildings comprise $2.5m. Its net assets at book value are $5.77m.
- The tax rate is 33%.

Required:

As the management accountant of Hall Co, prepare a report to the directors in which you analyse the performance of Wodgits compared with Bigwodge, and recommend a price which Hall Co ought to seek for the disposal of Wodgits.

Solution:

Report to the directors of Hall Co

Return on capital employed (ROCE)

Wodgits' inadequate ROCE seems to be mainly due to a low rate of asset turnover, which we must carefully investigate.

We know that land and buildings account for £2.5m of Wodgits' fixed asset total of £4.87m and it is important to establish how much of this property value represents redundant assets. As to plant and machinery, it may be that this is substantially new or revalued, in which case the assets may be of good value and the faults may lie mainly in under-capacity working or production inefficiencies. Much more serious, however, would be a situation where the plant is old and requiring heavy maintenance, and would be hard put to cope with increased volume of throughput.

If the first of these plant scenarios is correct, then Wodgits may well fetch a reasonable price, as a bidder, possibly Bigwodge themselves, would be obtaining good assets to add to their own evidently successful performance in their sector. If the second scenario applies, then we might find it difficult to obtain net asset value for the assets remaining after sale of the redundant properties.

Current ratio

Wodgits' current ratio and inventory holding period are fairly good, but before we put the unit up for sale, we would improve our prospects for a reasonable price by taking early action in regard to both receivables and payables. Both are too high and we should aim to tighten up credit control and also bring payables down to the more acceptable level which Bigwodge's payables payment period indicates is appropriate for the industry sector.

Conclusions

Assuming that we can find that, say, $1.5m of land and buildings are redundant and can be separately sold, and that the plant scenario is favourable or can be made so, then it would not seem to be too difficult to make the remainder of Wodgits a saleable proposition.

Thus if we can assume no debt interest, and taxation of 33%, then after-tax profits could be $576,000 ($860,000 × 0.67), and as Bigwodge's current P/E is 18, we might achieve for Wodgits a P/E of 9 or 10 which suggests a price of between $5.2 and $5.8m, which is comfortably above an asset value of $4.3m ($5.8m – $1.5m assets sold).

The impact of an acquisition on the acquirer's post-acquisition share price

A very important aspect for an acquirer is the post-acquisition effect on its earnings per share (EPS), and the impact on the share price and P/E ratio arising from the market's perceived views on the acquisition.

Once again, detailed analysis of the accounts, and comparison to other companies in similar business sectors can help to assess whether the likely impact will be favourable.

Simple example of the impact on EPS

Assume that the new entity starts with a prospective EPS of 13.1 cents based on combined profits of acquirer and acquired of $8.4m, and 64m shares in issue, and if these earnings could be maintained in year 1 (post-acquisition) they would appear not to be diluted.

However, if the acquirer is expected from its previous performances to attain 10% per annum growth in normal (money) terms, then for year 1 EPS of 13.1 cents × 1.10 would be 14.4 cents, and arguably if this is not attained then dilution will seem to have taken place.

A serious threat to an acquirer's EPS is the 'getting to know you' costs and also the 'reverse synergy' effects of 2+2 = 3, which sadly seems to be the fate of numerous acquisitions.

A major question is whether the present value of the combined earnings, including assumed longer-term profit improvements, really takes into account all the downside costs of putting two different entities together, each with its own management style.

Illustration of strategic issues

You are acting as financial adviser to a public entity, H plc, in the hotel business. H plc is considering a takeover bid for the shares of G Limited. Information relating to G ltd is given in the table below.

G Limited operates in the gaming and betting industry.

The company was established 7 years ago, and the two founder directors still provide the necessary technical and marketing skills. They own 60% of the issued share capital, the balance plus the long-term loan capital having been subscribed by a firm of venture capitalists.

Extracts from the annual reports of G Limited are given below.

Required:

Discuss the extent to which each of the following six reasons might apply to the proposed acquisition of G Limited by H plc. Support your answers with appropriate analysis of the data provided.

(i) Access to innovation

(ii) Growth in earnings per share

(iii) Achievement of operating economies

(iv) Reduction of risk through diversification

(v) Access to liquid funds

(vi) Improved asset backing for borrowing.

Data relating to G Ltd – extracts from annual reports

Year to 30 June	20X8	20X7	20X6
	£000	£000	£000
Revenue	860	684	547
Operating profit	55	68	16
Loan interest	(20)	(14)	(12)
Taxation	(9)	(6)	–
Net profit	26	48	4

Tangible non-current assets:

	20X8	20X7	20X6
Cost	224	174	133
Less depreciation	54	34	23
	170	140	110

Development costs

	20X8	20X7	20X6
Cost	254	189	129
Less written off	176	109	53
	78	80	76

Year to 30 June	20X8	20X7	20X6
	£000	£000	£000
Current assets			
Inventory	30	40	31
Receivables	109	72	57
Cash	1	14	5
	140	126	93
TOTAL ASSETS	388	346	279

Equity

Share capital (25p shares)	100	100	100
Retained profit reserve	61	35	(13)
	161	135	87
Long-term liabilities	160	160	160
Current liabilities	67	51	32
TOTAL EQUITY AND LIABILITIES	388	346	279

Solution:

(i) **Access to innovation**

To comment upon this fully would require detailed statement of profit or loss information. However, the development costs capitalised on the statement of financial position give an indication of considerable increase in development as opposed to research expenditure which has been undertaken, assuming that this does not reflect changes in accounting policy.

Against this, the high rate of write-off suggests that the life of developed products may well be short.

As innovation depends on people, H plc should identify and take steps to retain key staff in the event of a takeover.

(ii) **Growth in earnings per share**

The impact of the acquisition on the earnings per share of H plc will depend upon the price paid and whether the price included shares of H plc.

The past profit performance of G Limited and forecast earnings are certainly erratic and lower in relation to revenue. This may be due to poor management, in which case the firm could be turned around and earnings improved or it could be uncontrollable factors in which case earnings might be low and volatile in the future.

The counter-view would be to suggest that if the rapid growth of the past 3 years can be maintained, then there must be opportunities for boosting earnings even if the profit forecasts do not reflect this.

(iii) Achievement of operating economies

The achievement of such economies depends upon integration of similar businesses. Given that hotels and gaming and betting are closely linked there may be scope for such economies if gambling operations already occur or are planned at the hotels of H plc.

(iv) Reduction of risk through diversification

G Limited has volatile earnings and is more likely to increase the risk profile of H plc than reduce it.

(v) Access to liquid funds

Although there is no ready cash in G Limited, the entity has had a satisfactory liquidity position for several years with current ratios of between 2.9 (20X6) and 2.1 (20X8).

However, it should be noted that the position has worsened slightly over recent years. It is probable that since the hotel industry typically has fairly low liquidity, acquiring G Limited will improve the liquidity position of the combined entity as compared with H plc.

(vi) Improved asset backing for borrowings

Tangible non-current assets at cost less depreciation have increased dramatically during the period 20X6–20X8.

Obviously comments which can be made are limited due to a lack of categorisation of assets and detail of movements. However, the low depreciation charge suggests that there is land and buildings or long leasehold property among the assets.

Such assets provide good security for borrowing, and as assets are at cost the borrowing capacity may well be higher as it will reflect market values.

6 End of chapter objective test questions

Test your understanding 3 (Objective test question)

Mr A and Mr B incorporated a new company five years ago.

The company has grown extremely quickly and Mr A and Mr B still own 100% of the share capital in the company.

They now feel that the company needs an injection of funds to enable it to grow further. Mr A and Mr B want to keep a controlling interest in their company, and they feel that the company's growth prospects would be damaged by disposing of any part of it.

Which TWO of the following strategies could Mr A and Mr B consider?

A   Spin off

B   Initial public offering (IPO)

C   Private equity buy-in

D   Management buy-out

E   Trade sale of the whole company to a competitor

Test your understanding 4 (Objective test question)

Ravenglass Co is the subject of a takeover bid from Irton Co. An offer of $5 per share has been made to the Ravenglass Co shareholders.

Irton Co has recently taken over several other companies and has gained a reputation as an asset stripper. The directors of Ravenglass Co don't feel that the takeover would be in the best interests of the shareholders and other stakeholders of Ravenglass Co, so they are keen to prevent the takeover from going ahead.

Which THREE of the following strategic defence methods could be used by the directors of Ravenglass Co in this situation?

A   Poison pill

B   Super majority

C   White knight

D   Pacman

E   Appeal to the shareholders

Test your understanding 5 (Objective test question)

Paolo Co acquires another company and pays a price that represents a higher P/E valuation than the current P/E of Paolo Co.

The purchase consideration is paid by issuing new Paolo Co shares. There is no synergy arising from the takeover. Paolo Co has some debt in its capital structure.

Which of the following would be the LEAST likely consequence of this takeover?

A   A reduction in gearing for Paolo Co

B   A dilution of earnings of Paolo Co

C   An increase in the share price after the takeover

D   A reduction in the proportionate stake in the company of existing Paolo Co shareholders

Test your understanding 6 (Objective test question)

ASH Co has made a bid for GIANT Co, in an attempt to take it over.

The bid is a 1 for 2 share for share exchange.

Currently, ASH Co has 1 million shares in issue, trading at $6.33. GIANT Co has 200,000 shares in issue trading at $2.96.

It is expected that $100,000 of synergy will be generated by the takeover.

What is the expected share price in the combined company after the takeover?

A $5.92

B $6.33

C $6.38

D $7.02

Test your understanding 7 (Objective test question)

In Co is hoping to make a successful takeover offer for Out Co.

In Co is a successful company but it has relatively low cash reserves. Its gearing ratio has stayed fairly constant at around 15% in recent years (measured as debt / (debt + equity) by market values) and its interest cover is 5.50. 55% of the equity in In Co is still owned by the founding family. This holding has reduced from 75% in the last three years, as the family has sold off shares to generate much-needed income.

Which of the following is likely to be the best way of structuring an offer for Out Co?

A   Cash offer, funded from existing cash resources

B   Cash offer, funded by a rights issue

C   Cash offer, funded by borrowings

D   Share for share exchange

Test your understanding 8 (Objective test question)

Alpha Co has a P/E ratio of 16 and post-tax earnings of $200,000.

Beta Co has a P/E ratio of 21 and post-tax earnings of $800,000.

Beta's directors estimate that if they were to acquire Alpha they could save $100,000 (after tax) annually on administrative costs in running the new combined company. Additionally they estimate that the P/E ratio of the new company would be 20.

On the basis of these estimates, what is the maximum that Beta should pay for the entire share capital of Alpha?

A $6.3 million

B $5.2 million

C $4.2 million

D $2.0 million

Test your understanding 9 (Objective test question)

Two all-equity financed companies, R and S, have identical business risks.

Company R is valued at $40 million and Company S at $8 million. The two companies merge via a share exchange which results in R shareholders holding 80% of the shares of the new merged company.

As a result of synergy, surplus assets of $5 million are sold immediately without affecting the future profitability of the merged company. Half of the proceeds of the disposal are invested in a project with a net present value of $1 million.

What will be the gains to the shareholders of Company R?

A $4.8 million

B $3.2 million

C $1.2 million

D $0.8 million

7 End of chapter case style questions

Test your understanding 10 (Case style question)

(a) One theoretical method of valuing a company's shares is to calculate the present value of future dividends using a discount rate that reflects the risk of the business. In respect of large, listed companies, current evidence suggests that this is far too simplistic a view of how company values and share prices are determined.

   Required:

   Comment on the reasons why share prices may be substantially different from the level suggested by theory. Include brief comments on the relevance of P/E ratios and asset values in share price determination.

   (15 minutes)

(b) ML Co is an expanding clothes retailing company. It is all equity
financed by ordinary share capital of $10 million in shares of 50
cents nominal. The company's results to the end of March 20X9
have just been announced. Pre-tax profits were $4.6 million. The
chair's statement included a forecast that earnings might be
expected to rise by 5% per annum in the coming year and for the
foreseeable future.

CO, a children's clothes group, has an issued ordinary share capital
of $33 million in $1 shares. Pre-tax profits for the year to 31 March
20X9 were $5.2 million. Because of a recent programme of
reorganisation and rationalisation, no growth is forecast for the
current year but subsequently constant growth in earnings of
approximately 6% per annum is predicted. CO has had an erratic
growth and earnings record in the past and has not always achieved
it's often ambitious forecasts.

ML Co has approached the shareholders of CO with a bid of two
new shares in ML Co for every three CO shares. There is a cash
alternative of 135 cents per share.

Following the announcement of the bid, the market price of ML Co
shares fell while the price of shares in CO rose. Statistics for ML
Co, CO and two other listed companies in the same industry
immediately *prior* to the bid announcement are shown below. All
share prices are in cents.

20X8		Company	Dividend yield	P/E
High	Low		%	
225	185	ML Co	3.4	15
145	115	CO	3.6	13
187	122	HR	6	12
230	159	SZ	2.4	17

Both ML Co and CO pay tax at 33%. ML Co's cost of capital is 12%
per annum and CO's is 11% per annum.

Required:

Assume you are a financial analyst with a major fund manager. You have funds invested in both ML Co and CO.

- Assess whether the proposed share for share offer is likely to be beneficial to the shareholders in ML Co and CO, and recommend an investment strategy based on your calculations.

- Comment on other information that would be useful in your assessment of the bid. Assume that the estimates of growth given above are achieved and that the new company plans no further issues of equity.

State any assumptions that you make.

(30 minutes)

Test your understanding 11 (Case style question)

Oscar Wills is the chief executive of OW plc, a UK listed company. The entity has been trading for 5 years. Oscar is ambitious and aims to make his entity market leader within 5 years.

He makes an offer to acquire Wilde plc, an older quoted entity of similar size to OW but with a profit record that has been erratic in recent years. Wills is of the opinion that Wilde lacks marketing strength and feels that he could make the entity much more profitable.

A summary of the financial data before the bid is as follows:

	OW	Wilde
Number of shares in issue	40m	44m
Earnings available to ordinary shareholders	£4m	£4.4m
P/E ratio	20	10

OW – estimated financial data post-acquisition

Estimated market capitalisation	£167.7m
Estimated share price	262 p
Estimated EPS	13.1 p
Estimated equivalent value of one old Wilde share	143 p

- The offer is six OW shares for eleven Wilde shares.

- The offer is not expected to result in any immediate savings or increases in operational cash flows, but in future, Oscar Wills expects the EPS to grow by 10% per annum..

Required:

(a) Show how Oscar Wills calculated his estimate of post-acquisition values. Discuss the assumptions made by Oscar Wills, and calculate an alternative post-acquisition value for the company. State any assumptions that you make.

(15 minutes)

(b) If Wilde's shareholders rejected the bid, calculate the maximum price OW could afford pay without reducing its shareholders' wealth (assuming Oscar Wills' estimate of post-bid market value is correct).

(15 minutes)

(c) Explain why OW would wish to make the acquisition and comment on likely post-acquisition effects on the P/E ratio.

(15 minutes)

(d) Discuss other post-acquisition impacts that the directors of OW plc should consider.

(15 minutes)

Test your understanding answers

Test your understanding 1 (Case style question)

Calculations

Value of Mavers Co = $3.05 × 48m shares = $146.4m

Value of Power Co = $6.80 × 13m shares = $88.4m

Total value (assuming no synergistic gains) = 146.4 + 88.4 = $234.8m

Number of shares post-integration = 48 million + (2 × 13 million) = 74 million

So the post-integration share price will be:

$234.8m / 74 million = $3.173

	Shares	MV	Old wealth	Change
Mavers	48m	$152.3m	$146.4m	+$5.9m
Power	2 × 13m = 26m	$82.5m	$88.4m	−$5.9m

Advice

The Power Co shareholders will not accept a 2 for 1 share for share exchange since it causes their wealth to reduce.

Recommendation

In order for the Power Co shareholders to be encouraged to accept the offer, it must offer them a gain in wealth.

To make sure that Mavers Co is valuing Power Co at its current market value, the value of the offer needs to be ($6.80 × 13m shares) $88.4m in total.

Given the current Mavers Co share price of $3.05, this amounts to $88.4m / $3.05 = 28.98m shares in Mavers Co.

An exchange of 28.98m Mavers Co shares for the 13m Power Co shares represents a ratio of 28.98m to 13m or 2.23 to 1.

However, if the terms of the offer were to be exactly 2.23 Mavers Co shares for every 1 share in Power Co, there would be no incentive for the Power Co shareholders to sell (financially, they'd be indifferent between keeping their existing shares and exchanging them for Mavers Co shares).

In order to encourage Power Co's shareholders to sell, a premium would have to be offered.

Hence, an offer of (say) 2.5 Mavers Co shares for every 1 share in Power Co would probably be needed to encourage the Power Co shareholders to sell.

Position of Mavers Co shareholders

In this situation, where no synergistic gains are included in the calculations, a gain to Power Co's shareholders will result in a corresponding loss to the Mavers Co shareholders. Clearly Mavers Co would not want to proceed with the takeover in these circumstances.

Unless some synergies can be generated, to improve the wealth of the overall company after the acquisition, there is no way of structuring the deal so that both sets of shareholders will be satisfied.

Test your understanding 2 (Objective test question)

The answer is (C).

A forecast of cash flows before financing charges, discounted at an appropriate weighted average cost of capital, gives a valuation for the whole entity, both debt and equity.

Therefore, to acquire the shares and pay off the debt, this value ($130 million) should be paid.

Test your understanding 3 (Objective test question)

The answer is (B) and (C).

A spin-off would not actually generate any cash and a management buyout would split the business up or (if it was to be for the whole company) take a controlling interest away from Mr A and Mr B. A trade sale of the whole company would not leave Mr A and Mr B with a controlling interest.

Test your understanding 4 (Objective test question)

The answer is (C), (D) and (E).

(A) and (B) are defences that would have to be set up **before** a bid was made.

Test your understanding 5 (Objective test question)

The answer is (C).

If Paolo Co buys another company and values the target company on a higher P/E ratio, and if there is no synergy, there will be a reduction in the earnings per share of Paolo Co (B). Since the acquisition is paid for by using new shares, the gearing ratio of Paolo Co will fall (A), and existing shareholders will own a smaller proportionate stake in the company (D). It is unlikely that the share price will increase; in view of the reduction in earnings per share, it is more likely that the share price will fall after the takeover.

Test your understanding 6 (Objective test question)

The answer is (C).

Total value of the combined company will be:

(1m × $6.33) + (200,000 × $2.96) + 100,000 = $7,022,000

The number of shares in the combined company will be:

1 million + [(1/2) × 200,000] = 1,100,000

Therefore the share price will be $7,022,000 / 1,100,000 = $6.38

Test your understanding 7 (Objective test question)

The answer is (C).

In Co's gearing appears to be quite low and interest cover is quite high, so it shouldn't cause any problems to increase borrowings (C).

Low cash reserves would rule out a straight cash offer (A), and the fact that the family owners have been selling off shares would seem to rule out a rights issue (B).

A share for share exchange (D) would change the control of In Co, and would probably reduce the family's holding to lower than 50%, so should not be undertaken unless the family owners accept that they will lose their control of the company.

Test your understanding 8 (Objective test question)

The answer is (B).

Expected value of Alpha and Beta combined is:

$20 \times (200{,}000 + 800{,}000 + 100{,}000) = \$22$ million

Beta's current value is

$21 \times 800{,}000 = \$16.8$ million.

Therefore the value of Alpha to Beta is the difference between these two figures, i.e. $5.2 million.

Test your understanding 9 (Objective test question)

The answer is (B).

Value of merged company ($ million) = $40 + 8 + 5 + 1 = \$54$ million

R's shareholders have 80% (i.e. $43.2 million)

This is a gain of $3.2 million.

Test your understanding 10 (Case style question)

(a) *Given the wording, you really need to explain why the dividend valuation model may break down, as it is the 'theory' specifically mentioned in the question. You probably have time only to mention a couple of drawbacks with each approach.*

A common way of valuing the ordinary shares in a company is discounting all future dividends anticipated from holding the shares. Although having a ring of truth, it often fails to give a price which corresponds to the current market price, due to its inherent flaws:

– It requires constant dividend growth, which in turn implies a constant retention ratio and return on re-invested funds. It is possible to cope with varying growth rates but the calculation is awkward.

– It requires a continuous supply of investment opportunities through time to justify retention.

– It can give nonsensical results e.g. zero current dividend generates zero value, thus ignoring the value of the firm's assets and/or its earnings stream.

– It is only suitable for valuing minority stakes in a firm because it ignores the opportunities for managers to restructure firms to improve earnings and cash flow. The key to value is not the portion of profit paid out to shareholders but the earning power of the business.

Price earnings (P/E) ratios

This is not a method of valuing shares of quoted firms – P/E ratios are the *product* of valuation. When the market sets a value, the resulting share price divided by the last reported earnings gives the P/E ratio. Generally, a high P/E ratio indicates that a company is expected to grow its earnings rapidly in the future.

The P/E ratio can be used to cross-check against the value of other companies – if their relative P/E ratios look out of line, it may suggest under- or overvaluation somewhere. P/E ratios can also be used when valuing the shares of unquoted companies, taking due care when interpreting the accounting data used.

Asset Value (AV)

The AV is the value per share of the firm's assets net of all liabilities i.e. the owners' stake in the firm. It has some merit for unlisted companies whose shares are not traded, but it is highly unreliable for many reasons:

– Based on IFRS, asset values in the Statement of Financial Position are primarily designed to satisfy the directors' duty to account for past performance.

– It can be distorted by accounting practices e.g. different depreciation policies.

– Revaluation of assets is not mandatory (except in the property sector) so asset values could seriously understate market values.

– It is only valid at one point in time, the statement of financial position date.

– It (usually) ignores intangibles such as brands and market standing.

– It may exclude some liabilities – 'off-balance sheet' debts like operating lease obligations and warranty commitments.

– Inventory values quickly outdate in some industries, and some receivables / debtors may be doubtful.

The AV provides merely a floor to equity value – usually, the market value is many times the AV because the market is valuing future earnings capacity. A discounted cash flow approach is the most appropriate method of valuation.

(b) *The length of answer that you can offer will be limited. The bulk of your time will be spent on computation. The solution presented here gives a step-by-step guide that you would need to follow, rather than just a summary of the results.*

Basic information

	ML	CO	Combined
Profit after tax (PAT) for each firm is			
ML: $(0.67 \times \$4.6m)$	$3.082m	$3.484m	$6.566m
CO: $(0.67 \times \$5.2m)$			
Given respective P/E ratios, market values are:			
ML: $(15 \times \$3.082)$	$46.23m	$45.29m	$91.52m
CO: $(13 \times \$3.484)$			
Given the number of shares, share price is:			
ML: $(\$46.23m/20{,}000)$	$2.31	$1.37	
CO: $(\$45.29m/33{,}000)$			
EPS:			
ML: $(\$3.082/20{,}000)$	15.41c	10.56c	
CO: $(\$3.484/33{,}000)$			

Analysis

No. of shares post-bid:
$20{,}000 + (2/3 \times 33{,}000)$ = 42,000

Expected market prices post-bid = Total market value/no of shares

= $(91{,}520/42{,}000) = \$2.18$

Value of bid at post-issue price
= $(2 \text{ shares} \times \$2.18)$ = $4.36

Cash value of bid per 3 shares
offered: $(\$1.35 \times 3)$ = $4.05

Assessment

Assuming no changes in the level of market prices, and no re-rating of the sector, ML share price would fall post-acquisition to $2.18. At this price, the value of the 2-for-3 share offer should attract CO shareholders. They would be getting shares worth (2 × 2.18) = $4.36 in exchange for shares currently worth (3 × 1.37) = $4.11.

The share-for-share offer is also worth more than the cash alternative: $4.36 vs $4.05.

This is a 'reverse takeover', where the shareholders of the target end up holding a majority stake in the expanded company – but who gains from this?

Former CO shareholders would hold (22,000/42,000) × 91.52m = $47.939m of the value of the expanded firm, a gain of (47.939m – 45.290m pre-bid value of CO) = $2.649m.

ML shareholders would lose $2.649m, making the share-financed deal distinctly unattractive to them.

Conversely, the cash offer would create wealth for ML shareholders i.e. they give $4.05 for something worth $4.11 pre-bid.

The advice to the fund manager is: 'accept the bid in respect of CO shares and sell ML shares in the market if you can achieve a price above $2.18'.

Other information required

The advice given hinges on the behaviour of ML's share price – it has already fallen on the announcement, but by how much? It may already be too late if the market is efficient, as it would already have digested the information contained in the announcement.

Also:

- What benefits are expected from the merger i.e. cost savings and synergies? To make sense of the bid, ML must be setting the PV of these benefits above $2.649m to yield a positive NPV for the acquisition.

- How quickly are these benefits likely to show through? Any delay in exploiting these lowers the NPV.

– It is feasible that the market might apply a higher P/E ratio to the expanded company – maybe not as high as ML's but possibly at the market average, currently 14.25, compared to the weighted average P/E ratio for ML/CO of 14.

– Is ML likely to sell part of CO's operations? And to whom? If ML has already lined up a buyer, it must expect to turn a profit on the deal.

– Is the bid likely to be defended by the target's managers, fearful for their jobs? If so, a higher bid might be expected.

– Is a White Knight likely to appear with a higher bid on more favourable terms?

– Are there competition implications likely to attract the interest of the authorities?

Test your understanding 11 (Case style question)

(a)

	OW	Wilde	OW+Wilde
Earnings (£m)	4	4.4	8.4
Number of shares (m)	40	44	64
EPS (p)	10	10	13.1
P/E ratio	20	10	20
Share price (p)	200	100	262
MV (£m)	80	44	167.7 (estimate)

Post-acquisition:

% of entity owned by OW (40 / 64)	62.5%	
% of entity owned by Wilde (24 / 64)		37.5%
Market value (% × £167.7m)	104.8	62.9
No. of shares pre-acquisition (m)	40	44
Post-acquisition price per existing share (p)	262	143

Oscar Wills has applied his own pre-acquisition P/E ratio to the combined earnings of the new entity.

The difference between the combined market values pre-acquisition (£124m) and the estimated market value post-acquisition (£167.7m) is £43.7m.

This is Wilde's pre-acquisition earnings multiplied by the difference between the entity's pre-acquisition P/E and the combined post-acquisition P/E (20 – 10 = 10). EPS for Oscar Wills appears to have increased from 10 p to 13.1p because of this 'bootstrapping' effect.

In the absence of any immediate commercial benefits, or the disclosure of new information during the bid, there is no reason why the market value of the combined entity should be any different from the total of the two individual entities' market values – that is, £124m. This would suggest the following post-acquisition prices per existing share:

Wills: £124m × 62.5% = £77.5m or 194p per existing share compared with 200p per share now

Wilde: £124m × 37.5% = £46.5m or 106p per existing share compared with 100p per share now

There is a transfer of wealth from Wills' shareholders to Wilde's, because the terms of the offer are slightly more generous than the ratio of the old share prices.

The pre-acquisition prices suggest 1-for-2, not 6-for-11.

(b)

- Estimated value of combined firm (per OW) £168m
- Value of OW before merger £80m
- Maximum price £88m

This is £44m over the existing value of Wilde's shares. It can be reconciled by multiplying the historic earnings by the difference between Wilde's P/E and OW's P/E – that is £4.4m × (20 – 10).

(c) OW plc may have had the following among their reasons for making a bid for Wilde plc:

- *Expectation of growth.* OW is an ambitious entity and it sees in Wilde a means of growing faster and more cheaply than by internal expansion, especially as Wilde seems to be a 'slumbering heavyweight' relative to OW.

- *Management and technical staff.* Wilde's results may be erratic, but OW is aware that in terms of size and quality of main products Wilde is a significant player in its market sector. It is reasonable to assume therefore that Wilde may be suffering from poor administrative as well as marketing management, which could considerably undervalue the earning potential of its products. By means of more aggressive marketing and improved administration, OW believes that dramatic profit improvements are possible. Also Wilde may possess strong technical expertise which OW might find difficult and expensive to obtain by internal development.

- *Market share.* If Wilde is in the same industry sector as OW, this could well be a main reason for the bid, in which case OW's shareholders might have less reason to be concerned over the price. Thus if the acquisition led to OW's market share rising fairly quickly to make the new entity second or third in its sector, and not excessively far below the leader, it could begin to wield significantly greater influence in that sector.

- *Synergy savings.* Wilde may have a number of 'dogs' (Boston Consulting Group term for bad failure) among its business units, which OW may be much less prepared to pour resources into, even though some may be the Wilde chairman's 'pets'. However, if this aspect is known to the market, then the synergy savings may well attract a higher bidder.

- *Risk reduction.* From the comparative P/E ratios it seems evident that Wilde is regarded by the market as being much riskier than OW, and this could well be due to Wilde being an acquirer of struggling entities, bought at cheap prices, possibly even in sectors only remotely related to Wilde's core business. Such entities often turn out to be disasters, taking up disproportionate amounts of the acquirer's valuable management time. At OW, Mr Wills does not believe in keeping a 'kennelful of dogs'! and the profit improvement suggested is likely to come not only from more aggressive marketing but from a concentration of resources on key products, thereby reducing risk in the new entity.

Next, the acquirer needs to be concerned at the post-acquisition effects on its P/E ratio.

On the basis of the pre-acquisition estimates, Mr Wills looked to maintain OW's own P/E ratio of 20 (262p / 13.1p), but on the more realistic basis of assuming a value of 194 p per share – which assumes that OW inherits the greater risks of Wilde's current operations – then, as shown above, for the new entity the market capitalisations should be simply added together, making £124m and the P/E ratio becomes 194p / 13.1p = 14.8.

However, we must now consider the possibility of downside costs in year 1; thus even assuming that OW has taken several steps to improve Wilde's operations and perhaps made some significant asset sales, an upset to earnings caused by 'teething troubles' could do more than offset the effect of the improvements. Thus, EPS of, say, 13.5p for year 1 (instead of 14.4p, showing 10% expected growth), which one would expect to yield a P/E ratio of approximately 15.2 (13.5p /13.1p × 14.8), might well fall back to about 13, or even 12. Downside factors often seem to the market to be more significant than improvements.

Clearly then, at the time of making its bid, it would have been most unwise for OW to pay excessively for 'synergy savings' and not to give due regard to possible adverse post-acquisition impacts.

(d) **Further post-acquisition aspects**

Position audit

As an initial move, OW will need to do much more than analyse key financial factors of each of Wilde's units. OW's management will need to get a proper understanding of the main 'stakeholders' of each Wilde unit, for example, staff, customers and suppliers, and an appreciation of the products or services provided. In company planning, this wide-ranging survey is of the nature of a 'position audit', which should help considerably in speeding up the 'getting to know you' aspect which is so important if the full benefits of the acquisition are to be obtained.

Improving efficiency

It is better for OW to approach Wilde more as a management consultant rather than to demand immediate changes without adequate explanation. Administrative savings mainly involve people, and OW must try to ensure that the logic of its proposals is clearly explained to Wilde's management and staff, and as far as possible their cooperation gained.

Redundancies need to be worked out fairly but firmly with an emphasis on voluntary redundancy as far as possible; the main purpose must be to reduce the resentment of those who are losing their jobs and to provide as much help as possible by way of counselling or assistance in job seeking. In these situations uncertainty should be avoided, as it tends to demotivate the entire workforce, and rumour is liable to feed greedily on rumour.

Even if Mr Wills is convinced that Wilde's marketing needs to be more aggressive, he should first of all make himself fully aware of the nature of Wilde's marketing policies and of their customers and competitors. If Wilde is substantially in the same market sector as OW, there may be certain valuable niches occupied by Wilde which OW would do well to retain.

Profit improvement

The financial analysis of Wilde's units suggested above will help to pinpoint the areas where profit improvements can be obtained, but it is essential that a comprehensive action plan is then prepared, as far as possible in co-operation with Wilde's management, and reasonable time allowed for the phasing-in of significant changes.

It is not helpful to go 'stomping around' offices and factories, thereby emphasising the perceived incompetencies of Wilde personnel. It may be that many faults, especially of inadequate systems, may already be recognised by Wilde staff and, faced with the necessity of correcting them, they may be quite willing to join in making appropriate changes. Sadly, it is often the case that obstinate managers may be standing in the way of improvement, and in this situation OW is in a good position to take quick but fair and firm action, possibly by grasping the nettle of making major changes in Wilde's organisation structure if this is seen to be necessary for a more profitable operation.

Asset sales

Here it is often the reluctance of top management to dispose of redundant assets and 'dog' units, even though it is recognised that keeping them represents a serious waste of management time and scarce resources. OW will need to make it quite clear as to which activities are to be retained, which merged with OW units and which disposed of, but in all cases the logic of each move should be clearly explained to the Wilde management and staff affected. This assumes, of course, that OW has thought through what it intends to do, which again is a good reason for first carrying out a position audit before taking action on Wilde's operations.

Effective communication

Finally, a qualitative factor of the utmost importance, as by effective communication we mean that OW must do all possible to ensure that Wilde is on the same 'wavelength' as itself. New reporting systems and procedures should only be introduced after proper consultation, in which OW will need to make clear their purposes and ensure that changes will not cause serious disruption to Wilde's operations. This is especially true in seeking computer system compatibility, which will call not only for careful planning but an acceptance by OW that in this, as with other system changes, a sufficient period of parallel running may be an essential procedure.

There should be reasonable opportunities for Wilde staff to have contact with those of OW and vice versa, especially through participation in training procedures and conferences; also Wilde staff should be encouraged to feel that promotional prospects throughout the new entity will be open to them.

All the points made in this section concerning redundancies, changes and reorganisation created by the acquisition of Wilde apply equally to the need for OW to keep its own staff properly informed, otherwise demotivation may also affect OW with consequent damage to its own profitability whatever happens with Wilde.

Perhaps, in the end, the most effective post-acquisition strategy that OW can apply to Wilde and itself is to provide an atmosphere in which both sides are able to talk freely with each other, seeking co-operation wherever possible, and even though some of OW's actions – improving profitability and making asset sales – may be very hurtful to Wilde, at least things can probably be made somewhat more acceptable if the justification for them is properly explained to all concerned, and that includes any of OW's own staff who may also be affected.

Index

Index

Index

Index